Y0-BYF-539

NEIGHBOURHOOD ORGANIZATIONS AND THE WELFARE STATE

SHLOMO HASSON AND DAVID LEY

Neighbourhood Organizations and the Welfare State

UNIVERSITY OF TORONTO PRESS
Toronto   Buffalo   London

© University of Toronto Press Incorporated 1994
Toronto Buffalo London
Printed in Canada

ISBN 0-8020-2887-X (cloth)
ISBN 0-8020-7392-1 (paper)

Printed on acid-free paper

Canadian Cataloguing in Publication Data

Hasson, Shlomo, 1946-
   Neighbourhood organizations and the welfare
   state

   Includes index.
   ISBN 0-8020-2887-X (bound). ISBN 0-8020-7392-1 (pbk.)

   1. Citizens' associations – British Columbia –
   Vancouver – Case studies.   2. Citizens' associations –
   Jerusalem – Case studies.   I. Ley David. II. Title.

   HN110.Z9C65 1994   361.8′09711′33   C94-930321-6

This book has been published with the help of a grant from the Social Science
Federation of Canada, using funds provided by the Social Sciences and
Humanities Research Council of Canada.

Contents

Figures and Tables

TABLES

Preface

Like any other project, this book was born from a combination of purpose and circumstance. The purpose is derived from the long-standing interest of both of us in community organizations – in Hasson's case, from detailed work with a range of groups in Jerusalem, including urban social movements and neighbourhood councils, and in Ley's, an orientation nurtured by community involvement in Philadelphia's inner city, and sustained by work with neighbourhood groups in inner Vancouver. Besides a scholarly interest in the constitution and actions of grass-roots groups, and a political-moral perspective that there is much that warrants community mobilization, we are also attracted by the view, enunciated most recently by Václav Havel in *Disturbing the Peace*, that community action matters, and not only for its material results. Even when there remains little ground for optimism, wrote Havel in Czechoslovakia's dismal days of 1986, there remains hope, 'an ability to work for something because it is good, not just because it stands a chance to succeed.' This humanism stands in stark contrast to other voices in the past decade, invoking both a persisting theoretical functionalism (of the political right and the left) and a practical instrumentalism, which grant such processes as 'globalization' and 'privatization' an unassailable life of their own. Our broader theoretical position is that the city is both socially constructed and socially contested, and that the demystification of such umbrella categories not only permits the recovery of the human in human geography, but also confirms the status of individuals and groups in a squarely political process, albeit within a range of both enabling and inhibiting contexts. This project to remake the city, however partially, in their own image through political action was also the objective of the eight neighbourhood groups we will meet in the chapters that follow.

The circumstances that led to this book included two visits by Hasson to Vancouver and a visit by Ley to Jerusalem. In 1983/4, as a Fellow of the Centre for Human Settlements at the University of British Columbia, Hasson taught a course on the political geography of the city and began a project on community opposition to a new transportation corridor. On a second visit in 1985, discussion began in earnest concerning a comparative study of inner-city neighbourhood organizations in Vancouver and Jerusalem, and the selection of the districts was finalized during Ley's visit to Jerusalem in 1986. At first glance, such a comparison appears unlikely. But beyond the obvious historical and geopolitical differences between the two cities, some informative similarities exist. Both cities are located in young states where the process of nation building is far from complete. Both confront the existence of high levels of immigration, and the problem of incorporating an increasingly plural population into full citizenship. As democracies and mixed economies, welfare states are central players in national life, but face their own challenges to secure legitimacy and governability as they simultaneously pursue the often contradictory paths of economic growth and social welfare. And of course, in each city, beneath national geopolitical tensions, are another set of realities, as citizens encounter the needs of everyday life to procure social services such as housing, to block unwanted land-use intrusions, and, more radically, to acquire political empowerment and the capacity to build symbolic communities. At this level, as we shall see, the communalities in the relations between neighbourhood groups and the welfare state in each city become most instructive.

We have attempted to sharpen both the communalities and the differences by locating community activism in pairs of similar neighbourhoods in each city. This approach has led to a four-fold typology of neighbourhoods, according to their status as élite districts (Part I), districts of ethno-racial marginality (Part II), poverty districts (Part III), and districts undergoing social change, notably gentrification (Part IV). In this manner we are simultaneously undertaking a comparison of organizations between neighbourhoods and across cities, a strategy that we hope finds the middle ground between the search for discoverable order and the recognition of demonstrable difference. The interpretive approach we undertook in these eight communities was both enriching and time-consuming; participant observation, for example, was part of the methodology employed in six of the neighbourhoods. Fortunately we were able to benefit from parallel research projects at several points. Chapter 2 was written by James Duncan of Syracuse University, who kindly took time off from his own research monograph on Shaughnessy;

chapter 3, on Rehavia, was co-written by Hasson and Nili Shchory; and chapter 4 was written by Ley with assistance from Kay Anderson of the University of New South Wales, who recently completed a monograph on relationships between Chinatown and the state over the period from 1875 to 1980. As researcher for chapter 4, the late Doug Konrad was an integral member of the team, and his contribution is recognized in his honorary status as co-author. As for the remainder of the book, Hasson wrote chapters 5, 7, and 9, and Ley, chapters 6 and 8. Hasson prepared the first draft of many sections in chapters 1 and 10, which then underwent joint revision through several iterations. Ley wrote the introductions to the four parts, and provided editorial review of, and rewrites for, the entire text.

The manuscript benefited from a broader reservoir of goodwill. In Vancouver, Doug Konrad, Kris Olds, and Geraldine Pratt made useful critical observations on early drafts of individual chapters; in Jerusalem, Avner Amiel, Michael Paran, David Meiry, and Eyal Ben-Ari contributed from their experience and knowledge. We wish also to acknowledge Jim Green and Larry Bantleman, formerly of the Downtown Eastside Residents' Association, and Jacques Khouri, former leader of the West Broadway Citizens' Committee, for their observations on drafts of specific chapters. More generally, the generous cooperation of all eight neighbourhood organizations in the research process is gratefully acknowledged. We wish to thank also our typists, Joyce Poon, Jeanne Yang, and Chaym Weitzman, and cartographers Paul Jance, Eric Leinberger, and Tamar Sopher for their cheerful and excellent work. The research was supported by grants from the Canada-Israel Foundation, the Association for Canadian Studies in Israel, the International Council for Canadian Studies, the University of British Columbia, and The Jerusalem Institute for Israel studies. Publication has been made possible by a grant from the Aid to Scholarly Publications Programme of the Social Science Federation of Canada. We are grateful for the assistance from all these organizations. Finally, it is a pleasure to acknowledge the support and expertise of Virgil Duff and his colleagues at the University of Toronto Press.

Vancouver and Jerusalem
July 1993

NEIGHBOURHOOD ORGANIZATIONS AND THE WELFARE STATE

1

Neighbourhood Organizations, the City, and the State

The public's return to active political life in advanced industrial nations, and in Eastern Europe, has been expressed primarily by the rise of new social movements that have variously challenged traditional politics. The feminist, peace, green, gay, ethnic, civil rights, nationalist, and, most decisively, democracy movements have contested what had once been the exclusive domain of privileged social groups. Private-sector entrepreneurs in industrial, financial, and business institutions, along with politicians and bureaucrats at different levels of the state, have encountered a diversity of critical political cultures. If less cataclysmic, within the city different social groupings have also demanded an active role in shaping local landscapes, the provision of services, patterns of political discourse, and, ultimately, urban meaning. Disadvantaged groups, hitherto at the margins of society, have forcefully entered the urban scene, demanding social and political rights. They have appeared in the city's ghettos and slums in Western European and North American urban centres, and in the *barrios* and *favelas* of South American cities.[1] Working-class tenants' associations have emerged in the housing projects of France and Britain, striving to improve the provision of urban services and to protect their rights (Castells 1983; Lowe 1986). Citizens located in middle- to upper-class areas are demanding involvement in issues once considered the exclusive domain of various levels of government – that is, in decision making concerning land-use regulations, public amenities, educational programs, and the environment (Duncan and Duncan 1984). Local conflicts have emerged throughout the urban system as residents have attempted to introduce innovations (such as developing new school curricula) or to resist change (opposing the construction of a freeway, for example). Many of these conflicts focused on redevelopment, sections of networks, primarily roads, as well as facilities, such as schools, health clinics, and shopping centres (Cox 1973; Dear and Long 1978; Ley and Mercer 1980; Hasson 1984). Older communities defended themselves by political and social means against the penetration of new groups (ethnic, racial, or lower-class groups) perceived as threats (Suttles 1972; Evans 1984).

Over time, the nature of neighbourhood organizations has often undergone a notable metamorphosis. The protest movements of the 1960s and 1970s often displaced or reformed earlier organizations, the ratepayers' groups of more affluent districts (Higgins 1977), and the local boss associated with machine politics, notably in minority and immigrant areas in U.S., Canadian, British, and Israeli cities.[2] With the passage of time, however, protest organizations have frequently moderated their actions, and have become absorbed within the institutional-political system, a sequence typically running the gamut from paternalism to protest, and finally to partnership or co-production (Susskind and Elliot 1984). Despite the broad differences among these groups in terms of class and status affiliation, access to power, social orientation, and strategies of action, they have nevertheless symbolized the revival of urban politics and the apparent decentring of power. The unavoidable result has been the transformation of the political geography of the city into a mosaic of sociopolitical activity characterized by interests changing rapidly over space and by often short-lived community organizations.

The fragility and parochialism of particular neighbourhood organizations should not conceal the continuity of overall local activism. It seems that the messages of the 1960s – a social critique of the political-economic system, demands for local democracy, cultural self-expression, and, above all, an openness to resistance – have put down deep roots in civil society and the state. Within civil society, the institutionalization of these ideas is evident in an ongoing process of neighbourhood activism (Fischer 1984), and in the diversity of neighbourhood organizations. In the political sphere, group activism has been paralleled by the emergence of more flexible municipal systems, the adoption of some populist approaches, and sporadic attempts by the state to develop and institutionalize new forms of neighbourhood government (Morlan 1982; Nanneti 1985). A further ingredient in the changes within the state has been the development of a new middle class made up of younger and often reform-oriented professionals and politicians (Ley 1980, 1994). This class, invariably influential beyond its numbers, has typically assumed both a populist and an aesthetic orientation, seeking both to transfer resources to needy groups and to protect cultural and environmental values. This double code has provided points of entry for both lower- and upper-middle-class organizations to the emerging political process in the city.[3]

Parties of both the left and the right have tended to support the rise of neighbourhood organizations, at least initially, and always rhetorically, though for different reasons. The left has sought local empowerment to further the redistribution of social resources, while the right has sought to promote community self-help to relieve social expenditures and thereby release additional resources for capital investment (cf. Wolch 1989). In the course of this process, the innovations and challenges rising from below have been partly rejected and partly absorbed and routinized within the framework of the welfare state. As a result, local groups of different class origins have apparently acquired, over the past twenty years, a new, if variable, voice in the redistribution of public resources, resources which range from material goods such as housing to more intangible claims for the quality of life or, more radically, political decentralization.

Our intention here is to uncover the nature of different neighbourhood organizations, to clarify the processes whereby they come into being, to assess their significance in shaping urban life, and to analyze their relationships with different agents and levels of the state. Focusing on these issues, we wish to portray the magnitude of social diversity existing among neighbourhood organizations, and thereby to reveal the complexity of local cultures. In so doing, we endeavour to demonstrate that there are many geographies of social action at the neighbourhood level. The theoretical implication for the present study is that there is no such thing as an ideal or archetypical organization that serves as a standard for all the rest. By revealing different methods of neighbourhood action, we would like to offer a greater opportunity for diversified social groups, located in different cities and at different times, to speak in their own voices.

Analysing the systematic variations among neighbourhood organizations in terms of their development, urban significance, and relationships with the state suggests the wisdom of both a longitudinal and a cross-cultural interpretation, and it is precisely this that we are proposing: a study of the careers of eight neighbourhood organizations as they have evolved through time and across space; four of these are located in Vancouver, Canada, and four in Jerusalem, Israel. Like other advanced societies, Canada and Israel are welfare states, liberal democracies, market economies, and pluralist societies. These are the broad contexts within which neighbourhood organizations operate and according to whose changing character successful organizations define and redefine their strategies. Advanced democracies such as Canada and Israel bear some basic tensions as they seek simultaneously economic growth and the social redistribution of resources. Additional tensions in these relatively young states derive from the still unfinished task of nation building in societies that include large numbers of immigrants and other forms of social and cultural pluralism. The geopolitical differences between the two nations are evident. Less visible, but revealed by the case-studies, are some informative communalities, as residents in each place confront similar challenges in negotiating with the state to secure those material and symbolic resources deemed essential for everyday life. Besides the similarities, the differences in outcomes are also relevant, demonstrating the degrees of freedom in the political process as divergent results may lead from an engagement with equivalent structural conditions. The power of comparative study has been reasserted recently in several disciplines (see, for example, Agnew, Mercer, and Sopher 1984; Skocpol 1984), and it has been applied in research on community political organizations (Henig 1981; Castells 1983), though not without certain shortcomings (Pickvance 1985).

THE PRINCIPAL QUESTIONS

The four principal questions we ask in this study are: first, what different types of neighbourhood organizations have developed in Vancouver and Jerusalem? Second, how were the local residents mobilized into collective action? (This question relates to the social context in which the organizations were formed and to the role of human intervention in setting them up.) Third, what were the urban effects of the organizations studied? (This question relates to local effects as well as to broader social and political effects associated with the organizations' activities and their exchange with the state.) Finally, what were the relationships between the state and the neighbourhood organizations? (This question relates to both local and senior levels of the state – the provincial and federal governments in Canada and the central government in Israel.) We aim to reveal how the development of the welfare state and the changes in local government over time affected the nature of neighbourhood organizations.

TYPES OF NEIGHBOURHOOD ORGANIZATIONS

Our study encompasses different neighbourhood organizations: ratepayers' associations engaged in self-management and the preservation of heritage; racial and ethnic organizations, which, besides the preservation of old traditions, seek to improve the delivery of services; grass-roots organizations that challenge the existing order; and co-productive organizations involved in decentralization and experiments in empowerment. The conceptual question that arises at this point concerns the character of these organizations. The literature, whether empirical or theoretical, is considerably confused on this point, which may reflect both the diversity of organizational bases and orientations as well as the range of theoretical-cum-ideological perspectives through which they are viewed.

A key theoretical debate focuses on the nature of the social base and the consciousness of organizations. Are they a product of community or of class? The answers vary with the theoretical perspective. The legacy of the Chicago School has bequeathed to urban sociology the concept of 'natural community' as the fundamental social base for local organization. The natural area encompasses residential communities of distinctive social and cultural characteristics (Park, Burgess, and McKenzie 1925). Criticizing the concept of natural community, Suttles maintains that 'local communities and neighbourhoods, like other groups, acquire a corporate identity because they are held jointly responsible by other communities and external organizations' (1972, 13). Although he does not ignore distinct features of the ecological unit and local sentiments, Suttles shifts the discussion from the internal to the external functions of the community, thus emphasizing the social exchange, the tasks performed, and the reputation conveyed at the interface between the neighbourhood organization and external agencies.

Despite the increasing critique of the community as an analytical concept and as a practical base for social organization, the 1960s and 1970s saw the rise of numerous social movements demanding decentralization and community control (Kotler 1969). As Boggs (1991) points out, many of the bases for community mobilization still exist.[4] Studies in urban sociology have shown that the nature and characteristics of neighbourhood organizations are closely related to local sentiments, informal social networks, limited geographical mobility, and indifference or even hostility towards linkages between local problems and wider class-based conflicts.[5] For some urban scholars, neighbourhood resistance still represents popular radicalism, one that is associated with direct experience and local traditions and aspirations (Boyte 1980). Indeed, it is conceded by the neo-Marxist literature that the community still exists, and affects the values, orientations, and collective action of neighbourhood organizations (Castells 1983).

A somewhat different perspective on the social base is suggested by neo-Weberian studies. It has been suggested that differential access to urban public services (for example, housing and education) may form a basis for neighbourhood organization. As Rex (1968) showed, access to housing may not correspond with the social-class system. This disparity then leads to internal conflicts within the working class, based on social status and life chances.[6] Taking this point further, Dunleavy (1981) and Saunders (1986) suggest that local organizations at the urban level are constituted on the basis of consumption sectors (tenants, the elderly, public-transportation users, etc.). Adopting the model of consumption sectors, Lowe (1986, 72) writes that 'in terms of urban social movements there is a close link between sectoral consumption issues which unite or divide people according to their mode of access to key services, creating distinct material advantages and disadvantages.'

For the neo-Marxist literature, the very existence of community- and consumption-based organizations, which fail to make connections with class-based organizations, presents some serious theoretical and normative problems. The theoretical question is how these organizations fail to conceive the relationships between local problems and wider urban, political, and economic processes. The normative question is how to penetrate and harness established values and informal networks. The problem is fully exposed by Katznelson (1981, 6), who maintains that 'American urban politics has been governed by boundaries and rules that stress ethnicity, race, and territoriality, rather than class, and that emphasize the distribution of goods and services, while excluding questions of production or workplace relations.' Social inequality and local experience, Katznelson contends, are not linked to wider class consciousness. This may account for the instrumental and parochial orientations assumed quite often by local organizations. In the same vein, Plotkin (1991, 18) describes the community-based organization as one representing 'enclave consciousness,' which he defines as a tendency towards 'a rigid and undifferentiated exclusionism,' including fears of others, inward-looking tendencies, and minimization of outside risks. But beyond this critical conception of community-based organizations, Plotkin concedes that these organizations help to expand the realm of the public by offering 'a powerful rationale for empowerment' (ibid, 19).

Perhaps the most interesting synthesis between community-based organizations and class structure is suggested by Castells (1983), who explains how industrialized capitalism and the information system have commodified urban space, leading to highly differentiated, socially exploited, and culturally deprived urban areas. These areas have served as the bases for urban social movements that are not necessarily class-based. As Castells observed, these movements may reflect what residents in a certain neighbourhood regard as social exploitation, a threat to local or historical identity, or exclusion from political processes of decision making. Castells thus identifies three types of conflict in which the grass roots are involved: first, a conflict over the collective means of consumption, which revolves around residents' demands for quality of life (use value) and the capitalist drive for profit making (exchange value); second, a conflict over cultural meanings, where standardized values, imposed from above, collide with unique local, ethnic, and historical traditions; and, finally, a conflict over political participation, where the protesters challenge the state monopoly over planning, decision making, and the shaping of urban life. Thus, although an urban movement may take a non-class orientation, its very appearance is grounded in class structure. For some neo-Marxists, this implies that the nature of the movement is of minor importance compared with the fundamental macrosocietal features within which it is rooted. According to this view, the important task facing students of social change is 'to discover the relations in which non-class mobilizations stand to the class structure which shuttles through and environs them' (Kling and Posner 1991, 32).

Our approach towards the typification of neighbourhood organizations is thematic and incorporates recognition of the intricacies of the bases upon which mobilization is formed. We recognize the impact of class structure on the city, but at the same time incorporate local cultures and consumption cleavages, which shape collective grievances that often cannot be reduced to an individual's class position. The analysis points to the existence of inequalities between social classes of which local participants may be unaware, and shows how, on certain occasions, attempts were made to link local problems with wider political-economic issues. Such an approach enables us a more open-ended analysis than a tightly structured model of community, consumption sectors, or social class would suggest.

THE RISE OF NEIGHBOURHOOD ORGANIZATIONS

The literature dealing with the rise of neighbourhood organizations distinguishes between contextual or structural factors, on the one hand, and factors associated with human agency, on the other. Context encompasses the macrosocietal conditions existing prior to the mobilization process, and affecting the likelihood of mobilization, thus serving as necessary yet insufficient factors for mobilization. Human agency relates to intervention that mediates between the macrosocietal, initial conditions and collective action. Although there exists a great deal of cross-cutting between macrosocietal and agency-oriented explanations, the balance of causality is generally weighted towards one side or the other.[7]

Contextual Explanations

The contextual factors which affect mobilization may be analytically ordered in a sequence of causality, leading from universal, macrosocietal conditions to particularistic, local causes that precipitate social action.

Macrosocietal Features

Although aware of the role of human agency, functionalists and structural Marxists alike tend to focus on macrosocietal features, structural strains, and the ways in which they affect social mobilization. For advocates of the functionalist theory of collective behaviour, local activism (social and political protest) signifies the joint outcome of structural strains and weak integrative ideologies. Structural strains might be a result of accelerated urbanization, modernization, social mobility, rising social expectations (with heightened needs for public services and full employment) and political demands for participation, together with the inability of the public sector and the political apparatus to cope responsively with these changes (Smelser 1963; Gurr 1970; McCarthy and Zald 1977). The 'functional need' to keep the system intact may, however, eventually initiate a counter-process which puts society back in balance. One of the most comprehensive accounts of this school is provided by Smelser's explanatory scheme of social protest, which outlines six conditions that may lead to social mobilization.

Although inclined towards social change, some Marxist theory, much like functionalism, relates neighbourhood organizations to structural features of which they are part.[8] Theorizing the rise of social movements, Castells (1983) offers a valuable and more complex insight into the nature of crisis and change. In his view, as expressed in *The City and the Grassroots*, the social and spatial forms of the city are shaped by dominant actors – capitalists, technocrats, and bureaucrats – who operate through the specific institutions and mechanisms of the capitalist mode of production, the modes of industrial and information development, and state power. Although Castells emphasizes the crucial role of political, economic, and cultural structures, he is quite open to the role of social agents in shaping the movements (1983, 322).

In a critique of Castells, Pickvance (1985) identifies four macrosocietal factors that affect the rise and diversity of urban movements in different countries: rapid urbanization, the politicization of consumption issues, the skill of the political system in managing discontent, and the cycle of economic prosperity. Periods of prosperity may, according to Pickvance, lead to a rise in expectations and to social unrest, whereas periods of economic crisis may lead to a decline in social activity. Lowe (1986) sheds further light on the societal conditions that give rise to local activism by distinguishing between political processes (such as political history and the party system) and socio-economic processes that may generate or screen out protest.

The Nature of the Issue as Perceived at the Neighbourhood Level

Local residents do not organize in response to macrosocietal changes and general conflicts. Rather, they mobilize around specific issues perceived as critical at the local level. Moreover, as several studies have observed, the existence of tangible issues may not necessarily lead to mobilization, and one has also to consider the possibility of inaction. Such aspects of an issue as its visibility, geographic specificity, and a clear focus of responsibility for the issue, are among the conditions likely to facilitate mobilization (Henig 1982, 59–61).

Common and Individual Interests of the Residents

Common interest in social change may not necessarily result in social action. As Olson has perceived, individuals who seek to maximize their economic gains may rationally avoid any participation in the group's activity, leaving the burden of costs involved in social activity to others. Treating local issues as collective goods, individuals may rationally assume that they can enjoy the benefits of these goods without necessarily paying for their production. There is thus a basic, logical tension between the interests of the individual and those of the group. In Olson's words: 'Rational self-interested individuals will not act to achieve their common or group interests ... In sharing of the costs of efforts to achieve a common goal in small groups, there is however a surprising tendency for the "exploitation" of the great by the small' (1965, 2–3). Such a tension is likely to stifle mobilization, and to prevent the attainment or improvement of collective goods. To overcome the free-rider problem, Olson suggests the employment of some means of coercion or the distribution of selective rewards.

Explanations Favouring Human Agency

The fundamental question concerning mobilization that seems to arise at this point is: 'how is the connection to be established between the structure and the practices?' (Castells 1983, 298). In a similar vein, Pickvance (1978) has focused on the transformation of a 'social base' into a 'social force.' It is evident that neighbourhood mobilization is not a mere outcome of contextual factors. For mobilization to occur, residents must perceive the objective issues as worth acting upon, assess the risk and rewards involved in taking an action, and make a decision to act. What appears to influence the residents' decision at this point is the availability of leaders and organizers, and the strategies they assume, the available resources for mobilization, the political culture of the community, and a range of personal motives.[9]

Types of Leaders and Their Roles

There are, according to Henig (1982, 179–83), two types of neighbourhood leaders. On the one hand, there is the charismatic leader, who by virtue of some extraordinary qualities is in a position to affect human behaviour and to enhance mobilization. On the other hand, there is the more secular version of the entrepreneurial leader, who, by distributing selective rewards, sparks enthusiasm and convinces people to join the organization.

The role of leaders has been systematically explored by Lipsky (1970) in his study of relatively powerless groups which exposes the intricate, non-linear relationships between constituency and leadership. Leaders affect their constituency as much as they are affected by it. Also relevant is Henig's conclusion that 'it was primarily among the poorer and poorly organized neighbourhoods that variations in leadership and strategy had their greatest effect' (1982, 200). These variables proved to be contingent in their explanatory power, thus confirming the interwoven effects of leadership and context.

Availability of Resources

Besides the skills and styles of communication, the organizers must command some resources in order to secure mobilization and to sustain its momentum. Skilled professionals, likely community workers, lawyers, architects, planners, fund raisers, and volunteers who can handle the routine work, must be available to the organization. A crucial resource in affecting mobilization is the media (Lipsky 1970). The effectiveness of leadership is largely determined by the connection established with the communications media, ensuring the broadening and deepening of mobilization through media coverage.

Local Political Cultures

The timing and form organization takes, indeed whether it occurs at all, depend to a large extent on the character of local cultures. There is a wide consensus in the literature that residents of wealthier neighbourhoods, inasmuch as they command resources and enjoy easy access to the media and decision makers, are more likely to mobilize than residents in poor neighbourhoods. But there is some contrary evidence showing that relatively poor groups that acquire experience may overcome the impediments of scarcity of resources. The discussion of wealthier versus poorer neighbourhoods is restricted in the sense that it fails to consider internal variations within the same residential area in terms of interests, values, and norms; in actual conflicts the local community is often divided into at least two major groups with different concerns.[10]

Personal Motives

For some researchers, human agency appears to be guided by economic motives of profit maximization. This motivation implies a calculated assessment of risks and rewards, upon which a decision is made whether or not to take part in social action (Rich 1980). For others, human agency appears to be much more complex, reflecting such motives as fear, pride, or revenge (Ley 1974b; Perlman 1982).

It is evident from this brief discussion that the study of local activism is beset by one of the major theoretical dilemmas with which the social sciences struggle – the dualism of structure and agency. Grappling with this dilemma, Giddens (1977, 1984) has shown how human agency, explicated by concepts such as power, motives, and reasons, is reflexively and recursively implicated in social structures. These social structures are, however, conceived not as political-economic forces, which in Giddens's view are properties of the political-economic system, but as rules (conventions) and resources, which both condition and are reproduced by human action. The theory, as Bernstein (1989, 24) points out, 'is powerful and attractive because it expresses a deep understanding of what we are as reflexive knowledgeable human agents who are always conditioned by and are constantly reproducing social structures.' Evans (1988) has convincingly shown how this theory can be utilized in the study of neighbourhood organization. Noting Giddens's theorization, we aim to transcend the dualism of agency and structure and accomplish an integration through an interpretation (or thick description) of the manner in which social actors make sense of their circumstances and enveloping systems as a basis for action. Furthermore, we will explore the ways in which these actions may reproduce or redefine the system (for example, the state) in significant ways, and thereby consolidate or modify both agents and structures.

NEIGHBOURHOOD ORGANIZATIONS AND URBAN LIFE

Although neighbourhood organizations have become a widespread phenomenon, their impact on urban life is still highly debated. The literature, whether empirical or theoretical, discloses a considerable confusion on this point, which may reflect both the diversity of organizational orientations and the range of theoretical-cum-ideological perspectives through which they are viewed. For example, some Canadian writers minimize the impact of neighbourhood organizations. But this view is not shared by urban politicians, who in the 1980s treated neighbourhood power as the major obstacle to their desire for higher urban densities, a desire fuelled in large measure by the success of neighbourhoods in securing down-zoning in the 1970s.

Macro-social Effects

Neighbourhood organizations may occasionally problematize national social problems such as polarization between social classes, or racial and ethnic discrimination. Although the organizations are locally based, they deal with issues whose origins transcend the city, rooted in wider political, economic, and cultural systems.

It appears that most of Castells's attention has been directed towards these kinds of 'urban problems' and impacts. In his earlier writings, the radical neighbourhood organization or, in his terms, the 'urban social movement,' expresses the urban problematic in action 'that reopens the roads to revolution in our societies by linking other forms of conflict with those arising from the productive system and from political struggle' (1977, 318). The role of the organization is thus to produce a qualitative change both at the level of ownership relations and in the political balance of forces (Castells 1976, 151, 155). However, his later writing concerns the more modest role of the movement in shaping urban social life: 'Urban movements do, however, produce new historical meaning – in the twilight zone of pretending to build within the walls of a local community a new society they know to be unattainable. And they do so by nurturing the embryos of tomorrow's social movements within the local utopias that urban movements have constructed in order never to surrender to barbarism' (1983, 331).

The scope and content of Castells's urban movements suggest an interesting sociocultural link with the wider literature on the feminist, ecological, and peace movements. While it would be absurd to equate the two groupings, they do share several features. To begin with, they often transcend class boundaries and represent a wider interest that cuts across different social groupings within civil society. For Touraine, for instance, social actors are animated by a search for meaning. Such a search is defined by Touraine as 'the organized collective behaviour of a class actor struggling against his class adversary for the social control of historicity in a concrete community' (1981, 77). Historicity implies the way in which knowledge of social processes is used by social actors to reshape the social conditions of their existence. Social control of historicity is therefore a struggle over *all forms* of domination – political, scientific, moral, gender, and economic, in which the social actors confront their adversaries in the fields of action.

According to Habermas (1983, 33; cf. Offe 1984, ch. 12), these movements, 'no longer arise in the sphere of material reproduction, but rather in areas of cultural reproduction, social integration, and socialization.' Their major goal is to defend endangered lifestyles, to protect such issues as quality of life, equality, individual self-realization, participation, and human rights. Only rarely, as in the case of the women's movement (and today, one might add, the democracy, environmental, and peace movements), do these movements proclaim, so Habermas argues, universal messages. But more commonly, 'high value is placed on the particular, the provincial, small social places, decentralized forms of interaction, and de-specialized activities, simple interaction, and non-differentiated public spheres' (Habermas 1983, 36). The new movements thus seek to produce a change in the sphere of life-world, a sphere which, according to Habermas, has been colonized – that is, impoverished and unilaterally rationalized – by the political-economic system. It is not surprising, then, that Habermas views these movements as arising 'at the seam between system and life world,' with the aim of promoting 'the revitalization of buried possibilities for expression and communication' (ibid).

Despite some deep theoretical disagreements, there is much affinity between Habermas's interpretation of the role of the new movements and Foucault's emphasis on the 'forms of resistance' as a safeguard against the disciplinary effects associated with the political technologies of power throughout society (Dreyfus and Rabinow 1983, 185). These technologies, which are always localized within a specific institutional setting – such as schools, hospitals, and prisons – are marked by rigid scheduling, separation, surveillance, ranking, individuation, and imposed uniformity and anonymity. Against the dehumanizing nature of these techniques, Foucault asserts a radical refusal, 'the right to be different' (1983, 211–12).

Castells's notions of identity, cultural autonomy, communication, and self-management, which are revealed through neighbourhood life and neighbourhood decentralization, are plainly not so very far from Touraine's concept of a struggle over historicity, from Habermas's notions concerning the revitalization of the life-world, and from Foucault's assertion of the right to be different. The description of neighbourhood organizations as representative of a new society is not limited to Castells's work. Neighbourhood organizations, as Goldsmith writes, have increasingly become 'a primary means by which people seek to influence local events,' thus signifying within the context of city politics 'the decline of party as a means of aggregation and individual political participation,' (1980, 82).[11] For some authors, neighbourhood organizations are conceived of as enhancing internal participatory democracy and have been associated with such processes as self-actualization and overcoming social alienation.[12] Gottschalk, for instance, describes the organization as a spontaneous local entity, where the internal linkage is based on cooperation, social interaction, humanist response to the needs of others, and normative power (1975, 13–17). Other studies relate to the neighbourhood organization's political tasks, which range from moderate ones such as local control and making government responsive, to more radical tasks such as a piecemeal revolution, or a radical challenge to the status quo.[13]

The fundamental question that arises at this point is whether neighbourhood organizations, which occupy a large part of Castells's work, are indeed in a position to nurture the embryos of a new society. His answer is somewhat ambivalent. He concedes that, although the movements 'address the real issues of our time,' they do it 'neither on the scale nor terms adequate to the task.' Yet, as he moves on to argue, 'they are more than a last symbolic stand and desperate cry. They are symptoms of our contradictions, and therefore potentially capable of superseding these contradictions' (1983, 331).[14]

Urban Effects

Urban politics is essentially the politics of service delivery. It involves elected politicians, appointed officials, professionals, and participants in neighbourhood organizations. It is true that one of the major problems confronting these actors has to do with the scarcity of resources. Yet, as Yates (1977) has shown, the problem is much more complex. It involves conflicts between city-wide policy and neighbourhood-oriented aspirations; lack of trust between urban managers and politicians, on the one hand, and neighbourhood actors, on the other; low levels of responsiveness on the part of the local government, which is reflected in insensitivity to local needs; fragmentation of decision making, which is reflected in low levels of coordination between departments, duplication of services, and inefficiency. It has been argued by several studies (see, especially, Rich 1986) that decentralization and empowerment may help to solve some of these problems.

Neighbourhood Effects

The effects at this level are associated with material gains and social changes. Material gains entail the upgrading of the local quality of life through the employment of one of the following strategies: 1 / elimination of existing disamenities, like traffic congestion and air pollution; 2 / resistance to perceived new disamenities, like power plants or highways; 3 / retention of amenities against external threats, including environmental resources or heritage buildings; 4 / obtaining new facilities and services, like a new community centre or new school (Dabrowski, Haynor, and Cuervo 1986). Besides the material gains, neighbourhood organizations may serve a role in contributing to social control, social participation, and mutual support (Warren 1978, 9).

In performing these activities, the organization may assume some exclusionary functions such as social control in the case of the defended neighbourhood, and the pursuit of a specific limited interest in the case of the community of limited liability. It is precisely at this level that some of the most vehement criticism has been raised against neighbourhood organizations. Against the heroic representation of neighbourhood organizations as a central phenomenon in urban life, which ultimately leads to a progressive society, there is abundant empirical evidence that points to the contrary. Neighbourhood organizations may be characterized by a high degree of parochialism, modest aims, and a tendency to concentrate on seemingly trivial issues.[15] According to Hunter and Suttles (1972, 62–3), many organizations have 'a narrow support base and limited access to higher administrators' and therefore are often ignored. Furthermore, as Pahl (1975, 272–3) notes, they are short-lived and tend to dissolve following local reforms. Socially, their orientation might, in certain cases, be quite reactionary and conservative, revealing itself in the exclusion of minorities or other social groups from the neighbourhood (Cybriwsky 1978; Duncan and Duncan 1984) and, politically, they might be removed from participatory democracy (Warren and Warren 1977, 54–5; Cnaan 1989). Several of these shortcomings may be exacerbated among the organizations of disadvantaged groups, which form a substantial part of the literature. Saunders (1979, 129) maintains that 'disadvantaged groups are more likely to mobilize in reaction to a threat (such as urban renewal) than in response to a situation of ongoing deprivation.'

The defensive, often conservative, activity of neighbourhood organizations in poor areas (Cox 1976, 177) and their limited political effects seem to stem from a variety of political, social, and psychological circumstances. Consequently, the activity of such organizations is often hampered by the scarcity of material and time resources (Rich 1980), a high ratio of risk to reward (Oberschall 1973, 157–72), and a low level of intellectual input, sometimes resulting in irrational activity. Reflecting on the experience of these organizations, Harvey (1989) observes that they have not promoted municipal socialism, working-class community, localized struggle against capital, or a return to cultural rootedness. With few exceptions, he argues, they are not manifestations of regional resistance or the struggle for local autonomy.

An important task of this book is to come up with a more accurate description of the problems identified by neighbourhood organizations, and to distinguish between organizations according to their effects. Our argument is that the nature of the problem confronted by the organization is likely to shape the character of the political adversary, the strategy of action, and the prospects of attaining a solution. It is argued that radical grass-roots organizations would display an orientation towards broader social problems, confront higher levels of the state, and criticize the existing welfare policy. Neocorporatist organizations would tend to confront the power structure of the local state and the policy of service delivery. Finally, issue-oriented organizations are likely to be confined to the neighbourhood's specific needs, and to address the local or higher levels of the state only at those points that affect the organization's interests.

RELATIONSHIPS WITH THE STATE

One of our major arguments is that a typology of neighbourhood organizations is largely affected by the nature of municipal political regimes and the configuration of the welfare state. To be more specific, we argue that a typology of organizations is affected by the level of responsiveness of the state and by the level of development of its welfare infrastructure.

The Level of Responsiveness

The level of responsiveness of the state to neighbourhood organizations is depicted in varying ways by pluralist, élitist, Marxist, and neocorporatist theories. Following pluralism, the city is a pluralist democracy made up of multiple coalitions leading to the mayor (Dahl 1961, 1971). Power (in the sense of the capacity of an actor to influence the conduct of others) is conceived of as disaggregated, shared, and negotiated by multiple power centres and pressure groups, which represent diverse, fragmented, and competitive interests. The state is supposed to act as a neutral and responsive arbiter, and neighbourhood organizations are recommended to maintain their independence and to rely on advocacy and lobbying strategies (Gittle 1980). The central premises of the pluralist position have been heavily criticized by neo-élitist and Marxist theories, which, in spite of their differences, regard the pluralist theory as inadequate because it fails to take account of the systematic inequality in the distribution of wealth and power in urban politics.

The neo-élitist approach asserts that power is not diffuse and fragmented, as the pluralist theory would have it, but rather resides in the ability of certain groups to limit and even prevent the access of other individuals and groups to the process of decision making. Such asymmetry of power may affect which issues are to be raised on the public agenda (decision making) and which are not (non–decision making) (Bachrach and Baratz 1963). This is indeed a version of the élitist position that states that the self-conscious élite effectively runs the city. Friedland's study of urban renewal in American cities (1982) showed, for example, how the interests of the business sector and organized labour were represented on the public agenda, whereas the destruction of low-income housing and the displacement of inner-city blacks were excluded.[16] Lukes's critique of pluralism digs even deeper, pointing to the existence of latent conflicts, potential issues, and real interests that may even escape the participants themselves. In Lukes's view (1974, 21), the sources of the asymmetry of power and the bias of a system have to be sought not only in a series of individually chosen acts, 'but also in the socially structured and culturally patterned behaviour of groups, and practices of institutions.'

Approaching the relations between the state and neighbourhood organizations through the wider view of socially structured conflict is indeed one of the main tenets of Marxist positions. The state, according to Marxist theory, has to grapple with a self-contradictory task. On the one hand, the state must secure the process of wealth creation and private appropriation of resources. On the other hand, it must secure legitimation through the redistribution of resources. Political power is, then, sustained in a dual way: through material accumulation and through the employment of social and welfare policy.[17] The urban manifestation of the dual function of the state is succinctly demonstrated by Castells (1983), who shows how, torn between business interests and popular demands, the state proceeds to politicize the urban environment so that almost any attempt to improve urban services by local organizations is bound to bring about a political conflict within the state. In this conflict, Castells argues (p. 316), the state acts in a centralist, bureaucratized, and authoritarian manner.

In contrast, Saunders (1987, 307) seeks to integrate the Marxist conflict-oriented approach with the mainstream pluralist approach. He cautiously moves on to develop an ideal-type distinction which sets apart a centralized politics of production from a decentralized and more responsive politics of consumption. He develops his dualistic model of the welfare state within a specific Western European setting.[18] Whether these imputed changes also imply a loss of state capacity to govern is still an open question. At least one theoretical school, the neocorporatist one, tends to answer the question negatively. Since the 1970s, the steering capacity of the state has been enhanced (Schmitter 1974). In the post-liberal, advanced capitalist state, interests are represented through singular, strict, and hierarchically ordered associations (trade unions or business confederations) that are 'recognized or licensed (if not created) by the state and granted a deliberate representational monopoly within their respective categories in exchange for observing certain controls on their selection of leaders and articulation of demands and supports' (ibid, 93–4). True, neocorporatist theory represents a tripartite institutional arrangement that ties together government, organized labour, and business associations. None the less, this model might logically be extended to incorporate certain forms of neighbourhood government, initiated and legitimated by the state: little city halls in U.S. cities, local area planning in Canadian cities; and neighbourhood government in the Netherlands, Italy, and Israel. For all practical purposes, these forms of local government mark the ever-growing presence and the increased directive capacity of the state in the sphere of daily life. The relationships between the state and this type of organization are more institutionalized and coordinated than the voluntary organizations discussed by pluralist theory, built upon cooperation rather than competition and conflict, and focused on the delivery of services rather than societal change. In her discussion of the transformation of the voluntary sector into the 'shadow state,' Wolch (1990) has identified just such a neocorporatism in the welfare state's penetration of voluntary organizations.[19]

The Stage of Development of the Welfare State

How have historical changes in the relations between the welfare state and the public affected the nature of neighbourhood organizations? Some preliminary steps in addressing this question have been taken by several U.S. studies. These studies discern several phases in the development of the local state and trace the impact of each phase on the nature of neighbourhood government. First, in the colonial and post-colonial period, urban government was highly fragmented, the governing bodies were composed of dignitaries and wealthy citizens, and neighbourhood-based political organizations were almost non-existent. In a second phase, machine politics concentrated the political power in the hands of local bosses. The relations with the neighbourhoods were based on patronage and clientelism, where favours were exchanged for political support. The old-time neighbourhood bosses, as Yates (1973, 16) points out, 'established little baronies ... this is testimony to the existence of feudal power, not neighbourhood democracy.' Third, so-called progressive reform in the 1880–1920 period took power from neighbourhood bosses, placed urban government in the hands of expert administrators, advanced the idea of universalism in service provision, and reduced whatever neighbourhood power might have existed. Fourth, urban renewal in the 1960s, which entailed centralized intervention into the life of central city districts, resulted in the rise of neighbourhood movements. These movements sought to defend their territories, resist displacement, and participate in community-based decision making. In their struggle they were often aided by the civil rights movement, which emphasized the underserviced conditions of black neighbourhoods and demanded racial integration and social rights. Fifth, the war on poverty and the experience of community action and model-cities programs, in spite of their shortcomings, helped to develop neighbourhood organizations and to advance citizen participation in political decision making. Finally, the plethora of grass-roots and neighbourhood organizations since the 1970s is accounted for by continued conflicts over urban space as well as by the social learning of the 1960s. Fainstein and Fainstein (1991) shed some further light on the evolution of the relationships between state and neighbourhoods. They identify three phases in the postwar development of community representation in urban politics: 'an almost sole reliance on elected officials operating through city-wide institutions (1950–64); a period of social militancy aimed primarily at increasing the power of low-income and minority groups (1965–74); and the present phase of nonmilitant community activism' (p. 109).

It is worth noting that these useful descriptions have not gone beyond the level of cursory sketches, and were not developed into a comprehensive historical account. What appears to be needed at this point is a historical analysis that examines these relationships not only in the U.S. context, but also from a broader international perspective. This book tries to develop such a perspective through a comparative, historical study. Our point of departure is that both Canada and Israel went through several stages in the development of the welfare state: the nineteenth-century phase of the minimal state; the gradual rise of the welfare state since the beginning of the twentieth century; the crisis of the welfare state, which started in the 1960s and 1970s; and the advent of privatized consumption and self-provision in the 1980s and 1990s. Each of these phases has been characterized by a different set of relations with neighbourhood organizations. The existence of the minimal state corresponds with quasi-autonomous organizations, the rise of the welfare state has been associated with patron / client relationships, the crisis of the welfare state is linked with urban protest, while experiments in decentralization and empowerment in the mature, perhaps post-welfare state are the result of administrative decentralization and new patterns of co-production.

Our purpose here, then, is to provide a more differentiated perspective on neighbourhood organizations, one which is aware of the distinction between two nations while also viewing individual neighbourhood organizations as representative of larger historical trajectories.

THE WELFARE STATE AND LOCAL POLITICS

The welfare state has its origins in a series of urban reforms, of which perhaps the best known are the municipal initiatives in Birmingham in the late nineteenth century. The social maladies of the city led a social reformer like Joseph Chamberlain to advocate an active role for the local state in enhancing the social welfare of urban residents through the public delivery of essential services. This was a major innovation in the relationships between government and its urban citizenry. Reviewing the situation in Britain, Cox remarks: 'Planning and organizing the housing of considerable proportions of the population are responsibilities which did not exist when the 1888 Act was passed. There was no planning legislation, effectively, before 1909' (1976, 51). With time, however, the activities of the welfare state transcended the urban sphere to incorporate such general issues as income maintenance, pension programs, job training, education and health services, and social insurance. Yet the urban sphere has remained one of the major points of government intervention, and the site of both confrontation and endorsement by neighbourhood and welfare-rights organizations. Below, we review the development of the welfare state in Canada and Israel, and interrelations between the local state and neighbourhood organizations. In so doing, we aim to show that there is no one model capable of explaining the form and meaning of neighbourhood organizations. Understanding must be based on an integrated interpretation that considers the variations of historical context and the changing roles of the state.

The Welfare State in Canada

In the nineteenth century the services of a minimum state were introduced in Canada, notably compulsory education and public health acts. Rapid urbanization and industrialization in the generation prior to 1914 led to new degrees of poverty in the major immigrant centres, and the social surveys conducted in Britain and the United States were repeated in a number of Canadian cities. Among these the most enduring were the reports on the working-class city below the hill in Montreal by Ames (1972 [1897]), and the immigrant North End of Winnipeg by Woods-worth (1972 [1911]), then superintendent of All Peoples' Mission.[20] These publications both reflected and reinforced a momentum of urban reform that included attention to public ownership of utilities, urban planning, and local government reorganization, as well as to social welfare.

While there was some difference between the rhetoric and the reality of the reform movement, it did make palpable impacts in improving standards of health through the regulation of unhealthy environments. Local jurisdictions continued to be responsible for local needs, however, and by 1913 municipalities collectively spent more on health and welfare than the federal and provincial governments; indeed, for the thirty years up to 1913, expenditures by the City of Toronto exceeded those of the province of Ontario (Lemon 1993). Administrative reform produced a more professional cadre of urban managers, but the adoption of the bureaucratic model inspired by the private corporation served to create a distinct community of technical experts, who, over the decades, became increasingly isolated from, and inaccessible to, a broad public – an issue that became one basis for political mobilization in the late 1960s. The civic bureaucrats instead became accountable to the social class that benefited most fully from urban reform, the businessmen and boosters who were the dominant group among the successful candidates for civic office in the half-century following 1920.

The interwar period led to a significant transfer of responsibility for social welfare, which reflected more accurately the inferior constitutional position of local government beneath provincial and federal powers in the tripartite division of the Canadian state. The immense dislocation brought about by the Depression accelerated a process already under way, as municipal resources were overwhelmed by extensive poverty associated with the unemployment of up to a quarter of the workforce. Yet the response of senior government was slow and reluctant, and much was still left to private charities and philanthropy. In Vancouver's working-class Eastside, for example, Rev. Andrew Roddan of the First United Church wrote and broadcast on the plight of the homeless while his church was feeding 800–1,200 men a day by the winter of 1931, and counselling up to 15,000 people a year. A few blocks distant, among the yet more marginalized population of Chinatown, there were reports of deaths from starvation in the worst years of the Depression (Roddan 1932, 104; Anderson 1986).

Only late in the 1930s did the senior levels of government assume a greater share of the cost of health and social services, and the contribution of the hard-pressed municipalities fell below 20 per cent. In the 1940s, the welfare state began to take its present shape, goaded by wartime needs, the electoral success of the Co-operative Commonwealth Federation (CCF), a social-democratic movement that later became the New Democratic Party (NDP), and the growing recognition of the need for Keynesian state intervention with its strategy of demand management. By 1945, the federal government was responsible for 72 per cent of health and social spending, and the municipal share was down to 7 per cent. Progress in the postwar period was uneven, and it was not until the 1960s that Medicare (universal medical insurance), the Canada Pension Plan and Canada Assistance Plan, together with additional programs in health care, education, social assistance, and regional economic development, rounded out the major dimensions of the welfare state. Between 1963/4 and 1981/2, provincial social-service budgets increased sevenfold in real spending.

Meanwhile, an important development in the cities was the growing role of public-housing policy. Lagging again behind both British and U.S. precedents, Canadian public-housing policy was not legislated until revisions to the National Housing Act in 1944. The pace of development quickened under the sponsorship of the Central (later Canada) Mortgage and Housing Corporation (CMHC), and between 1964 and 1972 some ninety urban renewal projects were authorized. But, by the late 1960s, severe questions were being raised about existing models of public housing and comprehensive renewal: the problems of mass displacement and the stigma of high densities and stark design were noted in a federal report in 1969. There was equally an invidious side to the centralized administration of the renewal process, and revised federal housing policies issued by the Trudeau administration in the early 1970s pointed to a redirection of process as well as of product. A more decentralized and participatory administrative model was enunciated, with funds for new community-based non-profit and cooperative housing programs. A fundamental shift from renewal to conservation was simultaneously recorded in the new Neighbourhood Improvement Programme and in the Residential Rehabilitation Assistance Programme, a major initiative that was to direct over $3 billion of public funds into housing renovation over the next fifteen years.

This reorientation of the state did not occur in a political vacuum. Trudeau's promises of local accountability were themselves shaped in the context of a newly politicized citizenry, informed and sometimes animated by the growing professions of social work and social planning as well as the political currents of the counter-culture and the New Left.[21] Large-scale public and private redevelopment projects and infrastructure (notably urban freeway proposals) were resisted in city after city.[22] Activism was directed against not only the changes to the built environment, but also the cloistered decision-making process which lay behind it and the privileged access to power of the business voice, both outcomes of the administrative centralization of the earlier reform era. Propelled by newly elected reform politicians (though these were rarely in a majority on local councils), apparent decentralization of planning services occurred in more publicly accountable processes of neighbourhood, or local area, planning. In British Columbia, the NDP provincial government of 1972–5 also introduced the decentralization of some social services to be administered by locally elected community resources boards.

With some exceptions, the mid-1970s represented the high-water mark of an active and democratic welfare state. In the years following, shifts to the political right and growing public debt produced a more grudging view of further development. Restraint budgets, privatization of some services, and regressive taxation have all served to discipline the principles of the welfare state. There is some evidence of growing income polarization in the cities and of a deepening poverty among those with the lowest incomes, revealed in the spectre of urban homelessness. Once again, responsibility is being passed to charities, as is demonstrated by the remarkable growth of food banks. The first Canadian food bank was opened in 1981; by the end of 1984, 75 were in operation across the country, and by 1991 the total exceeded 300.[23]

A result was signs of a renewed politics of resistance at the grass-roots level by the end of the 1980s. The 1988 general election was fought over the proposed Free Trade Agreement (FTA) with the United States. Perhaps the major inspiration of opposition to the FTA was the threat to the Canadian welfare state posed by a union with the Americans and their more privatized social-service model. While FTA opponents garnered a majority of votes, they won a minority of seats, and the agreement was signed. But the election did mobilize large numbers of people around welfare-rights issues. Earlier, in 1983, massive opposition to the provincial government's social restraint program brought British Columbia within a few hours of a general strike. Anti-poverty and tenants' rights activists have been urging a return to the citizenship-rights model of the welfare state, and once again neighbourhoods have been activated by renewed public and private development pressures. Add to this re-awakened environmental sensitivities, and the legitimacy of government, together with its capacity to govern, are strained, not least because of a period of unprecedented public debt. Civic elections across the country showed some fresh successes for candidates advocating controlled growth and redistributive social policies. In 1990, and for the first time, the NDP was elected to the provincial government of Ontario; in 1991, further electoral successes followed in British Columbia and Saskatchewan.

Power and Politics in Vancouver, 1886–1966

Local politics has been framed by these developments in federal and provincial policy in Vancouver, a city of 450,000 residents at the core of a metropolitan area of 1.7 million people. Vancouver was established with the completion of the transcontinental Canadian Pacific Railway, which reached the small townsite of Granville in 1885.[24] Renamed by the president of the Montreal-based CPR, the city remained virtually a company town for a generation, as the CPR consolidated both its trading function and the property development of vast land holdings conceded to it as a condition of the extension of its Pacific terminus to Vancouver. The activity along the waterfront and the pollution pall which hung over the downtown peninsula confirmed the status of a successful trading and manufacturing centre. The city grew rapidly, particularly in the spectacular building boom from 1901 to 1911, with the arrival of thousands of families from central Canada and Britain.

In this frontier boom town, the primary law was the law of free enterprise. Real estate speculation was unfettered, land-use regulation was minimal, and the evolutionary processes of growth and change operated with Darwinian urgency. From the logic of the real estate market, no neighbourhood was sacrosanct. The élite district of the West End, with bourgeois homes that sported the Victorian excesses of picturesque eclecticism, exuded a glory which lasted for barely a generation, as apartment- and rooming-houses invaded the district, and the élite withdrew virtually *en masse*, with scarce a thought of resistance but many a thought of substantial capital gains, to be invested in their next property in the CPR's new suburb of Shaughnessy.

The regulating hand of the state in this free-enterprise land market was restrained. While rudimentary land-use by-laws were introduced relatively early in Point Grey, an independent suburb until amalgamation with Vancouver in 1929, in the adjacent suburb of East Vancouver urban development in a primarily working-class territory proceeded with gay, even anarchic, abandon. Following the city's annexation of these two inner suburbs, the ebbing tide of the Progressive era finally reached Vancouver, and the St Louis firm of Harland Bartholomew was contracted to prepare a land-use plan, completed in 1929. The Bartholomew plan largely consolidated the status quo, specifying concentric residential zones of declining population density with distance from the central business district, and a large industrial zone around downtown and extending through the city's east side along the waterfront and the reclaimed tideland adjacent to False Creek.

Civic rights were extended disproportionately to the privileged constituency of ratepayers. Homeownership was in fact enjoyed by a broad cross-section of the population, with large tracts of cut-over forest and a dense system of streetcar routes laid out in anticipation of development, together bringing enough land onto the market that crafts workers and junior functionaries were able to afford their own plot for a cottage or bungalow. But neighbourhood organization was most active in the middle-class areas. In middle-class Point Grey, land-use controls were introduced in 1922, and the ratepayers' association in Shaughnessy sustained the energetic earlier actions of the CPR to guarantee the longevity and exclusiveness of an élite suburb, instituting meticulous land-use and zoning controls and rigorously policing them. Still earlier, in 1909, the Kitsilano Ratepayers' Association was formed in an emerging district of comfortable homes to ensure the timely arrival of such urban services as sidewalks and lighting, and to keep a vigilant eye for any transgression in the landscape to the idyll of middle-class domesticity.

In contrast to the privileged status of ratepayers, other groups enjoyed minimal rights. Tenants and racial minorities experienced limited entitlement. The Chinese, huddled together for protection on the marshes of Dupont Street, were not enfranchised in municipal elections until 1949, and prior to that time were relieved to be left alone, as Chinatown was targeted by the police and health officials in unrelenting campaigns of by-law enforcement, often conducted in the undisguised discourse of racism. In contrast to the ratepayers, with their easy access to City Hall, the minorities of Chinatown and Japantown turned inward and, through benevolent associations and local bosses, established their own moral order and a modest system of mutual aid.

Vancouver was administered through a rather unwieldy ward system, and the rise of substantial leftist sympathy in the 1930s, coinciding with massive unemployment, together with the establishment of the social-democratic CCF, led to the abolition of the wards in 1936 and their replacement by an at-large electoral system. The CCF would have benefited from ward representation, but still did well enough in the first at-large election that, as a second defensive measure, the civic Non-Partisan Association (NPA) was formed in 1937 as a free-enterprise coalition, avowedly to keep formal political parties out of municipal politics. In an organizational sense, the NPA was not a party, but its members certainly shared a common ideology, an essential conviction that commerce was the principal civic virtue. For the next thirty years Vancouver enjoyed a stable period of one-party rule. The typical NPA candidate, invariably elected to office, was an independent businessman with close links to the city's Board of Trade. In 1969, as many as 73 per cent of leaders in the NPA were owners, managers, or agents of private companies (Easton and Tennant 1969). Tennant has well described the NPA as displaying 'an abhorrence of overt partisan activity, an acceptance of civic rule by business people (with a corresponding repugnance towards socialist and working class groups), a desire for unlimited commercial and physical growth and development in the city, and no desire at all for citizen participation in civic decision-making' (1980, 10–11).

The Neighbourhood Movement and the Emergence of Multi-Party Politics, 1967–1992

In the burgeoning welfare state, the federal Trudeau administration, which took office in 1968, upheld a bold urban policy, establishing the ministry of state for urban affairs in 1971, redirecting the course of urban renewal from demolition to rehabilitation, and introducing innovative Third Sector housing programs which gave considerable opportunity to non-profit and voluntary groups. By the end of the decade, however, the ministry had been terminated, the victim of Cabinet squabbles and federal-provincial wrangling, and through the 1980s the federal government progressively withdrew from urban policy, off-loading responsibility to provincial governments. In British Columbia, after the short-lived reform activity of the NDP administration between 1972 and 1975, the province was ruled until the end of 1991 by successive governments of the right-wing Social Credit party. Provincially inspired programs, which included community participation, were terminated (initially community-resources boards, and later certain regional government functions), power was recentralized, and social services were reduced as part of a neoconservative restraint strategy.

These contexts produced by senior governments offered variable degrees of empowerment and frustration to aspiring neighbourhood organizations and local politicians. Opportunities were most pronounced in the decade following 1968, and particularly in the early 1970s. At that time, a spirit of new beginnings and local empowerment was reinforced by all three levels of government in Vancouver, permitting fruitful cooperation. This led, for example, to the innovative public redevelopment of False Creek in Vancouver's inner city – a district which conveniently fell within the federal constituency of the minister of state for urban affairs.

A new-found turbulence in Vancouver civic politics after 1967 followed a thirty-year period of continuous NPA domination. By the 1960s the foundational tenets of the NPA were wearing thin, showing little sign of evolution, even as Vancouver itself was not only growing demographically, but also experiencing a significant economic and social transition. The city progressively left behind its origins as a raw frontier town. The lineaments of a 'post-industrial' service economy took shape in new government offices, health and educational institutions, and the mushrooming downtown office sector. A new middle class of young, highly educated professionals, both men and women, appeared in the city, a class in emergence which became increasingly critical of a municipal politics controlled by a male NPA dynasty that lacked sophistication and public accountability.[25] For this group, democracy entailed a more active process than the right to vote, and their urban vision extended beyond growth boosterism to include social justice and environmental quality. These oppositional sentiments were mobilized in 1967, when council announced, without public consultation, its intent to build a freeway system mandated by external technical consultants, in documents which subsequent enquiry showed council members did not understand. Not only did the devastating impacts of this plan upon the city's poorest neighbourhoods, Chinatown-Strathcona and the Downtown Eastside, pique middle-class anger; so did the characteristically highhanded style of decision making (see chapter 4). Middle-class energies crystallized into the founding of a new civic party, The Electors Action Movement (TEAM), dominated by liberal young professionals. TEAM enjoyed initial successes in the 1968 and 1970 elections, and was returned to power in a landslide victory in 1972.

However, with the reform coalition splintering from defections to the political left and right, TEAM's tenure in office was only six years. Its importance in nurturing a new generation of political leadership was, nevertheless, more enduring, and a number of its policy innovations were sustained by later administrations.[26] Moreover, a considerable policy agenda was implemented. TEAM's ideology and slogan of 'the livable city' was a complex concept that required a careful balancing of sometimes incompatible objectives of growth management, environmental quality, and social justice. These categories were also elastic enough that they could be manipulated by opportunistic interests, including the ratepayers of the élite neighbourhood of Shaughnessy (see chapter 2). Attempts were made by TEAM to democratize City Hall; control was removed from senior bureaucrats, information was shared with the public, council meetings were made far more accessible, some functions were decentralized in a policy of participatory neighbourhood planning, and tentative steps were taken towards the re-establishment of at least a partial ward system (an initiative which floundered following indecisive plebiscites in 1973 and 1979). Early in its term, openings for neighbourhood organizations were favourable, with a new and eager NDP provincial administration, and a minority Liberal government in Ottawa sustained by the federal NDP, which held the balance of power. It was a political climate 'most propitious for new departures' (Resnick 1977).

Yet TEAM, although a centrist party, did not have a broad base. It was the party of young, liberal professionals living in Vancouver's westside neighbourhoods. In 1969, 58 per cent of its leaders held professional or semi-professional jobs, while only 3 per cent were union officials or blue-collar workers (Easton and Tennant 1969). The political vacuum was filled by the Committee of Progressive Electors (COPE), a socialist party also organized in 1968 (in response to TEAM), around Alderman Harry Rankin, a lawyer with a practice in the poverty district of the Downtown Eastside. With union support, COPE pressed an agenda of democratic socialism to the left of the NDP, seeking a constituency among tenants, the working poor, and immigrants. Until 1980, Rankin was its only elected councillor, providing a frequent conundrum for grass-roots activists on the left (see chapters 6 and 8). However, COPE became a significant electoral force after 1980, benefiting in large measure from credible candidates drawn from the leadership of the Downtown Eastside Residents' Association (DERA, see chapter 6), and by 1990 it held half the seats on City Council. From 1982 to 1986, an unstable left-liberal grouping, presided over by Mayor Michael Harcourt, a former TEAM alderman, held numerical dominance at City Hall, extending the period of reform at the civic level long after it had been deflected by neoconservatism in Victoria and Ottawa. However, with Harcourt's move to provincial politics in 1986, and eventually to premier in 1991, a renewed NPA regained civic office in Vancouver under Mayor Gordon Campbell, and with the disappearance of TEAM, municipal politics became sharply polarized between COPE and NPA councillors.

Local politics in Vancouver has not been dissimilar from that of other large Canadian cities, where the simpler and scarcely contested growth boosterism of the pre-1968 era was also complicated by the mobilization of plural objectives leading to a multi-party system at City Hall. From 1968 to 1986 Vancouver fitted well a designation of Canadian municipal politics as incorporating 'the old guard, the progressives, and the soft middle' (Higgins 1981). The multiplication of political parties followed, rather than led, neighbourhood activism. It was the conflict over the freeway plan in 1967 which precipitated the formation of both TEAM and COPE in 1968; indeed, the parties comprised activism in an institutional form. Similarly, conflict over major land-use proposals between 1968 and 1972 prepared the ground for TEAM's victory in 1972; a majority of its councillors had been leaders in neighbourhood struggles. The same relationship has been no less true in the 1980s and early 1990s, when DERA provided COPE with two elected councillors and two mayoralty candidates.

The neighbourhood movement was most active in the period from 1967 to 1975. The freeway protest opened up a floodgate of frustrations, vented during a time of rapid growth and redevelopment of the built environment. The conservative and somewhat paternalistic community organizations of the poorest neighbourhoods, Chinatown-Strathcona and the Downtown Eastside, were outflanked in those districts by new protest groups with an unclouded expectation of citizenship rights. Middle-class heritage groups conducted sophisticated campaigns to protect historic sites during the redevelopment boom, and won a notable victory with the preservation of Gastown, under threat from both the freeway and Project 200, a vast rebuilding scheme sponsored by the CPR. Rapid social and land-use change was contested in the middle-class neighbourhoods, led by an Alinsky-style protest group in Kitsilano and the traditional ratepayers' association of Shaughnessy.

Neighbourhood activism was directed both at issues and at process, the insensitive style of the city's technocratic planning and centralized decision making. TEAM was a product of the neighbourhood movement, and once in office sought both to give a voice to community organizations and to channel their energies through the initiative of local area planning. Co-production was also achieved through provincial and federal programs of the early 1970s, the provincial community-resources boards, which permitted local administration of some social services, and the federal Neighbourhood Improvement Programme (NIP), pioneered in Strathcona, which provided funds for community enrichment, with priorities to be assigned by a neighbourhood committee.

These considerable initiatives of co-production were not sustained. The resources boards were eliminated in 1976 by the newly elected Social Credit party in Victoria, and NIP was phased out by the federal government. The slow-down of economic growth attenuated both development pressures and the state's revenues. Local area planning has been maintained by the city to the present, though the excessive early expectations for community participation have never been borne out in practice. Neighbourhood politics weakened, in part from achieved gains, in part from reduced redevelopment threats, in part from organizational weariness.

What is perhaps most surprising is that neighbourhood politics survived at all. Local organizations place substantial demands upon volunteer leaders, particularly in a city without a ward tradition, and during an era when the enabling hand of the state had been significantly withdrawn, in terms of funds, personnel, and even a willingness to listen. Moreover, quiescence should not be mistaken for extinction. Three of the four Vancouver organizations examined in later chapters have survived for more than twenty years. Neighbourhood participation has continued in more routinized forms, including the co-production activities of social-housing societies, some with a distinct geographic territory. Protest activities have flared up periodically, indicative of a seemingly irreversible socialization of the grass roots, which makes protest an ever-present possibility, even in the most unlikely places. In the late 1980s senior citizens in Kerrisdale, arguably the most conservative district in the city, mounted pickets to protest the demolition of affordable apartments. Indeed, a new round of neighbourhood activism erupted in a number of districts in the late 1980s. COPE attempted to build upon this widespread community dissent, and in the civic election of 1990 persuaded Jim Green, organizer of the Downtown Eastside Residents' Association for a decade, to run as mayoralty candidate. Astutely campaigning for enhanced neighbourhood powers under the slogan 'the Neighbourhood Green,' he won 45 per cent of the popular vote in his first election, against a well-established NPA incumbent.

Although neighbourhood interests have held a strong claim on liberal and socialist agendas, the response of the local state to a plural public has not been unproblematic. Party fortunes have been turbulent, with the collapse and subsequent revival of the NPA, the short-lived triumph and subsequent disappearance of TEAM, the repeated failure of the NDP to make inroads municipally, and the slow but steady ascension of COPE through the 1980s. Such instability reveals the difficulty of establishing municipal institutions which represent multiple publics and which adequately bind a fragmented urban vision. Relations between City Hall and the neighbourhoods have become far more intricate. The old model, where a privileged, indeed exclusive, role was afforded to ratepayers' associations of white, middle-class homeowners by earlier NPA councils is no longer tenable, although the power of such associations may still prove formidable (chapter 2). But other neighbourhood interests, formerly excluded from entitlement, have firmly pressed their democratic rights since the 1960s. The Chinese-origin minority, which did not receive the municipal vote until 1949, vigorously and successfully resisted the destruction of its territorial core by state freeway and urban-renewal policies through an organization with broader ambitions than the older and more conservative ethnic societies (chapter 4). An unlikely mobilization of poor tenants living in rooming-houses and residential hotels in the Downtown Eastside, triggered by liberal policies of community development, quickly evolved into a more radical protest organization beyond council's control (chapter 6). A response in Vancouver, as in

Jerusalem and many other cities in Western nations, to multiple publics has been a certain devolution of functions to neighbourhood groups. Such a strategy of co-production may open up genuine lines of local democracy; it may also permit a more insidious neocorporatism, a closer control by the state over local publics. But it is also a strategy with high risks for municipal government, as decentralization may sharpen and politicize neighbourhood issues, and provide a forum and legitimacy for critical grass-roots groups. In Vancouver's Kitsilano neighbourhood, rounds of local-area planning in the mid-1970s and again in the late 1980s precipitated precisely these unwanted consequences for the local state (chapter 8).

The Welfare State, Power, and Politics in Jerusalem

Jerusalem is a city of many contrasts. Enveloped in symbolism, it has been accorded the status of a cosmological centre, an *axis mundi* which marks an ontological transition between worlds. But for generations, perhaps with the exceptions of the Crusaders' kingdom of Jerusalem and the British mandate government, it has been a provincial city that lay at the periphery of the empires that ruled it. Rich in historical content but impoverished in economic terms, Jerusalem ranks low in its socio-economic status among the cities of Israel. It is a city where the rationality of democratic government collides with long-standing traditions of communal and territorial closure. Geopolitically, it is a united city, but from national, cultural, and social perspectives it is fundamentally divided between Jews and Arabs, ultra-orthodox and secular Jews, and lower- and upper-status groups. Today Jerusalem contains half a million people – 361,500 Jews and 142,600 Arabs – who share the same urban space but live separately. The neighbourhood organizations that developed in Jerusalem through the twentieth century are identified below, in the context of the evolution of the welfare state.

The British Mandate Government, 1917–1947

Under the British mandate government, the population of the city rose from 62,578 residents in 1922 to an estimated 165,000 in 1947. At the end of 1946, Jews comprised 62 per cent of the total population, as compared with 54 per cent in 1922 (Amiran 1973). This demographic growth resulted in further expansion of the built environment. The Arab population expanded in two directions: northeast and also south of the

Old City, founding the neighbourhood of Baka. Some spacious houses were built in the southwestern section of the city to accommodate British mandatory officials, consuls, and other foreigners who resided temporarily in Jerusalem. The Jewish settlement in the city took two major forms: organized neighbourhoods built by voluntary associations and unorganized neighbourhoods built by private developers. Quite often, residents in the neighbourhoods organized themselves in councils responsible for local affairs. This trend was encouraged by the British authorities, who occasionally appointed an influential figure in the community to serve as the neighbourhood's *muchtar*, that is, a local leader and liaison between the residents and the authorities. In 1945, there were twenty-three Jewish neighbourhoods headed by local *muchtars* (Bigger 1981, 15).

One of the most interesting urban innovations of the time was associated with the planning and design of garden suburbs such as Rehavia, Talpiyyot, and Beit ha-Kerem. These neighbourhoods were designed according to the principles of garden cities, then prevalent in urban development, and accommodated the modern segments of the Jewish population in Jerusalem. Moreover, unlike the traditional form of neighbourhood association headed by the *muchtar*, these neighbourhoods developed modern patterns of local organization (see chapter 3). They were headed by an elected neighbourhood council, which was responsible for the provision of social and physical services. The role of the councils was defined in local statutes, with which the residents had to comply. According to these statutes, the neighbourhood councils had the prerogative of preparing a planning scheme for the neighbourhood, and had the right to supervise and control the construction process. In addition, the neighbourhood councils and the *muchtars* handled such services as road paving, lighting, and garbage collection, as well as representing the community to the authorities.

Although the British authorities took little interest in communal-political organization, they had significantly changed the nature of urban government. It was under the British mandate government that the art of urban government and modern concepts and techniques of urban planning were introduced to Palestine. At the beginning of the British mandate over Palestine in 1920, there were twenty-two municipalities (sixteen Arab and six of mixed Jewish-Arab population). The British modernized the municipal system by passing a series of laws. In 1926 the urban franchise was extended to the entire male population, including those who did not own property but paid municipal taxes. In 1934 the Municipal Act was passed, defining the functions, authority, sources of income, and administrative procedures of local authorities (Elazar 1980).

At the end of the British mandate, in 1948, there were eleven Arab and twenty-six Jewish local authorities. The British impact on urban development was particularly significant in Jerusalem, where British planners prepared several master plans in order to rationalize urban development, including the final plan drawn up by Henry Kendall in 1944. As Shapiro (1973, 146) noted: 'The Kendall Plan is the most technically perfect of all the plans made for Jerusalem, including the Israeli Plans that were to follow, up to the 1968 Master Plan.' Indeed, planning as discourse and technique was the contribution of the British government to Jerusalem, and the Jerusalem plans shaped the Urban Building Ordinances of 1921, 1922, 1929, and 1936, which were valid until 1966, when the mandatory ordinance was replaced by the Israel Planning Law.

Modern city government soon affected the residents' quality of life. For the first time such basic issues as water supply, hygiene, private architecture, and zoning became the domain of the state. As a result, the health conditions of the population improved significantly. Thus, for instance, in the decade preceding the outbreak of the First World War, the rates of endemic malaria diagnosed in Jerusalem ranged from 53 per cent among young children to 18 per cent in the adult population (Amiran 1973, 29). Nothing contributed more at that time to infant mortality than malaria. This situation was rectified by the British authorities, who emptied all the cisterns in the city – the major breeding-ground for malaria-carrying mosquitoes – laid a water pipe from Solomon's pools, and allowed renewed use of those cisterns that had been properly cleaned and equipped with a cover and pump. Consequently, the disease sharply declined, and entirely disappeared from the city in 1930. Thus the intervention of a modern state led to an enormous improvement in the health conditions of Jerusalem's residents. Besides the amelioration of public services, which turned Jerusalem into one of the healthiest places in Palestine, the British mandate government granted Jerusalem the status of capital of the mandated territory and made it the seat of its government. The supreme authority under the British mandate government was the high commissioner, who, among other functions and roles, had the authority to appoint city mayors and their deputies. It is interesting to note that, in spite of a Jewish majority in Jerusalem, the city council throughout the British mandate had a Moslem majority, the city mayor (except for a short period in 1937 when the city was headed by a Jewish mayor) was a Moslem, and his deputies were a Christian and a Jew.

Besides the welfare functions assumed by the state, the mandate period saw the rise of 'voluntary welfarism.' A plethora of voluntary organizations emerged, organized along charitable, philanthropic, and sectoral party lines. These offered their members a variety of social services, among them economic assistance (especially the charitable organizations), employment, housing, education, and social services. Notable among these organizations was the Histadrut Ha'Ovdim Haklalit (General Federation of Labour, henceforth referred to by its popular name, the Histadrut), founded in 1920 by the socialist Zionist parties. Committed to the principle of a socialist society within a mixed (capitalist-socialist) economic system, the Histadrut functioned as a trade union and economic entrepreneur, as well as providing its members with a variety of social services and financial benefits – health care, old age and survivors' pensions, unemployment funds, day care, and educational and vocational services (Bar Yosef 1985).

The Divided City, 1948–1967

The establishment of the state of Israel brought in its wake some fundamental changes in the political and social organization of the city. Following the War of Independence, the city was divided into two sections: East Jerusalem, including the Old City and adjoining neighbourhoods to the east and northeast, under Jordanian control; and West Jerusalem, including all the neighbourhoods west and south of the Old City, under Israeli control. With certain exceptions, the armistice line separated those areas inhabited in 1947 by Jews from those inhabited by Arabs. During the nineteen years between the partition of the city in 1948 and its reunification in 1967, the population of West Jerusalem grew from 83,984 to 197,700. A census conducted by the Israeli authorities in East Jerusalem in September 1967 recorded some 66,000 people, of whom 82.1 per cent were Moslems and 16.4 per cent were Christians (Jerusalem Institute for Israel Studies and the Municipality of Jerusalem 1991).

Building activity in both parts of Jerusalem was determined to a large extent by the new geopolitical conditions. East Jerusalem expanded mostly northwards along the road to Ramallah and took the form of ribbon development. To block and defend the southern and northern flanks of West Jerusalem, a semicircular ribbon of housing projects was built along the 1948 armistice line, stretching from Ir Ganim (chapter 5) in the southwest through Katamonim (chapter 7) in the south, to southern Baka (chapter 9) in the southeast and to the neighbourhoods of Shmuel Hanavi and Musrara in the northeast. The residents in these housing projects were drawn from the new Middle Eastern (Sephardic) immigrants who arrived in the country after the establishment of the state. The majority of these immigrants came as refugees, and upon their arrival were entirely dependent on the state for housing, employment, and social services.

Indeed, the very act of providing the new immigrants with government housing attested to fundamental change in the role of the state. Whereas in preceding periods the establishment of new neighbourhoods was associated with voluntary organizations or with private building, it was now considered the responsibility of government. From its inception in 1948, the State of Israel assumed a welfare policy grounded in the governing Labour (Mapai) party ideology, the continuation of pre-state voluntary institutional patterns, and the needs created by mass immigration. The ideologies of the ingathering of the exiles, integrating the immigrants, and eventually rebuilding the nation were strongly associated with the adopted welfare policy. The welfare services and institutions were developed along universalistic and particularistic lines. Universalism entailed both catering to and developing the social rights of the public as a whole. Particularism entailed catering to the social needs of those who could not afford the services provided through the market mechanism (Bar Yosef 1985). Both universal and targeted services were primarily provided from the top through a corporatist link created between the government and the Histadrut, both headed by the Labour party. Besides its role as a trade union, the Histadrut continued to provide wage-linked retirement plans and to provide health-care services to a large segment (75 per cent in the mid-1980s) of the population. The state enacted a series of laws to guarantee the social and economic rights of the public as a whole: the National Insurance Act (1953), the Compulsory Education Act (1953), and the Social Welfare Act (1958). Besides its regulatory role, the state intervened directly in urban life by building (through the ministry of labour, and later through the ministry of housing) large housing projects to accommodate the newly arrived immigrants, and by establishing health clinics, schools, community centres, and roads.

The construction of state housing in Jerusalem, designed for new immigrants, had an enormous influence on the city's social structure. Close by its holy places, cultural centres, and architectural monuments, the city houses a large group of Middle Eastern (Sephardic or Oriental) immigrants of the lower class in dilapidated housing projects. In the 1950s these areas became centres of poverty, unemployment, and crime, and in some cases remain so to the present day. It was under these political and social circumstances that paternalist neighbourhood patterns of local bossism were fostered among immigrant communities by the Labour party, the Histadrut, and the local state. Key figures in the immigrant communities were thus co-opted by the political machine to serve as liaison between the residents and the state, and to secure local votes (see chapter 5).

The intervention of central government in local affairs was also reflected in relationships with the local state. Following the British colonial system, as set forth by the Municipal Act of 1934, the Israeli central government left the local state with only minor responsibilities. Municipal government is engaged in the improvement and upkeep of physical services and, along with the central government, provides education and welfare services. Housing and planning are handled by the central government. In many towns and cities local taxes are insufficient to cover expenditures, thus leaving the local state largely dependent upon financial support from the central state.

Relying on the political-economic resources located in central government, Mapai (Labour) managed to attain, in a relatively short period of time, political hegemony in most of the older urban centres, as well as in the newly founded towns in the peripheral regions. Jerusalem played a special role in this process. Municipal government in Jerusalem, hitherto a local affair, was quickly politicized by the national parties. In the first elections, held in 1950, the city's population clearly revealed its religious and right-wing inclinations. The leaders of Mapai at that time, who headed the central government, attached only minor importance to Jerusalem's local government. On the one hand, the Israeli government declared its ultimate devotion to Jerusalem, turned the city into the capital of the new state, and launched a fierce struggle against the United Nations resolution of 1947 mandating the internationalization of Jerusalem. On the other hand, the same government took little interest in the city's politics and economics. Thus at the time when Tel Aviv prospered as a commercial, administrative, and cultural centre, West Jerusalem lagged well behind. As a border city that had lost its economic hinterland, it developed a narrow economic base, specializing in public services. Until 1988, when the local authority and the central government joined together to establish the Association for Jerusalem Development, no serious attempt was undertaken by the government to develop and expand the economic base. The city to which all Israeli governments pledged allegiance has for decades been one of the country's poorest cities.

Labour dominance in Jerusalem's politics after the mid-1950s was partially challenged by the ascendancy of Teddy Kollek to the mayor's office in 1965. Riding a wave of popular support, Kollek ran at the head of his own local slate, One Jerusalem, which claims to be independent of all national parties. In reality, however, half of the slate is selected by Kollek personally and the other half by the Labour party.[27]

Unlike the situation in Vancouver, neighbourhood leaders are not represented on Kollek's slate. There are several reasons for their absence: at-large proportional elections, the Israeli method, do not encourage neighbourhood representation, and Kollek never fully endorsed neighbourhood participation in the city's politics, and attempted, with some success, to keep a distance between the two. As a charismatic leader, Kollek has succeeded in creating a large base of popular support in both upper- and lower-class residential areas, thus ensuring his hold on Jerusalem. During his tenure of more than a quarter of a century, Kollek has evinced little interest in economic development, devoting most of his efforts to the city's beautification. Perhaps like TEAM in Vancouver, he preferred the option of the livable city over the option of boosterism. Among the cultural facilities built during Kollek's incumbency one may count the Israeli Museum, the Jerusalem Theater, the Jerusalem Music Center, the Jerusalem stadium, the Jerusalem promenade, as well as numerous parks, gardens, and community and cultural centres. Under Teddy Kollek, Jerusalem became one of the most attractive cities in Israel; yet, in terms of employment, income level, and expenditures, it is one of the poorest cities in the country.

The Reunited City, 1967 to the Present

In the wake of the Six Day War in June 1967, the border that split Jerusalem was eliminated, and the city was reunited. A new wave of development swept the city, resulting in a new ribbon of neighbourhoods built beyond the 1948 armistice line. In addition, the Jewish quarter in the Old City, destroyed by the Jordanian authorities, was restored and reinhabited. Unlike the housing projects of the 1950s and 1960s, those constructed in the 1970s and 1980s were built to a higher standard, adopted modern principles of town planning, and were intended for the entire population of the city. Today, about one-third of the Jewish population in Jerusalem resides in areas previously considered part of East Jerusalem. The population of the city rose from 197,700 in West Jerusalem and 68,600 in East Jerusalem in 1967 to a total population of 504,000 people in 1989. Since 1967 the percentage of the Arab population in Jerusalem has slightly increased, to 28 per cent in 1989, while the percentage of the Jewish population has undergone marginal decline, but continues to exceed 70 per cent of the total (Jerusalem Institute for Israel Studies and the Municipality of Jerusalem 1991).

From the early 1970s Jerusalem's neighbourhoods became once again the centre of social ferment and social change. This process proceeded from the older immigrant-housing projects built in the 1950s and 1960s to the new projects built in the 1970s and 1980s. Social deprivation in the older immigrant projects, coupled with the anticipations accompanying the education of the younger generation, led to a huge discrepancy between expectations and opportunities. This gap provoked a growing critique of the government's welfare policy, and on certain occasions resulted in social mobilization and protest. Members of the younger generation, who grew up in the housing projects, criticized what, in their view, appeared as outright state discrimination against Sephardim. Unlike the established local bosses who tended to cooperate with the state, members of the younger generation were ready to confront the state and to assume militant protest strategies. It was among residents of these neighbourhoods that the urban social movements of the Black Panthers and the Ohalim (Tents) emerged in the 1970s and 1980s (see chapter 7), challenging inadequate state housing and social services. In the late 1970s these areas (with the exception of southern Baka) were targeted by the central government for urban renewal, which in Israel entailed rehabilitation of housing units and the upgrading of social and physical services.

The Urban Renewal Program, initiated by the right-wing Likud government that came to power in 1977, marked the major welfare project of the 1980s. The involvement of a right-wing government in a social program derives from the party's broad support among Sephardic Jews, who live in immigrant and poverty areas, and many of whom hold the Labour party responsible for poor housing and social conditions. It was quite natural under these circumstances that the Likud party would show sensitivity to the urban plight of its voters, and assume a welfare policy designed to upgrade their social and housing conditions. As a result, during the last decade, over $1 billion was invested in some hundred poverty neighbourhoods, six of which are located in Jerusalem. Moreover, the Likud government did not revise the welfare system developed by Labour, and maintained existing social expenditures per capita in the spheres of education, health, and social welfare. This policy may partly account for the disappearance of urban social movements during the 1980s and early 1990s. The Urban Renewal Program was planned, financed, and implemented by the central government, while the local state was accorded a marginal role in this project. Some decentralization of resources and decision making to the neighbourhood level has occurred, but at the expense of the local state. For many mayors, including Teddy Kollek, the Urban Renewal Program came to signify insensitive intervention of a centralized government in local affairs, and further attenuation of the local government's authority.

Perhaps to counter the central government's initiative during the 1980s, the local state in Jerusalem started to experiment in several neighbourhoods with the project of neighbourhood self-management. The local stimulus for the experiment came from neighbourhoods not included in urban renewal. Many of the new neighbourhoods built after 1967 lacked the basic social services required for smooth functioning: health clinics, schools and kindergartens, and community centres. They also lacked sufficiently developed physical infrastructure and other social services. Similar problems were noted in the older neighbourhoods. To cope with these problems, a suggestion was put forward to decentralize some municipal functions to the neighbourhoods and to encourage a process of neighbourhood self-management. Baka and Talpiyyot Mizrach were the first neighbourhoods singled out for the experiment of self-management (see chapter 9).

The dominant figure in encouraging the process of neighbourhood self-management has been Mayor Kollek. It seems that for Kollek such a project promised both the enhancement of democracy and social control over problem areas, i.e., new neighbourhoods which lack sufficient physical and social services; older and poorer areas; and Arab and ultra-orthodox districts, whose acceptance of Israeli authority is questionable. Therefore, Kollek has been willing to grant some policy-making autonomy to the neighbourhoods, to enhance cooperation in the delivery of services (co-production), and to have the neighbourhood councils involved as long as their representatives comply with the rules of the game. This is in essence neocorporatism that has been practised in Jerusalem in the consumption sphere (or service delivery) during the 1980s and 1990s. Much like the neocorporatist system in the production sphere, which is made up of government, labour unions, and the private sector, neocorporatism in the consumption sphere works in two ways. On the one hand, it may turn into a manipulative instrument in the hands of conservative politicians, leading to the co-optation of local leadership and to conflict absorption. On the other hand, it may turn into a progressive device through genuine collaboration between the local government and the neighbourhoods, thus not only advancing the social welfare of the city's residents, but also strengthening the power of the residents *and* the local state, not least in negotiating with the central government.

Under Teddy Kollek's long incumbency of almost thirty years, Jerusalem's municipal government has turned into an efficient organ, the level of the civil service has been upgraded, the collection of taxes has improved significantly (unlike other cities in Israel, Jerusalem has no financial deficit), and public confidence in the ability of local government to deliver services is high. However, while strengthening the local bureaucracy, Kollek has systematically eroded the power of the city council. It is not uncommon, therefore, that major decisions concerning municipal government and the delivery of services are taken within a small circle made up of the mayor and a few loyal bureaucrats; the city council functions on many occasions as a rubber stamp in approving decisions already made within a small circle. As one of the council members conceded, 'Everything is done in a democratic way; we are asked to approve decisions whose nature we do not entirely understand.' Kollek does not hide his disrespect for councillors, and in an interview described them as disloyal figures who seek to pursue their own hidden agendas. The negative attitude towards council and the positive support lent to the process of democratization at the neighbourhood level is indeed one of the striking contradictions of Kollek's long government, and points to a major weakness in his concept of urban democracy.

One interesting feature of Kollek's government is the sensitivity it shows to the Arab population of the city. But this sensitivity, which undoubtedly has a humanistic side, has to be interpreted carefully against the background of the conflict between Jews and Arabs. Kollek has advanced the idea of functional sovereignty as a solution to this divisive conflict. This principle entails that the Arab holy places will be served and run by Arab authorities, and that some of the municipal functions will be handled by Arab neighbourhood councils. Foreign affairs and security issues, however, are to remain in Israeli hands, and the city of Jerusalem is to remain undivided under Israeli authority. The Intifada (uprising) in the administered territories, in which East Jerusalem has played a leading role, casts a long shadow over Kollek's attempts to integrate the city through administrative decentralization.

Two key themes seem to run through this story of neighbourhood organizations and city government in Jerusalem. First, the development of neighbourhood organizations reflected historical circumstances; the relative development of the welfare state and its scope of intervention in daily life; and the residents' needs, aspirations, norms, and patterns of behaviour. Second, the interaction between these elements produced at different historical times quite different kinds of neighbourhood organizations: semi-autonomous organizations in the late nineteenth and early twentieth centuries, paternalist organizations in the 1950s and 1960s, protest movements in the 1970s and early 1980s, and neocorporatist organizations in the 1980s and 1990s – a sequence with similarities to the chronology in Vancouver discussed earlier. It is this convergence, inevitably incomplete, which provides the comparative moment of our interpretation.

THE PRINCIPAL THEMES

The two principal themes of this study concern the diversity of neighbourhood organizations through time, and their evolving relationships with the state. We argue that four types of neighbourhood organization may be identified in Vancouver and Jerusalem, reflecting current municipal circumstances and the specific stage of development of the welfare state. Granted certain general similarities, there were, of course, important differences between the two cities in terms of sociopolitical structure and human action. Each setting must be understood in its own terms, and particularly through the ways in which the social actors involved made sense of historical circumstances and welfare conditions as a basis for action. The following sketch, to be developed in detail in the case-studies, presents the general argument within a broader political, social, and historical perspective.

Ratepayers' Organizations

The period preceding the rise of the welfare state was marked by the emergence of self-help ratepayers' organizations that shaped the social and physical environment. In élite neighbourhoods they operated with some autonomy and limited intervention from local government. These organizations were associated in both Vancouver and Jerusalem with the opening up of new districts, and with privileged higher-status neighbourhoods with a considerable level of communal control over local life. Establishing their own separate aristocratic enclaves at the beginning of the twentieth century, these organizations are currently involved in protecting their turf against sociodemographic change and commercial incursion.

Ethno-racial Neighbourhood Organizations

Also preceding the rise of the welfare state, these groups maintained old patterns of community organization, based upon social closure, mutual support, and the traditional leadership of élite groups and local bosses. The rise of the welfare state has significantly affected these organizations in so far as it has been associated with the extension of the state apparatus into traditional life. Traditional groups have acted as political mediators between the state and the communities, serving the interests of both sides. But the relationship has always been marked by cultural and political asymmetry. The culture of the ethnic or racial communities were conceived as marginal and esoteric, and the local leadership was treated in a paternalistic manner by urban power élites. Consequently, a double pattern of patron-client relationships emerged between, first, the state and local leadership, and, second, local leadership and the community. In this structure, the ethnic / racial organizations, headed by élite groups and local bosses, have acted as agents of control, while serving their own interests as well as those of the state. They helped, if inadvertently, to maintain the existing political-economic system, and thus strengthened the political and cultural status quo.

During the late 1960s and 1970s these patterns of organization have been challenged from within by the younger generation. Criticizing the malfunctioning of the welfare state, and the strategies assumed by their elders, members of the younger generation turned to more active strategies of social protest. With a distinctive cultural politics, the newly emerged organizations strove for the incorporation of ethnic and racial groups from a position of marginal entitlement into one of political empowerment and cultural affirmation.

Grass-Roots Movements

The reach of the welfare state during the 1970s and 1980s, mostly felt in poor, ethnically or racially marginal neighbourhoods, was associated with a growing critique of its performance and policy. This critique culminated in some instances in the rise of radical grass-roots movements that challenged not only the performance of the state, but also its prejudicial constellation of interests and discourses. Against the dominant patterns of cultural hegemony, paternalism, and social injustice, the movements suggested alternative modes of city politics based upon decentralization, empowerment, and local management. In the course of this process, social organizers and community workers have quite often acted as agents of change. They helped to crystallize social and political ideologies, and along with local leaders took an active part in mobilizing the residents, and in negotiations with the state. In so doing these actors played a double role, encouraging both sociopolitical change and the socialization of the grass roots.

Co-production and Neocorporatism

Newly emergent patters of co-production and neocorporatism seem to mark the present phase of the welfare state, sometimes referred to as the mature or post-welfare phase. At the neighbourhood level these trends take the form of cooperation between the local state and neighbourhood organizations, and the emergence of blended corporate and local structures responsible for the delivery of certain services. Underlying the rise of these organizations are certain strands that characterize contemporary urban societies: a / the fiscal crisis of the welfare state, which is partly associated with the growing gaps between expectations and the available resources to realize these expectations; b / a political crisis, which is reflected in failures of legitimation and growing communication gaps between elected politicians and the general public; c / the remoteness of centralized government, and the growing realization within governmental bodies that centralized administration has become increasingly dysfunctional, impersonal, and insensitive to local needs; and d / growing public awareness of community needs, such as schools, protection from highways, and urban development and safeguarding of local and cultural heritage. There are several common features that seem to characterize these organizations. They press for greater municipal democratization through integration between representative and participatory democracy. The result is a tendency for administrative decentralization of some state functions to the local level, and collaboration between local government and neighbourhoods in the production and delivery of certain services, leading to variable degrees of neighbourhood self-administration. Unlike the earlier organizations, the leading actors in the phase, especially in its initial stages, are politicians and civil servants, who both shape and are shaped by local political cultures. It is too early to assess the long-term effects of these organizations, since the situation is full of contradictions. They are supported, for example, by both progressive and conservative politicians. The former seek to create a stronger democracy and to improve the delivery of services, whereas the latter seek to curtail the state's responsibilities and to co-opt local leadership. One thing, however, seems to be undeniable; in spite of strong arguments heralding the

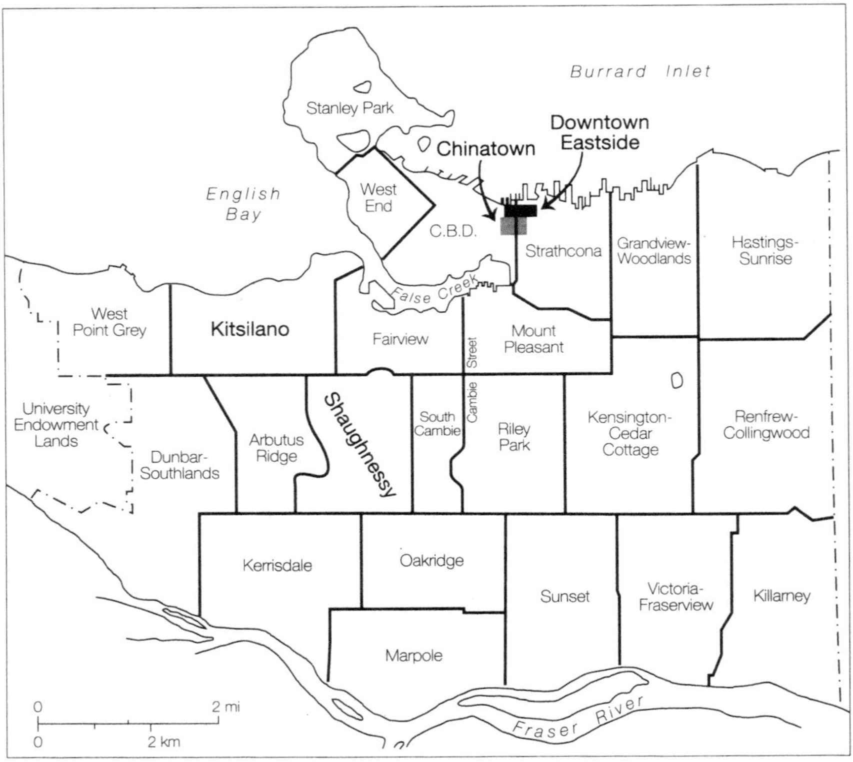

FIGURE 1.1.   The location of Vancouver neighbourhoods

eclipse of local community, neighbourhood organizations are still a viable entity for decision making and still affect the life of urban residents.

To summarize: our argument is that there is considerable diversity among neighbourhood organizations, but that the forms of organization are historically limited. In our study, diversity is revealed in four generic types: an older model which includes ratepayers' associations and groups focused around traditional cultural forms (including the local boss), and a more recent model which includes groups characterized by protest or co-production. Each type corresponds in general terms with a particular period and with a specific configuration of the state and its functions. The study thus traces in a historical manner the rise and fall of different types of organizations that were specific to their time and place. The eight case-studies represent two examples of each of these four types,

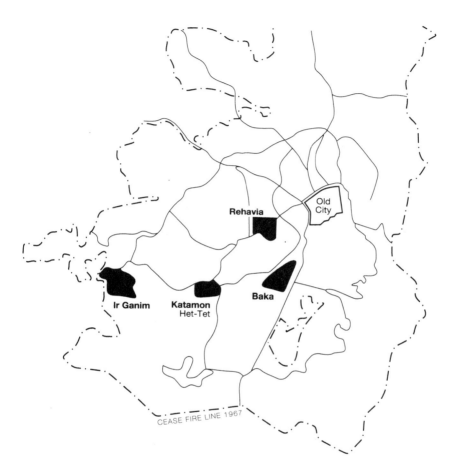

FIGURE 1.2.   The location of Jerusalem neighbourhoods

paired to include a neighbourhood organization drawn from both Vancouver and Jerusalem (figures 1.1, 1.2).

THE STRUCTURE OF THE BOOK

In detailed case-studies, we interpret neighbourhood organizations that emerged in disadvantaged, middle-class, and upper-class areas; older

organizations of ratepayers, and patronage organizations; and newer protest movements, and experiments in local democracy initiated from above.
Obviously, the idiosyncrasy of a case-study approach militates against
any attempt to transcend the specific findings and to formulate broader
generalizations. It is precisely at this point that the merits of comparative
study become most evident. By drawing comparisons between similar
communities and forms of local organizations, we are in a position to
assess the parallels and divergence between them, and thus to generate
certain generalizations. To attain this goal, we have paired chapters on
the Canadian and Israeli experience, thus allowing the reader to assess
similar types of social action (for example, protest or co-production) in
comparable neighbourhoods located in different cultural and sociopolitical frameworks.

We begin by presenting the earlier organizations that emerged in affluent neighbourhoods – the ratepayers' associations in Shaughnessy
Heights and Rehavia (chapters 2 and 3). Both neighbourhoods are élite
inner-city areas that, because of their proximity to downtown, experienced pressures from residential intensification (in Shaughnessy) and
business incursions (in Rehavia). The neighbourhood organizations in
these areas, whose origins go back to the 1920s and 1930s, struggled
to defend their districts. Skillfully employing the rhetoric of the livable
city, the Shaughnessy Heights Property Owners' Association has negotiated a new neighbourhood plan for the city, largely on its own terms,
which will aid the continued preservation of this élite district. The neighbourhood government of Rehavia fought to modify the Jerusalem master
plan so as to halt the penetration of offices into the area. Both organizations provide a classical case of co-production between the neighbourhood and the local government, oriented towards the preservation of
an old aristocratic area.

The second section presents the organizations that developed in immigrant lower-class neighbourhoods: Chinatown and Ir Ganim (chapters
4 and 5). Chinatown is an inner-city area dominated by Chinese-origin
residents, and has been under severe threat from urban renewal and freeway proposals. Ir Ganim is an outlying public-housing estate inhabited
by North African and Middle Eastern immigrants. Both areas were dominated by traditional and conservative neighbourhood organizations
whose relations with the state were either cooperative or deferential.
Moreover, in both places the state's policy towards the area and the traditional patterns of local organization have been resisted by a new, largely
native-born generation of young people, aided by outside professionals.
A citizens' group, the Strathcona Property Owners' and Tenants' As-

sociation, appeared in the late 1960s and upset a redevelopment program introduced by the local state. Ir Ganim witnessed, in the early 1980s, the rise of two grass-roots movements made up of second-generation immigrants, Youth for the Neighbourhood, and Improvement of Community Life, which challenged the local patronage system and its supporters within the state. Studying the development of the organizations in these two neighbourhoods has enabled us to assess the cultural variations and historical changes in the relationships between the state and minority groups in the city.

The third section presents the protest movements of the Downtown Eastside Residents' Association (DERA) and the Ohalim movement (chapters 6 and 7). These movements developed in the poorest sections of Vancouver and Jerusalem – the Downtown Eastside and Katamon Tet, respectively. The Downtown Eastside has been dominated by elderly men living in low-quality residential hotels. The population suffers severe social problems, dealt with in part by a set of public and private relief agencies. Katamon Tet is a public-housing estate settled by North African and Middle Eastern immigrants. Unlike other housing estates, it was built at a relatively high residential density, and some of its blocks were inhabited by large families with severe social problems. It was in these blocks that the Ohalim movement made its first appearance. The neighbourhood organizations in the Downtown Eastside and Katamon Tet were organized in the early 1970s around local charismatic figures. These leaders initiated a series of demonstrations and protest tactics that aggressively argued for their districts, especially on the issues of housing, social-service delivery, self-management, and territorial-cum-cultural identity. Over time, the two organizations developed some universal messages, pressing the case of other poor areas and distressed groups. The leaders of the two organizations became, in the 1980s, very active in urban affairs, though in different ways. The leaders of DERA were elected as council members, whereas the Ohalim leaders created a city-wide urban movement that championed the cause of disadvantaged neighbourhoods.

The fourth section presents organizations engaged in co-production, the West Broadway Citizens' Committee, formed in the Kitsilano district of Vancouver, and the neighbourhood government of the Baka district of Jerusalem (chapters 8 and 9). Kitsilano and Baka were lower-middle- and lower-class areas, respectively, which, because of their favourable location (Kitsilano's proximity to beaches and mountain views and Baka's nearness to the city centre), have undergone gentrification. The West Broadway Citizens' Committee emerged in the early 1970s, largely to resist the loss of affordable housing, and was involved in a stormy relationship with the city council over the co-production of local area planning. After some successes, it turned into a tenants' rights organization. The neighbourhood government of Baka was formed in the early 1980s by the Jerusalem municipality in order to assist the older lower-class residents in the area. Contrary to the municipality's original intentions, the organization was soon dominated by the gentrifiers, who used it in part to advance their specific sociocultural and educational needs. The unavoidable result has been tension and conflict between the gentrifiers and the older residents. Both Kitsilano and Baka are marked by the state's attempts to forge co-productive relations, manifested in joint planning and participation in decision making.

Finally, based on the empirical analysis, in chapter 10 we theorize our findings by delineating general principles concerning the emergence of neighbourhood organizations, the role they play in the formation of local landscapes and meanings, and their evolving relationships with the state.

In developing our case-studies, we move freely among different theoretical functions. From the Marxist tradition some basic notions are borrowed concerning power, conflict, and change, and at the same time Weberian notions are utilized on the role of the state, the place of charisma in institution building, and the processes of bureaucratization and routinization. In so doing, we employ models of both change and stability. Our data were collected through participant observation, in-depth interviews with social actors representing both the state and local organizations, and the analysis of relevant documents and reports. The presentation of these data relies on interpretations given by key actors, by the media, and by professionals involved in the organizations. However, these accounts are also subjected to critical interpretation based on empirical evidence, a double hermeneutic which seeks to separate the 'is' from the 'ought.'

PART ONE

Who Governs?
Élite Neighbourhoods and the State

Both Shaughnessy and Rehavia are old élite neighbourhoods, opened up as high-status suburbs in the early twentieth century, but later enveloped by urban growth and now sharing an inner-city location and confronting redevelopment pressures from an expanding downtown. Both were constructed in a largely European design idiom as symbolic communities to house a nation-building élite. Shaughnessy was built by the Canadian Pacific Railway (CPR), at the Pacific terminus of the transcontinental railway, the thin band of steel which was an integral element of the vast and improbable project of binding the Canadian nation. Vancouver itself was founded in 1886 with the arrival of the railway. The CPR's development of Shaughnessy on its vast land grant was an act of supreme confidence in the future, for the neighbourhood was carved out of the forest on the edge of a wilderness scarcely settled by Europeans. No less of a visionary project lay behind the construction of Rehavia in the 1920s. Built by the Zionist Palestine Land Development Company (PLDC), it represented part of a conscious settlement strategy in the making of a Jewish homeland. The Jewish professional and business leaders who settled the district from Europe in the interwar period may not have confronted the same environmental wilderness as the British and eastern Canadian bourgeois arriving in Vancouver, but in their own minds they may well have perceived an equivalent cultural wilderness in a land where, as an unwelcome minority, they faced an immense task of nation building.

Strong ratepayers' associations emerged at an early date in both districts, in Shaughnessy replacing the earlier guardianship of the CPR, in Rehavia working in a cooperative manner with the PLDC to provide a wide range of services in the context of the minimal state services provided under the British mandate. Fuller administrative powers were also sought directly from the government of British Columbia by Shaughnessy residents, in an attempt to secede and form a separate municipality. While this initiative was not rewarded, in a political compromise the privileged status of Shaughnessy was confirmed as it received special zoning protection in two acts passed by the provincial legislature. Thereafter its exclusive nature was reinforced, and like other élite districts the neighbourhood was empowered to preserve (although not without reverses) its high-status landscape.

The case-study carries the interpretation into the 1980s by charting through participant observation the campaign for protective zoning once the provincial legislation expired in 1970. In a city facing severe housing shortages, the Shaughnessy Heights Property Owners' Association devised a strategy not only to resist residential intensification, but also to encourage the deconversion of existing rooming-houses in large mansions back into single-family occupancy or into a few expensive flats. They accomplished their objectives in a new neighbourhood plan through a skilful discourse of representation, using the categories of liberal reform politics against itself. Through appropriating such reform categories as neighbourhood accountability, the preservation of open space, heritage protection, and the livable city they were able to argue their case successfully. The result is a striking demonstration of Lukes's (1974) argument of the capacity of élites to sustain their control not only by setting the agenda, but also through astute handling of the cultural politics of discourse. The outcome was also fraught with political irony as a second generation of Vancouver's frontier capitalists sought the state's protection against the incursions of the urban land market, while a reform-oriented local state overlooked city-wide housing needs to grant their request, and act as guarantor of the neighbourhood's longevity as an élite area.

That this outcome has been repeated in other high-status districts in Canada and elsewhere would seem to offer support for the neo-élitist theory of social relations within the local state.[1] But circumstances in Rehavia would seem to fit this position far less comfortably. Rehavia has offered remarkably little resistance to commercial and residential intensification which has spilled into it from the nearby business district. In this inactivity Rehavia repeats an older model of neighbourhood change in Canada when élite districts were readily invaded by the intensifying pressures of the urban land market – such indeed was the fate of Vancouver's first élite district, the West End, the source of many Shaughnessy households. So for a generation following the establishment of the Israeli state in 1948, Rehavia contained no neighbourhood council or, after 1969, an unambitious one, despite massive changes redefining the district, and despite also privileged connections to the powerful office of Mayor Kollek, a Rehavia resident. Indeed it was the local state, rather than the neighbourhood, which primed land-use conflict and neighbourhood activism in its unilateral decision to block the further invasion of professional offices into Rehavia, and to expel offices in existence without permits – precisely the task of neighbourhood policing pursued so vigorously by the Shaughnessy property owners before the threat of residential intensification. When surveyed, close to 90 per cent of Rehavia residents approved this initiative endorsed by the mayor, but they had been unwilling to press the issue themselves.

The outcome is a further round of paradoxes no less fundamental than those in Shaughnessy. Upper-middle-class residents find themselves in disagreement with upper-middle-class professionals who rent offices in their district; the city, which created the neighbourhood council at its own behest as part of a decentralized program of neighbourhood self-management, and which sought to protect Rehavia from the invasion of offices, is now the target of protest, and internally divided. The welfare state finds itself in the not-uncommon predicament of serving two masters in Rehavia, economic development and neighbourhood stability, each with conflicting interests. As the state brings its own interests to the issue, the outcome in this instance is a *ménage à trois* where there are, moreover, no clear heroes or villains.

2

Shaughnessy Heights:
The Protection of Privilege*

In the relatively young settlements of urban Canada, the oldest neighbourhood groups have been the ratepayers' associations, whose formation dates from the pre–welfare state era of the late nineteenth or early twentieth century. These associations, consisting of property owners, were located most often in developing middle- or upper-middle-class neighbourhoods. In Toronto, for example, the first ratepayers' association was established at the turn of the century in the new élite district of Rosedale, whereas in Vancouver, the Kitsilano Ratepayers' Association (KRA) was formed in 1909, when much of the district remained under forest cover, and berry pickers in the woods had need for caution because of the lingering presence of black bears. In the context of new settlement on the edge of the frontier under the auspices of a minimal state, the improvement of municipal services such as streets and lighting were significant objectives of ratepayers' groups. But so was the maintenance of the material and symbolic investment of homeownership, and from the earliest years, lobbying for improved services was matched by an exclusionary focus upon non-conforming land uses, or indeed, incompatible households. In a municipality where the preservation of property rights was the leitmotif of local government, easy and informal relations existed between ratepayers and the local state; the executive of the KRA typically included at least one elected member of city council, after 1937 always a member of the conservative Non-Partisan Association.

Among the city's ratepayer groups, few have shown such longevity, and none more success than the ratepayers of Shaughnessy, Vancouver's established inner-city, élite district. Like other privileged neighbourhoods

*This chapter was written by James Duncan. Parts of the discussion in this chapter previously appeared in Duncan 1992.

in Canada – Westmount in Montreal or Forest Hill in Toronto – the property owners of Shaughnessy sought monopoly power over their destiny through municipal self-government.[1] Though this initiative failed, they were able to secure a unique status for a generation in a customized relationship with the provincial government. When this agreement lapsed in 1970, the ratepayers sought to negotiate a similar unique standing with their new guardian, the City of Vancouver, in a process which is the principal focus of this chapter, a process where the earlier style of interaction between power élites was successfully transferred to the rather different procedures of the welfare state.

The Shaughnessy Heights Property Owners' Association (SHPOA) provides, then, an informative case of a successful neighbourhood association. It has in the half-century of its existence skilfully utilized its considerable assets, both organizational and financial, to convince the municipal and provincial levels of government that the area's residents, as represented by the association, have the right to exert considerable control over the destiny of their neighbourhood. In addition to having a highly committed and well-organized leadership and broad support within the neighbourhood, the association has had the unusual advantages of being well financed by its affluent membership, having legal services donated by association members, and having political and social connections within the highest levels of municipal and provincial government. The SHPOA provides a powerful example of the capacity of a privileged neighbourhood association to penetrate the policy-making powers of the state and subvert the state's discourse for its own objectives.

The first portion of this case-study traces the growth of Shaughnessy from its inception in the first decade of the twentieth century until the mid 1970s. Attention is focused on the role played by the Canadian Pacific Railway (CPR), which developed the area and managed its growth until the Depression when the mantle of responsibility shifted to the Property Owners' Association. We then consider the successful attempt of the property owners in the late 1970s and early 1980s to rezone their neighbourhood and institute a set of highly restrictive design guidelines on all future development. What is particularly interesting about this latter rezoning struggle is the manner in which the conservative, upper-class board of the Property Owners' Association astutely used an ideology and discourse of neighbourhood self-determination and 'livability' that had broad appeal to a middle-class city council composed nearly equally of conservatives, liberals, and socialists.

THE CANADIAN PACIFIC RAILWAY AND THE CONSTRUCTION OF AN
ÉLITE NEIGHBOURHOOD

In 1884 the CPR, in exchange for extending the transcontinental railway
to Vancouver, was granted 6,000 acres of land south of False Creek
in Vancouver, as well as parcels of land in the West End of the city
and what was to become the central business district.[2] The railway first
developed approximately 550 acres in the West End during the 1890s
and then turned to its large southern holding. It carved this parcel into
what it projected as two middle-class neighbourhoods, Kitsilano and Fair-
view, and an upper-class one, Shaughnessy Heights.

In 1907 the CPR began clearing the 345 acres of land bounded by
Sixteenth Avenue in the north, the Lulu Island Railway in the west,
King Edward Avenue in the south, and Oak Street in the east. This
area, which the CPR hoped to convert into the most prestigious residential suburb in the city, was named after Lord Thomas Shaughnessy,
president of the railway from 1898 until 1918.[3] Over the next year the
valuable timber on the land was cut, graded, and sold. The CPR then
retained the services of Mr Frederick Todd, a landscape architect from
Montreal who had earlier laid out the adjacent district of Point Grey,
and a Danish engineer by the name of Davisk to clear and prepare the
subdivision. Their subdivision plans were put into effect by Gzowski
and Company, who at one time employed 1,200 men on the project
(City of Vancouver Planning Department 1982b, 2). Todd was greatly
influenced by the work of Frederick Law Olmsted, the American landscape architect whose romantic 'country in the city' designs were the
rage during the latter part of the nineteenth century. The hilly topography of the subdivision was used to advantage; streets were laid out
in a sinuous fashion to follow contours, and sewer and water lines were
built. The lots ranged in size from one-fifth of an acre to an acre and
a half, and the area was transected by several handsome boulevards and
a five-acre park, The Crescent (see figure 2.1). It is estimated that, before
a single house was built, $1 million was spent on developing the land
(Eaton 1974, 4). The CPR planned, however, to recover this sum many
times over through the sale of lots to the wealthy citizens of this rapidly
growing city. The *Vancouver Province* reported on 9 May 1908 that 'the
CPR plans to do everything possible to restrict the value and the location
of all the buildings to establish a residential community of the highest
character' (p. 13). This sentence, written as the land for development
was being cleared, captures in epigrammatic form the arguments that
were to be presented to the Vancouver City Council nearly seventy-

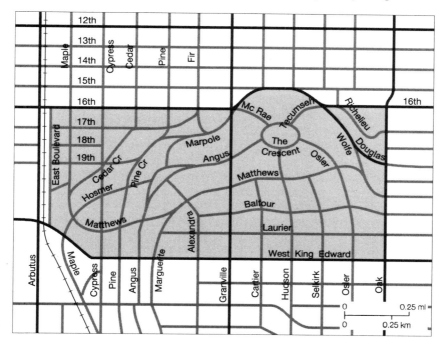

FIGURE 2.1.   The curvilinear street pattern of First Shaughnessy. This layout, continued in more qualified form in Second Shaughnessy to the south, establishes a distinctive difference with the regular street grid of the surrounding inner city. This distinction has been sharpened in the 1980s by the closure of several access streets into Shaughnessy.

five years later, in 1981, by the Property Owners' Association, the later custodian of the neighbourhood. Among the key terms in the *Province*'s statement is the word *restrict*. The capitalists who built and lived in the area had not the slightest intention of allowing a free market in land to operate. Indeed, the free market was (and continues to be) seen as a destabilizing force. Shaughnessy has always needed institutional controls to shape its growth in the manner that the railway and the Property Owners' Association envisioned. The second key theme is a 'residential community of the highest character.' Here we have a myth that has persisted for three-quarters of a century – that wealth and property such as Shaughnessy Heights contains are to be equated with high social as well as environmental character. The myth, however, is subverted by the need for controls against 'mere' wealth in the area, but as always the power of myth lies in its ability to mask its contradictions.

In 1909 the Granville Street Bridge was completed, providing a fast route connecting Shaughnessy Heights to the downtown where its future residents would work. The CPR threw the full weight of its prestige behind the development of Shaughnessy to make it the kind of high-status environment that would appeal to businessmen and professionals in this young city. The district's nomenclature was suffused with the idiom of a nation-building élite. In addition to naming the subdivision after the railway's president, streets were named after four of its directors – R.B. Angus, C.R. Hosmer, W.D. Matthews, and Sir Edmund Osler (Matthews, n.d.) – prominent local figures, such as General A.D. McRae; the recently retired Canadian prime minister, Sir Wilfrid Laurier, and also the current British prime minister, Lord Balfour. In that same year the first house was built for Richard Marpole, the local head of the CPR.

Land was sold in the subdivision for $10,000 per acre, a large sum of money for undeveloped land; only single-family dwellings were permitted, with a minimum price of $6,000. In order to entice investors to build in Shaughnessy Heights, the CPR lent buyers 90 per cent of the price of the land (at 6 per cent for eight years) and two-thirds of the price of the building (up to a maximum of $5,000). Altogether the company set aside $5 million for loans on homes. Such loans were, however, available only if the plans for the building met the standards set by the CPR. Building plans were carefully checked not only to assure that they adhered to the price guidelines, but also for their overall appearance, including positioning on the lot, house style, and the quality of building materials.[4] Thus, from the beginning there were design controls on housing. The only zoning restrictions at this time, however, were that the area remain single-family residential. The result was a residential area of very large lots with mansions, many of which had gate-houses and stables. The average lot size was 16,000 square feet, as compared with 4,000 square feet for single-family detached housing in the middle-class sections of the city. Approximately 50 per cent of the Shaughnessy Heights houses are still over 4,000 square feet in area. In other words, these houses exceed the average *lot* size of nearby middle-class areas.

By 1914, 243 houses had been completed, some 40 per cent of the present stock.[5] The company sought to further protect its investment by safeguarding the exclusive nature of its development. It paid the expenses of a group of Shaughnessy residents to travel to Victoria in order to convince the provincial government to allow Shaughnessy Heights to break away from the Municipality of Point Grey (then an independent suburb of Vancouver) and become a separate municipality. Point Grey also sent a delegation to oppose this secession. Although the provincial legislature rejected the proposal for secession, it allowed the area to become a separate ward of Point Grey with the important proviso that taxes collected in the area were to be used for its benefit. Shaughnessy was also to elect one representative to the Point Grey municipal council.[6] The Shaughnessy Heights Settlement Act of 1914 reaffirmed the controls that the CPR had put in place, and revealed the combined influence of the railway and the 243 households, 80 per cent of whom were listed in the Vancouver Social Register in 1914 (City of Vancouver Planning Department 1982b, 3).

The First World War halted the torrid pace of building, and there was little new development in the area until 1920. In September 1922, Point Grey became the first municipality in Canada to pass zoning regulations as part of its town-planning policy. Under these regulations, residential areas in addition to private dwellings could contain the offices of physicians, lawyers, dentists, artists or musicians. In addition they could contain certain select institutions such as clubs, churches, schools, libraries, public museums, and other philanthropic institutions. Apartments and tenements were banned from these areas (Corporation of Point Grey 1922, 2). Such legislation, which was designed to keep Point Grey middle class, was not restrictive enough to suit the taste of either the railway or Shaughnessy Heights. The CPR, therefore, anticipating a wave of postwar development, once again turned to the provincial government. In December 1922, the Shaughnessy Heights Building Restriction Act removed zoning control from the Municipality of Point Grey and created a special provincial zoning category prohibiting the subdivision of lots (Province of British Columbia 1922). Under the act the area was to remain residential, with any religious, educational, or governmental use to be approved by the Royal Trust, the trustee for the CPR. The act further stipulated that any resident was entitled to take out an injunction against a zoning violator. It was assumed correctly that the threat of legal action by the company or affluent residents would dissuade any would-be violator. The railway, anticipating demand for their lands to the south of King Edward Avenue, also convinced the provincial legislature to extend the 1914 Settlement Act to cover their undeveloped lands up to Thirty-Third Avenue. They called this new area 'Second Shaughnessy.' This residential area, which contained the CPR-built golf club, was very much an appendage of the older Shaughnessy Heights. It is perhaps best seen as an attempt by the railway to capture some of the prestige of its successful development by associating its name with this adjacent undeveloped area which it owned. To further safeguard the single-family character of the area, which was seen as crucial to maintaining high property values, the CPR placed restrictive covenants on Shaughnessy deeds (City of Vancouver Planning Department 1982b, 3). All of these controls were apparently secured with the approval of the residents, who saw a convergence of their interests with those of the CPR.

THE RISE OF THE PROPERTY OWNERS' ASSOCIATION

The Depression brought to an end both the period of growth and the era of harmony between the interests of the CPR and property owners. As a result of the city's financial crisis, a number of the area's most prominent residents filed for bankruptcy and were forced to sell their mansions. So many properties were repossessed during the 1930s (more than 250 in First and Second Shaughnessy) that the neighbourhood was referred to locally as 'Mortgage Heights' and 'Poverty Heights' (City of Vancouver Planning Department 1982b, 3). Although property values declined to a fraction of their earlier market value, taxes remained at their previous levels, contributing to acute financial crisis. To give a prominent example of decline in property value, 'Glen Brae,' one of the finest mansions in the area, valued at $75,000 in 1920, sold for $7,500 in 1939 (City of Vancouver Planning Department 1979, 2). While the residents and the CPR had previously cooperated in lobbying the provincial government to help them retain the exclusively single-family-residential nature of the area, under the financial pressure of the Depression such unity of interest quickly fell apart. Residents began to take in boarders illegally, and many single-family homes were converted to rooming-houses.

In 1938 the Shaughnessy Heights Property Owners' Association was formed. Its primary goal was to combat the trend towards the conversion of large houses into multiple-occupancy units.[7] The early leaders of the SHPOA were successful professionals and businessmen who were committed to the area as a place to live and could afford to maintain their property. One of the SHPOA's first official acts was to file a petition in 1939 with the provincial government, extending the Building Restriction Act to 1970. The provincial government not only accepted this proposal, but granted the SHPOA the right to register complaints against, and prosecute violators of, the act (City of Vancouver Planning Department 1979, 2).

An intensive lobbying campaign to reduce local property taxes was a second initiative, also intended to arrest the decline of single-family units. But the Second World War further undermined the SHPOA's goal of maintaining a financially stable single-family area. Because of a housing shortage in Canada during the war years, the federal government, by a 1942 order-in-council and under the authority of the War Measures Act, permitted the establishment of multi-family dwellings in all areas previously zoned as single-family (City of Vancouver Planning Department 1982b, 4). As there were nearly two dozen vacant houses in Shaughnessy in that year, it seemed unpatriotic to members of the SHPOA to protest the conversion of houses into guest lodges or rooming-houses (Davis 1972, 4). This law accelerated what the Depression had started; the wholesale conversion of single-family houses into rooming-houses. Furthermore, subdivisions of large properties were also occurring. In that same year, as a sop to the SHPOA which was smarting from the legalization of rooming-houses, property taxes were lowered in Shaughnessy. At this juncture, the SHPOA's effectiveness was at its nadir. The rooming-house owners even formed an association – the First Shaughnessy Residents' Association (FSRA) – to represent their interests and oppose the SHPOA. After the war the SHPOA tried to turn back the clock to the prewar status quo, while the FSRA lobbied for the retention of rooming-houses (City of Vancouver Planning Department 1982b, 4). The province settled the dispute in 1955 by offering the following compromise: all rooming-houses that were in existence before April 1955 could continue as non-conforming uses, but no new ones could come into existence. In 1957 a census of rooming-houses showed that 30 per cent of the houses in First Shaughnessy were in multiple-occupancy use (ibid). In addition, in 1955, the provincial government, tired of having to adjudicate Vancouver's land disputes, added an amendment to the Building Restrictions Act, which stated that control over Shaughnessy's zoning would be turned over to the city as soon as the city requested it. The City Planning Department prepared itself for such an eventuality by creating a new zoning district for First Shaughnessy to come into effect when the city eventually assumed control over the area (ibid).

THE END OF PROVINCIAL ZONING

During the postwar economic recovery, Shaughnessy regained a good measure of its former prestige and popularity with executives, who found

FIGURE 2.2.   What Shaughnessy is not. The label was applied by SHPOA to this landscape at a public hearing: 1950s or 1960s catalogue-style houses on smaller lots, aspiring to a suburban, and not an estate, landscape (Photograph: James Duncan).

the area close to the downtown and the house prices, which had still not recovered from the effects of the Depression, affordable. Existing houses and undeveloped building lots sold quickly. Most of the houses that were built during these decades, though large by city standards, were small in contrast to the mansions built forty years earlier. These bungalows were also built on smaller lots, causing a shift in landscape aesthetics.[8] With the advent of prosperity, rooming-houses slowly began to be converted back to single-family housing. Although the SHPOA was delighted by these reversions, it was dismayed by the increase in smaller houses which undermined the 'exclusive' character of the area. But once again, the SHPOA discovered its limits. As long as the minimum lot size was adhered to, there was nothing that the association could do if someone wished to put up a bungalow or a Spanish colonial house with a red tile roof, objectionable as the SHPOA members found these houses to be (see figure 2.2).

After the status of the rooming-houses had been clarified in 1955, the SHPOA used its powers vigorously to oppose any violations of the code. The nature of its membership was well suited to perform this watchdog function. Although the organization had broad support within the neighbourhood (in the sense that many residents paid the nominal $5 per annum membership fee),[9] there was a small, though shifting, core of activists who were elected to the board of directors and who ran the organization. This core was drawn from the business and professional élite of the city, and although popularly elected to the board by the membership, a slate of new candidates was in fact hand-picked by the existing board.[10] The board of directors then chose a president from among its number.[11] In this way the board managed to keep individuals whom they did not trust out of positions of power in the association. Although men usually comprised the executive, their wives, the vast majority of whom were not employed outside the home, acted as foot soldiers, patrolling the streets looking for any sign of building activity or for violations of code. Any suspected violators were written a letter of warning by the SHPOA and were reported to its legal committee, who either informed the province or commenced legal action on behalf of the association. For example, in 1959 the SHPOA's legal committee took action against the owners of three private residences that had been illegally converted to revenue properties and won each case.[12] Reporting violations to the province, however, was less effective, to the frustration of the SHPOA board, as the province did not always choose to prosecute violators.

In the late 1960s, the lease on the golf course located in Second Shaughnessy, and owned by the CPR, expired. The company, as we have seen, had long ceased to act as a spokesman for the preservation of the élite nature of Shaughnessy as it had already sold the vast majority of its holdings. Now, for the first time, however, the SHPOA found itself in direct conflict with the CPR since the railway wished to subdivide the golf course. The issue for the SHPOA was no longer simply single-family housing, but rather a rejection of any more housing in or near First Shaughnessy. The SHPOA's strategy was to convince the city and the province to preserve the land for the 'public good.' The first attempt was to have it converted into a park in memory of the late Sir Winston Churchill. Although playing on the anglophilia of British Columbian politicians was an astute gambit, the idea of a park, even one to honour Churchill, failed to generate sufficient political support because of the high cost of purchasing the land.[13] Subsequently, the Botanical Gardens

Association was established in order to convince the city and province to set aside a large portion of the golf course as a botanical garden for the 'education of the residents of the city.' A letter dated 21 June 1966 was sent by the Botanical Gardens Association to the rank-and-file membership of the SHPOA informing them that it was in the SHPOA's interests that they become members of the Botanical Gardens Association. The letter stated that 'the "Save Shaughnessy" effort has resulted in the formation of the *Botanical Gardens Association* and that this Association is endeavoring to have 67 acres of the area set aside for the development of a botanical garden.'[14] The plan received the blessing of the Vancouver Parks Board, whose chairman was later to become the president of the board of directors of the SHPOA. After intense lobbying it also received the support of the mayor and the premier of the province. The city subsequently purchased the land from the CPR, and a botanical garden was constructed, protecting the southern flank of First Shaughnessy from unwanted residential development. Despite this great victory, there were storm clouds on the horizon, because with the anticipated expiry of the Shaughnessy Heights Building Restriction Act in 1970, the association was bracing itself for a new round of zoning battles.

SHAUGHNESSY RELUCTANTLY REJOINS THE CITY

It appears that the provincial government had been growing increasingly unwilling to continue to involve itself in what was seen as a local zoning issue. The province had invited the city to reclaim Shaughnessy in 1959, but the city council preferred to wait until the Building Restriction Act expired in 1970. In this jurisdictional impasse the SHPOA lobbied the provincial legislature, sending it a preliminary memorandum in December 1966 entitled 'Why Shaughnessy Heights Building Restriction Act Is Good For Vancouver and British Columbia and Should Be Extended for a Further Period of Twenty Five Years.' This was followed by similar petitions in February 1967 and February 1968 entitled 'Memorandum Regarding Application for Extension of Shaughnessy Heights Building Restriction Act.' These petitions stated that Shaughnessy was a historic district worth protecting, and that the act was the best guarantee that it would be preserved. The First Shaughnessy Rate Payers' Association, a group representing the non-conforming uses in the area, attempted to counter the SHPOA's petition by submitting a memorandum of its own in 1967 opposing the extension of the Building Restriction Act and accusing the SHPOA of allowing its members to violate the act. At the end of December 1969, the act was allowed to expire by the provincial legislature, much to the dismay of the SHPOA. It appears that this happened, not because of the opposition of the Rate Payers' Association, but because the act seemed an anachronism and the province wished to refer responsibility to a seemingly reluctant Vancouver city council.

With the expiry of the act the new (RS-4) zoning for First Shaughnessy came into effect, setting the minimum lot area at 9,500 square feet and the minimum frontage at 85 feet. It was hoped by both the SHPOA and the city planning department that this would provide greater protection against subdivision than had previously existed. However, as the average lot size in the heart of the area was 42,500 square feet and the average frontage 156 feet, there still remained the possibility of subdivision. As an added safeguard, therefore, the city's director of planning was given some discretion over subdivision. Since the SHPOA felt that the city in the past had been insufficiently vigorous in prosecuting zoning violators, it convinced the city to change its charter to allow the SHPOA to continue to prosecute such violators. As it turned out, even these extraordinary provisions were not sufficient to preserve all of the houses and large lots. Although the pace of subdivision and demolition were slowed, they could not be halted. The SHPOA fought each subdivision application with briefs presented to the planning department. Although there were many such cases, the most interesting was a three-year court battle over the subdivision of a large lot on Hudson Street. Because the city planning department had ruled in favour of the owner of the property, the SHPOA took both the owner and the city to court. The SHPOA won the case, but it was appealed to the Supreme Court of British Columbia, which reversed the lower court's ruling.[15] The core group of active SHPOA members also maintained a constant vigil against violators of the code, either reporting them to the planning department or the board of permits, or prosecuting them directly. For example, in late 1971, the SHPOA notified the Department of Permits and Licences of what it suspected were violations of the zoning code on six properties. In January 1972, these properties were inspected, and four were found to be in illegal multiple occupancy. The city then took action against them.[16] In spite of these efforts, the SHPOA was unable to prevent a small but constant reduction in the average lot size, the demolition of a few old houses, and the building of a number of new ones.

By the mid 1970s, after six years of trying to work within the context of RS-4 zoning, the SHPOA decided that it was slowly losing the battle to stop demolition, subdivision, and the building of new houses. A new zoning law would better conserve the landscape. To this end, in 1976 a private firm was commissioned to propose a new plan for Shaughnessy that would reflect the association's landscape taste and desire to retain an élite character (Shaughnessy Heights Property Owners' Association 1977). The resulting plan, which not only covered the question of subdivision and demolition of old houses, but also proposed design guidelines on all new construction, was accepted only in part as it was not seen to reflect the SHPOA's views adequately. Core members of the association conducted their own study and subsequently modified the firm's plans. The board's recommendations were accepted at the 1978 annual meeting of the association, and were then submitted along with the firm's proposals to the city planning department for consideration.

The city planning department in turn was broadly supportive of the SHPOA's proposals, recommending that the First Shaughnessy Study Planning Committee be formed to draw up new by-laws for the area.[17] The committee which was to 'assist' the planning department in drawing up a new Shaughnessy plan was composed of ten members of the SHPOA, three owners of rooming-houses, two tenants, a member of the Vancouver Heritage Advisory Committee, and a representative of the city planning department. The composition of this committee, which had the blessing of the city planning department, was a clear acknowledgment of the pre-eminence of the SHPOA within Shaughnessy.[18] Its members numerically dominated the committee, thereby ensuring that any vote would reflect their views. They were chosen from the core group of board members and had, with one exception, grown up in Shaughnessy. Half of the SHPOA members on the committee were either lawyers or the wives of lawyers; indeed half of the committee were women, reflecting the important role that women had always played in the association.[19]

Although there was broad agreement among the SHPOA group, one member quarrelled regularly with the others. Though similar in background, having grown up in Shaughnessy, he had somewhat different interests as he was a property developer. I was told that, although he was admitted to the board of directors of the SHPOA, he was denied the presidency of the association because it was feared that he was more interested in his own business ventures than in preserving the area. The fact that he was responsible for demolishing an old mansion and replacing it with smaller new houses was etched in the minds of board members. He was included, however, because he was from a prominent old family, and because it was thought that he could be better controlled if he were on the committee than if he were kept off it.

Of the three owners of rooming-houses, only one attended regularly, a rather ineffectual person who was treated with benign condescension by the members of the SHPOA. The tenants did not represent real tenants' interests within the area. They had been 'recruited' onto the committee by the SHPOA because they were perceived to be harmless. The most flagrant violation of the spirit of neighbourhood representation was the selection of one tenant who was employed by one of the directors of the SHPOA. The other was an inexperienced university undergraduate who was overwhelmed by the older, more articulate and aggressive SHPOA members of the committee. Later she was replaced by another tenant who was interested in aesthetics rather than tenants' rights. The representative of the Vancouver Heritage Advisory Committee rarely attended the meetings and also had virtually no influence over the proceedings.

During the two years that this committee met two successive planners were assigned as liaison between the committee and the planning department. Their task in the meetings was to represent the point of view of the planning department, and to advise the committee on what was technically and legally possible. The first planner was overwhelmed by the strong personalities on the committee who had little interest in the opinion of the planning department when it did not coincide with their own. He was replaced by a more forceful planner who refused to be bullied by the members of the SHPOA. Although he broadly shared the SHPOA's goal of preserving the nature of Shaughnessy, he saw his task on the committee as trying to 'educate' the members on what would be acceptable to both the planning department and city council.

The Creation of the Shaughnessy Plan

Before discussing the workings of the committee, it is important to establish the sociopolitical context within which these deliberations were taking place. With the expiry of the act in 1970, the SHPOA was forced to deal with a council that they feared might have more plural objectives than fostering the élite nature of Shaughnessy. The immediate political context during the early to mid 1970s was a city council dominated by The Electors Action Movement (TEAM), a liberal political party whose platform was the 'livable city.'[20] It included a concern on the part of both the city council and the TEAM-appointed director of plan-

ing for the issues of quality of life, landscape aesthetics, and neighbourhood protection. Its actions included historic designation and the revitalization of old 'character' neighbourhoods like Chinatown and Gastown, in a process of participatory and consultative local area planning.
These calls for the creation of a 'livable city' were met with widespread
enthusiasm and survived the loss of a TEAM majority in the late 1970s.
The city planning department still espoused these ideas, and, more important, so did the public.

The 'Goals for Vancouver' survey of 5,000 people in 1979 sampled
attitudes in order to help set the goals for city planning in the 1980s
(City of Vancouver Planning Commission 1980). The responses to this
survey placed great stress upon aesthetics, preserving green spaces, supporting the individual character and identity of neighbourhoods, and preserving heritage and character areas. The planning department and the
city council adopted these goals, goals that well suited the arguments
that the SHPOA had been making about Shaughnessy for the past forty
years. The association could argue that its desire for heritage preservation
and green space was not merely in its own interest, but was endorsed
by the city as a whole. The SHPOA, then, could claim legitimacy from
a broader ideology, as well as from friends on council who included
Mayor Volrich (1976–80), the leader of an action by Shaughnessy residents to block the construction of a shopping centre on its margins some
years earlier.

But there was a countervailing reality: a housing shortage of near crisis
proportions. A rental vacancy rate consistently below 1 per cent and
a shortage of land for building were driving housing costs to unprecedented levels. Shaughnessy, of course, contained very low densities on
land near the heart of the city. What remained to be seen was whether
arguments for green space, heritage, and neighbourhood protection
would prevail over the arguments for more plentiful and affordable
housing.

The very general goals that the Shaughnessy planning committee
began with in 1979 were as follows: first and foremost, to try to preserve
the 'English country house in the city' appearance of the area and maintain its single-family residential status (see figure 2.3). This overall goal
implied several subgoals: first, to halt subdivision of large lots; second,
to provide financial incentives to owners of the largest mansions so that
they would not demolish them; third, to encourage owners of rooming-
houses to convert them either to single-family structures or to strata title
tenure so that the houses would be owner-occupied by a small number

FIGURE 2.3.   How Shaughnessy sees itself: a spacious, single-family Tudor Revival mansion (c.1910) on a large lot, peeking modestly through mature deciduous landscaping, and displaying the icons of territory and possession (Photograph: James Duncan).

of people; and, fourth, to create a set of design guidelines so that all new building in the area would be in keeping with the ideal of the early-twentieth-century English country house that the SHPOA has always espoused. What the committee did not know, however, was how to translate these goals into a planning document that would be acceptable to council.

Establishing the Discourse

Although the First Shaughnessy Study Planning Committee began by opposing any housing type other than single-family use, it rapidly became aware that it had to provide some financial incentives to owners of mansions, which, because of their size, were at risk of being demolished in the future, and to owners of rooming-houses that they hoped would convert to owner-occupied dwellings. Similarly they realized that not all subdivision could be blocked, and as a result there would inevitably be a certain amount of new construction in the area. These two issues soon came to be seen as linked, for a primary incentive to the owners of mansions was to allow them either to 'strata title' so that the existing structure could be divided into two or more very expensive condominiums without changing the exterior of the house, or to 'infill,' whereby a large lot could be subdivided on condition that the main house be kept intact.

Once it was agreed that there was no choice but to have some subdivision and strata titling of properties, then the central question that the committee focused upon was how best to ensure that all new development conformed to the tastes of the board members of the SHPOA. Whereas the rhetoric of the CPR and the SHPOA from the beginning had been about single-family housing, it was equally concerned with legislating landscape taste (remember that the CPR's loan program was tied to design controls). The committee therefore set about defining how they wished their neighbourhood to look so that, through the medium of the zoning code, they could legislate it into existence. What emerged in the meetings was not only a concern over the mansions that had been turned into rooming-houses but a generally agreed-upon distaste for the new smaller houses that had been built since the war (see figure 2.2). In fact in some respects there was less concern over the former than over the latter, for it was felt that the mansions could be restored to their former glory while the smaller houses, because of their size and design, would always detract from the English-country-house styles (see figure 2.3). Furthermore, no more rooming-houses could be created, whereas any new development could produce houses that failed to conform to the SHPOA's image of the area.

When quite early on in the proceedings I asked one of the committee members what kind of a landscape the SHPOA wished to create, he replied by citing what he thought they liked and disliked: 'We are striving for tasteful seclusion, privacy, trees, [and] setbacks. We hate the tacky bungalows with their open lots. They look functional, like they are for living and nothing else. We love old Tudors, Victorians, things which are authentic.'[21] It should be pointed out that these 'tacky bungalows' were selling for between $300,000 and $400,000 at the time (1979), although this price was primarily lot value. This view of bungalows came to be accepted by the city planning department, for, in the final draft of the *Design Guidelines* (1982a), all houses in Shaughnessy were given a rating of architectural merit. An 'A' rating meant that the house was of exceptional merit; 'B' rating meant that it contributed to the 'Shaughnessy image'; while a 'C' rating signified that 'the building could be removed entirely with little or no regrettable loss to the architectural fabric of Shaughnessy. Often these are buildings which, from the outset, ignored the social and architectural tradition of First Shaughnessy. Houses in this category have been neglected, and redevelopment may be the only alternative for these properties.'[22] 'The majority of these properties had not in fact been neglected. Rather, the real reason that they were candidates for redevelopment was that they did not fit in with the 'Shaughnessy image.' But how to allow for redevelopment that would enhance the image? A member of the committee provided the following example of the problem: 'A new house has gone up on Angus which is Tudor imitation. But the timbers are match sticks and the leaded windows are tape. This is simply awful. How can we avoid it? How can we legislate against it? We want houses built with traditional materials.'[23] A sympathetic member of city council who occasionally sat in on the committee's meetings hit the nail on the head when she said, 'The problem is you want to come up with design guidelines to make people imitate a 1920 imitation Tudor.'[24]

Another problem that the committee faced in regard to new development was the size of new housing to be built. There was disagreement over this issue. One view was: 'We don't want big houses that look crummy. If it's small, say, 2,000 to 4,000 square feet, it must be exquisite.'[25] Another view was: 'Big houses are a part of the Shaughnessy concept. Part of the magic of Shaughnessy is big houses on big lots. The impression the area gives is large scale.'[26] Another member of the committee countered: 'The problem is that if we impose new mansions of, say, 6,000 to 8,000 square feet as the smallest house able to contribute to the Shaughnessy image, then we could get ugly monsters.'[27] A senior planner who attended several of the meetings offered a solution with the right nuances, the coach house: 'If you have an 8,000 square foot house, you don't want one 5,000 square feet of the same height behind it. Probably you want a smaller house beside it that would look like a coach house. This then wouldn't spoil the character of the 8,000 foot house.'[28] Over the months broad support emerged for this idea. As one SHPOA member observed: 'We want coach houses next to large houses to make it appear like an estate.'[29]

One of the most interesting changes in the attitudes of the SHPOA members of the committee over the nearly three years that they met was that they discovered the characteristics of the Shaughnessy landscape that were most important to them. At the beginning they were unwilling to concede any deviation from their ideal, but over time as they tried to develop a neighbourhood plan they became willing to compromise certain demands. In spite of their rhetoric of authenticity, of 'honest design,' they came to see that, as the alderman had told them, they were trying to create guidelines to design 1980s imitations of 1920s imitation Tudor houses. Although the full implications of the idea were never fully articulated, an awareness emerged that the committee was essentially dealing with illusions. Hence they were content with imitation coach houses, with places that looked like estates but were not. Eventually most of them were even willing to compromise their cherished goal of single-family detached housing as long as this compromise could be disguised in the landscape: 'If the house is well designed, who cares what the use is, so long as it looks single-family and the parking is concealed.'[30] With one exception, all of the SHPOA members on the committee agreed that even duplexes were acceptable as long as the properties looked as if they were single-family dwellings and conformed to local architectural tastes.

The one continuing source of tension on the committee was not between the SHPOA and the tenants or the rooming-house interests, for the representatives of these latter groups were effectively neutralized. The developer and his fellow SHPOA members found themselves repeatedly at odds. The developer was aggressive in his belief that the other members of the committee did not understand local land economics. Other SHPOA members saw him as a Philistine who too often placed his financial interests over the interests of the neighbourhood. Their assessments of each other were, in fact, quite accurate, for the issue of profits versus sentiment was a recurrent theme throughout the meetings. The following is a typical exchange, beginning with the developer: 'I want it so that the present residents can profit from the area as well [as speculators from outside the district].'[31] The following week another committee member opposed this view: 'The purpose of this whole exercise is to help a few poor[32] people hold on to their homes, not to make a few people into millionaires. I have heard of people drawing up plans for eight townhouses on their property. This makes me damn mad.' Another added, indignantly: 'I can point to 50% of the houses in the area. People who have been in the area for a long time and who live there because they like it. I won't sell no matter what the zoning – until the kids leave the house.' To which the developer responded, with a condescending smile: 'I know people who are holding out for higher prices and then will sell.'[33]

Since the appearance of the landscape was of crucial importance to the SHPOA committee members, their attention focused on both the content of the proposed design guidelines and its implementation. The plan was written to ensure that new buildings in Shaughnessy would blend with the English-country-house ideal that had characterized construction in the area before the Depression.[34] The guidelines controlled everything from house style and siting on the lot to types of windows and planting. The issue of who would ensure that the guidelines were followed was the subject of intense debate. Essentially the SHPOA did not trust the city planning department to implement the guidelines. The final advisory committee that was to judge all building plans therefore was to be comprised of four property owners, and three members drawn one each from the Heritage Advisory Committee, the Architectural Institute of British Columbia, and the British Columbia Society of Landscape Architects. The SHPOA had won a key victory as they could retain control of this all-important design committee.

Much of the discussion in the planning meetings revealed the upper-class prejudices of SHPOA members against the middle class and those whom they considered to be *parvenus*. However, for political reasons, in the official minutes of their meetings, and for the final draft of the plan, they tried their best to downplay the area as a haven of the upper class and portray it as a park-like, heritage landscape for all Vancouver citizens to enjoy. Judicious wording of the draft plan was necessary:

First SHPOA member: We should decrease in emphasis the 'well to do exclusiveness' of the area [which had appeared in an early draft of the plan]. Is this good public relations? Does it add to our claim of historic preservation? We must present Shaughnessy as an area of historical significance to people in Burnaby [an outer suburb], etc. Perhaps the mention of rich people will turn them off.

Second SHPOA member: Yes, remove the reference to helping people maintain large properties. The press will pick this up as a preoccupation of ours. Do you want to see this printed in the press?[35]

The SHPOA members of the committee were also aware that there were a variety of conflicting pressures on them from both the political right and the left. Most of these pressures centred around the issue of the strata titling of large pre-1940 houses and infill on large lots. By late 1980, the SHPOA members of the committee had reversed their initial opposition to even very limited subdivision and conversion of certain large houses into condominiums. They had come to believe that strata titling and infill were the best way to save certain large pre-1940 houses from demolition. This strategy would also, they believed, maintain the 'English country look' that they wished to preserve and help to subsidize the owners of large properties. It would also allow for density increases in the area, which city council was keen to encourage in hopes of addressing the housing shortage in the city. The committee was warned by a sympathetic ally on council that there would be opposition from some people within Shaughnessy to the plan as envisioned: 'A number of Shaughnessy people don't want any conversion [of large houses into condominiums]. They want it to remain an expensive high class, heritage area.' To which a SHPOA member responded, 'Yes, we have to be conscious of political opposition by going too low [in terms of the minimum size of a house to be subdivided].'[36]

However, the committee was also aware of pressures from the political left. One of the goals of the SHPOA was to offer the owners of the rooming-houses sufficient financial inducements that they would convert their houses back into single-family dwellings or strata title them into a maximum of four units having an average size of 1,800 square feet. During 1980, however, the committee was told that it could run into opposition to this plan from the city council. This became especially clear after October 1980 when three council members from the socialist Committee of Progressive Electors (COPE) were elected to the ten-member council, and a social-democratic mayor was also elected. As one SHPOA member of the committee put it, in the first planning meeting after the civic elections, the new city council 'will be less sympathetic to the rich people in Shaughnessy, so we [the committee] will have to be more careful.'[37] More to the point with regard to the conversion of rooming-houses, another member noted: 'The new city council will not let us get away with getting rid of hundreds of people at the low end of the scale by converting rooming houses into expensive units.'

The sympathetic councillor, present to advise the committee on the political implications of the election, observed: 'COPE will see this as driving out the poor. I wouldn't single out this use for attention. It will just get you in trouble ... Council will only see you putting out poor people. Some of the tenants will organize and storm city hall. Then your whole plan is down the drain.'[38] The councillor continued to offer advice: 'Look, you have to avoid having all these people thrown out at once. This would create a mess.' The planner who acted as a liaison with the committee confided to me, rather defensively, after this meeting: 'Property owners should be protected, not just renters. After all, they spent their money buying into a prestige, single-family neighbourhood and their investment should be protected. Renters are a minority in the area.'

The Passage of the Shaughnessy Plan

In 1981 the city planning department approved the plan, and at the end of the year the city council decided to have a 'vote in principle' on it. Before the vote, the planner who had acted as liaison with the group showed attractive slides of the area and argued that it should be preserved for future generations. He then went on to state that, while there was a housing shortage in the city, there was 'a particular shortage of prestige single-family homes near the downtown.'[39] The plan passed unanimously. The two most left-wing aldermen observed, respectively: 'It's a great plan. This is a special area'; and 'There's no question that everyone agrees with the goal to save the plan [from being defeated]'. The mayor commented that 'it is in the interest of the city to preserve Shaughnessy.' The issue of the housing shortage and of renters was not raised by anyone. The ideology of livability, of green space, heritage, and neighbourhood protection had prevailed.

In March 1982, when council met to give final approval to the plan, a group of property owners in Shaughnessy who felt that the SHPOA members on the committee did not represent their interests submitted seventy-five letters asking councillors to delay their decision so that a new public hearing could be convened. City council, in deference to divided neighbourhood opinion, rescheduled a hearing and vote on the plan. The cause of this dissension was a draft of the plan that had been circulated in Shaughnessy by the planning department. The irony of this opposition was that the dissenting property owners held views similar to those that had been held by the SHPOA members of the committee several years earlier. They felt that the SHPOA leadership had compromised them, and that no strata titling or infill concessions should be made at all. The leadership of the SHPOA were not prepared for this challenge from within their own ranks and set about at once to convince the dissidents to withdraw their opposition. Hours were spent in persuasion, and finally thirty-nine retractions were secured. One of the more convincing arguments used by the leadership was that the dissenters represented over half of the properties that could be strata titled or infilled and that there would be relatively little of either unless they wanted it. The dissenters also had to be reassured by the city that their taxes would not be increased to reflect the new development potential of their property. However, those who remained unconvinced in turn canvassed the neighbourhood to uncover more people willing to oppose the plan at the public hearing. Both the leadership of the SHPOA and the dissenters also strenuously lobbied city council.

The planning department's prestige was now on the line as they had endorsed the plan, and it likewise canvassed both in Shaughnessy and with council. During the public hearing the planning department and the SHPOA leadership argued for the plan, while the leaders of the dissidents argued that a small group of activists in the SHPOA were foisting unwanted changes onto the district. The supporters of each side were in the crowd loudly supporting their speakers. When it came to a vote, the mayor, the two liberal members of TEAM, and four members of the right-of-centre Non-Partisan Association (NPA) voted for the plan, citing heritage, green space, and the importance of the area to the city as their reasons. One member of the NPA and the three members of COPE voted against the plan on the grounds that they did not want to force zoning changes and design guidelines upon a divided neighbourhood. There was no mention at the meeting of the potential eviction of tenants nor of the housing shortage. Thus the Shaughnessy plan was approved by a seven-to-four margin. The terms of the debate both by those in favour and those against concerned the discourse of the livable city. The only threat to the plan had come from conservatives within the neighbourhood. The left ultimately opposed it not because it was élitist, nor because its intent was to remove renters from the area, but because the district was divided and thus the ideology of local self-determination could not be brought to bear in its support. In effect, the left threw its support behind a faction that was more conservative than the Shaughnessy Heights Property Owners' Association.

CONCLUSION

In a city with a land shortage and a severe housing crisis how is it that the planning department and city council could support such a plan? Why is it that a scheme which increased the minimum lot size in the area was designed to displace hundreds of lower-income renters and encode into law upper-class anglophile taste, was not only deemed acceptable but seen as commendable? It is too simple to say that we have witnessed a conspiracy by a small élite pulling strings behind closed doors to achieve something that the citizenry did not want. Rather, the plan was brought into being because it appears to be what the citizens and bureaucrats did want. The upper-class members of the SHPOA did not invent the ideology of the livable city, of green space, of architectural heritage, of neighbourhood protection. It had been espoused primarily by middle-class liberal academics, bureaucrats, and politicians with an eye to improving the quality of life in middle- and working-class districts. The SHPOA skilfully used the contradictions of this ideology in large part because they genuinely believed in the importance of green space and heritage and the right to control their neighbourhood. They found the ideology of the livable city congenial not simply because it was useful to them, but because they recognized in it the traditional English upper-class sentiments about the importance of aesthetics, locality, and history. Now the ideology of the livable city had made traditional upper-class landscape taste and ideals acceptable to the political left, centre, and right alike. The class interest of the SHPOA had been masked by a rhetoric of the general interest, ensuring that the livable city would continue to remain more livable for some than for others.

This masking hides a more secret history of Shaughnessy. Some of the contradictions of both early and late twentieth-century capitalism can be traced in this history of Shaughnessy and its relationship to the rest of the city. Since its inception, the residents of Shaughnessy have been deeply enmeshed in a capitalism which they have attempted to deny, not simply through protective zoning, but also by adopting one of the most prominent symbols of the English aristocracy during the industrial age: the country house. This denial, which Wiener (1981) traces back to nineteenth-century English *nouveau riche* industrialists, requires an elaborate illusion, for the 'old families' of Shaughnessy are not aristocrats, but the children and grandchildren of frontier capitalists; the heritage houses are not eighteenth- or nineteenth-century English mansions, but twentieth-century copies often built in the lifetime of the residents; and furthermore they are not country estates, but urban plots laid out by a developer.

If the mystifying relationship which the Shaughnessy élite has with capital is a historical trace of one of the contradictions of early capitalism, then the relationship the élite has with the state (the liberal bureaucrats and city politicians of various political stripes) is a manifestation of one of the contradictions of late capitalism, and the contortions of the welfare state. For now the state sanctions the 'escape' from the world of capitalism into a world of precapitalist values, not as the privileged fantasy of the élite, but as a right to which all citizens are entitled, though in reality only as *voyeurs*. The cultural heritage of all Vancouver residents is thought to lie in the dream world of English country houses which is Shaughnessy. And in the acceptance of green space as an unquestioned good, we can see anti-urbanism which is a rejection of the city as the seat of capitalism. Thus when the SHPOA asks the planners and politicians to help it preserve heritage or green space in Shaughnessy, they cannot be denied. In the name of democracy (read: local control) as well as in the interests of making the secret denial of capitalism available to the masses, the state subsidizes upper-class interests.

The contortions of the welfare state are in part a product of the ambivalence of neighbourhood politics. The exclusionary tendencies of community control provide a sharp check to any simplistic notion of local democracy emerging from neighbourhood participation (a point to which we shall return in chapter 10). It is in a sense paradoxical that community participation in decision making should be pressed at all during the same period as the regressive effects of local monopoly power have been so forcefully evident in the exclusionary zoning practices of some U.S. suburbs. Arguably these tendencies may be stronger among old-style ratepayers' associations, but there are no grounds for seeing privatism as being exclusive to them.

The success of the Shaughnessy Heights Property Owners' Association also displays the survival of an earlier model of neighbourhood organization into the present era of the welfare state. Both the rights, and the politics, of property-owning ratepayers were upheld in Shaughnessy by the local state. The politics of influence, of informal relations as joint members of a power élite, have aided the association's relations with the state in the present as in the past. These relations are not, however, guarantors of goal achievement, for the SHPOA has suffered significant reversals as well as victories over the course of its history. We shall see a clear demonstration in chapter 3 of the contingent nature of even élite status in securing desired outcomes in the neighbourhood politics of Rehavia, in Jerusalem's inner city.

3

Rehavia: A Jewel in the Urban Crown*

On a hillside just off Jerusalem's city centre lies the middle-class neighbourhood of Rehavia. Its eastern boundary is King George Street, a major artery leading downtown; to the north and northwest lie the religious neighbourhood of Sha'arei Hessed and the working-class neighbourhood of Nahlat Ahim. The southern border between Rehavia and the affluent Talbiya and Kiryat Shmuel neighbourhoods is less distinct (see figure 3.1). The neighbourhood has developed gradually over a period of fifty years, and consequently its staged subdivisions – known as Rehavia Alef, Bet, Gimel, and Daled – represent a variety of planning concepts and architectural styles. Some sections were spaciously laid out, in line with the garden-city style, while others were densely built, featuring some modern urban concepts (Kroyanker 1989).

The land on which Rehavia was to be built, known in the 1920s as Zanzarya, had been purchased during the First World War from the Greek Orthodox Church by the Palestine Land Development Company (PLDC), a land-purchasing company run by the Zionist movement (Bigger 1977, 121). When the first houses of Rehavia Alef were built in the early 1920s, it was considered an outlying area and the PLDC encountered some difficulties in selling the land. To encourage families to move into the area, the PLDC advertised Rehavia as a modern neighbourhood conveniently near the train station and the commercial centre (Eshbal 1954).

In sharp contrast to the architecturally traditional neighbourhoods built outside the Old City walls from the 1860s onward, Rehavia was planned to be modern. Its modernity was partly the result of geopolitical changes

*This chapter was written by Shlomo Hasson and Nili Shchory.

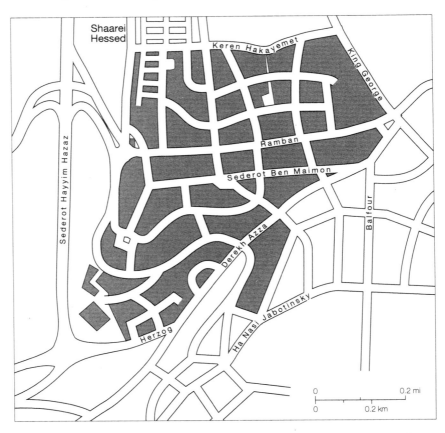

FIGURE 3.1.   The street plan of Rehavia: the first section of Rehavia Alef

that took place in the area in the aftermath of the First World War, when Britain, under a League of nations mandate, succeeded the dismembered Ottoman Empire as administrator of Palestine. One of the British mandate's first acts was to make Jerusalem the capital of Palestine and to draw up a modern town plan for the city. This act served as impetus for modern experiments in architecture and planning (Bigger 1977, 108). Richard Kaufman, a Jewish architect trained in Germany, where he was exposed to the garden-city concept, drew up several schemes for modern garden-city neighbourhoods in Jerusalem, among them Rehavia, Beit Hakerem, Bayit Vegan, and Talpiot. His plan for Rehavia (later known as Rehavia Alef) is a typical manifestation of garden-city principles. Like

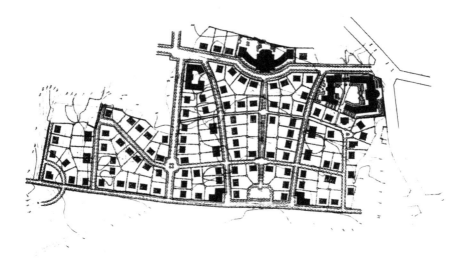

FIGURE 3.2. Kaufman's garden-city plan. The first plan of Rehavia was drawn by Richard Kaufman in 1922 along garden-city principles. The neighbourhood has a grid pattern of roads, rectangular housing lots facing the street, and a central pedestrian boulevard cutting across the area from north to south (Source: Palestine Land Development Company 1923).

Shaughnessy it contains curvilinear streets, and also a central pedestrian boulevard cutting across the neighbourhood from north to south, leading at both ends to public land uses: the Gymnasia Rehavia high school at the north and a public park at the south. Also like Shaughnessy, Rehavia has large rectangular housing lots, here of a quarter-acre, facing the street at their narrow side, so as to allow for a maximum number of houses with a view of the road; each house has a small garden in front (see figure 3.2). Describing Kaufman's plan, Yehuda Ezrahi (an author and Rehavia resident) wrote: 'The plan reminds one of an abstract-geometric painting and possesses a meticulous beauty. It relates to the topography of the hill and seeks to introduce harmony, aesthetics, and order. It seems like a human body with a head and arms formed by public institutions and the Gymnasia' (1968, 75). Remnants of the original neighbourhood can still be seen. There are many intersecting tree-lined streets winding along the slope, large boulevards, some segments of a pedestrian walkway, and here and there one can still find one-storey houses with small, quite often neglected gardens in front.

During the 1930s and 1940s, new residential sections were laid out – Rehavia Beit, Gimel, and Daled. Hecker and Yelin, who planned Rehavia Beit, sought to maintain the original idea of a garden-city neighbourhood, and saw to it that all the houses were of two storeys with small gardens. This concept was, however, abruptly abandoned in Rehavia Gimel and Daled in favour of three- or four-storey apartment buildings. The pace of construction speeded up during the 1930s and reached an unprecedented peak in the years 1933–6 with the arrival of Jewish immigrants who had fled Nazi Germany. Of the 246 buildings constructed between 1924 and 1936, 144 were built during these three years (Kroyanker 1989, 273).

Rehavia of the 1920s and 1930s had a distinctive social character. Among its first residents were such prominent Jewish community figures as Yitzhak Ben-Zvi, later Israel's second president; Daniel Oster, who would be Jerusalem's first Jewish mayor; Arthur Ruppin, head of the Palestine Office of the World Zionist Organization, which oversaw Zionist planned settlement in Palestine; as well as a judge, an architect, and several affluent businessmen (Shabbetai 1986). The immigration of the 1930s brought with it a large group of intellectuals and scholars trained at Central European universities (mainly in Germany, Austria, and Czechoslovakia). By that time, many Hebrew University professors were living in Rehavia: Gershom Scholem, Hugo Bergman, Martin Buber, and Akibba Ernst-Simon, to name but a few. Soon the area became identified with the local élite. A 1936 poll shows the preponderance of white-collar occupations. Out of 1,000 residents, 12 were university professors, 46 engineers, 56 doctors, 145 business people, and 247 administrators (ibid). The establishment of the major offices of the Zionist movement in the neighbourhood's northeastern corner further added to its prestige. Its cafés hosted the local intelligentsia, top officials working nearby, and off-duty British soldiers. There was a European-colonial atmosphere to the neighbourhood in those days, manifested physically in the Bauhaus and International Style architecture, art-deco railings and window grilles, all mixed with oriental decorations and the pine and palm trees that lined the boulevards (see figure 3.3).

Today most of this is gone. The 1950s and 1960s witnessed a huge wave of construction that brought the population over the 10,000 mark, with the resulting conversion of old houses into apartment buildings and the unavoidable slippage of social distinctiveness (Kroyanker 1989). The

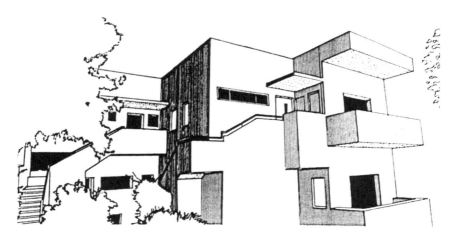

FIGURE 3.3.   The international style in Rehavia: a two-storey cooperative
housing project (Meonot Ovdim A) built in the 1930s around a central
courtyard (Source: David Kroyanker).

expansion of the city centre turned Rehavia into an inner-city neighbourhood threatened by the encroachment of traffic, commerce, and business. Since these issues will be dealt with in much more detail later on,
suffice it to say here that, despite these changes, Rehavia still retains a
high measure of respectability hardly to be found in the 'nouveau' middle-
class areas that now ring Jerusalem. The 1983 census shows that over
80 per cent of Rehavia's residents are of European descent and that 32
per cent of them have a university degree (Shabbetai 1986). Rehavia
still ranks at the top of Jerusalem's neighbourhoods in a wide variety
of socio-economic indicators.

Against this background, we examine the role of the first neighbourhood councils in creating a distinctive locality and the struggle currently
being pursued by the council to defend Rehavia from the physical encroachment of business offices. We will demonstrate that, while the issues
under debate and the strategies employed have changed over time, the
basic principle of preserving the neighbourhood's character through local
activism has remained intact.

REHAVIA AT ITS HEIGHT

A *Gemeinschaft*-like Community

On 30 April 1923, twelve of the first twenty landowners in Zanzarya assembled in the office of the PLDC to discuss administrative and financial matters concerning the neighbourhood's future. The name 'Rehavia' (meaning, approximately, 'open' or 'spacious') was chosen, and a council was elected to represent the interests of the residents. There was an urgent need for such a council, since the PLDC policy was to purchase land, draw up a physical scheme, sell the land to Jewish settlers, and leave construction to them (Eshbal 1954, 74). There were six members in this first council – two rabbis, one doctor, one high-ranking official representing the PLDC, an engineer, and a businessman. The council's chairperson came from one of the city's oldest and most respected Sephardic families (Eshbal 1954). In the years that followed, council members included a lawyer, a judge, and a businessman who served as the chairman of the Jerusalem Chamber of Commerce. There were members of both European and Sephardic descent.

To attain judicial status, the neighbourhood was registered with the local magistrate as the Mutual Association of Rehavia Ltd. In addition, the council composed a set of guidelines to define its role and the rights and obligations of the association's members, compiling these in a book of regulations. According to these regulations, the association's council and its chairperson were to be elected by an assembly made up of the registered residents; newcomers were obliged to join the association and comply with its rules, and membership could be revoked if a member was convicted of a felony. The regulations specified that the council was the neighbourhood's responsible organization with regard to planning, development, and social life. The council was, then, given a wide range of municipal functions: the paving of roads, installation of water and sewage pipelines and a street-lighting system, development of public facilities (gardens and parks) and of public institutions, and street cleaning. At one point the council even provided regular bus service with a vehicle it leased for that purpose.[1] In addition to provision of services, the council assumed a regulative role, vehemently ensuring adherence to zoning codes. When the Jerusalem Workers' Council, for example, launched an industrial development plan for an area within the confines of Rehavia, the council appealed to the city planning commission (a statutory body) and convinced it to reject the proposal (Bigger 1977, 121).

Only those commercial services deemed necessary to public welfare were allowed, among them schools, kindergartens, public institutions, grocery stores, cafés, and some medical clinics. To facilitate its activities and to improve the delivery of services, the council levied taxes.[2]

Though lacking municipal authority, the council managed to run Rehavia as if the neighbourhood were a city within a city. The question that arises, then, is what the council's sources of power were, and how it could impose its authority on the residents. On this subject, Katan and Cnaan (1986) observe that neighbourhoods at the time were practically social communities: 'The first neighbourhoods established at the end of the 19th and beginning of the 20th century in Jerusalem and Tel Aviv had distinct and clear geographic boundaries. They did not constitute only a territorial fact but also a social entity; in fact, most of them were characterized by some basic features typical to a "Gemeinschaft" kind of a community' (p. 23).

Apparently, there were sociodemographic features that made self-government possible, even desirable: the small size of the community, its socio-economic homogeneity, commonly held norms and aspirations, and a strong local identity. Reflecting on Rehavia's social composition, Kroyanker wrote: 'Rehavia had a special charm nourished by the original homogeneous population living there during its first 20 years ... Rehavia of those days, sometimes described as a "Prussian island in an Oriental sea," fostered the German heritage with its norms and manners. People used to say that the last Prussian lives in Rehavia' (1989, 280). Another cohesive group was made up of affluent or high-status Sephardic families.

Social cohesiveness, sense of place, and self-management were not limited to Rehavia. As Katan and Cnaan (1986) maintain, these features were quite widespread among newly emerging neighbourhoods, although their specific forms varied from one place to another. For instance, the communal life in Sha'arei-Hessed and Nahlat Ahim (the neighbourhoods northwest of Rehavia) revolved around the synagogues, and local authority resided with the rabbis. In Arab neighbourhoods, both new and old, the leader was the *mukhtar*, who generally came from the largest and most powerful *hamula* (clan) in the area. In modern neighbourhoods, such as Rehavia, Beit Hakerem, or Kiryat Moshe, the ratepayers' association has represented and to a certain extent administered the community.

Much like the case in Rehavia, many of the Jewish neighbourhood councils promulgated and codified regulations governing social and physical aspects of neighbourhood life. Local residents were expected to comply with the regulations and commit themselves to the neighbourhood (Kark 1978).

The *Gemeinschaft* type of neighbourhood organization, much sought after by Tonnies (1963), shed some light on the legitimization of local councils like those emerging in Rehavia and Beit Hakerem. We would argue, however, that the *gemeinschaft* type of community has been somewhat overidealized, and that the result has been to overlook substantive political issues – not the least among them being the role of the state. The policy of the British administration in Palestine was to deliver a minimum level of national and municipal services and to leave any further development in the hands of the local community (Bigger 1977). Under such circumstances, it was almost a necessity for neighbourhood residents to create their own organizations and to become involved in planning and in the delivery of services. In other words, voluntary organizations were not merely the product of an altruistic 'general will,' as Tonnies and some of his disciples would have it, but also a rational-utilitarian response to practical collective needs at the neighbourhood level. Had the residents of Rehavia failed to organize they would probably have had to live with a lower level of services and consequently a lower quality of life.

Another source of political support which Rehavia as well as other neighbourhood organizations could rely upon was the colonization policy of the Zionist movement. Underlying the purchase of land and the support given to the Jewish settlers of Rehavia, Beit Hakerem, and Ahuzat Bayit (the nucleus of Tel Aviv) was a deliberate Zionist policy of strengthening the Jewish hold on territory (Ruppin 1936; Frumkin 1954). Outlying industrious and self-administered neighbourhoods were eminently in line with this policy. Hence the PLDC's willingness to cooperate with the Rehavia council, to accept its reservations and complaints, and to comply with the association's regulations. There was minor though persistent opposition to the council's authority – some residents even unsuccessfully petitioned the courts to exempt them from the association's regulations – but, under the circumstances, this opposition proved to be fruitless (Eshbal 1954).

The deficiencies of such a diffuse political system are not hard to discern: duplication of services, lack of cooperation and coordination, social inequality in service provision stemming from tax-base variation. To overcome some of these problems, Rehavia's council approached some adjacent neighbourhoods and suggested the creation of a larger territorial entity that could be more efficient in the delivery of services, but no concrete steps were taken to pursue this goal.[3]

Rehavia's residents were not the only people to recognize the drawbacks of such a decentralized municipal system. In an attempt to modernize it, the British administration in the 1930s issued a series of acts to regularize municipal government and town-planning procedures.[4] These acts, along with the growing recognition of the need for a strong municipality, made the situation of the neighbourhood organizations, including the one in Rehavia, somewhat precarious. Services, regulation, and taxation were now to be managed from the top, with the obvious result of reducing the authority of the neighbourhood councils. During the late 1930s and the 1940s, many newcomers did not join the Mutual Aid Association, and the neighbourhood council lost most of its administrative functions. The result was the loss of legitimacy and authority. Continuing demographic growth further exacerbated this process. Many residents, including some of the most affluent and respectable, stopped paying their taxes to the neighbourhood association.[5] In an effort to counter growing opposition and apathy, the council sent the residents a letter saying that 'the good of the neighbourhood requires that the residents emerge from their apathy, join the Association, and become more active in local affairs.'[6] In another appeal, the council wrote:

The annual general assembly of the Association's membership was surprised to discover that a large number of property owners and residents are not members of the Association and are not committed to improving and developing the neighbourhood ... Although most of our services are now provided by the municipality (in response to the Council's own demands), there are still many services not included in the municipal domain, and for which our modest income is insufficient ... If all the residents of Rehavia were members of the Association, the meagre tax payments would add up to a considerable amount of money, making local improvements possible.[7]

Further decline in neighbourhood authority was checked by the outbreak of Arab-Jewish hostilities. The large waves of Jewish immigration, especially the arrivals from Central Europe in the 1930s, and nationalist agitations in neighbouring countries, led to the Arab uprising of 1936-9. In response to the rebellion, the organized Jewish community, known in Hebrew as the *Yishuv*, defended itself in various ways. One of these was by organizing neighbourhood civil guard corps; the Rehavia council helped recruit volunteers for the local contingent, oversaw the stationing of policemen and guards within the neighbourhood, and levied taxes to pay for this protection.[8] The council maintained these functions until the establishment of the state in 1948. In 1949, the council and the Voluntary Mutual Aid Association were disbanded and, up until 1969, there was no successor to the pre-state council.

The Role of the State

The decline of neighbourhood life, of which Rehavia is just one example, has been quite often attributed to the rise of the central state. It has been argued that the development of a comprehensive welfare system, directed from the top by bureaucrats, led to the demise of the voluntary organizations that flourished during the pre-state period (Elazar 1987). Although this line of argument is essentially correct, it too easily ignores some developments that predate the rise of the central state, not the least of which is the emergence of strong municipalities governed by modern laws and planning regulations. The rise of strong municipalities and the erosion of neighbourhood power was felt not only in Rehavia, but in other neighbourhoods as well. Katan and Cnaan, who examined the situation in Tel Aviv, observed: 'the creation of a joint local municipality that assumed responsibility for services previously delivered by the neighbourhood itself and by the LNC (local neighbourhood committee) have eroded the power of both the indigenous leadership and the local committee. This process of decline was non-uniform. While it was strongly felt in certain neighbourhoods, others have succeeded in keeping at least part of their "Gemeinschaft" dimensions' (1986, 24).

Rehavia was among those neighbourhoods which managed to survive the rise of a strong municipal system, apparently by adapting its functions and especially by becoming involved in civil defence. The War of Independence (1948), which was felt particularly in Jerusalem, further deepened Rehavia's involvement in civil-defence tasks. Shortly after the war broke out, the new western Jewish neighbourhoods, as well as the Jewish Quarter of the Old City, came under Arab siege. As water and food supplies diminished, the Israeli government established a special committee, in Hebrew called Va'adat Hamatsav (the Situation Committee), to handle all municipal affairs, including the rationing of food supplies. The neighbourhood councils were considered local branches of this body and were required to implement its policies. Rehavia's consequently became involved in the distribution of food and water and took part in civil defence. Yet the end of the war saw the dissolution of the council; as one of its members explained: 'We realized that there was nothing left for us to do.'[9]

From that point onward there was no neighbourhood council in Rehavia. Here and there groups of residents, bothered generally by some land-use decision, responded with short-lived single-issue organizations. No serious steps were taken, however, to revive local organizations with overall territorial responsibility.[10]

The change came much later, as an outcome of the state's self-critique of excessive centralization, bureaucratization, and the removal of the public from community life (Hasson 1989; Kollek 1988). In response to this critique, the Jerusalem municipality in 1980 initiated the Jerusalem Project for Neighborhood Self-Management (JPNSM). But before turning to this project, we need to address several questions concerning the break-up of neighbourhood organizations in the late 1940s. Was there really nothing left to do, as the Rehavia council member thought? Was there nothing in the neighbourhood, socially or physically, that was of concern to the residents? Were the residents really content with the quality of services and the physical and social changes that took place in their locality? Had the welfare state proved itself a genuine substitute for communal management? The decline of services in Rehavia and Beit Hakerem, the contemporary threat to the very existence of these neighbourhoods, and the manifest nostalgia for the past vividly expressed in the attempt made by Beit Hakerem residents to preserve the old Council House, seem to suggest not. The welfare state, as has increasingly become evident, could not replace a committed local council in close contact with local needs. What was it, then, that stifled community organizations at a time when even lower-class neighbourhoods settled by new immigrants (see chapters 5 and 7) went on to create their locally based organizations?

The answer to these questions seem to lie in some general urban processes that particularly affected older neighbourhoods like Rehavia. The residents of the 1920s and 1930s who remained in the neighbourhood aged and lost their initiative, while no younger generation emerged. As one of the older residents said: 'We do not have the old social network we once possessed. People passed away and new ones have not come.'[11] But this is only part of the story. The large wave of construction which swept the area during the 1950s and 1960s led to substantial population growth – from 1,235 in 1939 to 10,237 in 1961 and 11,213 in 1972.[12] With this growth, Rehavia lost much of its distinctive social character and became, as Kroyanker (1989) maintains, just another middle-class neighbourhood. To sum up, the disappearance of neighbourhood politics, including Rehavia's council, coincided with the rise of strong municipalities and with the emergence of the central state. Nevertheless, it would be too simplistic to attribute too much to the state, while ignoring the role of sociodemographic changes and, especially, the rise of local apathy. At a time when the immigrant housing estates built in the 1950s and 1960s saw the rise of local bosses and protest movements, the residents of Rehavia, the city's jewel, remained dormant, failing to organize to counter trends threatening their locality (Hasson 1987).

THE STRUGGLE FOR SURVIVAL

Background

During the 1950s and 1960s, the outlying garden neighbourhood of Rehavia was transformed, as Yehuda Ezrahi (1968) observed, into another inner-city area. The original internal roads, he noted, became major traffic arteries; some of the one-family houses were converted into apartment buildings; municipal services deteriorated, and the residents of the 1930s and 1940s aged. Many of them found themselves unable to keep up their houses and gardens and put them up for sale; the younger generation, unable to compete with businesses willing to pay high prices for prime office space, has been moving out as well.[13] The Jerusalem master plan of 1965 only exacerbated these processes by allowing professional and business offices, as well as art studios, to operate within residential areas.[14] As a result, many residential units in Rehavia passed into the commercial sector, and the number of offices increased steadily. In 1982 there were 100 offices in the neighbourhood; in 1986 there were already 236 – equivalent to 7.5 per cent of the local housing stock.[15] Concomitant with the penetration of Rehavia by offices, the local population dropped from 11,213 in 1972 to 8,276 in 1983. Yet the proportion of the elderly (65 years and above) has increased significantly, reaching an estimated level of 30 per cent, three times higher than the national average, while the proportion of young families with children has sharply decreased.[16] School-enrolment statistics clearly attest to the magnitude of the ageing phenomenon. In 1987, two kindergartens were closed, leaving only two others to serve the entire neighbourhood population and some adjacent neighbourhoods as well. The Gymnasia Ha'ivrit school, once the pride of Rehavia, was by 1987 serving mainly students from outside the neighbourhood, only 8.5 per cent of its students then coming from Rehavia.[17] One resident complains: 'This neighbourhood, once the city's jewel, has now been transformed into a business district with all that implies. Many houses accommodate only a few residents, most of whom are old.' Another complains: 'We do not have any social relations with the office owners and there is a growing sense of alienation and insecurity. During recent years Rehavia has become a place I have little empathy for. In the evenings there is almost no one here and the streets are empty. At night the building looming above me looks like a dark slab and we are afraid to go out to the corridor for fear that someone is hiding on the staircase.' Still another resident adds: 'The sense of a place of residence has been lost.'[18]

Reorganizing the Neighbourhood

Faced with rapid social changes, some residents tried to set up a neighbourhood council that would counter the 'office invasion.' In 1969 they called a meeting to discuss the issue, but only a few residents attended. Those who came nevertheless appointed a neighbourhood council, which worked, in low gear, over the next twelve years to improve physical conditions.[19] The notorious apathy of Rehavia's residents remained greatly unchanged during the early 1980s, despite a deliberate attempt, undertaken by the Jerusalem municipality through the JPNSM, to encourage neighbourhood self-management. As an extension of a previous experiment in school integration, the municipality in 1982 established a neighbourhood council (Minhelet, in Hebrew) for both Rehavia and the adjacent working-class neighbourhood of Nahlat Ahim. The concept behind this was to foster social integration and self-management through a semi-institutionalized organization partly financed by the municipality.

The full scope of the Jerusalem experiment in self-management and its underlying ideology, methods, and achievements, will be discussed in the study of Baka (chapter 9). Suffice it to say that here, as in other residential areas experimenting with self-management, the Rehavia–Nahlat Ahim neighbourhood council consists of two components: a professional staff whose salaries are paid by the municipality and an elected council of residents who serve on a voluntary basis. The professional staff includes a manager, an architect, a community worker, and a secretary. In addition, there are several committees charged with specific issues such as environmental quality, the elderly, and education. The residents' council makes policy, while the professional staff is responsible for implementation and for handling routine affairs (Hasson 1989).

In its first five years, from 1982 to 1987 (before the first neighbourhood elections), the Rehavia–Nahlat Ahim neighbourhood council was an appointed one made up of members of the previous council, and proved to be one of the weakest in the Jerusalem project. No leadership emerged, and for a long time the council lacked a chairperson. Moreover, the council suffered from a high professional staff turnover, creating a sense of instability and insecurity with regard to the future of the council.[20] When elections were finally held in 1987, a Nahlat Ahim resident won the post of council chairperson – an indication that the Rehavia population had failed to assume responsibility and produce a genuine leadership. A 1988 poll revealed that 52.1 per cent of Rehavia's inhabitants were unaware of the council's existence; of those who were aware, 50 per cent knew nothing of its activities. With one exception, such low levels of public awareness were not recorded in any other neighbourhood (Hasson 1989).

In the absence of strong leadership of both the voluntary and professional sort, the two neighbourhoods failed to set a long-range agenda for local development. Instead, a pragmatic-reactive approach was adopted, focusing on what were seen as critical issues: the elderly population, the quality of the environment, education, and the office issue. Four committees were established to pursue these issues. The committee on the elderly understandably attracted the largest number of participants.

A cursory look at the letters, documents, and local newspapers produced by the council reveal that office penetration is considered the neighbourhood's major problem, having been tied to a list of maladies:

1 / The presence of business clients in residential buildings, interfering with daily life;
2 / The office owners' lack of interest in the state of the buildings and surrounding areas, leading to environmental neglect;
3 / A parking shortage resulting from the use by workers and customers of residential parking;
4 / A sense of isolation and fear at night, when offices are closed;
5 / Demographic decline, the ageing of the population, and the out-migration of the younger generation as a result of the high rents paid by office owners.

Based on previous studies of local organizations in affluent neighbour-hoods, including Shaughnessy Heights, one might have expected to find an active committee devoted to halting the office invasion.[21] Reality proved, however, to be quite different. The level of citizen participation has been almost nil. For a long time the offices committee has been run by just two individuals, its chairperson (a local volunteer) and the community worker. Personal negotiations – based on close contacts with Jerusalem mayor Teddy Kollek, himself a Rehavia resident, and with the deputy mayor, Yossef Gadish – have been preferred to mass mobilization and pressure-group politics. The first chairperson of the committee, an urban planner, believed that the best way to handle the problem was through partisan politics, based on private negotiations with the municipality. The second chairperson enjoyed informal access to the mayor, and she relied on these to pursue her goals. It was also apparently in the municipality's interest to handle the whole issue far away from the public and the media. In 1982 the deputy mayor, who headed the Jerusalem Association for the Advancement of Self-Management (JAASM), suggested to the offices committee chairperson that the offices issue not be put on the public agenda and that the city's planning department be allowed to handle the problem. Consequently, letters were exchanged and negotiations conducted, resulting in the transformation of the offices issue from a public into a private one. In other words, avoidance of public discussion has not been a sign of indecision, but rather of a deliberate decision to search for common ground without public debate.

On the practical level, the committee has produced some short- and long-range proposals. The short-range proposals suggest that the Jerusalem municipality should move to expel those offices operating in residential units without a legal permit. According to the law, a residential unit should not be put to any other use unless its land-use status has been legally changed, or unless the user received a special permit authorizing an exceptional land use. Relying on the 1965 master plan, which allowed office decentralization into residential areas, many newly arrived business people have not bothered to attain such exceptional permits, and could therefore be removed legally. The long-run proposal was for the municipality to amend the 1965 master plan by curbing office operation in the Rehavia and Nahlat Ahim neighbourhoods.[22] Such a modification requires a large-scale rezoning operation in order to define which streets should remain strictly residential and which should be set aside for mixed land uses. Personal politics proved to be very effective in influencing municipal decisions. In 1983 the city council formally declared that Rehavia should remain a residential area, and the city's planning department was ordered to draw up a city-wide plan which would amend item 6, the relevant provision in the 1965 master plan, and prevent office penetration of residential areas.[23] Moreover, in 1984, the city's construction department sent letters to those offices operating in Rehavia without permits and ordered them to move out of the area. None have left so far. In order to remove an office, the municipality has to prove that, according to the original building permit, an apartment currently being used as an office had been assigned for residential use. Since most of the permits have been lost, the municipality does not have much to base its case on. It has nevertheless applied to the courts in several cases, on which a verdict is still pending.

Partisan politics and behind-the-scenes negotiations seem to be quite effective in a middle-class area. But the Rehavia case has proven to be somewhat more complicated. Opposition to partisan politics has emerged within the neighbourhood organization. At the city-wide level, white-collar professionals in the business sector have created a strong lobby and pressed for the maintenance of the status quo. As a result, the offices issue quickly re-emerged onto the city's public agenda and has been accompanied by a heated sociopolitical debate.

In 1984, while criticizing the partisan politics adopted by the offices committee, the chairperson of the neighbourhood council publicly expressed his doubts as to whether the committee was genuinely representing the residents' interests. He said: 'It is quite possible that a large number of residents might oppose the activities undertaken by the committee, for example, those seeking to rent their apartments out to businessmen.'[24] In response to the chairperson's challenge, the committee turned to the community and asked for its support. A leaflet handed out to the residents at the end of 1985 brought 300 letters of support and 40 containing reservations about the removal of the offices. (One letter of support came from the mayor.)[25] A 1986 petition demanding the closing of offices was signed by 500 residents. A media campaign launched against the offices resulted in very favourable coverage by the local newspapers. The public has been kept informed of developments and encouraged to present complaints and provide information on the intrusion of new offices. The 1987 neighbourhood elections brought the organization strong leadership from Nahlat Ahim, which continued to pursue the offices issue.

Rehavia's struggle against office penetration coincided with the adoption of a new urban concept by the city's planning department. Surveys conducted by the department in the late 1970s and early 1980s showed a significant spread of offices into residential areas. The number of offices in residential areas, it was found, increased from 234 in 1968 to 631 in 1976, and of the 500 new offices opened between 1976 and 1980, about 80 per cent were in residential areas. The surveys also revealed Rehavia to be the neighbourhood most affected by these trends.[26] For the department's urban planners, the data indicated a twofold negative process: the declining viability of the city centre and the deterioration of neighbourhoods with the concomitant loss of identity and vitality. Yet these serious findings, as the head of the planning department said, 'might still be lying in a drawer somewhere had Rehavia not pressed for municipal intervention.'[27]

As a result of Rehavia's pressure, the city council in 1983 ordered the planning department to prepare a new plan, whose major goals were defined as: 1 / To abolish item 6 in the 1965 master plan, which allowed offices to operate in residential areas; and 2 / To formulate a new zoning ordinance that would regulate the distribution of offices throughout the city.[28]

Members of the planning department hoped that, once their proposal was legally endorsed, office penetration of residential areas in all parts of the city would come to a halt. To sum up, pressures eventually exerted by Rehavia in order to solve what was conceived of as a neighbourhood problem resulted in a city-wide scheme in line with the interests of the city planning department. The Rehavia delegates have not endorsed the large scheme, while white-collar professionals and business people vehemently criticized it and mobilized their members in an effort to reject the plan.

The Business-Sector Response

For the white-collar professionals who established business offices in Jerusalem's residential areas, and in Rehavia in particular, any legal procedure that might entail relocation has been considered a threat that should be firmly opposed. Not only are their economic interests at stake – they stand to incur relocation costs, higher city-centre rents, and higher parking costs – their access to customers and their local reputation stood to be affected.[29] Those located in Rehavia enjoy free parking and quiet surroundings, so their costs might have been particularly high. The Rehavia council's offices committee has been blamed for not representing the interests of the inhabitants, while its interest in making the neighbourhood more youthful was called a dream.[30] To counter the scheme, white-collar professionals in the private sector in 1985 formed an action committee called the Business Sector Committee (BSC). The BSC represented the following organizations: the Institute of Town Planners and Architects, the self-employed, and the local branches of organizations representing lawyers and accountants. Following its first meeting, the BSC declared: 'representatives of the above-mentioned organizations have reached the conclusion that the scheme is unreasonable from a town-planning point of view and its social damage would be much greater than its benefits. It impairs traffic movement, worsens the parking situation, stands in opposition to modern trends of mixed land uses, and harms our legitimate economic interests.'[31] The goal of the BSC has been accordingly defined as either scuttling the plan or at least mitigating its effects. To pursue their campaign against the new scheme, members of the BSC met with the deputy mayor, the head of the town planning subcommittee, with some city council members and with the city engineer. They also petitioned the chairperson of the leading municipal party, Yerushalaim Ahat ('One Jerusalem'), and in a letter dated July 1985 they wrote: 'The group that might be hurt [by the scheme] supported the party quite actively during the last municipal elections. Though we do not expect anything in return we certainly do not deserve outright rejection of our demands.'[32]

Following receipt of this letter, there was a tense meeting between the party's leaders, the BSC, and the Rehavia neighbourhood council chairperson and architect. The BSC delegates argued that the council did not represent the residents' opinions and demanded the rejection of the plan. The deputy mayor did not accept this and told both parties that their arguments would be seriously considered. The plan then went into the public-hearing phase.

Having failed to halt the scheme at the initial stage, the BSC has tried to mitigate and neutralize its impact in public hearing. The strategy adopted by the BSC was to obstruct the decision-making process by raising dozens of objections. Members of the organization were carefully instructed in how to submit objections and what kinds of arguments – economic, social, and moral – they should raise. In one letter they were advised 'to combine traffic, parking, and access arguments together with any other possible rubbish.'[33] The purpose was to obstruct the decision-making process. As the BSC chairperson once boasted, 'I have created a filibuster.'[34] It is hard to determine whether it is the filibuster that slowed down the decision-making process or the political initiative of those members of the town planning subcommittee in charge of the hearings. What seems clear is that the scheme was seriously diluted during the hearings and that, by the time it was submitted to the district planning committee, it looked quite different from the planning department's original proposal.

SOME REFLECTIONS ON THE ROLE OF THE STATE

The conflict over land use in Rehavia is not unusual, and several similar examples have already been discussed at some length in the literature (Lojkine 1976). Theorizing on this sort of conflict, Castells (1983) describes it as a collision between 'use' and 'exchange' values, where the residents are interested in the continuity of their interests (reproduction) and the business sector seeks to secure higher rates of profit and capital accumulation (production). Similar conflicts have been read as an expression of deeper class conflict, whereby the working class, deprived of its natural-environmental rights, encounters its antagonist in the bourgeois-capitalist class.

Rehavia's case obviously does not fit easily into such a model, as it involves two groups coming from the same upper-middle class. The theoretical questions suggested by such a case-study are: what happens when members of the same class collide over such conflicting interests as profit making and environmental (neighbourhood) protection? How may the state (the agencies of local and national government) react to conflicting interests pursued by two powerful groups? The instrumental-Marxist theory, advanced by Miliband (1969) and corroborated to some extent by Saunders's study in Croydon (1979), would probably meet with difficulties in the present case, since politicians and top administrators have social ties with both residents and business groups and have simultaneously endorsed the interests of both.

The state quickly found itself in the well-known predicament of the welfare state – that of serving two masters with conflicting interests. The state's difficult problem is of both a concrete and an abstract nature. Who should be supported, business or people? Which values are to be defended, those of freedom of profit making and wealth creation or those of livable neighbourhoods and maintenance of public welfare? Wealth creation, in this particular case, implies the rejection of the neighbourhood plan and freeing market forces to encourage office penetration. Maintenance of public welfare requires approval of the scheme, which sets geographic limits to free economic activity. Opting for either solution will lose the state something – the support of its citizens or urban economic growth.

Caught in such a dilemma, Habermas noted, the welfare state tends to react with confusion, trying to do two opposite things at the same time, or rather to conceal what it is really doing by means that are contrary to its true purpose. These contradictory efforts result in an 'increasingly visible conflict between the promise and experience, form and content of state policies [which] can lead ... to a growing difficulty for state policies to win acceptance' (1975, 144).

The sociopolitical conduct of the Jerusalem municipality throughout the conflict lends some support to Habermas's observations. First, there are the historical facts. In 1965, decentralization of business offices was permitted, while in the 1980s there has been an effort to check this trend. Recognizing the fact that Jerusalem's city centre had become too small to accommodate the growing demand for office space, the municipality began in the 1960s to adopt a pro-business policy. The early 1980s, in sharp contrast, witnessed a change of mood as the city government adopted a pro-neighbourhood policy. There is nothing wrong with revitalizing the city centre, but the state ought to be consistent once it has embarked on a given policy. Frequent policy changes, as in the offices issue, can cause financial loss and is bound to arouse resentment and opposition.

There has also been a wide gap between policy statements and practical action. As early as 1983 the Jerusalem city council stated very clearly that its policy was to remove offices from residential areas. In line with this policy, the municipal planning department launched a rezoning scheme and the city's legal counsel wrote to those offices operating illegally and demanded their immediate removal.[35] The municipality has repeatedly confirmed this policy. Three years later the municipal counsel assured the Rehavia neighbourhood council: 'As I notified you on 23 November 1986, the municipal policy is to remove offices from residential areas, and the Rehavia neighbourhood is the first and most important area in which this policy is to be implemented.'[36] In practice, nothing happened. Since 1983 not even one office has been removed. On the contrary, the number of offices has steadily increased. One of the new offices belongs to a city-council member, while others are owned by lawyers formerly employed by the municipality.[37]

This apparent conflict between form (statements) and content (effective action), familiar by now to the residents, is not a product of state conspiracy. Rather, it indicates disagreement and conflict within the state itself with regard to urban priorities and political interests. The mayor and the members of the planning department have stood on one side, while the deputy mayor and the town planning subcommittee, a local statutory body with the authority to recommend city plans (like the one discussed here), stood on the opposite side. The conflict first came into the open in 1985, when the mayor demanded swift action to remove offices, while his deputy objected and suggested a more favourable time-table of five years.[38] This disagreement resulted in a scheme that lacks any schedule whatsoever. The deputy mayor has not been alone in ob-jecting to the original scheme. During the hearing process, begun in September 1985, the town planning subcommittee has proved to be very considerate of, and sensitive to, the needs of the business sector. As re-quired by law, there was a two-month waiting period to allow the public to raise objections. Yet the process in the end took almost three years, until November 1988. The chairperson of the town planning subcom-mittee found it endlessly necessary to extend the process, since, in his words, 'the whole issue requires further study.' Such a lengthy process was indeed in the interests of the BSC, which sought to extend the hear-ings indefinitely. This was, of course, contrary to the interests of the neighbourhood council, which tried to speed up the hearing process. The town planning subcommittee, for its part, used the time thus gained to advance a compromise that would make the plan more favourable to the business sector. To this end, the subcommittee even decided, in June 1987, to rezone three residential streets into mixed land-use areas.[39] An article in the local newspaper *Kol Ha'ir* reported this decision under the headline: 'The scheme was readjusted to the needs of the lawyers,' and disclosed that five offices had recently been opened on the three streets involved, all of them for the use of former top municipal and national officials.[40]

Prompted by the chairperson of Rehavia's offices committee, the mayor alluded to this decision in a reproving letter:

I was surprised to discover that you have decided to remove another three streets from the area in which office operation is banned. It is unseemly that in the five years since I demanded that offices withdraw from residential areas there has not been even one case in which we have succeeded ... It is unseemly that before taking any significant step to implement the scheme we are already making concessions. I therefore condemn your decision regarding the said streets and request that you bring the whole matter up for further discussion.[41]

In the wake of the mayor's letter, the town planning subcommittee con-ducted another discussion and decided to revoke the concession and revert to the original scheme. The minutes of the meeting acknowledge the mayor's influence, noting that the decision came 'following Teddy's letter of 6 July 1987.'[42]

In order to break the deadlock, the mayor finally gave up on his city-wide conception and in 1988 accepted that the offices restriction would be limited to Rehavia and Nahlat Ahim. Commenting on the mayor's decision, the head of the town planning subcommittee said: 'The mayor wanted a city-wide scheme. But, realizing that the whole issue is bogged down in endless objections, he has pressed for a swift solution. Teddy was very wise to understand that the decision process could have lasted for years and that the only way to get the scheme out of the mud was by limiting its scope.'[43] The scheme endorsed by the subcommittee in November 1988 was not only limited geographically, but also made many concessions to the offices. They were allowed in residential areas as long as they were located in basements, apartments with separate entrances, or apartments that also served as dwellings. The subcommittee also reserved the right to grant an exceptional-use permit to an office operating in a residential area, thus bypassing the zoning ordinance. The neighbourhood council won two points. First, the scheme included a timetable (albeit one more extended than the council had demanded); second, specific criteria were adopted to define when and where an exceptional-use permit could be granted. In 1988, the revised scheme was submitted to the district planning committee under the auspices of the ministry of the interior, where it was to be legally approved, only to be rejected on technical grounds (lack of distinctions among types of offices) in May 1989. In its decision the district planning committee (an organ of the central government) advised the municipality to draw up a new plan, and for the time being instructed the city to freeze the situation in Rehavia and prevent the introduction of new offices. In an interview with the secretary of the district planning committee, a professional much respected for his political neutrality, he granted that the situation is complex. Both sides, in his view, are right. The business sector, which significantly contributes to the city economy, he noted, needs more space and it is hard to envision its removal en masse from Rehavia. Yet, he added, the residents have justice on their side as well and their interests need to be protected. The solution, in his view, requires a compromise: mixed land uses alongside strictly residential areas.[44] The complexity of the issue is also evident from the fact that, prior to the district planning committee's decision, both parties anticipated rejection, each side for its own good reasons.[45] The head of the city planning department believed that such a revised and curtailed document would not be approved. The head of the BSC believed that the scheme conceded too much and should therefore not be approved. Both parties were proved correct, leaving one to wonder if this is the underlying message of the state through the district planning committee.

Rehavia's struggle against urban market forces is an interesting study whose theoretical ramifications should be carefully interpreted. There is nothing in the data to suggest a coalition, either covert or overt, between the state and capital interests. The state, as this study shows, was not an extension of the bourgeois class, nor was it a mere reflection of social conflicts. True, it related to a social conflict, but it did so while bringing in its own interests, so that in the end it represented and modified interests originating in civil society. The mayor and the planning department transcended the parochial view of Rehavia's residents by seeking a genuinely universal solution to a city-wide problem. The deputy mayor and the town planning subcommittee did not succumb to business interests; rather, they sought a compromise that would serve both parties.

The study further reveals that there are frequently neither angels nor villains in urban politics, a point too easily passed over, as Pickvance (1976) has noted, by those who tend to overidentify with neighbourhood organizations. Approval of the original scheme and the mass removal of offices from Rehavia could have damaged the city's economy, already slack, by alienating local entrepreneurs and deterring further investment. In this light the conflict looks quite different. It may be that the deputy mayor and the head of the town planning subcommittee took a wider view of urban needs than did the mayor, the city planning department, and the Rehavia–Nahlat Ahim neighbourhood council. It may be that the planning department was too ambitious in its plans and failed to consider macro-urban processes beyond its control, such as the continuing decay of Jerusalem's city centre and the conversion of apartments and houses by the elderly in order to meet their personal and health-care needs. Perhaps Rehavia's residents, as they age, do not care very much about their neighbourhood and take action only in the face of a threat, thus failing to produce a long-term policy that would determine what their neighbourhood should look like. Checking office penetration is not a substitute for comprehensive policy, and the residents have already noticed that new problems await them – not the least the penetration of the neighbourhood by conservative religious groups. So far, there has been no genuine attempt to formulate a vision of Rehavia; most of the council's activities are either reactive – halting office penetration – or short term – dealing with immediate environmental and social issues. We do not mean to side with those who criticize neighbourhood organizations for being overly myopic and reactive.[46] There is much value in serving the elderly and in solving immediate physical problems. Yet there is also a need for long-term policy, and this has so far failed to emerge.

Instead of initiating long-term policy, the neighbourhood feeds upon hopes. Commenting on the district planning committee's indecision, the council's newspaper stated: 'we can only hope that the new scheme will be better than the previous one ... and we must insist that the freeze provision [on office penetration] ordered by the district planning committee be strictly enforced by the municipality.'[47] Time, however, plays into the hands of the business sector. None of the older offices has moved out, and new ones continue to open in converted residential units.

PART TWO

The Incorporation of Ethno-racial Minorities

If districts like Shaughnessy and Rehavia have historically provided a model to which middle-class residents aspire, a pole of emulation, Chinatown-Strathcona and Ir Ganim have presented its other, a model which the middle class define themselves against, a region of stigma. The inner-city tract of Chinatown-Strathcona has, since Vancouver's inception, been home to its poorest residents, for long stigmatized culturally and disenfranchised politically; a low-lying and poorly drained district unwanted by other residents, it was claimed by Chinese immigrants as a defensive position in a hostile Euro-Canadian society. Ir Ganim is of more recent vintage, but bears witness to a number of the same marginalizing sentiments. The vast immigration of Sephardic Jews from North Africa and the Middle East following 1948 brought considerable strain to the Israeli state. The new settlers were linguistically and culturally distant from the European-origin majority, the Ashkenazim. They were members of a traditional society, conditioned by the conservative impulses of the Muslim states in which they had survived as ethnic enclaves. Housed initially in Israeli transit camps, they were resettled in hastily constructed housing estates, often in the outskirts of the larger cities. In these austere surroundings, poorly serviced, and separated from jobs and other opportunities, districts like Ir Ganim offered their residents minimal citizenship rights.

As a result, both communities looked inwards and developed their own style of leadership and self-help. In Chinatown, excluded by the full force of racist sentiment from all but a minimal entitlement, a dense network of benevolent societies and other voluntary organizations, based on clan groupings and regions of origin, provided a semblance of mutual aid. Local leaders emerged through the societies, invariably merchants, who acted as cultural brokers with the different levels of the Canadian state. In different circumstances they could have played the role of the immigrant ward boss, delivering votes and distributing services, but in a polarized frontier society, the electoral disenfranchisement of the Chinese meant that for decades there were no votes to deliver, nor were there significant state resources to distribute. Events in Ir Ganim were necessarily different. The national project in Israel placed a high premium on absorbing the immigrants into the life of the nation. This provided a context where traditional leaders were courted and cultivated, as a means of reaching the broader immigrant population. Traditional and non-democratically selected figures were thereby empowered to act as local bosses with considerable authority and access to the resources of the state.

The primary theme of the two case-studies here is the penetration of the modern state into these two inward-looking, culturally and economically marginalized communities, and their response and engagement in turn with the state. In Chinatown-Strathcona, penetration took the form of a destructive program of modernization, extensive urban renewal and freeway proposals, which would have substantially erased the community. In Ir Ganim, penetration took the form of incursions of modern political parties, notably the Israeli Labour Party, whose secular, socialist message scarcely connected with a traditional, theocentric world-view. In both communities vigorous local responses occurred against the marginalization of minorities by the modern state, a form of cultural resistance by new immigrant voices which included a better educated and youthful second generation. As the cultural hegemonies of a Eurocentric Canada and an Ashkenazi-dominated Israel were challenged, alternative and more plural realities were sought. Not only were urban renewal and the freeway threat repelled by the Strathcona Property Owners' and Tenants' Association (SPOTA), and the co-optation of local leaders challenged in Ir Ganim by the Youth for the Neighbourhood (YFN) movement, but these successes were followed by degrees of local empowerment: SPOTA-managed housing renovation and a neighbourhood improvement program in Strathcona, and in Ir Ganim greater citizenship rights implemented democratically by YFN rather than through the ward boss.

While they engaged briefly in protest actions, both SPOTA and YFN were fundamentally oriented to a strategy of co-production with the state. A radical protest group, Improvement of Community Life (ICL) which was parachuted into Ir Ganim by external middle-class activists, received no significant local support. Not that middle-class allies were unwelcome; the expertise of community workers and other sympathetic professionals was integral to the success especially of SPOTA in both its mobilization and its co-production phases. And for both groups a limited co-production was the extent of their objectives. Although the struggles in Chinatown-Strathcona were an important ingredient in the reversal of national urban policy in Canada after 1968, SPOTA's energies were largely spent by the late 1970s, and in the subsequent engagement with multicultural policy, established it seemed to incorporate and focus precisely the ethnic and racial voices that had formerly been marginalized, the Chinese community returned to a more accommodating stance in its relation with the state. Similarly, in Ir Ganim, the conservative reformers of the YFN, by leaving most of the responsibility with their chairperson, essentially restored the status of the ward boss. Indeed as the chairperson himself moved into high political office, the vacuum of leadership in Ir Ganim encouraged the return of the influence of the deposed and unelected traditional boss.

Events in Chinatown-Strathcona and Ir Ganim bring some pressing issues to bear on current discussion about entitlement and citizenship rights.[1] First, in both neighbourhoods, resistance to marginality was pressed in a culturally specific manner, in popular movements moulded by particularistic values and aspirations, a model presumably in accord with post-modern and post-structural sensibilities. Second, while aiding mobilization, particularism in this instance limited both the geographical and the political extent of social change. Once immediate threats were diverted and immediate needs were met, organizational energies were spent, alternative visions began to dissipate before more traditional and accommodating patterns. The massive familiarity of everyday life and its established thinking-as-usual can easily stifle dissent in the absence of an abiding oppositional ideology.

4

Chinatown-Strathcona: Gaining an Entitlement*

The low, tideland setting of Chinatown-Strathcona has always offered an image that is the inverse of Shaughnessy Heights. If Shaughnessy is the wealthiest district in the metropolitan region (average family incomes in census tract 21 exceeded $116,000 in 1986), Chinatown-Strathcona is among the poorest, its residents being scarcely better off than the male pensioners of the Downtown Eastside (see chapter 6). If Shaughnessy has historically been the home of an Anglo-Canadian élite, Chinatown-Strathcona has provided an entry point for a succession of non–English speaking European immigrants as well as an abiding population of Chinese-origin residents. But despite their evident dissimilarity, the two districts have been functionally linked, at least in their origins, through that most Canadian of ties that bind, the Canadian Pacific Railway. Both bear the name and the mark of Montreal railway barons who were among the leaders of a national power élite. Lord Strathcona was founder and director of the CPR, and Lord Shaughnessy its president after 1898. Their railway was built through the Rocky Mountains principally by Chinese labour, and at a great cost; as many as 600 or more Chinese fatalities occurred as the route to Vancouver was blasted through hazardous terrain. In their view over Strathcona, members of the local power élite living in the CPR's subdivision of Shaughnessy Heights might see, even if they do not acknowledge it, a certain reflection of themselves.

Generations of Chinese children have relived the imprint of capitalist paternalism as they have passed through Strathcona Elementary School on East Pender Street. Indeed, colonial social relations transferred freely

*This chapter was written by David Ley, Kay Anderson, and Doug Konrad.

from the place of work to the place of residence, and in the shaping of these relations the state played a major part.

From the earliest years the story of Chinese settlement in Canada has also been the story of the Canadian state, and no less than in other examples of the West's dealings with 'the Orient,' in its relations with its Chinese residents the Canadian state has revealed its own partisan ideology, an ideology which until recently vacillated between a positive espousal of European origins and a narrow and destructive sinophobia.[1] Examples of the latter are legion and many of them have their setting in Vancouver, for long the principal centre of Asian immigrants in Canada. The Chinese in Vancouver have, over the course of a century, experienced the full range of informal and institutional discrimination: an inequitable head tax and other immigration controls, anti-Asian riots (in 1887 and 1907) in which people and property were attacked while the authorities (in 1887) refrained from intervention, occupational restrictions, electoral disenfranchisement, selective harassment, minimal services, restrictive covenants – as citizens their ordained status for many decades was one of minimum entitlement, and the state's objective was exclusion, not absorption. Over the course of the twentieth century, the policies and practices of the state have most certainly evolved, but, we shall argue, even in the current benign policy of multiculturalism, the assigned role of the Chinese community is to be different, and to flaunt its ethnic difference in a landscape carefully managed by the state.

Until the 1970s, Chinese settlement in Vancouver was strongly confined to the area in and around Chinatown, in part a result of the local state's policy of geographic containment to confirm the community's excluded status. The initial site of residents in the 1880s was along two blocks of Dupont (now Pender) Street (see figure 4.1). By 1901, 2,000 Chinese immigrants lived in this district, a population which included only 53 women and children as a direct and intended consequence of immigration statutes. This location, while only three blocks south of the Vancouver townsite, was a poorly drained area on the edge of the False Creek tidal flats. The Royal City Mill, the city gas works, the Canadian Pacific Railway, and the depot of the Great Northern Railway were immediate neighbours, giving the settlement a highly stigmatized image from the start. Over the decades, as settlement expanded, particularly with the liberalization of immigration in 1947, land-use specialization occurred. The original Pender Street strip became the commercial heart of Chinatown, while the residential community spilled east of Main Street (Westminster Street on figure 4.1), and particularly east

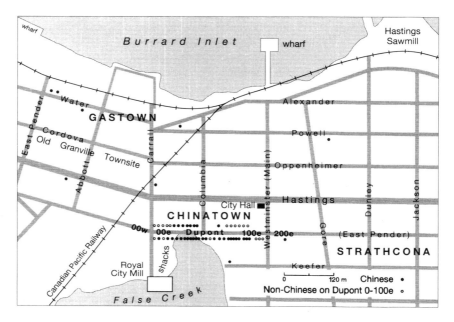

FIGURE 4.1.   The geography of Chinese-origin settlement in Vancouver in 1892. Chinese residents were substantially undercounted; enumerators, for example, did not venture into the shacks on the tidal flats which housed significant numbers of labourers (Source: based on Anderson 1986).

of Gore into the immigrant reception area of Strathcona, with some movement northwards across Hastings Street into Japantown (now part of the Downtown Eastside) following the wartime internment of the entire Japanese community (Kobayashi 1988; see also chapter 6). Strathcona had been home to an earlier immigrant population, including Italians, Jews, and Eastern Europeans, and ethnic churches and retirement homes from this period remain in the neighbourhood. In the postwar period, the Chinese share of the population grew rapidly in Strathcona from a quarter in 1947 to a half in 1957. In census tract 57, the residential core of the district, 53 per cent identified with 'Asian' ethnicity in 1971, and 62 per cent with Chinese ethnicity in 1986; in the latter year, 60 per cent (or 4,810 persons) were immigrants born in Asia, and almost the same number used Chinese as their home language. At least in terms of social and economic indicators, the district continued to be disadvantaged. In 1986, at the end of a deep recession, the male unemployment rate of 29 per cent in tract 57 was among the highest in the metropolitan area. Poorly paying service jobs formed the major occupational category, while half the families and 80 per cent of unattached individuals were classified by the census as of low income.

As a segregated racial enclave, the Chinese community was obliged to turn inwards for support groups and voluntary organizations. A network of some eighty fraternal and mutual-aid associations were formed following old-world traits – and often reviving old-world divisions – half of them around clan groupings and regions of origin.[2] They offered a range of services of a social, economic, and legal nature, and attempted, not often successfully, to mediate between their members and the three levels of the Canadian state. Small, without influence, and culturally marginal, the community was typically ignored by municipal and provincial government, aside from the police and the health department. In their relations with the city's power élite, the differences between the districts named after Lord Shaughnessy and Lord Strathcona could not have been greater. Prior to enfranchisement in 1947, the Chinese were excluded from formal political entitlement, and English-speaking leaders (usually merchants), as the only point of contact with the state, assumed the role of the ward boss – with the important difference that, unlike the ward bosses of Ir Ganim (see chapter 5), they had little in the way of City Hall largesse to distribute, as long as the state was bent upon exclusion. Significantly, enfranchisement was secured only with the substantial backing of labour, church, and civil-liberties groups (Yee 1983). However, by the 1960s, slow acculturation and access to the fuller rights of citizenship diminished somewhat the importance of traditional associations. A new generation of leaders was emerging, many of them Canadian-born, well-educated, and often living outside Chinatown-Strathcona, including a small, youthful, group of activists. They were impatient with the old-world orientation of the traditional leaders and their persistent failure in negotiating on behalf of the district, most notably in the urban-renewal program which had begun to bulldoze Strathcona in 1959. It was from this group that effective opposition to the state would develop.

FOUNDING STRUGGLES: URBAN RENEWAL AND THE CHINATOWN FREEWAY

In Canada, as elsewhere, the urban-renewal programs initiated in the 1950s were characterized by rational planners operating in a centralized and inaccessible bureaucracy.³ If their views in general were insensitive, when dealing with the Chinese community they were condescending. Strathcona, the first area designated for renewal in Vancouver, was described as a 'revenue sink,' 'its state of deterioration a menace' (Marsh 1950). A later city report could find some redeeming features for the older district west of Main Street as 'a tourist attraction, [but] the remainder of the Chinese quarter to the east of Main Street is at present of significance only to the people who live there' (City of Vancouver Technical Planning Board 1956). With such a deprecating view of the citizens' entitlement, city council overrode local opposition. It 'was concerned with the best and most appropriate use of the City's most valuable asset, its land. When the development on part of that land becomes blighted, the asset is being wasted' (ibid, 1957). With these words, Council was continuing in the time-honoured tradition of reducing the Chinese community to objects for the projects of others. Strathcona was declared a redevelopment area, no further public works were undertaken, property prices were frozen, and building permits were forbidden to private owners (Kim and Lai 1982). A survey recorded that 78 per cent of Strathcona homeowners wanted to remain in the area; however, as details were released it became clear that the city and the federal government did not intend any private ownership to continue in the renewal district. The first phase of renewal saw the construction of two high-density public-housing projects with 535 units, and a further 234 units constructed five miles away. By the time the second phase was underway in 1965, a total of more than 3,300 people had been displaced. The human costs of relocation were substantial.⁴ Former owners became state tenants, their compensation (at prices frozen several years earlier) being inadequate to enable them to re-enter the housing market, while some, relocated out of Strathcona, found their cultural networks broken and faced the traumatic spectre of living outside a secure linguistic enclave.

There was, to be sure, considerable community opposition to the renewal process voiced primarily by traditional organizations like the Chinese Benevolent Association. But their strenuous appeals fell on deaf ears. No sooner had Council received a delegation of fifty protesters in October 1960 than it decided to hold a special meeting to arrange for the second renewal phase (Anderson 1988). However, as the decade advanced a broadening opposition arose to the autocratic style of the local state, which brought into Strathcona articulate external allies with a more determined style of protest. The catalytic issue was the latest in a series of proposals to establish a freeway network in the city, an important

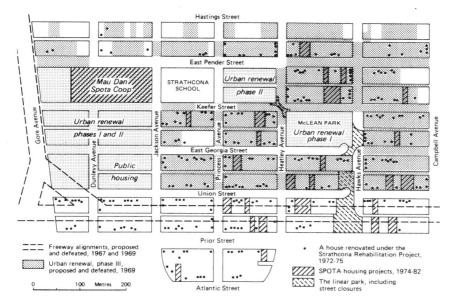

FIGURE 4.2.   The SPOTA-induced landscape of Strathcona: the difference a neighbourhood organization can make (Source: City of Vancouver 1967, Ptarmigan 1976).

element in a twenty-year downtown plan which included also vast urban renewal projects covering 2,500 acres of land on the margins of the central business district (Wong 1978). Two options for an eight-lane freeway prepared by traffic engineers were before the NPA Council: an alignment that would erase the western half of Chinatown, or a route through Gore Street that would separate the Chinese commercial district from its residential partner by a concrete barrier (Figure 4.2).[5] Without calling any public hearings, Council unanimously adopted the Chinatown alignment in October 1967.

The response of the Chinese community was intense, against not only the project, but also the inaccessible decision-making process which it exemplified. The leadership of the Chinese Benevolent Association seethed: 'They didn't even consult us. We didn't even know that the question was to be considered by council on Tuesday ... The whole community is very angry ... It means the death of Chinatown.'[6] Other Chinese leaders saw the connection not only with urban renewal, but with a long history of indignities the community had endured at the hands of the state: Mr Foon Sien regarded the freeway as 'the latest abuse in 81 years of discrimination.'[7] But perhaps more important for the outcome, new allies appeared, aroused by Council's insensitivity to Chinatown, critical of the broader implications of its downtown plan, and indignant at the cloistered process of land-use decision making.[8] University social scientists, planners, and architects spearheaded the protest, but they were joined by tourism interests and influential downtown business people. Bending before the pressure, a majority of Council voted to hold a public-information meeting, to the displeasure of Mayor Campbell, a developer. 'The calling of the meeting is a public disgrace and a tempest in a Chinese teapot,' he fumed with startling insensitivity. 'Do we have to hire a playhouse to put on a puppet show for objectors?'[9]

The terms of reference were changing in the relations between the city and Chinatown, and more broadly in terms of the city's paternal and autocratic decision-making style. By the end of 1967 the entire freeway plan was dead, and a newly mobilized citizenry was created. The white leaders of the freeway protest reappeared in 1968 as organizers in the formation of two new civic parties, The Electors Action Movement (TEAM), a liberal reform grouping of young white professionals and some business people, and the Committee of Progressive Electors (COPE), a left-wing party concerned particularly with tenants' and poverty issues (Miller 1975; Ley 1980). These two parties and their allies were to share control of city council for much of the 1972–86 period. However, unlike the public endorsement of political candidates representing the nearby Downtown Eastside (chapter 6), only one of the candidates returned to office during this period was a Chinese Canadian, a lawyer who served for two terms as a member of Mayor Harcourt's party in the 1980s.

The success of the freeway struggle created a new cultural and political context when the city submitted its plan for the third phase of urban renewal in Chinatown in August 1968, approved in principle by Council four years earlier. In the largest project yet, 15 blocks were cited for demolition, with another 3,000 people to be displaced. But the lessons of the freeway protest were well learned. The conservative style of the old Chinatown leadership, its merchant bias, and its reliance on private lobbying had not proven effective. A new group including better-educated younger activists, both Chinese and white professionals, responded to the new challenge of urban renewal. At a public meeting in December 1968, 600 persons voted to establish the Strathcona Property Owners' and Tenants' Association (SPOTA).

BUILDING A LEADERSHIP

Bessie Lee, in 1990 still a Strathcona resident, was an early president of SPOTA: 'I stopped by this large meeting in Strathcona School (November 1968). Well, the city planners were down there explaining the beautiful concept of this urban renewal project and they asked for questions. So I asked a couple of questions and I got just a very negative attitude ... [social worker] Margaret Mitchell happened to be sitting near me and she said "Look if you *really* want to find out more and do something, about this, give your name to that girl over there"' (Marlatt and Itter 1979, 181). Bessie Lee's experience with the civic bureaucracy showed how little had changed at City Hall despite the great freeway debate. But the community had learned some important lessons. Bessie Lee, her neighbours Walter and Mary Chan, and others mobilized the district on a house-by-house basis, making effective use of block captains. The Chan family were indicative of a new spirit of community organization in Chinatown-Strathcona, a new politics which went hand in hand with a new identity, separate from the often influential lobbying of traditional groups like the Chinese Benevolent Association (CBA). As Mary Chan saw it: 'My husband said we must have faith and work together, and if the CBA doesn't want to fight for it, we will. He said the Chinese have to *show* that they're capable of winning the fight with City Hall, and we mustn't look down on ourselves as a people – we *can do* it' (Marlatt and Itter 1979, 180). Walter Chan, like his wife a teacher, as a young man in China, was one of three co-presidents elected at SPOTA's inaugural meeting. Their daughter, Shirley, in 1968 studying English and Social Sciences at the politically radical campus of Simon Fraser University in the suburbs, was a model of a new generation of young and well-educated Chinese activists. Like many others in the neighbourhood, she was roused to action by the expropriation of homes and destruction of the area by urban renewal:[10] 'I was a student at Simon Fraser. And there was a meeting one night at First United Church, and I came home and dad asked me if I would go – mother was already there. So I went to the meeting, and I just heard the incredible anger that the community was feeling, and the frustration. I heard people saying, "All I want is a fair shake," and these were my neighbours. Or I heard Mr. and Mrs. Wong say in Chinese, "We worked very hard to build ourselves a nest, and now you're going to take it away from us." So that was enough. That was how I got involved' (ibid, 178). Shirley Chan was a leading voice of SPOTA for almost a decade, and her subsequent career is symptomatic of the new generation of community leadership, not cowed by existing power élites and recognizing the need for political struggle to gain entitlement and its rights. She served on the boards of various inner-city social agencies, ran once (unsuccessfully) for municipal office in 1970, worked in Ottawa, and was assistant to Mayor Harcourt in the early 1980s.[11]

This association with Harcourt is particularly informative. From the beginning, SPOTA discerned a second lesson from the successful freeway fight: the necessity for allies outside the Chinese community to serve as bridges to broader support and enabling resources. At the gathering prior to the large public meeting where SPOTA was formally founded, Bessie Lee recalls that 'we decided right then and there to get English-speaking or bilingual people into the group to make it strong.' At the inaugural meeting, 'we had two secretaries and two treasurers,' one English-speaking and one Chinese-speaking (Marlatt and Itter 1979, 181). Tom Mesic, a letter carrier who had grown up in Strathcona and had been a school friend of Shirley Chan, was elected as English-speaking treasurer in 1968, and became SPOTA president, serving from 1972 to 1976.[12] Among the other leaders of SPOTA was Harry Con, one of the three initial co-presidents and an abiding influence (vice-president in 1989). In some respects Con is a more traditional leader, a merchant and on the executive (later national chairman) of the Chinese Freemasons, a benevolent society. According to Shirley Chan, he was 'pulled into' the group because he was bilingual, had 'good Liberal connections' to Ottawa, and understood 'a bit about government bureaucracy.' Mr Con's links to government were reinforced by his appointment, as first chairperson, to the city-inspired Chinatown Historic Area Planning Committee in 1976. He represents one of the clearest tendencies towards the development of a ward boss in Chinatown, though, with the neighbourhood's many interests, the concentration of power with a few individuals has never approached the level reached in Ir-Ganim (chapter 5).

But in addition to those inside the group as residents, there was a critical retinue of external advisers, mainly professional community-development workers with common objectives and political connections, and for whom engagement in Strathcona was itself a learning process which, for several, later consolidated into a social-democratic (NDP) political career. In this manner, as in others, it is important not to overlook the dialectical relationship between the community and the state. Experiences in the community can mould front-stage and back-stage leaders, encouraging them to penetrate the state in the electoral process and seek to recast its policies and practices. We have already encountered Margaret

Mitchell, who encouraged Bessie Lee's further participation in the formation of SPOTA. Mitchell, then recently appointed as a community worker to Strathcona by the locally funded United Community Services, mediated between SPOTA and the state. Later (like Nathal Karmel, appointed community worker in Kitsilano [see chapter 8]) she would act as area manager for the decentralized community resources board, and in the 1980s was elected as NDP member of Parliament for Vancouver East.

Mitchell introduced SPOTA to a range of resource people, including a group of law students, among them Michael Harcourt, who provided the organization with background legal documentation in preparation for negotiating meetings.[13] For example, minutes of a SPOTA executive meeting in September 1969 record the presence of Harcourt and five other professionals who briefed the executive on negotiating with the three levels of government over a rehabilitation plan for Strathcona.[14] Harcourt was elected to city council as a member of the TEAM slate in 1972, became NDP mayor in 1980, and led the opposition in the provincial legislature from 1986 until his election as premier of an NDP government in 1991. Both Mitchell and Harcourt were themselves directed to Strathcona by Darlene Marzari, then employed by the city as a social-planning coordinator, like Harcourt a member of the 1972 TEAM sweep of City Hall, in the late 1980s, NDP member in Victoria for Vancouver Point Grey, and in 1991 one of Harcourt's cabinet ministers. While prominent in Strathcona and the most visible subsequently, Mitchell, Harcourt, and Marzari were part of a broader cluster of social workers, planners, architects, and lawyers who acted as unpaid consultants to SPOTA and, through that interaction, both enabled the group's actions and consolidated their own ideology and politics.

RECLAIMING STRATHCONA: THE PROCESS OF CO-PRODUCTION

The formation of SPOTA was not the beginning of concerted opposition to urban renewal. Though ineffective prior to that time, opposition had been brewing across Canada through the 1960s, with Strathcona and Trefann Court in Toronto the most celebrated cases, and it had attracted the ear of the new Liberal administration of Pierre Trudeau, which came to power in Ottawa in 1968 amid the reverberations of campus unrest and popular social movements in Europe and the United States. With a sense of innovation more than a little sympathetic to the spirit of the times, the federal Task Force on Housing and Urban Development toured

Canada in autumn 1968 and, led by the minister, visited Vancouver, where it met with Strathcona residents protesting the injustices of urban renewal, during a walking tour of the neighbourhood, an event which Darlene Marzari helped organize.[15] With precipitous speed, just over a week later the city was informed that the federal government would withdraw or severely limit funds for urban renewal; the task force issued a formal moratorium on urban renewal across Canada early in 1969 (Kim and Lai 1982).

In this promising national context, there was incentive to mobilize the community to press for a redirection of the city's redevelopment plans. Soon after its formation, SPOTA submitted a brief accompanied by 578 signatures to Council with six recommendations.

1 / The people who have signed the enclosed petition demand their right to continue to live in the Strathcona area ...

2 / People who have been forced to move due to urban renewal have not been dealt with fairly. In future citizens must be assured of adequate information, legal aid, choices of accommodation and fair exchange value if homes are expropriated by the city ...

3 / We urge that present plans for urban renewal be revised to allow for preservation and rehabilitation of present homes and to provide land for rebuilding private homes ...

4 / There must be a variety of privately owned accommodation available in the community in addition to public housing and large private developments ...

5 / People who have a business or an income-producing property should have an opportunity to improve buildings if necessary or to relocate their business within the area ...

6 / We request the Vancouver City Council and the Provincial and Federal Governments to recognize the Strathcona Property Owners and Tenants Association as an official body for negotiations on these and other matters ... [16]

The recommendations included both a reaction to the immediate threat of expropriation and clearance and the beginnings of a proactive position which would take shape more fully in the following months. But, for now, the threat of the city's decade-old renewal plan continued as an abiding concern, a concern only intensified by Council's intransigence towards the brief. For a majority of Council and key City Hall staff were opposed to the urban-renewal freeze, and sent letters to Ottawa requesting there be no further delay in re-enacting the program.[17]

SPOTA extended its own network of support, enlisting the aid of members of the provincial legislative assembly (MLAs) as well as the minority of sympathetic members of city council. Following the suggestion of two local MLAs, a survey of residents was undertaken to provide grounds for a constructive counter-proposal. Of 375 questionnaires (representing 1,644 people) returned (at 75 per cent a high response rate), only 4 households had indicated a wish to leave the area and the remainder approved a strategy of housing rehabilitation. The results formed the basis for a second brief which strategically took the initiative in offering the city 'fresh proposals' for resolving the impasse of the renewal freeze. Remarkably, federal government officials had recommended this tactic to SPOTA in order to loosen the city's entrenched position.[18] The significance of this relationship should not be overlooked: the members of a federal ministry were advising a protest group less than six months old how to divert the urban-planning policies of the elected council of the nation's third-largest city. The partnership was soon to be made even more visible.

The thrust of the 'fresh proposals' in the second brief was an experimental rehabilitation program in Strathcona with government grant and loan subsidies, and other major revisions of the renewal guidelines.[19] Following the advice of the MLA for Vancouver Centre, SPOTA canvassed for a meeting with all three levels of government to establish the rehabilitation program. Robert Andras, the newly appointed federal minister of state for urban affairs, was the first to respond favourably; his office set up a three-day session in August 1969 for the meeting and, as if this facilitation was not enough, wrote directly to the president of SPOTA suggesting a private meeting *in advance* of the tri-level government session.[20] The city, meanwhile, had not given up on renewal and, without informing SPOTA of its results, told the minister on 6 August that preliminary assessments indicated that rehabilitation was not economically feasible. But unknown to the city, Andras had already met with SPOTA officials and had made his own commitments. As Bessie Lee reported: 'Robert Andras came out to Vancouver and met with us privately before he met with the city officials. When they found that out they were really angry because they still thought they were going to get their way, you know. So then at the meeting at City Hall in the afternoon he stood up and said that he would not allow the program without the community having full participation in the planning. So we were recognized as the fourth level of government for this area, and that was the first time this ever happened anywhere' (Marlatt and Itter 1979, 184). Moreover, Andras added, the federal government was prepared to fund only a rehabilitation program.

The provincial government was also pushing the city, and in September 1969 recommended a unique four-level Strathcona Working Committee (SWC) to formulate a planning and funding program for rehabilitation. The committee, chaired by the city's chief social planner, included three SPOTA representatives and one each from the city, provincial, and federal governments. It was the first time in Canada that citizens had been involved with the state as equal partners in a planning process.

The Strathcona renewal story highlights how the Canadian state may be fragmented, and that its fragmentation allows windows of opportunity for enterprising neighbourhood interests. Moreover, fragmentation may occur not only by jurisdiction but also by department. While the city's social planner who chaired the SWC was supportive of the rehabilitation process, he felt his task was undermined by other civic bureaucrats and by aldermen who remained committed to renewal and a non-participatory planning process (Ptarmigan Planning Associates 1976, 16). SPOTA remained suspicious of the city's intent, and most observers of the SWC saw the two groups as antagonists with senior government officials as mediators (ibid, 4, 11).

This caution was well placed as the city persistently showed itself to be bargaining in bad faith. In late 1969 it sprung a renewed freeway scheme upon the community without any prior consultation. Both the proposal and the non-consultative process were vigorously resisted, and the city, prodded by the province, reluctantly included the eight-block area which fell in the path of the projected freeway within the boundaries of the rehabilitation district. Then, in 1971, the city attempted to abrogate responsibility for its share of funds for rehabilitation loans and grants. Again intervention from the province was required to effect a reconsideration. Third, the same year, and again without prior consultation, the city decided at an *in camera* meeting to build a large firehall on a three-acre site expropriated in the mid 1960s as part of the urban-renewal program, welching on earlier promises that low-cost housing would be built on the site.[21] Having sold the land at a discount price to a private developer to build low-cost housing, the city had to expend three times as much to repurchase it. As these facts surfaced through leaked documents, SPOTA made political hay of Council's incompetence (or worse, it appeared) and bad faith, and vigorous opposition was carried into the Vancouver dailies.[22] A rally in Chinatown in December 1972, the first to carry social protest into the streets, attracted 1,000 angry residents one day before a civic election was held. The next day, a reform council of TEAM candidates was swept to power, and the old guard of NPA politicians who had sought to dismember Chinatown and had controlled City Hall for thirty years were dismissed from office. Within a month the new council killed the firehall plan and soon after agreed on a family and seniors housing proposal for the site, to be coordinated by SPOTA. After legal delays, SPOTA's 120-unit Mau Dan housing project was completed in 1982, including an 82-unit co-op.[23]

Meanwhile, the progress of the Strathcona Working Committee was delayed by these tussles between the two principal parties, and the rehabilitation formula took two years to hammer out. Details of the Strathcona Rehabilitation Project were finally announced by the area's Liberal MP (and federal cabinet minister) in October 1971.[24] A budget of some $5 million was allocated to housing rehabilitation and improved public works – a pilot project for the state's Residential Rehabilitation Assistance Programme and Neighbourhood Improvement Programme, promoting enhancement and preservation, which were the major initiatives to replace now discredited urban renewal. Over the next three years, 382 dwelling units were rehabilitated, roads resurfaced, sidewalks rebuilt, and new lighting and sewerage lines installed (see figure 4.2). Income eligibility and other restrictions led to limits on participation, which was less than projected for rooming-houses in particular (a significant failure). Strathcona residents urged that unspent funds be dedicated to other improvements, including tree plantings and a linear park, formed in part by selective street closures and providing the additional benefit of restricting truck and commuter traffic through the area.

Buoyed by these successes, SPOTA maintained its lobbying to establish a non-profit housing society. The electoral success of the provincial New Democratic Party in 1972 opened the door to build some fifty infill housing units on land leased from the provincial government, who had bought it from the city (Marlatt and Itter 1979, 184). By 1977, and with the NDP out of office in Victoria, housing funds were less accessible, and SPOTA's final and largest project, Mau Dan, was funded by the federal government. When Mau Dan was completed in 1982, the result of fourteen years of activism was a remarkable remaking of the Strathcona landscape (see figure 4.2).

While SPOTA's style certainly departed from that of traditional Chinatown organizations, its relationship with the state is more accurately described as a co-production rather than a conflict model. The difference was marked in comparison with groups like DERA and the West Broadway Citizens' Committee (chapters 6 and 8), who were active in the city during the early 1970s. 'In contrast to the social activism of the period, the community did not use confrontation as a tactic. They presented their views, yet were careful to back off in order that the other party did not lose face' (Bell 1975, 17). An interview in 1983 suggested that a new generation of leaders held to the same style of respect and inclusiveness: 'Relationships with all levels of government have been struggles but respectful and ending in positive results ... The private sector has been comfortably absorbed by the community. In fact developers have complemented the community's goals in their recent developments.'[25] The ethos is not only respectful but also conservative.

Indeed, in many respects SPOTA was a single-issue organization primarily composed of homeowners, with strictly local goals, resisting urban renewal and advocating rehabilitation and infill housing. At the founding meetings, as Bessie Lee pointed out, 'people that you didn't think would come turned up because their home was at stake' (Marlatt and Itter 1979, 182). But with a successful outcome to the immediate crisis, such a high level of commitment was not sustained, so that, after the first year or two, SPOTA's membership rarely exceeded 200, and it was carried by a hard-worked volunteer executive. Little wonder that by the mid 1970s, with the housing goals accomplished, there were discernible signs of quiescence. In April 1976 a membership meeting considered dissolution or amalgamation as possible future options.[26] The completion of Mau Dan was the last significant project, and through much of the 1980s SPOTA continued as a paper organization but with limited energy or sense of purpose. The original leaders were ageing, some had died, others moved away. Ironically, but consistent with the history of co-production in Strathcona since 1968, it has taken a municipally sponsored initiative, a local area plan for the district, to breathe new life into the organization in 1989.

And by 1989 there was a changing SPOTA for a changing Strathcona. The old Schara Tzedeck Synagogue built in 1917, which, converted to the Gibbs Boys' Club, had been the site of SPOTA's founding meeting in December 1968, was recycled once more to the Alexandra Court condominiums in 1987.[27] And while Mary Chan and Bessie Lee remain members of SPOTA, the current president is a white architect and homeowner who has lived in the district for two years. He is anxious to stem gentrification of the area ...

CHINATOWN: MULTICULTURALISM AND THE MAKING OF AN ETHNIC NEIGHBOURHOOD

A rather different, but no less informative, process of co-production has brought together Chinese business interests and various arms of the state in a joint effort to manage the landscape of Chinatown. If the 1960s represented a period of conflict as the community resisted 'the latest abuse' (in Mr Foon Sien's well-chosen words) from the state, the 1970s and 1980s promised a more harmonious union. Chinatown has become one of the city's key 'ethnic neighbourhoods,' a civic asset to be courted for its distinctive contribution to Canadian multiculturalism. But the apparent correspondence of interests between the state and the community should not conceal the fact that it is primarily the state that is asserting its conceptions of race and place and the community that is receiving and interpreting them. The ideology of race has been part of a European cultural tradition for centuries, and while, to be sure, it has more often been wielded in situations of conflict, it can equally serve as a category of inclusion / exclusion in situations of positive stereotyping. Indeed it is the deeper process of racial classification that warrants research attention, both in the past and the apparently more 'tolerant' present.[28]

During the late 1960s and early 1970s, enthusiasm for the distinctiveness of Canada's 'ethnic groups' was loudly acclaimed in the House of Commons and elsewhere. It was precisely this diversity, not only ethnic but regional, which held the key to the nation's elusive identity – or so it was often, nervously, offered. In 1963 Prime Minister Pearson declared that 'the only way in which we can maintain unity in Canada is by recognizing and glorying in our diversity.'[29] Eight years later the Liberal government of Pierre Trudeau institutionalized the long-standing idea of the Canadian cultural mosaic in its policy of multiculturalism. In the words of the prime minister, the program of 'Multiculturalism' would 'support and encourage the various cultures and ethnic groups that give structure and vitality to our society. They will be encouraged to share their cultural expression and values with other Canadians and so contribute to a richer life for us all.'[30] People of Chinese origin and other such 'ethnic' Canadians would now be sponsored, through a program of grants and advertising, to promote themselves as 'Chinese,' as if this were a living whole that transcended generation, context, citizenship, and place of birth. In this subtle way, the hegemony of British-

and French-origin 'charter groups' in Canada has been reasserted into the present.

Overseeing a 'Chinese Landscape': The State as Suitor

Since the initiation of the policy of multiculturalism, a variety of means has been brought to bear to indicate a public commitment to the new 'multicultural fact of Canada' (Kallen 1983). Important among them have been initiatives to promote 'ethnic neighbourhoods,' of which Chinatown in Vancouver has been considered a key example. In 1969, a city-commissioned restoration report on Vancouver's Old Granville townsite said: 'The Chinese community is the only truly ethnic group within the study area'; it is one which 'the general urban population finds both agreeable and enriching' and which 'can contribute to the quality and richness of city life' (City of Vancouver Planning Department 1969, 5, 16). Within a year of the report's publication, the city's planning department prepared its own set of recommendations for protecting 'the charm of [this] honestly evolved area.'[31] Provincial officials in Victoria also saw the exotic potential of Vancouver's Chinatown. Protective legislation was unanimously supported, and in February 1971 Cabinet approved an order-in-council which designated the area a 'Historic Site' and vested authority with the province over all major changes to and demolitions and renovations of Chinatown's buildings. The new form of external control was not lost on the editors of the *Chinatown News*: 'Our preservation and restoration regulations require the Planning Department approval for all facelifting work done to buildings in Chinatown before a single penny is spent.'[32]

Indeed, enabling legislation to preserve Chinatown, while a victory for the city's planning department, was not considered such a triumph by those who were expected to bear (in taxes) a large part of the cost. Government targeting of this kind was met with suspicion from Chinese property owners who even 'burst into laughter' at a Chinatown beautification proposal presented by the planning director at a meeting in November 1972.[33] In time, however, the economic opportunity afforded by the city's vision became clear to some property owners, and early in 1973 they formed the Chinatown Property Owners' and Merchants' Association (CTPOMA) to try to steer government resources to purposes of their own choosing. Their representative, Mr H. Fan, quickly informed planners it was parking space for customers – not Chinatown's face-lift – that local business people and residents were most interested in.[34]

But those in charge of the power of definition did not share this priority, and sought ways of ensuring that the city's concept of neighbourhood improvement was implemented in Chinatown. As the deputy director of planning put it: 'I believe that the approach should be that we consider recommending to Council the purchase of property for parking, but only tying it to some kind of undertaking by the CTPOMA to carry out a beautification project.'[35] The CTPOMA's other suggestion that funds be used to build continuous free-standing canopies along the three-block length of Pender Street met with an equally cool response. In the words of the new Chinatown planner, Mr M. Kemble, the association's canopy designs had 'little regard to the variety of actual building facade conditions that exist on Pender Street and which give the street its charm and visual interest.'[36] The canopy idea was quashed, parking space made conditional on the initiation of a joint street beautification scheme, and Pender Street's 'Oriental' façade secured, unencumbered, for mainstream consumption.

The CTPOMA was unmoved by the planner's efforts to fashion Chinatown to a Western image, and refused to commit themselves to street improvements. But the city, far from directing its attention elsewhere when it did not get the merchants on side, pursued its own Chinatown concept more actively. In 1974, the City Charter was amended to give Council itself the power to designate heritage buildings or areas, and, in preparation for bestowing this special status on Chinatown, planners devised a set of sign guidelines, intended to make Vancouver's Chinatown more legible as an 'Oriental' turf. Rezoning of the district also gave objective status to mainstream images of place. The new zoning schedule would 'recognize the area's unique ethnic quality and ensure the protection, restoration and maintenance of Chinatown's historical, architectural and cultural character.'[37] These proposals became policy in July 1974, when Council approved a Chinatown Historic Area, and the Chinatown Historic Area Planning Committee (CHAPC) of mostly Chinese-origin members was established to help the city 'preserve and protect the character and heritage of Chinatown.'[38]

Just as the City of Vancouver had once targeted Chinatown for its putative difference in earlier decades, so in the 1970s was Chinatown defined against European society. Praise had certainly taken the place of stigma, but Chinatown was as 'Chinese' in the eyes of Europeans in the 1970s as it had been in the past. Through rezoning, the city even drew the physical contours of the area, and further objectified the enduring idea of the 'East' in the 'West' – a distinction that for a century had involved the use of place and geographical boundaries to affirm cultural and political ones.

Chinatown merchants were not without their criticisms of the city's image and practice, however. One CTPOMA member levelled a charge in a letter to the planning department: 'It is my view that the City Hall powers that be are trying to force new or rebuilding type construction to conform to copies of tourist photos of temples in Asia. In other words construction cannot proceed unless it would be a museumized version with artificial red posts and verticle [sic] window stripes.'39 Such merchants were not blind to the exercise of external control, and their actions reveal, as we have seen, a combination of resistance and accommodation. In the 1970s, some 'Chinese' identified – often for sound reasons – with the currents of the dominant culture. In the case of Chinatown's rezoning, for example, the CTPOMA chairman acknowledged its potential to boost tourism, and the fact that 'the defined boundary of Chinatown will give us some elbow space for expansion of business activities.'40

Broad support for the much-delayed beautification project was more difficult to enlist, however, and again the record tells of an interaction between state and community that was subtler than the simple imposition of a socially based hegemony. For one thing, lack of interest on the part of the CTPOMA forced city planners to scale down the scope of their streetscaping scheme. Even by November 1976, when improvement guidelines were unveiled at a Chinatown meeting by city planners, reaction of the mere thirty-six property owners in attendance was restrained. It was an impasse that concerned the newly established CHAPC, and its chairperson, the ubiquitous Harry Con, quickly assumed the role the organization had originally been assigned. 'If merchants and property owners still manifest indifference and disinterest, I doubt whether City planners would come up with any more plans to improve this area for a long, long time,' Con warned in the New Year.41 Indeed, many CHAPC members saw the value of promoting Chinatown's profile for people of Chinese origin in Vancouver. Whether out of pride in the Chinese experience in Canada, interest in Chinatown's tourist trade, or personal political ambition, CHAPC members saw an opportunity in Chinatown's definition, and orchestrated a strenuous campaign among Pender Street's merchants. The organization's efforts, as with those of the relentless Mr Kemble and other Chinatown planners, were finally rewarded in the spring of 1977 when 75 merchants saw their way to committing $300,000 to the beautification project. By that time, the scheme to 'Orientalize' Chinatown had been modified to include a special sidewalk and cross-walk treatment, new stone curbing, planting of trees native to China, Oriental sidewalk furniture, brass bilingual name signs, and special 'lantern-like' street lighting. Council registered its approval with a $200,000 contribution; a year later, in November 1978, the provincial government took the opportunity of an impending election to announce a grant for the remaining $200,000.

The Chinatown streetscape project was opened in February 1980 by the Hon. Grace McCarthy (deputy premier) and Vancouver mayor Jack Volrich. It was a symbolic occasion that signalled the magnitude of change that had, in one sense, taken place in the reception of Chinese-origin residents in Canada. But links to the past were equally transparent in the 1980 celebrations. Indeed, lest one misconstrue the novelty of the 'multicultural' present, it is equally important to note the endurance – in a new guise – of racial ideology in mainstream culture and institutional practice. For Canada's planners and politicians, Chinatown's 'Chineseness' had become its very asset. And with the eventual cooperation of Chinese organizations themselves, who adapted the spatial and racial classifications to their own interests, it was a perception that continued to re-create the vision and reality of a neighbourhood apart.

Consolidating the Ethnic Turf: The Chinese Cultural Centre and the Dr Sun Yat-sen Garden

One of the main responsibilities of Canada's Multiculturalism Directorate after 1972 was 'to encourage and assist ... the full realization of the multicultural nature of Canadian society through programs which promote the preservation and sharing of cultural heritages.'[42] Although the involvement of the directorate itself in Vancouver's Chinatown was limited during the 1970s, the federal government made public its commitment to 'multicultural' Canada by undertaking some substantial capital-works projects in the district. The other two levels of government also moved quickly to facilitate this expression of difference at the local level, and joined Ottawa in a significant project, the Chinese Cultural Centre and the adjacent Dr Sun Yat-sen Classical Garden. In 1970, at a Chinatown reception, the premier of British Columbia and federal dignitaries roundly endorsed an idea, already being circulated, of a Chinese Cultural Centre. One officer from the department of the secretary of state urged the Wong

Association 'to give some serious thought to such an offer ... [and] act as chairman of the ad hoc committee on a Chinese Cultural Centre.'[43] The official visitors were so enthusiastic, said architect Mr Joe Wai, that in the course of the Cantonese banquet, the three levels of government made public pledges to cover 160 per cent of the estimated cost of the project (Rossiter 1983).

Whereas earlier in the century, people of Chinese origin had contested the liabilities of their racial definition by mobilizing as an ethnic bloc, in the 1970s they combined in a context of government deference to the status 'Chinese.' Within weeks of the reception, the editor of the *Chinatown News* urged cohesion and cooperation from the Chinese community. 'If we want something done for our community' he said, 'we'd do well to compose our differences. The time has come for a massive coalition to get the centre built. We have the functional resources in the community. And the three levels of government have already pledged their support. But we need to coalesce and move toward a unified goal ... Chinatown merchants and property owners should be eager to participate too ... It is to their interest and profitability to bring the Centre plan to fruition.'[44] In the event, site negotiations for the Cultural Centre complex turned out to be protracted, and political pledges of financial support proved hard to extract. Throughout these deliberations, a Chinese Cultural Centre organization, a Chinese Cultural Centre site committee, and the CHAPC adopted an advocacy position, appealing to the 'contribution' that Chinatown was often said to make to Vancouver. The CHAPC traded in the language city planners well understood when it tried to convince Council to grant the 3.5-acre site at the corner of Carrall and Pender streets: 'The Chinese Cultural Centre project and garden / park development will provide an impetus and the first step toward changing the entire area back to an exciting focus for Chinatown and Vancouver.'[45] Council fully concurred and agreed to negotiate a land-lease arrangement with the 3,000-member Chinese Cultural Centre organization. 'We want to encourage you to preserve and continue the great traditions and customs of the Chinese people,' Mayor Volrich said in an election speech in Chinatown soon after the decision.[46]

The perception of Vancouver's Chinatown as an 'ethnic neighbourhood' whose 'difference' was its virtue was fully endorsed by the most senior level of Canadian government. Indeed, a significant boost to the Chinese Cultural Centre complex came in May 1977, when Ottawa committed $1.5 million of Urban Demonstration capital to the establishment of a classical Chinese garden. The garden was also expected to 'aid in the re-establishment of a viable Chinatown and arrest the eastward drift and dispersal of this unique community.'[47] The CHAPC and members of the Chinese Cultural Centre organization were again eager, and knew how to deliver the landscape symbolism that had become Chinatown's signature, as they mounted the proposal for an 'authentic Chinese garden, conforming to traditional concepts and incorporating traditional elements of Chinese garden design.'[48]

The classical garden idea seems to have appealed to all the romantic conceptions of the 'Flowery Kingdom' that had captivated the earliest Western visitors to China. One Vancouver magazine recalled them in 1981: 'The garden will be a mecca for Far Eastern scholars and a tourist showpiece unique in the Western hemisphere,' while Mayor Volrich told the consul general for the People's Republic in 1980: 'We wish our Vancouver "Chung Shan" Garden to be of world-class calibre and a great asset to our city and to the Chinese community.'[49] No pagodas, no chinoiserie, no willow patterns, no dragons – this was to be the pure East re-created anew in (and for) the West.

Other state practices indicate the sense in which the mosaic ideology was being discovered and realized through Chinatown. As with all development permit applications in Chinatown, the winning architectural submission for the Chinese Cultural Centre was reviewed by the planning department. The input of its officials is evidence, like the garden, of the vision the levels of government were trying to achieve through the manipulation of landscape imagery in Chinatown. Mr Kemble, for example, was especially concerned to integrate the design of the centre's exterior with the wider Chinatown streetscape. For this reason he objected to the lack of 'Chinese' architectural features in the application; for example, the lack of a 'recessed entrance balcony' and 'bright accent colours on the exterior of the building.'[50] He also suggested that 'stepped gable walls' be incorporated into the entry area because of 'their possible association with the form of traditional ancestral halls common to south China,' while a Chinese Cultural Centre logo 'backlit with neon tubing' might be more 'in keeping,' he said, 'with the sign guidelines of the Chinatown Historic Area.' All of these recommendations for a stronger 'Chinese' motif were incorporated into the final design.[51]

On 14 September 1980, representatives of all three levels of government and numerous other officials were on hand at the opening of the $900,000 first stage of the Chinese Cultural Centre in Vancouver's Chinatown. 'I want to underline the policy of our organization to help fund these centres as one of the best opportunities to preserve the cultures that will strengthen our country,' said Premier Bill Bennett, in presenting a cheque for $400,000 towards the centre's construction.[52] Mayor Volrich also underscored the value of Canada's 'multicultural fact.' 'The project reflects the great culture of the Chinese people,' he declared amidst, in the words of the *Chinatown News*, 'a colourful extravaganza of lanterns, lions, unicorn dances, songs and firecrackers.'[53] Yet if the project reflected that 'great culture,' it also surely identified Chinatown's representers who, through all the rhetoric, ambience, and government largesse, were ceaselessly inventing a Chinatown of Western characterization.

CONCLUSION: THE COMMUNITY AND THE STATE

For more than a century the state has been an abiding presence in the making of both Chinese identity and Chinatown, and thereby in defining the extent of the community's entitlement. From the late 1880s, all three levels of Canadian government have lent moral and legal authority to the twin ideas of a 'Chinese' race and place, set apart, and forever, it seemed, an object for the project of others. As we have noted, this cultural hegemony continues to be reworked in a different form in the current era of multiculturalism. The community's engagement with this en-trenched ideology must not, however, be oversimplified. Over the course of the generations the community has expressed both resistance and ac-commodation. The period of most organized and successful resistance occurred in the late 1960s and 1970s against the state-engineered threats of urban renewal and freeway building, which would have reduced the district to a shell. Taking advantage of distinct cleavages between the three levels of the state, the Chinese community and its supporters were able to forge an alliance which was successful in its strategy of neigh-bourhood preservation and enhancement.

Even in apparent accommodation to cultural domination, the Chinese have always met the state with a critical, if respectful, response. The meetings of the Chinatown Historic Area Planning Committee during the 1980s were frequently a tugging match as Chinatown merchants and property owners sought to redefine the committee's mandate, as laid out by the city, which was primarily to respond to the 'ethnic' design features of proposed changes. But the members' objectives were rather more pro-saic than was the cultural program of government: 'Don't be too stringent or developers will go to Richmond [an emerging suburban "China-town"]. The developers are getting pretty cheesed off around here.'[54]

The tone of Chinatown members was not infrequently sceptical of 'Oriental roof, all that garbage ... '[55]

The process of neighbourhood organization in Chinatown-Strathcona throws an illuminating light on the practices of several involved parties. First, the abrupt termination of urban-renewal funding in Strathcona shows the potential permeability of senior government to grass-roots lobbying, even if the local state has proven obdurate in its dealings with neighbourhood concerns. Indeed, all four Vancouver neighbourhood associations have made successful representations to higher levels of the state, when denied by city council. The fact that it is possible to go over the head of local government not only demonstrates the simple point of the state's complexity and heterogeneity, sometimes forgotten in highly abstract discussions, but also challenges a theoretical tendency to see populist, consumption-based politics as necessarily a politics of the local state.

Second, mediations between SPOTA and the state were organized both overtly and behind the scenes by a group of sympathetic but non-resident professionals, in community work, planning and architecture, and law. In several instances these grass-roots experiences led to a personal shift among the professionals into a career in social-democratic (NDP) politics. Their election in a sense institutionalized the lessons and values confirmed from neighbourhood conflict, and thus both perpetuated those experiences and projected them into the decision making of the state itself, no small matter when one of the professionals, Michael Harcourt, later became mayor of Vancouver (1980-6), provincial member for the Strathcona area (1986-), and premier of British Columbia (1991-). In this manner, neighbourhood activism may leave a trace of considerable longevity, which certainly survives long after any initial conflict has disappeared, and yet needs to be factored into a reckoning of the ultimate impacts of neighbourhood politics.

This trace is more important, particularly in traditional communities, as the period of conflict may be short-lived, to be replaced by more habitual and accommodating forms of thought and practice. In Strathcona the remarkable successes of the 1968–72 period carried only limited forward momentum, and by 1976 the few remaining members of SPOTA were considering disbanding. It is significant that one of the few abiding community leaders over the more than twenty years since SPOTA's formation in 1968 has been Harry Con, a traditional-style figure, prominent as a merchant and through the executive of a benevolent society prior to and accompanying his work for SPOTA, and later the CHAPC. The story of neighbourhood organization in Ir Ganim which follows (chapter 5) provides a fuller illustration of the tenacity with which older and more traditional forms of social organization can survive the shock of neighbourhood activism. Theoretically, this return of tradition alerts us to refrain from taking any evolutionary model of neighbourhood organization too literally.

5

Ir Ganim:
Between Bossism and Protest

The establishment of the state of Israel in May 1948 brought in its wake
a large wave of immigration into the country. Between May 1948 and
December 1951, 690,000 Jews arrived in Israel, almost doubling its population. The newcomers entered a social structure that contained a variety
of social classes: petty bourgeois, small capitalists, managerial and intellectual social groups, and a large working class. The power élite of
the working class had, in the pre-state period, achieved political control
of the national power centres (including the Va'ad Leumi, the Jewish
community's proto-government, and the Jewish Agency), and in the
1950s it achieved political hegemony in the Knesset (parliament) and
cabinet and tried, not without success, to take control of municipal power
centres (Gonen and Hasson 1983). Within this system, the new immigrants formed a distinctive outgroup. Most of them lacked private economic resources, and their educational level and occupational skills were
lower than those of the rest of the absorbing society. Furthermore, in
contrast with the pre-state European immigration, known as *Ashkenazim*,
a large proportion of the new state's immigrants came from pre-modern
Muslim countries in Asia and Africa. Accordingly, the proportion of
Jews born in Asia and Africa, known as *Sephardim*, increased from 10.9
per cent in the 1914–48 period to 51.2 per cent in the 1948–72 period
(Bachi 1977, 93).

As a result, the Israeli social structure became more varied, comprising
three major classes: a middle class with private property; an established
working class made up of people who had arrived before the establishment
of the state, mostly from Eastern Europe, and who, because of their training and their knowledge of the system and their social connections, had
preferred access to centres of political power and public resources; and

a new fraction of the working class, consisting largely of Sephardim, whose members had no private property and had only limited access to centres of political power. Buried in this historical-social situation were the seeds of social conflict over political-cultural orientations and over socio-economic resources. In particular there was a potential threat to the ruling political Party Mapai (the Israel Workers Party, later the Labour Party), because the new immigrants, who came from traditional societies, were far from adhering to a socialist ideology. As Ishai (1982, 92) argues, 'The idea of struggle between the capitalists and the working class and the development of historical materialism was completely foreign to them. In their native countries, where the Muslim ethos ruled, authority was in the hands of a single ruler, whose sovereignty was sanctified by the religious establishment.' In the social culture of the new working class there was nothing to grant legitimacy and political support to the workers' party that was founded by the members of the established European-born working class. Hypothetically, the demographic change that occurred in the wake of the wave of immigration could even have led to a cultural-political conflict, to changes in the social structure, and to a challenge to the status quo that had been established in pre-state days. In the short run, however (and the emphasis is on the short run), the conflict remained under the surface. The reasons for this are tied to the historical heritage the immigrants brought with them, and to the central role the state played in upholding the political system.

The members of the new working class lacked organizational-political experience; in their countries of origin, political parties had not developed to the extent they had in Europe. (The argument that Communist parties developed in the Islamic countries and that Jews were among their main activists is true, but this was but a marginal phenomenon within a much wider reality.) The absence of political experience, of class consciousness, and of economic ability prevented the creation of a broad party based on the new working class of Sephardic origin. This tendency to abstain from political organization was strengthened by state intervention. Many state interests were tied up with absorption of the immigrants, like the building up of the nation, the ingathering of the exiles, the need to settle border areas, welfare considerations of a just distribution of resources, and considerations associated with the maintenance of the sociopolitical status quo.

The political hegemony of the power élite of the established working class was maintained through a series of sociopolitical interventions in daily life. In the first stages of absorption, the state's institutions, controlled by the power élite (Mapai Party), were in charge of almost every aspect of daily life. These institutions provided the immigrants with housing, employment, education, and health and other social services, and in this way were able to put pressure on them, directly or indirectly, in order to ensure their political support (Horowitz and Lissak 1972, 294). The existing political system began to make itself felt at the very earliest stages of absorption in the immigrants' transit camps (Ma'abarot, in Hebrew). The heads of large families, who could enlist a large number of voters, received various incentives in order to recruit supporters and voters for the party. With the elimination of the transit camps in the late 1950s and the settlement of the newcomers in public-housing estates, there was a search for a local equivalent of the same function, that is, a local mediator between the leading party and the local community. The local boss was born of this sociohistorical situation.

This chapter, based on a study of Ir Ganim (Garden City) – an immigrant housing estate at the southwestern part of Jerusalem – describes the rise of the local boss system and its challenge by grass-roots movements. The study was carried out over a period of five years, between 1980 and 1985, and is based on participant observation; interviews; and analysis of minutes, reports, and documents produced by the parties involved.

IR GANIM

Throughout the late 1950s and 1960s Jerusalem had witnessed a massive development of immigrant neighbourhoods and housing estates. Large tracts of land were transformed almost overnight into monotonous, strictly laid out housing projects accommodating thousands of new immigrants. The newcomers, being highly dependent on the state in terms of social services and employment, needed a go-between to represent their needs before the state's senior officials and bureaucrats. Consequently, as was the case in nineteenth-century U.S. cities, charismatic local figures raised from among the immigrants became the community representatives (Sait 1963; Banfield and Wilson 1967).

Ir Ganim is one example of this situation. The neighbourhood was built and populated in several stages between 1958 and 1972. It consists of four subsections: Kiryat Menahem to the north, Ir Ganim Alef to the east, Ir Ganim Beit at the centre, and Ir Ganim Gimel to the south (see figure 5.1). The largest wave of population arrived in the 1960s and settled in Ir Ganim Alef, Beit, and Gimel. In 1972 the neighbourhood

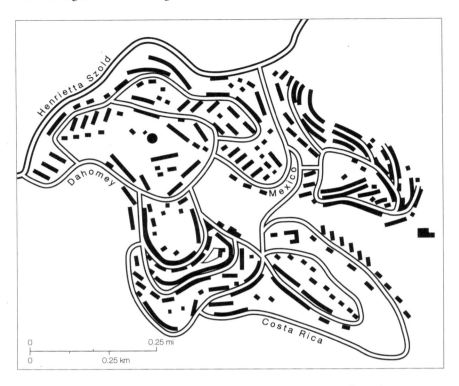

FIGURE 5.1.   The street plan of Ir Ganim. A typical layout of immigrant
housing estates is represented by the Ir Ganim project: curved streets,
monotonous buildings, and the absence of a well-defined centre.

accommodated 8,730 inhabitants, most of whom (77 per cent) were of
Asian and North African origin. The average income of a head of household in the area was about half that found in older neighbourhoods,
and the educational level (measured by median years of schooling) was
about a third lower. Over the years an internal socio-economic differentiation has occurred within the neighbourhood. Kiryat Menahem, built
in the 1970s with a relatively higher standard of housing, has accommodated a large stratum of old-timers and middle-class residents. Ir
Ganim Alef, designed as a garden-city neighbourhood, has witnessed
gentrification and become the respectable section of the area. Ir Ganim
Beit, which presents a variety of public-housing styles, comprises a large

FIGURE 5.2.   State brutalism in the housing landscape. A typical concrete building for new immigrants which accommodates several dozen families. The modernist style of Le Corbusier is adapted here to the state's immediate needs and limited budget. The result is drab and anonymous architecture.

group of socially less-advantaged groups. The socially disadvantaged part of the neighbourhood is Ir Ganim Gimel, where several multi-storey buildings were built, each accommodating 64 families (see figure 5.2). In 1981 the total population in the four sections was 12,000, of which about two-thirds were Sephardic, mainly of North African origin (NRP 1982, 12).

To provide for the residents' social well-being, the government has developed a variety of public facilities: several nursery schools and kindergartens, two elementary schools, a community centre, a public health centre, a dental clinic, and many synagogues. The neighbourhood's most acute problem, as identified in 1981 by a local planning team, was the large number of socially disadvantaged families. Most of these families were located in Ir Ganim Beit and Gimel. Other social problems found in the neighbourhood were the existence of a large group of young couples who did not have accommodation of their own and therefore had to live with their parents; poor housing quality; young delinquents and socially detached youths; and a relatively high proportion of unskilled workers and the unemployed (NRP 1982, 10–31).

As these findings may suggest, the immigrants who arrived in Ir Ganim needed frequent and close contacts with administrators and politicians responsible for allocating public services. A need thus emerged within the community itself for a link with public-welfare agencies to find solutions in the spheres of production (employment) and consumption (housing and other human-oriented services). The stage was then set for the appearance of the neighbourhood boss.

The future local boss, David Ohayon, was born in Casablanca, Morocco, to a respectable family. His father was the head of the local Jewish community and represented its interests before the authorities. Following in the footsteps of his father, David Ohayon entered public activity at an early age. Upon completing his high school studies, he joined the Jewish Agency in Marseilles, and for six years, from 1956 to 1962, he helped in organizing the immigration of Moroccan Jews to Israel. In 1962 he arrived in Israel and was sent by the absorbing institutions to a transit camp near Ir Ganim. At that time he earned his living as a factory worker. Lamenting the absorption of the Sephardic community by the older European community, he says: 'I have nothing against the European culture, but I would like the Europeans to know that we too have a significant culture of our own. Now I gradually forget my culture, and my children unfortunately would never know that we had once possessed a wonderful Andalusian music. So where is the integration of exiles they talk about?'[1]

The hardship of absorption was augmented by the housing and environmental conditions. The houses where he and his neighbours lived were made up of asbestos blocks, and their surroundings were undeveloped. Most of the roads were unpaved, and social services were minimal. Under these conditions, a communal need emerged within the transit camp for a mediator to provide a link between the residents and government agencies. Given Ohayon's background and experience, it was only natural for him to become the community's representative in dealing with the authorities. Indeed, at that time people like Ohayon were much sought after by the political parties. In general, they were themselves immigrants, and spoke the language, knew the local culture, were aware of the needs of the immigrants, and could function as a cultural-political liaison between the political élite and the community. The political élite consequently fostered these local representatives, offered them a wide variety of social and political rewards, and in return expected them to render some sociopolitical services, the most important of which was to ensure local political support.

For the Mapai/Labour Party that was in power until 1977, these services were of crucial importance, since, as noted before, its ideology was quite alien to the majority of the North African and Middle Eastern residents of Ir Ganim. Under these circumstances David Ohayon became an attractive target for political co-optation. Recounting his personal experience, Ohayon says:

Of course, it was a robbery by the parties. All the parties chased after the new immigrants in order to incorporate them ... Each party wanted to acquire the largest public share in the neighbourhoods, so we the activists, who wanted, really, the residents' good, turned into vote contractors to bring people to the parties. Of course, it's true that they used us for their political interests because we were green then, we didn't know anything about politics or parties, that was something that belonged to European Jews, and we certainly didn't have anything like that in the Arab countries, in Morocco, and we became their political slaves. Of course, I won't hide that we learned their methods, their whole social and party system. We had no choice but to enter the public-political affairs. Without a doubt, the people I met in the establishment were close to Mapai. It was impossible to get anything done without having connections with those people, and I'll mention Akiva Azulai, deputy mayor and chairman of the Moroccan community in Jerusalem; when I went to him, he asked me to become associated with the Labour Party. Of course, I had no socialist ideological background, I didn't know what socialism was before I came here, I didn't know the difference between right and left and all those things. But we had to be partners with the people who were our friends, who helped us when they were, then, in the establishment – members of the city council, of the Histadrut, of all those institutions. Of course, that was the ruling party in the country and we had to be with them and we helped them and became part of the same party, and then we picked up the ideology of the Labour Party too.[2]

The Labour Party and its apparatus resorted to Ohayon's help in different ways and offered him a large number of powerful positions within the neighbourhood. In the late 1960s he was appointed a manager of the neighbourhood's Histadrut (labour) union federation club, where he had an office, and then the service of a secretary. At the same time he served as the secretary of the Labour Party chapter in the neighbourhood, and as a member of the directorate of the municipal religious council, a post of great importance in a neighbourhood that has twenty-eight synagogues. In the mid 1970s he was appointed director of the neighbourhood centre for vocational training, a position that involved providing information on employment possibilities as well as organizing vocational training courses. With the establishment of the local community centre, which is in charge of informal education and social activities, he became a member of the centre's directorate. In 1978, he was elected chair of the neighbourhood council and thus added public legitimacy to his already powerful position. Over this period he was sent by the Histadrut federation union to take several courses in community work at the Tel Aviv University and then at the Hebrew University of Jerusalem. But, as he conceded, 'leadership is something you are born with; either you have it or you have not. This is something one may cultivate but never acquire through learning. This is why I am against people who seek to teach leadership.'[3] David Ohayon, who became over the years a powerful local boss, has been also vested with some municipal and national roles. He served two terms as a member of the city council and was a member of the Labour Party executive committee. Through these positions he developed a wide network of contacts with the mayor and his deputies, with the Labour Party district committee, and with Jerusalem's members of the Knesset (parliament).

The 1977 general elections marked the end of thirty years of Labour government and the rise of the right-wing Likud Party to power. Although numerous reasons may be cited for the 1977 political change, there is much evidence to suggest that it was rooted in a sociopolitical process whereby residents of poverty and immigrant neighbourhoods, including Ir Ganim, increasingly distanced themselves from the Labour Party (Gonen 1982). The new prime minister, Menachem Begin, perhaps touched by human misery or perhaps as an act of political pay-back, declared in 1978 the beginning of the Neighbourhood Renewal Programme (NRP, known also as Project Renewal) in Israeli cities. In Jerusalem, six neighbourhoods, among them Ir Ganim, were included in the project. David Ohayon, in spite of his numerous links with the former government, has not been affected by the political change. On the contrary, in the absence of any alternative local organization, and because of Ohayon's position as chair of the neighbourhood councils, he was entrusted by the city mayor with the most important and influential role in the local renewal program, that is, as chair of the neighbourhood's steering committee. The steering committee was made up of twenty-two members, eleven residents and eleven professionals, and was responsible for policy making, prioritizing of projects, and resource allocation. Beside the steering committee, there were several subcommittees engaged in detailed work in such specific fields as housing, community services, religion, the elderly, young people, and recreation. Apart from this powerful position as head of the steering committee, where he had far-reaching control over local budgets, he also chaired the housing subcommittee, a body that provided solutions for the housing problems of young couples, and the student grant committee, which supported local students through Project Renewal's grants, and he participated in the religious affairs subcommittee. To facilitate his remarkable public activity he has been offered a job in the ministry of communication (a well-known refuge for public activists and rivalled only by a job with the Sick Health Fund) and is currently employed by the Histadrut union federation as manager of the local vocational training centre.

What motivated the local boss of Ir Ganim? Perhaps a psychological-Nietzschean desire for a 'will to power'? As Ohayon says of himself, 'Sometimes, when I meet people who tell that thanks to you we were able to expand our house, thanks to you we could do this, thanks to you we could do that ... that gives me a lot of strength, a lot of motivation.'[4]

THE MANAGEMENT OF PLACE BY THE LOCAL BOSS

The sociophysical shaping of the neighbourhood by the local boss was based on his territorial monopoly of power positions. This monopoly, which arose against the background of a historically specific situation, put the boss at the intersection of contacts between the neighbourhood and the state, and gave him a double role. On the one hand, he served as a local advocate, representing the interests and needs of the neighbourhood residents to the state, and seeing the transfer of resources and services to his constituents. On the other hand, he served as the designated representative of a political apparatus – the Mapai/Labour Party, the Histadrut union federation, and the municipality – acting to advance its goals in the neighbourhood. He thus acted as vote contractor in many of the national, municipal, and Histadrut elections, and until 1977 succeeded in delivering the required political services. Yet his field of action was fraught with tensions and problems. At the personal level he had to steer a middle way between community and state expectations, a task which, in his words, 'borders with insanity.' As he goes on to say, 'Sometimes you are elevated upwards and sometimes you are dragged downwards to be cursed and hated.'[5]

Beyond the personal problems there was another contradiction structured into the role of the state. Alongside a modern welfare system that strived for universalism in the supply of services and in political-social activity, a particularist-paternalist system developed, with traditional characteristics based on personal connections, the solution of individual problems, the distribution of personal benefits, loyalty, and social dependence. This tension was expressed in the system of relations with both the local setting and the political-institutional system.

The boss's connection with the neighbourhood had the character of an individualistic approach that prevented the creation of broad frameworks functioning with a neighbourhood-wide view and based on broad resident participation. Most of Ohayon's personal connections were confined to residents of the boss's ethnic background, i.e., immigrants from North Africa and, to a lesser extent, immigrants from Romania. Over the years these contacts became limited to socially problematic cases.

Attempts to set up broader, either sectoral or locally based organizations were seen as a threat, that is, as attempts to undermine the boss's position, and therefore were generally aborted in their early stages. An attempt to organize a group of unemployed young people with criminal records was frustrated by creating personal tensions between members of the group that, in the end, led to its dissolution. A community worker who tried to found a representative neighbourhood council was transferred out of the area. An attempt made by Ohalim movement activists (see chapter 7) to set up an 'Ohel' organization in the neighbourhood was prevented, and the first steps of the younger generation's organizations, to be discussed shortly, were met with forceful opposition.

From the point of view of communication between the state and the neighbourhood, the local-boss system signified a narrow channel of exchange between the centre (the party, the Histadrut union federation, and the municipality) and the periphery (the neighbourhood), in which the residents were cut off from decision-making processes, from establishing priorities, and from allocating resources. The political relations with the institutional environment were based on mediation and consent through the offices of one person. The role of the local boss as a mediator had no formal basis, but was supported by the state, which strengthened his position in the neighbourhood. This informal relation required the boss to be loyal to the state, to maintain harmonious relations with it, and to refrain from acting outside the system. Though the boss took a confrontational approach from time to time, it was always for a short period and was controlled, and meant to serve as a means of applying pressure and not as a goal in itself. Thus, for instance, the neighbourhood boss threatened to bring the Neighbourhood Renewal Programme (NRP) to a standstill, and then proposed, in order to work out the existing problems, that the deputy mayor be appointed to head the local steering committee. At base, the reciprocal relations between the neighbourhood boss and establishment were founded on mutual loyalty and obligation, as Ohayon noted: 'If I go out today, even as a neighbourhood leader, and help the mayor ... I have no doubt that the mayor will remain obligated to me for a full four years. His door will be open to me, he knows that he has a leader who is his man ... It's impossible to separate the political and the public realms; they go together.'[6]

Given this context, it is interesting to examine the relationships developed between the local boss and the national policy of neighbourhood renewal. To be sure, the major social message conveyed by the NRP was to have the public involved in upgrading the neighbourhood. To this end, half of the steering committee members and most of the subcommittee participants were to be local residents, while the rest were appointed administrators or professionals. It was expected of the participants to take an active part in setting goals and objectives for the renewal program, to set priorities, to launch social and physical schemes, and to allocate resources. In this manner, the NRP strived to reshape the relationship between the Israeli centralist state and the public by working towards greater rationalization and democratization of local social life – hence, the introduction of such principles as rational planning, budgeting, an action program, division of labour, task differentiation, recruitment of resources, structured bureaucratic procedures, and citizen participation (Carmon 1988).

Under such changes one could have expected the community power structure in Ir Ganim to become more diffused. It is no wonder, then, that the local boss had an ambivalent attitude towards the renewal program. On the one hand, the program and its budget were seen as a source of power and control; on the other hand, they were a source of constant fear concerning the rise, with the encouragement of the state, of local alternative organizations. In order to minimize what the local boss saw as a possible threat to his leadership, he put his own people in key positions in the NRP's institutions, thus establishing his hold on them. The first director of the NRP indicated that he was 'the chairman's man.' The position was offered to him by the boss, and, as he claimed, 'I decided from the very beginning to work only with him, because it was easier to work with him than against him ... had he wanted to he could have destroyed the entire project. So I always saw to it that I reached an agreement with him before bringing matters before the steering committee.'[7] These facts of life were well known to the second director of the NRP. When giving instructions to planning staff, who had been hired to do physical and social planning in the neighbourhood, the director made it clear that the staff had no mandate to interfere with the responsibilities of the local organization, 'even when the neighbourhood organization is not democratic.'[8]

A detailed examination of the composition of the subcommittees that functioned in the framework of the NRP demonstrated that most of their heads were loyal to the local boss. One of the prime examples is that of the head of the services and community subcommittee, who also served as editor of the local newspaper. This position was of great importance because the local paper was delivered to every family in the neighbourhood, as well as to the city council, government offices, and the offices of the city's weekly newspapers. During the local election campaign in 1982 the local boss was interviewed and an entire page was devoted to the coverage without provoking comment, even though most of the newspaper staff members agreed to the interview only on condition that a response from rival candidates would also be published. Both the local boss and the editor benefited from the interview. In response to a comment made by the editor about the notable presence of the boss in every neighbourhood forum, the boss said, 'I am not a member of all those forums, and the claim that I control them is baseless. The fact is that on the services and community subcommittee, which functions as it should, there are no claims of that sort.'[9]

Eventually the neighbourhood press turned into a tool of the local boss, who used it to cover up the clashes between political democratization and the local power structure, a structure that neutralizes genuine citizen participation. In an interview, the local boss said of himself: 'The concentration of too many functions in the hands of one person is not at all healthy, neither for the person nor for the community. I myself am known as one who opposes having one man take on so many positions himself. I would be very happy if residents of the neighbourhood shared an interest in what is being done in the neighbourhood and took an active part in the sub-committees.'[10] The boss's comments presented an image of himself as a supporter of broadly based democratic organization, which apparently contradicted the actual situation.

The NRP was implicated, therefore, in a deep-seated tension which sprang from an explicit emphasis placed on professionalism, rationalism, and democracy, on the one hand, and an implicit acceptance of the boss's supremacy, on the other. But this was just an apparent contradiction. Modernization, professionalism, and certain types of citizen participation do not necessarily collide with traditional patronage patterns, and the two systems may even interpenetrate each other in hitherto unknown ways. Indeed, as the present case seems to suggest, the modern bureau-cratic model applied by the NRP opened up new political-economic avenues and opportunities for the local boss. Practically speaking, Ohayon acquired a set of new offices, some of which he retained while others he generously distributed among his supporters, thus further aug-menting his power position. Above all, however, he was now able to control the vast resources directed into the neighbourhood through the NRP channels.

Even citizen participation turned into a powerful tool in his hands. Professional recommendations put forward by the local planning team on the basis of a neighbourhood-wide survey, which suggested focusing attention on less-advantaged families, were vehemently criticized by Ohayon. Reproaching the team, he said, 'I was stunned to read your recommendations ... The residents have already expressed their prefer-ences: first, housing; second, detached youth – finding them a job – and finally education. You have heard our will and I don't want you to repeat your ideas.'[11] Eventually, the professional team succumbed to the res-idents' will as presented by Ohayon. Soon the local boss became the prime defender of the residents' right to participate in decision making. As he observed: 'Citizen participation changed the neighbourhood work-ing patterns. But the state still regards us as people who are allowed to be superficially involved, that is, to be involved only to approve the state's already designated goals. The state does not consider us as real partners ... It is true that we are not professionals but neither are the establishment's people. Sometimes I think that 50 per cent of them are mere bureaucrats.'[12] Genuine protest, manipulation, suspicion, and a des-perate attempt to withhold power positions seem to be intertwined in these statements. The bottom line, none the less, has been that the NRP never seriously challenged the local boss and, indirectly, even increased his grip upon the neighbourhood.

THE CHALLENGE TO THE LOCAL BOSS

The challenge to the local boss has come from elsewhere, and is associated with such broader social processes as the socio-economic mobility of local residents, the rise of social discontent, and, as is the case in Chinatown-Strathcona, the appearance of the younger generation as an active actor on the neighbourhood scene. Already in 1980, as the director of the NRP reported, the client group of the local boss had markedly shrunk, to encompass only the most distressed families in the area, most of whom were of Moroccan origin. Groups that witnessed upward social mobility, as the director observed, refused to cooperate with Ohayon.[13] Among these groups were the local parent-teacher associations, as well as a local street organization that was involved in a struggle over the expansion of residential flats. A community worker associated with these organizations said: 'We don't turn to him because we don't trust him.'[14]

Throughout 1981 and 1982, social resentment and discontent rapidly spread across the neighbourhood as several different forces coalesced to destabilize the hitherto unchallenged authority of the local boss. For one thing, the very existence of the NRP in the neighbourhood signalled the importance attached to local politics. It did not take long for certain groups to visualize the vast potential associated with the neighbourhood's leadership and its corollary control over the NRP resources. And although the NRP's director and the associated professional team did not venture to challenge the boss's authority, such a challenge eventually arose from the local younger generation. Another source of social unrest was associated with the political change in the national elections of 1977. For many middle-class Labour-oriented members, this change, sometimes conceived as a 'political upheaval,' signalled the Labour Party's inability to establish a genuine link with residents in immigrant and poverty-stricken neighbourhoods. This failure is indicated by their emphasis on the need to re-enter right wing–oriented neighbourhoods (such as Ir Ganim), to bridge the widening gap between the party and the community, to re-educate the residents by establishing a cognitive link with the party's goals, and finally to create grass-roots movements that would challenge the Likud Party in its very own stronghold. Practically, this ideological-political task was to be carried out by two or three members of the 77 circle, a Labour-oriented academic group formed in the aftermath of the 1977 general elections.[15]

The Jerusalem municipality, for its own reasons, tacitly approved the 77 circle's strategy. Although the leading party in the city council, Jerusalem One, is presented as politically independent, half of its members on the city council are appointed through consultation with the Labour Party. Following the 1977 political change, it was feared that a similar fate might face the Jerusalem One party also. Moreover, Ohayon's failure to deliver the votes gave urgency to the need to develop new links with local groups, even behind his back. To this end an agreement was reached whereby the municipality would assign two community workers to set up grass-roots organizations in Ir Ganim and Musrara, and the organizations thus set up would challenge the Likud's policy.[16]

Over a relatively short period of time, between September and December 1981, through an intensive process of community action, a left-wing organization – Improvement of Community Life (ICL) – was created. There is no explicit evidence that the Likud Party resorted to a similar activity. Yet, between February and December 1981, another grass-roots organization – Youth for the Neighbourhood (YFN) – was formed, and its chairperson and some of its leading members had close contacts with the Likud.

Despite the significant cultural and political differences existing between the ICL and the YFN movements, they nevertheless had several basic features in common. Members of the two groups were drawn from the neighbourhood's young generation cohort, most of them being in their twenties and aspiring to achieve political power. Though differing in their political views, they shared deep antipathy for the politicized-patronage system fostered by the local boss, and sought to replace it with another more democratic one. In a leaflet published by the ICL movement in late 1981, the local residents were called to organize against 'a one man neighbourhood committee ... a dictator ... [against] Ohayon, a smart politician who managed to take over the neighbourhood.' The leaflet concluded with a call to put an end to the 'party's pimps from the immigrant transit camps era' and encouraged the residents 'to act so as to make possible greater public involvement in neighbourhood affairs in order to allow for the democratisation of our life.'[17] The generational gap was further elaborated by the leader of the YFN movement, who said:

I think there is really something interesting about the younger generation, even people who identify politically with a certain party ... those people criticize their own parties much more stringently than the older generation did ... The older generation had a problem ... Sometimes political considerations and neighbourhood considerations were opposed and there was the little leader in the neighbourhood who was allowed by the party to stick his nose up a bit ... They gave him a few little incentives, and he felt that he had no choice but to do what the party told him to do ... The party's interests took precedence over the neighbourhood's interests.[18]

The significance of these conceptions for local social action was that social protest, originating on either the left or the right, closely intertwined with an intergenerational conflict, and with an attempt to mitigate party control over neighbourhood affairs.

The Rise of the YFN Movement

The members of the YFN consisted of a group of young people who shared a common background of religious education. Members of the group, though of Middle Eastern and North African origin, attended the local Habad school and continued as adults to pray and meet at the local Habad synagogue. This is in itself an interesting phenomenon, since the Habad Hassidic movement, led by the Lubavitz Rabbi in Brooklyn, is of an Ashkenazic origin, and its presence in impoverished neighbourhoods is part of a deliberate missionary attempt to recruit disadvantaged Jewish families to its ranks.

By February 1981, some members of the group, who were students at the Hebrew University, offered extracurricular classes to 150 schoolchildren aged six to seventeen and taught illiterate women the preliminaries of reading and writing. Chaim Amar, a local resident who was later to become the chairperson of the YFN, led the educational program and acted as a liaison between the Hebrew University program that sponsored the students and the NRP that paid for their work. From this point onwards, Chaim Amar was to play an important role in neighbourhood politics. He was born in 1958 in Casablanca. In 1962 his family moved to Israel and, like David Ohayon, was sent to live in the transit camp made of asbestos houses near Ir Ganim. He studied for eight years in the local Habad school, completed his studies at a prestigious religious high school, and served three years in the army tank corps. Upon completing his military service, he went to the Hebrew University to study Jewish philosophy. During his university studies he started taking part in public affairs – for three years he was a member of the Hebrew University student council, ran the university's training program for public activists, and served as a council intermediary between the university and the neighbourhood.[19] His public activity brought him into contact with some right-wing leaders, and he joined the Likud Party and supported Likud territorial policy in the West Bank and Gaza Strip.

The identification of housing and youth problems as the major issues to be confronted by the NRP served as a springboard for Amar's local political activity. On 1 July 1981, he summoned a meeting of his group in the Habad synagogue to discuss the establishment of a local social movement, and on 26 July the group declared itself as a social movement that 'strives to run the neighbourhood as a legitimate force.'[20] The idea was to create a popular movement that would eventually replace the local boss with a neighbourhood-wide democratic organization. A leaflet distributed to the public at that time read: 'We will change the neighbourhood elections system to let each street have its own representative ... In this way we strive to create a close contact between the neighbourhood committee and the different parts of the neighbourhood, and to have the residents involved in local activities and struggles.'[21] Referring to the neighbourhood committee itself, the movement declared: 'Our innovation, then, is productive cooperation between the residents and the committee, with the committee acting as a group; there cannot be a situation in which only one member of the committee functions.'[22] The messages delivered by the movement indicated a strong sense of innovation and a deliberate attempt to present a vanguard alternative to what had been presented as an already outdated neighbourhood organization. In a letter sent to the mayor, the movement's chairman wrote: 'We tried to present a new approach that combines ideology and innovation. We tried to prove that even in disadvantaged neighbourhoods an intelligentsia may spring up, a second generation can emerge that tries to solve problems rather than run away from them.'[23] The YFN was presented as a model not only for the neighbourhood as such but also for Israeli society as a whole. When registered as a non-profit organization, the movement proclaimed a universal message – that is, a message that transcended neighbourhood boundaries: 'The YFN movement wishes, both on the local and national levels, to aid Israeli society with both physical and communal concerns. The movement sees its purpose as explaining, all over the country, its goals and activities with the intention of serving as a model to be imitated – as a trail blazer for the social future of the state of Israel.'[24]

To mobilize local support, the movement held meetings every Saturday, between January and March 1982, at the twenty-eight local synagogues to inform the congregations of its ideals and strategies. In this way, the unanimous support of the local rabbis was secured, and the rabbis later used their networks to disseminate the movement's ideas. Meetings were also held with the secretary of the World Sephardic Federation and with Knesset members of the Likud and Tchiya (right of the Likud) parties in order to attain social legitimation and economic support. A community worker was consequently assigned to accompany the YFN movement, and some of its expenditures were covered by the municipality. Unexpectedly, the movement was also aided by the head of the municipal unit responsible for Youth Advancement, a person well known for his left-wing orientation and affiliation with the United Labour Party. It was suggested that, infuriated with being passed over by his supervisors, who supported the rival ICL movement, the head of the Youth Advancement unit asserted himself by cooperating with the YFN movement.[25]

Being aware of the YFN's growing influence, the local boss tried to negotiate a political deal, and in April 1982 suggested a combining of effort for coming neighbourhood elections. YFN's negative response severed the social relations with the boss, who now diverted his efforts towards the ICL movement.

The Rise of the ICL Movement

Unlike the YFN, which arose spontaneously from the neighbourhood, the ICL was created by forces originating outside Ir Ganim, among them radical community workers designated by the municipality, and representatives of the 77 circle and the United Labour Party. Moreover, whereas the YFN assumed political neutrality at the neighbourhood level (though its head did not hide his affiliation with the right), the ICL was the favourite of the left and maintained close connections with the United Labour Party and with the 'Peace Now' movement.

The first action to initiate a left wing–oriented organization was made in September 1981 by Avner Amiel, the head of the unit for Community Action in the city department of youth, sport, and community. Avner Amiel has had a long record of inciting grass-roots activity in Jerusalem. During the early 1970s, along with some of his colleagues, he helped to initiate and organize the Israeli Black Panthers Movement and acted as a liaison between the movement and the national and international media. In the late 1970s he was one of the founders of the Ohalim Movement, and in 1981 he was trying to stimulate a similar social change in Ir Ganim. To this end, he summoned the neighbourhood community workers to a meeting on 21 September, where he said:

There is a growing discontent in Ir Ganim associated with problems of socially detached youths, housing and overcrowdedness. There is also the beginning of spontaneous organizations around block committees ... We can use the territorial problems in order to advance new values and promote social change. An earlier experience in the Bucharim neighbourhood showed that this can be done by linking residents and academics and making them work together on some specific problems ... The strategy, then, is as follows: to create a new local force that will confront local problems, to create an academic movement that will advance new social values, to foster solidarity between the two groups through community action from below, and to initiate public activity on a large scale so that it will eventually attract other neighbourhoods' attention.[26]

Coalition building, consciousness heightening, universalization of local problems and grass-roots activity directed against the right-wing government were present in Amiel's thoughts. In his words: 'The idea is to knock out the government by inciting social unrest all over the city.' The community workers, although sympathizing with the general idea, remained sceptical and hesitant with regard to its practicality. One of them noted that Ir Ganim is the most apathetic neighbourhood in the city, and another argued: 'People who live in a large building along with another 64 families would like to see first basic services getting improved. They would like to have hot water, a nice building and an environment where they can live in. They could not care less about other things. A hungry person does not take much interest in philosophy.'[27] The message delivered by the community workers was then quite clear: community work should focus on tangible and concrete issues, leaving aside Amiel's grand ideology. In a second meeting, held on 24 September 1981, Amiel informed the community workers that members of the 77 circle would soon begin to tackle the neighbourhood's housing problems. His question as to how the community workers view the cooperation with the academics triggered the following discussion:

Community Worker A: What can we do together?
Avner: I've some ideas, but maybe you've given it some thought.
Community Worker B: I think we should join the academics in performing something really big, but the issues we handle here are very small.[28]

Frustrated with the community workers' responses, Amiel turned to his supervisors and asked for a radical community worker in order to pursue his plan.[29] Consequently, Yair Fidel, a community worker associated with the United Labour Party and the 'Peace Now' movement and who, on one occasion, declared himself to be 'an anarchist,' was sent to Ir Ganim to help out in creating the organization. Over a short period of time, Fidel and a member of the 77 circle managed to mobilize several well-to-do residents from the socially established section of Kiryat Menahem, and to turn them into the nucleus of the movement, adding Dede Ben-Shitrit, a youth leader in his early thirties. In addition, several young families in search of housing, and living in overcrowded conditions or in houses suffering dampness, were identified to form the movement's target group. Commenting on the mobilization process, one of the local community workers noted: 'They created a political leadership without a social base and a social base without a political leadership. I think that up until now the ICL movement lacks a broad social base of committed residents, because at a certain point along the arduous process of citizen mobilization from below they gave up and imposed instead a political leadership from the top.'[30] Leadership was quite vague an issue at that stage, since Fidel and one member of the 77 circle took upon themselves to heighten social consciousness and subsequently served as the ideological leaders of the movement. In line with Amiel's ideological beliefs, themselves reminiscent of Alinsky's ideas, they strove to transform personal and local problems into universal-political conflicts. One immediate target was the local NRP, which, as Fidel maintained, turned the residents into charity recipients. As he put it: 'Our duty is to show other neighbourhoods the truth, the truth of an alternative possibility, a possibility of new rules, and along with them to struggle for a new social order.'[31] The ministry of housing, led by the charismatic Likud leader David Levy, was singled out for practical critique, and was blamed for the dilapidated housing conditions in disadvantaged neighbourhoods. In a call for the residents of Ir Ganim to attend a demonstration against the ministry of housing, the movement proclaimed:

Enough of horrible overcrowding, enough of leaky buildings ... 1,200 apartments in the neighbourhood are damp and leaky, 600 apartments are not fit for human habitation, 1,700 are overcrowded so that people live on top of each other ... in the case of a small number of families in 'Yakir' [a settlement in the West Bank] the Ministry of Housing spends $200,000 on 30 families. In Ir Ganim and Kiryat Menahem, the same Ministry is spending only $70,000 over four years of the Neighbourhood Renewal Project.[32]

The demonstration, held in Ir Ganim on 2 November 1982, challenged the Likud's settlement policy in the occupied territories, and described it as detrimental to the social cause of disadvantaged neighbourhoods. Money, it was argued, should be spent on disadvantaged neighbourhoods and not on new settlements in the occupied territories.

In a prompt action, the minister of housing called the deputy mayor, directed his attention to the political-agitating role played by municipal employees, and demanded his quick intervention. Consequently, Yair Fidel was condemned for breaking the professional codes and was removed to another neighbourhood. (A similar fate faced another community worker who fostered a grass-roots movement in Musrara.) Unimpressed by his removal from the neighbourhood, Fidel changed his place of residence to Ir Ganim and joined the ICL as the movement's mouthpiece. In anticipation of the neighbourhood's coming elections he now helped in shaping the ICL's 1982 platform, which alongside its cry to improve the housing conditions, put forward the following demands: to treat Ir Ganim as a small town and not as a neighbourhood, to raise the local standards of living, to establish medical clinics and pharmacies, to improve public transportation, to install telephones, and to improve the public lighting.

Seven groups campaigned in the neighbourhood elections held in December 1982, of which the most important ones were a group headed by David Ohayon, the YFN movement headed by Chaim Amar, and the ICL movement headed by Dede Ben-Shitrit. Fourteen hundred residents voted. Of the fifteen neighbourhood council seats, fourteen were won by the YFN movement, and one by Ohayon. The ICL movement, in other words, did not get even a single representative in the new council, and the local boss lost his chair to the youth's local movement.

The neighbourhood residents, though overwhelmingly in support of the younger generation, were not ready to endorse the left-wing messages delivered by the ICL movement. Ir Ganim's culture appears in this light as a kind of heritage from the past, or in Gramsci's words (1971, ch. 1), as a kind of 'ideological hegemony' that shaped the interpretation and attitude towards society. This cultural-political tradition was characterized by the following features: closure around ethnicity, a traditional-religious spirit, a tendency to support the right-wing on the national level, conformism, and avoidance of conflict. The nature of this tradition was, subsequently, opposed to radical left-oriented protest, as advanced by the ICL movement, and tended to support the YFN's pragmatic orientation. The local culture was indirectly strengthened by those community workers who assumed an apolitical approach and aspired to solve concrete local problems. Under these circumstances the YFN movement's victory was unavoidable.

THE MANAGEMENT OF THE NEIGHBOURHOOD BY GRASS-ROOTS MOVEMENTS

The young people of the YFN movement, who had won the election, were all in their twenties and early thirties. Some of them were university graduates, others had a high school education, and many of them were well established in their jobs. The chairperson was head of a student program at the university and worked also as a youth leader. His two deputies also had university education: one taught at an elementary school, and the other was a lecturer at the Betzalel Art Academy. The movement's secretary had a high-school education and worked as a book-keeper at the local health clinic. The ten other representatives included two electrical engineers, a former army captain who completed a college degree after his tour of duty, a computer operator, a teacher, a youth leader, a policeman, a student at Yeshiva (a religious seminary), and two blue-collar workers. They were all males of Sephardic origin, and all but two had a religious background. As Chaim Amar correctly commented, this was the intelligentsia of the young generation. And one can understand the scale of disappointment, when the newly elected group discovered that it had won a hollow prize, since the main centres of power had already moved elsewhere – to the steering committee, and to the community centre directorate, to be headed by David Ohayon! Throughout 1983 and 1984 the movement launched a stubborn struggle to realize its rights and to establish its control over local power positions.

Addressing the mayor of Jerusalem in 1984, Chaim Amar wrote:

Today one year and three months after being elected to the neighbourhood committee, we have not yet been incorporated into the system operating within the neighbourhood. Everyone pushes us aside and tries to fail us. Where are all your promises to change the situation after 15 January 1983 ... what about having our delegates in the steering committee? ... What about having our delegates in the community centre directorate? ... Unfortunately our members gradually begin to realise that in the atmosphere that has been created in Jerusalem there is no practical possibility of serving as a conventional committee. The only way to get things moving is still the way we have not chosen, the way that is so opposed to our principles and to our central idea – the way of violence and demonstrations and turning tables over etc. ... We reached a crossroads and the problem we face had to do with our future and the future of our neighbourhood. We are not willing to be a mere decoration. We were not elected for that! The mentality of the young generation from which we come does not allow us to remain in our present situation. We have come to act, and there are alternative ways of action outside the system in which we operate at the moment.[33]

Through persistent pressures and actions according to the established rules, the movement finally changed the municipality's attitude, and the latter went from ignoring the new council to co-productive activity with it. Gradually, local centres of power passed into the movement's hands: leadership of the NRP's steering committee, directorship of the NRP, partnership in responsibility for the Histadrut club, and membership in the employment committee and in the centre for vocational training. When this process was completed, the YFN movement had achieved local control while institutionalizing itself as an organization oriented towards improvement through co-production.

Reports published in 1983 and in 1984 indicated a high level of co-production with the state, which had resulted in the improvement of housing conditions, roads, public transport, and educational facilities. Consequently, some residents enlarged their apartments, the public transportation system improved, new classes for adult education were opened, and the physical infrastructure was upgraded. In addition, the movement initiated some public events, among them a communal bar mitzvah celebration for fifty boys. These activities were well adapted to local expectations, as expressed by residents' letters and requests. In one of these letters, which may serve as an illustration, a local resident addresses the chairman: 'I write to you with a great request as chairman of the neighbourhood council that you help me find the most efficient possible solution for a loan to complete a construction job. I turn to you with this request since I am a resident of the neighbourhood and have a right to assistance from the head of the neighbourhood council.'[34] Community needs, traditions, and expectations thus channelled the movement's activity towards concrete material problems with the result of further intensifying its local-pragmatic orientation.

While the YFN movement had deeply immersed itself in local affairs, the ICL movement went on to develop a broader political orientation. On 15 January 1983, members of the movement participated for the first time in a Peace Now demonstration, and protest against the government's settlement policy in the occupied territories. In the course of the demonstration, which was held in one of the Jewish settlements in the West Bank, Dede Ben-Shitrit, the ICL chairman, said: 'The struggle for peace is primarily the struggle of the exploited groups in this country ... The ICL movement is a movement of disadvantaged Sephardim and Ashkenazim (Oriental and European born Jews) who see the link between foreign and defence policy and the economic and social situation in the disadvantaged neighbourhoods.'[35]

In the following months, ICL members cooperated with the Peace Now movement, and occasionally three to five of them took part in the Peace Now demonstrations. Collaboration was also fostered with other social movements operating in Musrara and Katamons in order to protest against government economic and defence policy. Reacting to the ICL activity, the NRP subcommittee in charge of religious affairs condemned ICL cooperation with the Peace Now movement. As Dede Ben-Shitrit noted, he and his friends were consequently conceived in the neighbourhood as leftists and PLO (the Palestine Liberation Organization) supporters, and were blamed for evoking violence and social division among the people.[36] In sharp contrast to the neighbourhood's response, the media were very sympathetic to the movement, giving its activities broad coverage and almost entirely ignoring the YFN movement. The ICL was represented through the media as a 'class-based movement' that signalled the growing discontent in disadvantaged neighbourhoods with the Likud's policy.[37] Israeli TV broadcast two special reports on the movement, and Dede Ben-Shitrit was interviewed on a popular TV program. Several Kibbutzim affiliated with the United Labour Party invited Ben-Shitrit to lecture on the movement, and gradually he became a public figure.

Inwardly, however, the movement was slowly rotting. Beyond the vanguard image skilfully created through the media lay the gloomy reality of inactivity; trivial cooperation with the local boss in the NRP; and, above all, the great failure to mobilize a supportive social base. Since the first demonstration in the West Bank, the number of activists on which the movement could have relied shrank significantly. One hundred people took part in the first demonstration, forty in the second, and then the number declined to only a handful thereafter. This reality sharply collided with the movement's high image as fostered through the media – one that posited the movement as a local vanguard which symbolized the beginning of ideological change in hitherto Likud strongholds.[38] Whether the public believed this image is hard to tell; members of the movement, however, were not seduced into transforming the image into reality. In a meeting held on 12 April 1983, Yair Fidel, in an act of self-critique, exposed the movement's weaknesses one by one. First, he blamed himself for creating in the movement a high image that markedly contrasted with its low level of social activity. Second, he pointed out that the movement's leadership was made up of well-to-do residents who socially did not represent the disadvantaged groups of Ir Ganim. Finally, he complained that the lion's share of the work fell on his shoulders and that informally he had been the driving motor behind the movement.[39]

The soul-searching process, steered by Fidel, ended up in a decision to organize a group of disadvantaged families living in dilapidated housing conditions and, along with them, to launch a protest squat in an adjacent, unsettled area, and to establish a 'Tent Settlement.' Tents, mattresses, a generator, and volunteers to instruct the squatters were secured at meetings held with members of Peace Now and Kibbutz Negba (affiliated with the United Labour Party). On the night of 11 June 1983, in a well-planned operation to which representatives of the media were cordially invited, about twenty families, headed by members of Peace Now and Kibbutz Negba, pitched their tents on a hill, Giva'at Masua, south of Ir Ganim. Large placards of ICL and Peace Now were posted all around. One of them read: 'We called our settlement "upper ICL" in order to protest the government's policy of spending billions on settlements like upper Shechem [a settlement on the West Bank overlooking Nablus] and pennies on solutions to the problems of disadvantaged neighbourhoods.'

The fourth day of the protest squat shed some light on the movement's achievement. Most of those present in the 'new settlement' were members of Peace Now and Kibbutz Negba, and there was only a small group of residents from Ir Ganim. At the foot of the hill, in the house of one of the residents, Yair Fidel, who was now wanted by the police, met with a number of members of Kibbutz Negba. He claimed angrily that he had been deserted by the residents, and said: 'Dede and I were the only ones who spent the night there, so I am not surprised that the police saw us.' Referring to the residents, he said: 'They're of no use, they want me to sit in prison for them.' Descending from the hill after dismantling the settlement (without any help from the residents), one member of Peace Now said that he felt exploited by the residents, another said that the residents were ready to join the devil in order to get housing solutions, and still another, a member of Kibbutz Negba, advised Yair Fidel to let the residents carry the struggle by themselves; 'perhaps this,' he added, 'will teach them some responsibility.'

THE END?

Yair Fidel, probably accepting the Kibbutz members' advice, has left his job as a community worker and severed his ties with the ICL, and has become a correspondent for the *Hadashot* daily newspaper. Dede Ben-Shitrit, capitalizing on the ICL vanguard image, has become a city-council member and, in the 1984–9 period, held the municipal portfolio of neighbourhood affairs. Chaim Amar has delved deeply into the neighbourhood's affairs only to discover that 'a large burden of 90 per cent of the work falls on the chairman of the neighbourhood council.'[40] The unavoidable result was concentration of power in his hands. Reflecting in 1985 somewhat reprovingly on his movement's volunteer activity he noted: 'Sometimes you are disappointed at your best friends, I should have understood that not everyone has the same bug, and to tell the truth, alongside the disappointment, when you see it realistically, you understand that it really is hard for a person to push himself voluntarily and to keep up the same level of excitement over many years.' This led to a change in his attitude towards the local boss: 'Today, in hindsight, I respect David Ohayon much more, and maybe I'm the only one who can really appreciate what he did, as one who has gone through the same thing, To be a chairman is not a simple job.' The change in outlook and interpretation led to close contacts between Amar and Ohayon, and to cooperation between them. The YFN chairman described the change as follows:

Today, for instance, I cooperate very closely with Ohayon. It's not a secret that we've been cooperating for an entire year ... The relations have improved. There were crises, but today he helps me because he's accepted it. By the way, it was a difficult process because of the fact that he isn't chairman, he isn't a member of the steering committee. I've changed a lot of things in my conception of him ... For instance, it's not fair only to criticize him, sometimes you have to see things from inside, the pressures that are on the chairman. Only I or another chairman can understand what the problems of a chairman are, and I and Ohayon reached the point of talking. Sometimes I tell him about the shortcomings of the council, too. Our level of trust is very high. Ohayon cares, in the end, about the neighbourhood. I think he is an example of a political tragedy.[41]

These changes, which brought the movement closer to the former organizational-political model, angered some of its members and led to a split and to a crisis. The deputy chairperson claimed that the movement had lost the confidence of the public, abandoned its social commitment, and turned into a tool for a few people to pursue 'totally questionable personal advancement.'[42]

In 1986 Amar completed his term as the neighbourhood council's chairperson and was appointed as a special social aide to the prime minister, Itzhak Shamir. New neighbourhood elections were not held, and currently there are no local followers of either the YFN or the ICL movement. David Ohayon is the head of the vocational training centre, and as such plays an important role in helping young people to find jobs.

With the phasing out of the NRP and the lessening of interest in housing investments, a governmental shift occurred towards employment programs, and once again Ohayon resumed a central social role at the local level.

What was it, then, all about, and how are we to interpret the events in Ir Ganim? It appears that, at a certain time, Ir Ganim reached a juncture at which a variety of neighbourhood organizational forms – a traditional neighbourhood boss, a co-production form represented by the YFN, and a protest-oriented form symbolized, though in mock form, by the ICL – collided with one another. The result has been that, beyond the instrumental gains, there emerged an interesting debate concerning the meaning of neighbourhood politics.

For the local boss, neighbourhood politics implied a double patronage system – party / local boss, and local boss / clients-residents – which served both the community's basic needs and the interests of the political system. At base, this conception reflected a traditional type of organization that fit the old customs, norms, and values prevailing among Oriental Jewish communities. The Israeli political apparatus capitalized on this tradition and utilized the local boss as a communicator in order to recruit the community's political support. The Israeli experience resembles U.S. urban politics of the late nineteenth century. The emergence of ethnic neighbourhoods in the American city inhabited by lower-class immigrants; the existence of an electoral system based on geographical districts (the ward system), which turned the immigrant neighbourhood into the basic unit of political organization; and the political machine's need to control votes gave the local boss a firm position in urban politics. As in the American city, the local boss in Ir Ganim originated from among the new immigrants, spoke their language, was aware of their needs, and as a result could function as a cultural-political liaison between the political apparatus and the new immigrants. Apparently, the need for a mediator is a common feature of immigrant groups in the city; groups that, despite sociocultural differences, need a go-between with the local bureaucracy and politicians, and assistance in obtaining resources, especially at the initial phase of absorption.

This traditional conception of urban politics came under heavy criticism over time as people witnessed upward social mobility, developed their own networks with the bureaucratic-political system, and subsequently reduced their dependency on the local boss. These processes were felt in particular, as the Ir Ganim case shows, among members of the younger generation. For members of this group, neighbourhood politics entailed an entirely different project. Essentially, they sought to uproot the patronage system, to enhance residents' involvement in local affairs, and to grapple with needs that were both material (allocation of physical and social resources) and post-material (fostering a sense of belonging and self-management).

Alongside these general tendencies, there emerged some conspicuous divergencies among subgroups within the younger generation. One group, the YFN movement, saw neighbourhood politics as a pragmatic enterprise designed to serve the particularistic needs of the local residents, and thus to bring about tangible improvements within the neighbourhood sphere. In contrast, the ICL movement used neighbourhood politics as leverage to raise some universal messages, such as critique of the Likud party's expenditures in the occupied territories at the expense of poor neighbourhoods. Accordingly, the YFN adopted a co-productive strategy, while the ICL relied heavily on social protest.

The local residents proved to be quite receptive towards the particularistic–co-productive orientation and tended to remain reserved in relation to and even alienated from the universalistic-protest orientation. Apparently, a traditional community, whose members adhere to the right and seek to advance material interests, tends to favour a pragmatic organization and to distance itself from an ideological-left wing–oriented organization. Members of the lower class in Ir Ganim, as well as in other poor neighbourhoods in Jerusalem (and, by extension, in Israel), are not necessarily the supporters of radical protest organizations. Moreover, over time, the prevailing local conventions, which emphasize the dominant role of the chairperson in local politics and cooperation with the state, helped to re-create the local boss system. Within this traditional political context, the very rise of a universalistic–protest-oriented organization like the ICL was an act of swimming against the current, an attempt to deroutinize old habits and patterns of behaviour. This attempt was supported by liberal community workers, members of the peace movement, and the media, who sought to give the ICL an image of a popular movement challenging the Likud in its own stronghold. This hyper-real image did not stand the test of reality, and collapsed in the face of the community's apathy and resentment of the ICL's political messages.

Viewed through the eyes of these organizations, neighbourhood politics appears to oscillate between popular (particularistic–co-productive) and high (universalistic-protest) cultures. The question that arises at this point is whether popular and high culture can be drawn together in a unified action, thus mobilizing the local base, or whether they are doomed to remain worlds apart. Whatever the answer may be, one thing seems to be quite certain: by raising this question, the different social actors who appeared on the Ir Ganim stage signalled that the major debate in the area was not only between state and society, but also within civil society itself. In an interesting manner, the ensuing debate touched some deeper cultural and moral issues. It highlighted the struggle of the immigrants' younger generation to assert itself, it problematized the cry for the depoliticization of daily life, and it exposed in local events a deep-seated cultural and moral conflict which besets Israeli society today.

PART THREE

Engaging the 'Underclass'

Beyond the racialized minorities of Chinatown and Ir Ganim is a further level of marginality in Vancouver and Jerusalem. The Downtown Eastside, Vancouver's oldest district, has been labelled 'skid row' for forty years, and its high concentration of social transients, beer parlours, public drunkenness, and crime seems to confirm its underclass status. It is a neighbourhood whose residents are dependent upon the welfare state, a public city (Dear and Wolch 1987) of primarily middle-aged and elderly men, a number of them handicapped physically or mentally, living in single rooms in low-quality hotels, and with up to 80 per cent of the population retired or unemployed. Katamon Tet is in Jerusalem's poverty belt, and its public-housing projects are among the poorest in the city. In the worst areas, where the Ohalim (tents) movement began, densities were highest, 40 per cent of young adults were unemployed, and crime was rife; a third of the teenagers had criminal records. In both districts marginality was acute, defined in the Downtown Eastside by poverty, age, and poor health, in Katamon Tet by poverty and (Sephardic) ethnicity, and in each instance compounded by the presence of lifestyles which appeared deviant by middle-class standards. Residents experienced minimal citizenship rights.

Neighbourhood mobilization in each district bore the distinct character of poor people's movements seeking justice, not charity. Both were initially inspired by community social workers; in the Downtown Eastside local leadership quickly took over, but in Katamon Tet a community worker continued to give direction in conjunction with a local juvenile gang leader. In each instance charismatic leadership was integral to the success of activism, with key individuals energizing the groups by example, through inspiration, perseverance, and personal sacrifice. Existing organizational structures provided the framework for group formation; the Downtown Eastside Residents Association (DERA), with a large number of retired workers from the unionized resource industries, employed a trades-union model of organization, while in Katamon Tet the structure of the juvenile gang was preserved in form but politicized in content.

Both DERA and the Ohalim movement were protest organizations, though as they evolved they fluctuated between protest and co-production in their relations to the state. Demonstrations, squats, sit-ins, and the embarrassment of government over the contradictions of its policy (for example, the gap between legislation and enforcement) were integral to their strategy and bared the vulnerable ambiguities of the welfare state. In welfare-dependent neighbourhoods they were strong advocates of a self-help model, and in DERA's case expressed strong scepticism about the contribution of even sympathetic community workers. In each instance the protest voice was informed by socialist philosophy, even if in practice it embodied a good dose of pragmatism. As such the message was universal rather than particular; both groups sought to encourage mobilization in other districts and lent their support to broader national movements, including the peace movement (in both cities), the labour and welfare-rights movements in Vancouver, and opposition to West Bank settlement in Jerusalem.

Such political mobilization required a significant cultural reorientation, a defamiliarization of everyday life which made suddenly problematic the limiting cultural worlds of the beer parlour (in the Downtown Eastside) and the juvenile gang (in Katamon Tet). This symbolic struggle of redefinition was waged by DERA pressing the discourse of community and control, while rejecting the image of skid row, an image of pathology and dependence. In Katamon Tet alternative realities were first opened up by an innovative use of community theatre, which challenged the taken-for-granted world of neighbourhood adolescents and, by offering a new interpretation of their everyday life, sought to transform criminal activity into political activism.

Most interesting has been the response of the welfare state to groups whose protest activities have often been irritating, and have exposed the soft underside of its conflicting objectives. The state, if not the parent of DERA and the Ohalim movement, was the midwife present at their birth, providing social workers to aid initial community development. Both groups also benefited from a surprising largesse of funding from the state and other agencies in their untested early years, and relatively easy access to high-ranking political figures. This empowerment was a result of the liberalism of the 1968–75 period in social policy at all three levels of government in British Columbia, and federal Neighbourhood Renewal funds and the liberal Kollek administration in Jerusalem after 1977. With a keen sense of the realities of power, DERA in particular sought to penetrate the state through the electoral process, a strategy which through perseverance has been remarkably successful. The outcome has been an inevitable shift towards co-production, which has led to significantly enhanced public services entering each neighbourhood. The risk, of course, is total incorporation of the groups by the state. By 1990 such incorporation was near to being complete with the Ohalim movement; DERA, in contrast, while confronting major challenges from the erosion of the welfare state and urban redevelopment in the Downtown Eastside, showed remarkable longevity. Active for twenty years, it provides an informative model of neighbourhood organization and community development from within a multiply deprived setting.

6

The Downtown Eastside: 'One Hundred Years of Struggle'[1]

Canadian municipal government was for decades almost exclusively government by and for business and pro-development groups, while serving a broader public interest defined by large and small property owners. Those residents who fell outside this definition of citizenship also fell outside the terms of full civic entitlement: racial minorities (chapter 4), the poor, even tenants. The Downtown Eastside, long known as Vancouver's skid row, was the most marginalized district in the city, for even tenants' rights were denied to this population of elderly men, long-term occupants of residential hotels and rooming-houses, until 1989. For many years the state neglected the district, treating its residents as stereotypical objects, and even when municipal government began to attend to the area in the mid 1960s it was in the discourse of skid row, and with the language of 'tax sinks' – the city's planning director noted that municipal expenditures in the district were twenty to twenty-five times greater than municipal tax revenues[2] – a language which has repeatedly preceded state-driven redevelopment in many Canadian and U.S. cities.

But events were not to unfold in this manner in Vancouver during the 1970s. The open society espoused by the federal Liberals under Pierre Trudeau in 1968 provided an enabling context in which other voices might enter the municipal arena. The city's reform council, elected in 1972, cautiously maintained an open door to include groups who had historically been excluded from civic decision making. We have seen the effects of this new-found openness on the part of the state in the empowerment of the residents of Chinatown-Strathcona (chapter 4). In the adjacent neighbourhood of the Downtown Eastside, such an enabling context also aided the formation of a grass-roots group, though common origins have not meant that the two associations have shared either an identical character nor have they followed a similar trajectory. Both groups have drawn upon distinctive local histories in their evolution. The Strathcona Property Owners' and Tenants' Association (SPOTA), after a short period of protest, quickly returned to a co-productive relationship with the state and a somewhat conservative ideology. The Downtown Eastside in contrast has historically been a district of labour-based strife, and it was the genius of the Downtown Eastside Residents' Association (DERA) to translate a past of activism over labour rights into a present of activism over neighbourhood rights, while maintaining the protest model in the course of community mobilization. As in Chinatown-Strathcona, this achievement involved a challenge to earlier traditional associations, primarily the churches and missions in the district. In the Downtown Eastside (as in Strathcona) the displacement of traditional groupings is far from complete, for the religious organizations continue to offer a wide range of social services. But the division between the groups is sharp. Particularly among the missions, the underlying ideology is Christian charity to individuals in need, while DERA demands social justice and citizenship rights. While the missions are primarily non-political and individualistic in their outreach, DERA is strongly political and systemic in its analysis. Indeed its universalistic message of social inequality, redistribution, and community control necessarily have brought the association into a relationship with the welfare state that has frequently been marked by conflict. Among the paradoxes of DERA are its longevity as a protest organization for poor people, and the success of its socialist strategy in a political culture which, aside from short periods, has been dominated by conservative parties.

Unwittingly, then, in the Downtown Eastside, the permissive environment of benevolent liberalism helped create a political subject, the Downtown Eastside Residents' Association. Quickly DERA found its own socialist ideology, an ideology not of consultation but of control, informed by a trades-union model of tough negotiation backed up by a 'strike' (conflict) mandate, a model familiar to a largely retired workforce with many former union members. In an intriguing instance of organizational crossover, a political model learned in the realm of production has been practised in the realm of consumption. Benefiting from a large membership, charismatic leadership, and a shifting and sometimes surprising network of allies, DERA has forcibly pressed its case before often resistant levels of the state for twenty years. Its objectives have been advanced on several fronts: a symbolic-cultural struggle to remake the identity of the district, a political struggle with the city over legitimacy, a welfare struggle over the provision of services (notably housing), and, most recently, a territorial struggle to defend the district before the incursions of corporate redevelopment.

A LANDSCAPE OF MARGINALITY

The Downtown Eastside, Vancouver's original townsite, is the city's oldest neighbourhood.[3] As the central business district and middle-class residences moved westwards, the East End became home to a working-class community employed on the waterfront and, in Chinatown and Japantown, included two racial enclaves. It became the metropolitan extension of the provincial resource economy. Along the waterfront, canneries, sawmills, meat-packing plants, and metal-working shops were either processors or suppliers of the province's staple industries. At the foot of Carrall Street, the Union Steamship Docks represented the hub from which a human cargo departed to replenish the work camps and small resource-based settlements up and down the coast. From these same camps workers returned with the exhilaration of release after a stretch of three or four months in isolation. Alighting at the foot of Carrall, it was a mere two blocks to the intersection with Cordova. 'For fifty years it has been the unchanged main stem of the loggers' district' noted an observer in the 1940s, and within two or three blocks of Cordova and Carrall were a dozen hotels with beer parlours frequented by loggers and other resource workers, as well as cafés, outfitting shops, employment agencies, tailors, and barbers – a commercial entourage dedicated to servicing the needs of single men with a 'lucky stake' (Knight 1980, 29).

During the poverty of the 1930s the Downtown Eastside became a hotbed of political mobilization, with its union halls and the Powell Street Grounds (today, Oppenheimer Park) a rallying place for demonstrations and labour marches, leading to several bitter conflicts with the police. In 1935 a thousand striking longshoremen approaching Ballantyne Pier hurled bricks and stones against the tear gas and batons of city and provincial police. The same spring the latest of numerous demonstrations of the unemployed ended with Mayor McGeer reading the Riot Act in Victory Square to a group of unemployed men who had occupied the Hudson's Bay Store. The next month, following a May Day rally of 15,000 at the Powell Street Grounds, a division of unemployed men based in the East End Ukrainian Hall occupied the Carnegie Library at Hastings and Main.[4] Confrontations were renewed in 1938 when another delegation of men out of work occupied the Post Office and Art

Gallery for a month before being broken up by a tear-gas assault by police (Roy 1980, 102).

This rich and conflictual labour history has provided both an inspiration and an object lesson to community organizers over the past two decades. Progress means struggle for the underdog, and the unchanged old landscape of the Downtown Eastside is full of symbolic associations: the Carnegie Library, Victory Square, Ballantyne Pier, the Powell Street Grounds, the various labour halls – all remain landmarks charged with a collective memory of conflict. Struggle is far more than an intellectual abstraction; it is a central preoccupation of everyday life. The task of the community organizer, like the union organizer of an earlier period, has been to make individual troubles the basis for a shared social project.

Following wartime recovery, the landscape and its residents became yet more marginal to mainstream society. By the end of the 1940s there was a high concentration of retired resource workers living in small, inexpensive units, and including a surprising number who had been injured and handicapped in industrial accidents. 'There were old bachelors living in rooming houses, old bunkhouses and row cabins scattered in profusion all along the No. 20 line from Victoria Drive to the city's inner core. On one stretch of Pender Street every second building was a pensioners' hotel' (Knight 1980, 50-1). By the 1960s they had been joined by a transient population of middle-aged and elderly men, some alcoholic, Native people, and transient youth. Substance abuse became rife: 'In 1957, at the age of thirteen, I began living in this community. Hastings and Main was then called "the corner" ... I turned out on heroin at thirteen, in Mission. Then, it was just a matter of coming down to 'the corner' here in Vancouver to buy ... When I was fourteen or fifteen I got charged with living off the avails of prostitution. Gloria, the woman I was living with, was in her twenties and we got busted in the Balmoral ... I was more bisexual than gay; certainly I had sexual relations with men as well as women, but I would work men in terms of raising money.'[5] To those who had known the district, a qualitative change had taken place: 'I used to spend so much time down around Carrall and along the waterfront ... It used to be a lively place where the action was. But today it's sleazy, worse than sleazy.'[6]

The neighbourhood was now addressed publicly in the discourse of skid road (see figure 6.1).[7] Its forty to fifty city blocks included twenty-six beer parlours, two liquor stores, and eleven missions. With less than 2 per cent of Vancouver's population, it accounted for one-third of the city's homicides, aggravated assaults, and robberies, and two-thirds of

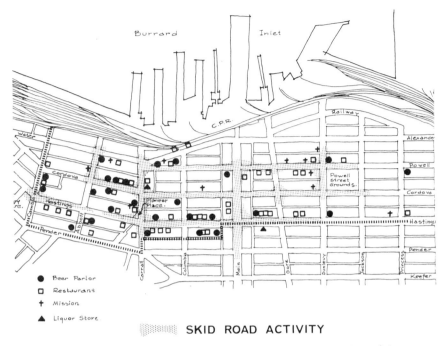

- ● Beer Parlor
- □ Restaurant
- † Mission
- ▲ Liquor Store

SKID ROAD ACTIVITY

FIGURE 6.1.   The discourse of skid road: the city's representation of the Downtown Eastside in 1965 (Source: City of Vancouver 1965).

drunkenness charges, though these numbers included repeat offenders plus non-resident 'tourists' on a spree.[8] A second city report six years later described 'Skid Road Vancouver' as having expanded farther, with a five-block extension southwards on Main Street (City of Vancouver, Social Planning Department 1971).

Meanwhile, a second and very different assault was being made upon the character of the Downtown Eastside. In 1965 the Canadian Pacific Railway (CPR) announced plans for Project 200, a vast redevelopment which would demolish much of Gastown, the blocks along Water Street, closest to the central business district (see figure 6.1). Preservation interests began to mobilize in defence of Vancouver's townsite and its buildings, and in 1968 the Community Arts Council organized a successful walking tour of 700 interested persons (Astles 1972). The publicity attending the tour turned back the threat of Project 200, gave momentum to reinvestment and renovation in Gastown, and by mid 1971 more than a hundred new businesses were established, including restaurants, boutiques, and import shops. While there was, as one journalist saw it, a strange blend of 'Crêpe Suzette and cockroaches,' renovation was also directed to several Gastown hotels and rooming-houses, and with it came eviction notices to low-income and often long-time residents (Lautens 1970).

Simultaneously, then, the Downtown Eastside faced the contradictory impulses of decline and gentrification, frustrating any attempts to consolidate a stable, decent, and affordable district for low-income people. Such an outcome seemed implausible, if not impossible, for a neighbourhood of poor, elderly, handicapped, and politically disorganized residents facing the powerful forces of slumming, on the one hand, and up-market reinvestment, on the other. One long-time resident of the district saw the need clearly: 'The peculiar thing about poor people is they live helplessly, and without experience of helping others. All they have to do is sign a petition or come to a meeting, talk, do something for their own sake. But they don't. That's why we have to have a leader better suited to our type of people. One that's persuasive, with the kind of personality to gather people and convince people. But the leader must come from our area ... We need a big man, we really need a big man.'[9] In many respects, it was precisely this unlikely development which took place in the early 1970s.

THE DOWNTOWN EASTSIDE RESIDENTS' ASSOCIATION (DERA)

A survey undertaken in 1970 shortly in advance of DERA's founding, indicated the scale of the needs and challenges confronting any aspiring neighbourhood association (City of Vancouver, Social Planning Department 1971). Among a population of almost 7,000, 80 per cent were white males, with 46 per cent over 55 years of age; Asians and native Indians completed the racial mix. Among the housing stock, three of every four units was a sleeping room, without kitchen and washroom facilities, and generally less than one hundred square feet in size; not surprisingly, 85 per cent of residents lived alone. Only half the respondents had a personal doctor, in a community where all seven tuberculosis deaths in Vancouver occurred in 1977, where suicides were eight times greater than the city average, and where life expectancies lagged behind the norm by four years for men and a disturbing seventeen years for women.[10] The proportion of physically, emotionally, and psychologically handicapped persons was high; a later estimate placed the figure at near 50 per cent.[11] In summer 1970, 86 per cent were retired or unemployed, and supported by various forms of social assistance.

This profile accorded with the popular stereotype of the district. Far more discordant, however, were other characteristics of the population. The community was highly stable; indeed, the second most stable in the city; 40 per cent of those interviewed had lived in the district over ten years, and a similar proportion had lived at their present address for three years or more. Transiency was a visible, but a minority, feature in the area. If given an opportunity to move elsewhere, half the respondents would elect to remain in the district. For those living alone in small rooms, outside sources of socialization were inevitably significant, but, none the less, 40 per cent never drank in beer parlours. Alternative recreational options were limited, although in fine weather a number of older men used the small parks of Victory Square or Oppenheimer as a communal living-room (Hall 1974). Beneath the veneer of skid row was a more complex reality incorporating a substantial opportunity for community building; DERA's mission became one of transforming a potential social community into an actual political one, of making a social base into a social force.

Following its social reports on skid row in 1965 and 1971, the city's social planning department sponsored a federally funded People's Aide program in the district in 1972. It was administered by Peter Davies, a social planner who had previously been a community worker at First United Church. Its objective was to hire neighbourhood non-professionals as community problem solvers in such areas as housing, pension, and welfare issues. Bruce Eriksen noticed an advertisement for the program while recovering from a back injury sustained on the job as a steelworker. To that point he had sensed an absence of any political entitlement: 'Before that time when I went past City Hall I thought it was some high class place that I couldn't even go into. I don't think I even voted up to that time. But I soon formed an opinion that the City was a corporation and that we're all equal shareholders. We want our share.'[12] Eriksen applied successfully for a position as a People's Aide. The neighbourhood's 'big man' had arrived.

Up to 1972, Eriksen's life was an incarnation of the Downtown Eastside. His schooling had ended at Grade 3, and by his teenage years he was a resident of the Downtown Eastside, taking advantage of the wartime boom in manufacturing and the resource sector. He worked in the Burrard Inlet shipyards, in logging camps, as an ironworker, on con-

FIGURE 6.2.   Bruce Eriksen, redundant in 1978 following the city's denial of
DERA's grant, as political artist in the Downtown Eastside (Photograph:
Downtown East 48, July 1978).

struction, and even as an artist (see figure 6.2).[13] The daily round of
the beer parlours took its toll and he became an alcoholic who reha-
bilitated in 1958. As a People's Aide, and reflecting more analytically
on the daily life he knew at first hand, Eriksen's political judgment was
quickly refined. He began to argue with Davies about the scope of the
People's Aide program: 'It was the same strategy as the agencies and
the churches. Take each individual by the hand. But the problem was
not with individuals in the first instance. We need to educate people
about their rights and how to fight for them. Fight to have our rights
enforced or the law changed.'[14] Following Eriksen's urging, Davies called

a public meeting at First United Church and it was decided to form the Downtown Eastside Residents' Association; formal incorporation occurred in August 1973.[15] Eriksen's style was uncompromising. As a candidate for the Community Resources Board elections in 1975 he described himself as a Downtown Eastside resident for over twenty years and 'tough, outspoken and never gives up,'[16] an assessment fully endorsed in his tenure as organizer and executive member of DERA from 1973 until the end of 1980, when, as a newly elected alderman, he relinquished formal leadership of the group.

Eriksen's strong personality attracted considerable media attention, and tended to overshadow other workers, to the extent that criticism emerged at City Hall that DERA was a one-man show. But in fact leadership was broadly based, and, depending on the state of government grants, up to ten workers were on the DERA payroll at any one time. Among these the most persevering were Libby Davies (daughter of Peter Davies) and Jean Swanson. Ms. Davies moved into the Downtown Eastside in 1973, as a university graduate working on a government grant; she took on a number of DERA projects as member of the executive, including day care, the Community Resources Board, and the Neighbourhood Improvement Programme. Married later to Bruce Eriksen, she too was eventually successful in running for municipal office. Jean Swanson was a bar waitress at the Patricia Hotel until persuaded by Eriksen to join DERA's federally funded employment program; for a number of years she was elected secretary on the DERA executive. Later involved in anti-poverty programs she ran unsuccessfully as a candidate in several elections, including the 1988 mayoralty race.

Following the election of Eriksen and Davies in 1980, a second generation of leaders joined the Association. The principal figure was Jim Green as organizer. A neighbourhood resident and old friend of Jean Swanson, Green presented points of continuity in leadership.[17] Having been a steelworker and a former union shop steward, he maintained connections, during his tenure, with the Downtown Eastside's heavy-manufacturing and union tradition. But there were also some differences. Green came to Canada in 1968 to avoid call-up for Vietnam. He did some college teaching and completed a Master's thesis in anthropology; a book-length manuscript on the Canadian Seamen's Union has been published (Green 1986). While Green's style and appearance are tough ('He's solidly built, with a rugged face, and the hands of a steelworker'),[18] more careful attention is paid to public relations, as DERA in the 1980s

FIGURE 6.3.   Jim Green addressing followers during an action by the CRAB Park committee (Photograph: Kris Olds).

moved from a conflict model in its dealings with the state to one which alternates between conflict and co-production. None the less, despite a group of hard-working and able co-workers like Stephen Learey, Green's powerful presence continued the pattern of 'a big man' leading DERA (see figure 6.3).

   While charisma and persistence have been associated with DERA's success, a major factor has been the size of its membership. The announcement of the Association's founding in 1973 was joined by a report of a petition with 232 names to urge an improvement of street lighting.[19] Numbers grew steadily: to 520 a year later, to 1,250 in September 1975, and topping 2,000 by the end of 1976. At the annual general meeting of October 1983, 3,746 members were claimed, and by 1989 a total of 4,500.[20] Like few other organizations, DERA was characterized by an inclusiveness that transcended racial boundaries. Bilingual membership cards were printed in English and Cantonese in its first year, and translation services were available at monthly meetings. A successful seniors' club was begun in 1976 and, in the capable hands of Anna Wong, grew in numbers. By 1989 a third of DERA members were Chinese Canadians, mainly women.

These numbers have been of political importance, for, like other groups with enemies at City Hall, DERA constantly had to resist challenges to its legitimacy in the community. Convincing endorsement was also received from its performance in community elections: eight of ten DERA candidates were elected to the Downtown Community Resources Board in 1975, and the same year the Association also won control of the elected local planning committee for neighbourhood improvement.[21] Most impressive, at least to the media, and most embarrassing to City Council, was DERA's ability to mobilize support when its annual operating grant was denied by Council. In the late 1970s it assembled 52 delegations who urged Council to change its mind and, in 1983, in a setting which approached high farce, signed up 150 delegations to present briefs to Council in support of its appeal.

Challenges of non-representativeness could be readily made in a district where social agencies and church groups were thick on the ground. A quick count identified 39 agencies active in the mid 1980s, with often competing agendas and definite views on their respective turfs.[22] The churches had already well-established ministries before DERA's founding. First United has maintained a very visible set of neighbourhood services, including in recent years a social housing association; St James Anglican Church similarly has a strong community program. Of a rather different character are the missions. The Central City Mission was founded in 1910, and by the 1960s its 300-bed hostel was offering clothing and serving 115,000 meals a year. The Salvation Army offers a hostel, medical care, food and clothing, job placement, and a detoxification centre. These were only the principal religious actors; others included the Franciscan Sisters of Atonement, Catholic Charities, Union Gospel Mission, and a number of smaller outreach groups.[23]

DERA's relationship to the churches and social agencies has been ambivalent. Fundamentally, there was an ideological difference, particularly with the missions, in the diagnosis of the district's problems. 'We have the church, state and social agencies all joining in to "alleviate" the misery and suffering of the exploited poor,' declared an early DERA statement:

'the church can be said to have failed in its mission. A program that replaces incentive with dependence cannot be said to have worked.'[24] By the end of each month the missions were serving close to 2,000 meals a day, but to Jean Swanson it was a case of 'hunger, handouts and humiliation.'[25] Conflict arose with more secular local agencies. Disagreement with the Downtown Community Health Society over a site for a new health facility led to the society's director recommending rejection of DERA's grant application before City Council.[26] Relations soured with the administration of the Carnegie Centre, a community library and leisure facility for which DERA had strenuously lobbied over a six-year period. In 1983 the Carnegie Centre's director, a former DERA ally, resigned, citing pressure from DERA to 'discredit board members and myself' in an alleged struggle over influence in the community.[27] As members of City Council in the 1980s, Eriksen and Davies also consistently voted against civic funding for the Downtown Eastside Economic Development Society; ironically the frequent appearance of DEEDS before Council is reminiscent of the persistent appeals of DERA for its own civic grant.[28]

Nor was there undue respect for social workers and other outside professionals as they related to the community. An early viewpoint assailed 'the hordes of social workers who hover like vultures over the place ... keeping it half-dead by their very presence, existing off that half-deadness which they sustain and which is beneficial only to them.'[29] Even the departure of Peter Davies, the social planner who had helped found DERA, evoked little sentimentality; indeed, it 'will be welcomed by all of us in this community who are striving to take charge of our collective destiny.'[30] Libby Davies presented the DERA viewpoint succinctly: 'It's time we told City Hall we have no use for expensive hired hands. We have competent workers of our own.'[31]

Ideology, Strategy, Tactics

For the third issue of *Downtown East*, Bruce Eriksen wrote a letter to the editor, outlining 'the purpose of the Downtown Eastside Residents' Association.'[32] Four objectives were listed:

1. To help the people of the Downtown Eastside gain control over the forces which affect their lives.
2. To inform the people as to how to go about demanding change and/or preventing disruption in the community.

3. To make the people aware of *their own power* to make changes of political importance.
4. To set the processes of change in motion by honest collaboration between the people and the organization. The targets of the Association include the following:

> Unconcerned, inadequate or corrupt officials, public planners and bureaucratic units such as Welfare Departments; ... individual oppressors such as landlords, exploitable [*sic*] business owners such as beer parlor owners ...

It was not long before these objectives were restated in politically more soothing language, and in this form they have been adhered to by the second-generation leadership in the 1980s. But perhaps the original formulation laid bare the underlying ideology more clearly.

Community control for community change is the underpinning dynamic. DERA stands opposed to exploitation, but it is equally wary of paternalism, a stand consistent with its scepticism concerning agencies, planners, and 'outside' organizations with a local presence. Implicit is a superior local knowledge and commitment among residents, equipping them more fully to engage in social planning. Help therefore means self-help. In the words of the Association's unpublished autobiography: 'DERA is an example of a community group that has grown organically from the people in the community rather than from outsiders. Since the early 1970s, DERA has followed the principles in the tradition of many unions. With this re-birth has come a regaining of power and control by many now-elderly builders and citizens of the community' (Green 1983, 1). The union model has exerted an abiding influence on DERA. Both Eriksen and Green have been union members, Green a shop steward in the Marine Workers and Boilermakers Union, Eriksen a member of the militant Canadian Seamen's Union (the subject of Green's book) and the Iron Workers Union. With his strong union background, Green has seen the parallel most clearly, identifying DERA 'in organization, structure and philosophy as a trade union for the people of this community.'[33] Thus there are monthly meetings when the elected executive is accountable to its membership, the rank and file. Like a union closed shop, members must be local residents, living within prescribed boundaries, or else, if outside the district, elderly, and thus part of the distinctive cohort that DERA represents. In this manner local control is upheld.

The pursuit of local goals has not led to a flawed parochialism. DERA workers have been supportive of broader coalitions and special needs.

They have been associated with city-wide housing and tenants' initiatives and welfare-rights issues, while endorsing the peace movement and labour movements, including the Solidarity Coalition (supported in rallies by 'hundreds of DERA members') which brought the province to the verge of a general strike in 1983. Besides neighbourhood issues, telegrammes to the prime minister have included protests at cruise-missile testing in Canada, and advice that the prime minister 'demand the immediate withdrawal of all foreign troops from Grenada.'[34] Its view of society, then, is one which is systemic and does not lose sight of 'the bigger picture when we take on a small issue.'[35] From its early years, DERA has distanced itself from agencies which limit themselves to treating the symptoms of victims. There was an initial disagreement over the goals of the People's Aide project, which amounted ultimately, in Libby Davies's view, to 'a babysitting service' (Priest, Harris, and Wong 1983, ch. 9, 1). Rather than dealing with victims, DERA went to 'the source.'[36] Its view of causality, together with its activism, rhetoric, and endorsement of democratic socialist politicians, have incited red-baiting by political opponents. Eriksen has been extremely resistant to this political labelling: 'We got this left-wing image because we were labelled by businessmen. But the real issue was enforcement of the law. We had to be organized and fight for our rights. Fight to have them enforced or the laws changed. My philosophy was formed by [Mayor] Art Phillips who said people must obey the law. But everywhere I looked I saw people breaking the law. We were fighting for equal treatment for all, wherever you live ... I have never ever read communist philosophy, Karl Marx and all that shit. I made my own conclusions. What I saw was unfair. That had nothing to do with socialism.'[37] Eriksen's testiness is understandable in light of the crass political caricatures directed at him; for other DERA leaders, however, evidence of a theoretical class analysis is apparent. However, its socialism is not abstract, but rather a socialism with a pragmatic face, confronting real issues oppressing real people and offering real strategies to resolve them. Solutions require access to power: 'I learned one thing as a shop steward. Justice, morality, decency ... don't count for anything to the people making decisions. If you want to get treated fairly you have to have power.'[38]

DERA has engaged in a range of strategies to give substance to its objectives. The initial task has been to lobby, to be visible, to make community needs known. Politicians of every stripe were invited on, and usually undertook, walking tours of the district to view conditions and needs at first hand. Unusual more in size than in character was a walking tour in July 1984 with forty-two politicians from all three levels of government, the chairman of the Expo 86 Corporation and the directors of the Port of Vancouver and the Regional Office of Canada Mortgage and Housing Corporation (CMHC).[39] Following the tour, DERA presented an eight-point proposal to the group 'to save the neighbourhood.'

Walking tours were only one of a multifaceted lobbying and information strategy. Frequent delegations to City Council, the Provincial Legislature in Victoria, and in later years a few trips to Ottawa were part of pressuring the various levels of the state. As necessary, these were joined by petitions, rallies, pickets, and suits in the courts to force the issue. In a 1983 letter, Glenn Bullard, DERA president, wrote with diplomatic understatement that, 'to achieve our objective, DERA has often taken strong positions calling for the enactment of new laws or the enforcement of existing laws.'[40] An elaboration of 'strong positions' by Bruce Eriksen more faithfully captured the spirit of tactics during the 1970s: 'We raised hell with City Council if we didn't get what we wanted.'[41]

An escalation of tactics was the norm in dealing with government: 'We used their own laws and by-laws against them. Every argument we used was based on their alleged position. We tried to do it the nice way first. When that wasn't forthcoming, we had to embarrass them.'[42] Embarrassment typically took the form of picket lines or a well-publicized delegation before Council. The delegations were blunt and devoid of the niceties a middle-class Council had grown accustomed to. In October 1973 five men died in a hotel fire in the Downtown Eastside. While the liberal councillors of The Electors Action Movement (TEAM) laboriously debated the matter, council chambers filled with a motley gathering of DERA members carrying placards reading 'TEAM fiddles while skid road burns' and 'Slumlord abuses, council excuses.'[43] Raucous gatherings before Council became an unwelcome experience of elected officials and personal vendettas were instigated which took their toll during DERA's annual quest before Council for a civic grant to support organizers.

Embarrassment was frequently a successful tactic. In 1974 a construction strike halted work on projects across the city, including Oppenheimer Lodge, a social-housing project in the Downtown Eastside, which was already much delayed. A deal, however, was struck between the City and the construction unions to continue work on the Granville Mall, a pet downtown project of the new mayor and Council. DERA picketed the mall and persuaded construction workers to walk off the job. The picket line would be lifted, Libby Davies promised, when 'the city can work out a similar agreement to get work going again on Oppenheimer Lodge.'[44] A furious mayor sent DERA a letter assuring them their action would 'not have any effect on the construction of Oppenheimer Lodge.' But four days later the building trades decided to exempt Oppenheimer Lodge from strike action, and DERA lifted its picket line on the mall. Aside from this embarrassment, the mayor earned a week of bad press from Vancouver's dailies.[45]

A celebrated ruse using embarrassment as a tactic was the widely reported Crummy Cockroach Haven Contest in which Downtown Eastside residents were invited to submit entries nominating the 'three sleaziest dives' in the district.[46] The contest was part of a campaign to have the city enforce its own by-laws covering the standards of maintenance of downtown rooms and businesses. The results of the contest were handed over to the Human Services Committee of Council, and a month later the health department laid charges against four premises, including the 'winner' of the Cockroach Haven award. The charges against a second hotel were laid the day after DERA called in a television crew who broadcast its conditions to a large viewing public. The citizens seemed to be setting the city's agenda. Following continuous pressure from DERA, an interdepartmental team, the Downtown Housing Implementation Committee, was formed, consisting of senior officials of the fire, health, permits, and social planning departments at City Hall and charged to develop a coherent city strategy. Working-class humour was successfully applying pressure to have the city acknowledge its legal responsibilities. In the single-minded pursuit of neighbourhood improvement, not even erstwhile allies were exempt from embarrassment. While endorsing the governing New Democratic Party (NDP) in the 1975 provincial elections, DERA none the less picketed the attorney general's campaign office to protest non-enforcement of fire by-laws.[47]

In the 1980s, DERA's tactics seemed less abrasive, in part because of the very real achievements of the past. As Jim Green said, 'There's less necessity for picketing and rallies now. We can often accomplish with a telephone call what took a picket line in the 1970s. But when we need to, we will do it. I'm involved in a lot of negotiations, meetings with government and so on. I expect to get what I ask for. I tell them I'd rather not embarrass them with 500 pickets and the media.'[48] In the feisty early years, interaction was more physical, and nowhere was this more evident than in relations with hotel operations. Within a few months

TABLE 6.1. Electoral Support for DERA Candidates in Vancouver Civic Elections (in thousands)

	1974	1976	1978	1980	1982	1984	1986	1988	1990
Bruce Eriksen	11.6	21.7	29.4	44.8	52.1	60.8	56.2	52.5	59.1
position	24th	17th	11th	3rd	4th	5th	10th	9th	3rd
Libby Davies		15.3	16.8	*	41.9	57.4	58.2	60.4	69.3
position		22nd	20th		9th	8th	7th	4th	1st
Jean Swanson			18.0	31.7		50.4	47.7	**	
position			19th	16th		13th	16th		
Jim Green								***	

*Elected to Parks Board
**Unsuccessful mayoralty candidate (45,200 votes, or 37 per cent of popular vote)
***Unsuccessful mayoralty candidate (56,800 votes, or 45 per cent of popular vote)

of the founding of DERA, Bruce Eriksen had been banned from five hotels and received verbal and physical threats. On one occasion he was beaten up by bar waiters while challenging the practice of overserving in their establishment. At the end of 1973 he was advised by police to leave town as word had reached them that there was a contract out on his life.

While all of these actions were a means to empowerment, the political deck was stacked against DERA. At City Council, during the 1970s there were only two or three votes that could be counted on, while, at the provincial level, the 1975–86 period was one of almost total frustration. There had to be an electoral as well as a pressure-group strategy. 'The only possible way,' observed Eriksen, 'for the people of this city to realize their ambitions for this city is to elect a group of politicians who are willing to carry out their platform' (Priest, Harris, and Wong 1983, ch. 9, 23). Never one to lead from behind, he ran for Council in the 1974 election. In an at-large civic system, with ten elected councillors, he came in twenty-fourth, with more than 11,000 votes, a commendable-enough performance for a first-time candidate with a narrow base (see table 6.1). Libby Davies also ran for office in 1976, both of them with the socialist Committee of Progressive Electors (COPE), and, in 1978, with Jean Swanson as a third candidate, all three DERA organizers had their names on the ballot paper. Just missing election in 1978, Eriksen was swept to office in 1980, with Libby Davies elected as a parks commissioner. Two years later she joined Eriksen on Council, a position she sustained through the 1980s. With Harry Rankin, a lawyer with a Downtown Eastside office, and the only COPE incumbent on Council during the 1970s, the ten-person council has, since 1982, included no fewer than three members with roots in the Downtown Eastside, a district with 2 per cent of Vancouver's population. During the 1980-6 period of Mayor Harcourt's tenure, the effect on city politics towards the Downtown Eastside was palpable, if contested by feuding groups on Council. As Jim Green aptly, if modestly, observed, 'More can be accomplished in one election than DERA can accomplish in 10 years.'[49]   Electoral success indicated also DERA's broadening civic role in left-wing politics. Aside from Eriksen and Davies, Jean Swanson ran as COPE's mayoralty candidate in 1988, followed by Jim Green in 1990, winning 45 per cent of the popular vote. Moreover, present and former DERA workers assumed prominent positions in the Waterfront Coalition, the CRAB Park organization,[50] the Tenants' Rights Coalition, the End Legislated Poverty group, and the Grandview-Woodlands Area Council (the district east of the Downtown Eastside). DERA has become a training school for leaders of progressive causes – a point that has not escaped the attention of conservative politicians, as we shall see.

Cultural-Symbolic Struggles

A fundamental objective of DERA has been to redefine the meaning of its district. As long as the discourse of skid row prevailed, so too did a characteristic set of labelling perceptions and practices which became self-fulfilling. At least one alderman imputed that Downtown Eastside residents did not (could not?) read and thus did not warrant the cost of a renovated Carnegie Centre; judges, in levying minimal fines on slum landlords, imputed responsibility on the lifestyle of their tenants; and City Hall, in zoning much of the district as industrial, imputed that residents ultimately could only be transients.

An initial objective, then, was to reclaim the district at the level of meaning. DERA's president noted in a 1983 letter to two area members of Parliament that 'for ten years, DERA has pursued its constitutional objective to improve the life of the community. Our fundamental strategy has been to organize our members, and other local residents and merchants to demand that the Downtown Eastside be recognized by all as a residential neighbourhood and not simply Skid Road.'[51] Or, as Jim Green (1983) put it, 'we hope to challenge the erroneous attitude that the Downtown Eastside is a "second class neighbourhood" or a "skid row" – labels created by outsiders.' Skid road was a construct of the outsider, whether social agency, business person, government, or 'suburban yahoo' looking for a night on the town: 'They have invented "Skid Road" and they intend to sustain the invention.'[52]

DERA challenged the discourse of skid road with the discourse of community. Tirelessly it reminded outsiders of the district's stability, of the loyalty of many elderly men to it, of the small minority who were transients and alcoholics. The media were an important aid in public education, with in-depth investigative articles opening up the plural and contested meanings of the Downtown Eastside.[53] Under the heading of community advocacy, DERA's president wrote to the director of Social Planning that 'the organizer recently assisted the producers of CKVU's Vancouver Show to develop a television series on people who live in the Downtown Eastside, to present neighbourhood residents as they really are, rather than as stereotypes.'[54] As one of its first tasks in 1973, DERA promoted the concept not of skid row but of the Downtown Eastside: a new name for a new identity. Contested too were the boundaries of the district. While the city had limited its designation to a small area with the most pronounced skid-row indicators, DERA claimed a far more expansive territory of downtown districts characterized by unorganized poor and elderly residents in rooming-houses and residential hotels.

A residential area should not have industrial zoning, and in the 1970s DERA pressed successfully for rezoning and, consequently, designation as a neighbourhood-improvement area, thereby achieving both confirmation of status as a stable community, and also government funds for community improvement. Like any other neighbourhood group, DERA negotiated for new facilities in the language of what was appropriate for a residential area. Improved services – the Carnegie Centre, CRAB Park, new social housing – were appropriate and successfully lobbied for, while noxious facilities were resisted both successfully (the closure of the liquor store at Main and Hastings) and unsuccessfully (the 'dumping' of a heroin addiction centre and a 'monstrous remand centre' in the district by the provincial government). But if overruled by the province, DERA was able to reformulate the meaning of its territory with important figures in the city. With the new terms of reference from neighbourhood-improvement designation in place, the director of planning had rejected the heroin centre as a non-conforming land use which 'detracts from the residential character of the area.'[55] And a civic citation from Mayor Harcourt's office in 1983 declared that 'the Downtown Eastside Residents Association has helped to change the concept of an area of our city formerly known as "Skid Road" to the Downtown Eastside.'[56]

Political-Organizational Struggles: The Civic Grant

In an important respect, DERA was a creation of the state. The 1972 liberal council sought to extend entitlement to the Downtown Eastside, and supported the People's Aide program which led to the formation of DERA. Like any neighbourhood organization, DERA lacked core funding, and while the federal government, with a remarkable spirit of boldness, showered the Association with a quarter of a million dollars over its first three years for a job-training program, the city provided annual grants for the salary of staff. For 1974 and 1975, the annual grant program endorsed by Council funded two DERA organizers.[57] But this honeymoon with the local state was short-lived. The persistent and abrasive nature of the Association's tactics annoyed the thin-skinned liberals on council. Rather than being orchestrated from City Hall, DERA was developing its own agenda, its own style, and its own politics in its relation with COPE – and all of this was focused on the strong personality of Eriksen, who, month after month, publicly assailed Council over its policy failures in the Downtown Eastside.

In 1976 DERA's civic grant was rejected and there began what for almost ten years was an annual pantomime of rejection, appeal, mass delegations to Council, and widespread and sympathetic publicity from the media, which had the quite unintended effect of broadening the Association's base and advertising its issues in a city-wide forum – contributing, no doubt, to the electoral success of its candidates for public office in 1980, after the Association had been mauled by Council three years in a row. Council members accused DERA of being 'too political' and conservatives, of 'promoting class warfare.'[58] Despite a raking over the coals by City Hall reporters, councillors did not reduce their criticism in subsequent years, although it entailed a calculated political risk. Indeed, at least one liberal may well have lost her seat on Council in part because of her opposition to DERA. Alderwoman Ford spearheaded the 1983 rejection of DERA's grant, which represented the most carnivalesque conflict of all, with DERA lining up 150 delegations and applying to use a sound truck for three days to rally its forces. Mrs Ford suffered a surprising lapse of support in the 1984 election, while the three DERA candidates for Council enjoyed their best year. Thereafter conservative members of council realized the political cost of opposition, in terms of both inflating public sympathy for DERA and damaging their own electoral base. Despite a right-wing majority, the city councils of the late 1980s have given almost *pro forma* approval to DERA's annual grant request.

The struggle over the civic grant was waged over both charisma and content. Eriksen's style irritated many council members; one moved to support funds for two DERA organizers in 1978 as long as Eriksen was not one of them.[59] But, as the years passed, a greater concern was that DERA was establishing its own and competing power base. In an astonishing tirade at a public hearing on redevelopment of the Expo lands in 1989, a former conservative alderman alleged that DERA lobbied for social housing on the site only so that it could stuff it with 'vote fodder.' 'That seemed to be the feeling of council, they were too political,' observed Alderwoman Brown in 1983 when DERA's was the only submission rejected of seventy-two for a civic grant. 'Jim Green spent an awful lot of time at City Hall and council felt that if he spent half his time on political work, and half his time on community work, we should only pay half the salary.'[60]

Jim Green was not fazed by Council's rejection: 'Our presence is a continuous thorn in their sides. I'm sure we've insulted them. We represent the people and they represent special interests ... This is going to make things tough, but we will come back even tougher.'[61]

Welfare Struggles: The Housing Question

Good-quality housing has been an abiding central objective of DERA lobbyists. In the 1970s the goal was to ensure the most rudimentary standards of safety and hygiene. In the 1980s the association's mandate broadened to the provision of locally managed social housing. But, in both instances, achieving its objective was dependent upon its dealings with the welfare state, and it is through the housing question that the dialectical relationship between the community organization and the state may be seen most clearly, as it has evolved from conflict towards a cautious co-production.

In the early 1970s by-law standards in the Downtown Eastside were lax and irregularly enforced. Fire was a serious hazard, and during 1973 ten men perished in hotel and rooming-house fires. Over the course of the year, no fewer than 107 skid-road fires occurred; the Cobalt Hotel was in flames on seven separate occasions.[62] Following a fatal October fire in the Commercial Hotel, DERA picketed City Hall and attended

Council chambers *en masse*, demanding the upgrading and enforcement of fire standards. A flurry of activity at City Hall followed, with new fire regulations and a new promise of enforcement; ten hotels were said to have been closed down in the previous year for violating the existing code. But hotel owners confronting a significant bill were slow to comply, and the fires continued. Following a further fatal fire at the end of October 1974, a demonstration of 150 DERA supporters issued a statement to Council: 'You have succumbed to the whims of landlords when they threaten to close down their premises rather than comply with health and fire standards ... We urge Council to assume the responsibility it was elected with. You are playing with people's lives and we will not stand by and watch it happen any longer.'[63] Thereafter compliance and enforcement were practised, and with the installation of sprinkler systems the fire hazard almost disappeared.

One reason why hotel owners hesitated in upgrading was the economics of operating residential rooms. While this is a controversial question, the frequent closures and conversions to other uses suggest that some operations at least were marginal. The critical variable in a hotel's profit margin was its beer parlour. It was said that in 1982 the Europe Hotel earned revenues of $550,000 from its pub, but management was not prepared to transfer its profits into repairs and maintenance. Before it was converted into social-housing units, the owner of the architecturally distinct Europe Hotel had plans to capitalize on its heritage designation and Gastown location with an upmarket renovation. But these improvements would not benefit existing tenants. Despite a net income of $220,000 in 1982, the Europe had complied with only a quarter of the improvements ordered by the City up to three years before. 'I have held off the improvements waiting for this [renovation] plan,' observed the owner. 'You don't think I would restore it for the derelicts living there now, do you?'[64]

It was this prejudice which DERA confronted in its attempt to improve living standards, and with it a laggardly pattern of code enforcement plus a forgiving judiciary. Following success with the fire by-law, DERA directed its attention to the Standards of Maintenance code. Here it confronted a foot-dragging civic bureaucracy, which was challenged by a prolonged campaign in 1978.[65] DERA noted that the Warren Hotel had been visited seventeen times by inspectors before orders were issued, while the Cascade Hotel was visited eighteen times in a year, given a list of orders seven pages long, and then granted a licence before these were followed up.[66] The scale of violations was staggering. In an exhaustive joint investigation of 23 hotels by DERA and city inspectors in 1978, close to 10,000 code violations were detected, an average of 7-8 violations per room.[67] Yet attacking code enforcement simply released a hydra's head of attendant problems. First, the effort and expense of prosecutions produced no deterrents in the courts. The Warren Hotel (winner of the Crummy Cockroach Haven award) was found guilty of infringing by-laws and fined $100; the Cascade Hotel was found guilty on 12 counts and fined $600, the minimum penalty.[68] In a DERA-supported action, 37 tenants, primarily Chinese pensioners, at the East Hotel took their landlord to Small Claims Court on breach of contract for not providing heat or hot water and not cleaning filthy premises. This promising precedent was torpedoed by the court's response; after an eighteen-month struggle it found in the tenants' favour, and awarded each of them damages of $25.[69]

Code enforcement also raised the risk of closure. A defence of the East Hotel was that it was losing money and could not afford a sprinkler system and other mandated improvements; refused a redevelopment permit, it was still empty in 1982. By the autumn of 1974, 21 hotels faced closure notices for non-compliance with the new by-laws; two years later more than 1,500 rooms had been closed.[70] Closures for non-compliance of by-laws and summary evictions of tenants have continued through the 1980s.[71] The carrying out of improvements has also proven a two-edged sword, accompanied as it often has been by rent increases and evictions. In one instance, 63 tenants of a rooming-house fought successfully to turn back rent increases of up to 118 per cent, after the owner had spent $50,000 on a sprinkler system and new wiring.[72]

So the solution of code enforcement raised a new series of problems. DERA addressed each of these in turn, but also, as we shall see, turned to a broader housing strategy. Rent increases and summary evictions were a daily fact of life in the Downtown Eastside because occupants of residential hotels had no legal protections, falling outside the terms of the Landlord and Tenant Act passed by the NDP government in the early 1970s to establish tenants' rights. DERA files are full of the human cost of non-protection, for example, of a case thrown out by the courts against the Columbia Hotel for evicting a tenant of twenty years' standing with one day's notice on Good Friday[73] – though worse was to come with the evictions and rent increases accompanying Expo in 1985-6. A subsequent Residential Tenancy Act required each resident of a hotel or rooming-house to apply separately for designation, and thus protection, as a tenant. It was a hopeless task, but DERA staff gamely aided residents on an individual basis to seek designation. After intensive lobbying, picketing of government agencies, and mounting frustration over fifteen years, some measure of success was finally attained with the passage of amendments to the Residential Tenancy Act in 1989, extending normal tenant protections to hotel and rooming-house residents by right.[74]

But the difficulties with code enforcement also prompted a broader vision of necessary change. Strong and enforced by-laws and tenant protection were important, but so too was some protection from the vagaries of a purely market-driven housing stock. The role of the state was critical, not only as regulator, but also as housing supplier. In the summer of 1976, Bruce Eriksen took the federal minister for urban affairs and the constituency member of Parliament on a walkabout, and proposed to them that the new federal Residential Rehabilitation Assistance Programme (RRAP), with loans and grants for targeted older neighbourhoods, be extended to rooming-houses and residential hotels. Six months later, the new minister announced an amendment to RRAP incorporating this proposal, with the Downtown Eastside serving as the first area to be designated.[75] An advantage of RRAP funded renovation was its linkage to rent controls, thus precluding arbitrary rent increases. The program has proven a useful one, and, by the end of 1986, 1,200 units in the Downtown Eastside had been upgraded using RRAP funds.[76]

The third leg of DERA's housing strategy was new social housing. This initiative was already afoot in the early 1970s, primed by the liberal reform councils. The United Housing Foundation purchased and renovated three hotels for low-rent housing.[77] These were followed by three lodges with 381 units built with funding from all three levels of government over the next three years; promises of a total of ten projects were made. DERA, assisting in the settling of tenants, accumulated a waiting-list of 1,100 applicants. But then shifts in government policy, particularly at the provincial level, eroded the funding sources. DERA had strongly endorsed this building program and continued to lobby for it: 'the real solution must be massive construction of low cost housing in our area.'[78] But its appeal fell upon deaf ears at the city council. Following its vigorous enforcement campaign in 1978, DERA presented a policy document to Council in September 1978 with its three-point plan to 'eliminate slum housing': (a) by-law enforcement, (b) renovation, and (c) new housing.[79] The proposal was opposed by twenty hotel owners and a city staff report rejecting new housing; an unfriendly Council eventually disapproved DERA's proposal by a 6–2 margin. The following spring a newly constituted group of city staff, the Downtown Housing Implementation Committee, issued its report with no mention of new housing; its principal author was quoted as claiming that 'non-profit housing would directly compete with private owners.'[80] The report had its genesis in the meeting of Council members with DERA and hotel owners the previous September, and there was no doubting which interest group had caught the ear of Council and its staff.

There was only one avenue to pursue. If the city and province would not sponsor social housing, then DERA would form its own corporation and build the units. This initiative was greeted with considerable scepticism, and the CMHC forwarded a grant of only $500 for the development of a non-profit housing proposal. As so often, DERA broke the rules with a bold and innovative application to the CMHC to purchase and renovate the Stratford Hotel. Room sizes would be doubled, and profits from the beer parlour used to subsidize rents. The CMHC's regional office was 'stumped' at this finessing of due process, and after long deliberations the application was turned back.[81] It was a deeply demoralizing defeat. A full year's work – and hopes – had borne no fruit, and the DERA office had been shut for six months without funds. But within a few months the organization had been turned around. Eriksen and Davies were elected alderman and parks commissioner, and Jim Green had been appointed DERA organizer. DERA's second phase in its housing strategy was underway.

As Jim Green remembers it, DERA backed into the sponsorship of social housing. In the early 1980s, DERA won a huge victory in persuading the provincial government to close its profitable but troublesome liquor store at Main and Hastings. But DERA members were not satisfied 'and wanted to seek retribution for what the liquor store had done to the neighbourhood all those years':[82] they demanded the site from the province for social housing. This was not forthcoming, but the city's social planning department promised that, if DERA would relinquish this demand, there was a good chance that a better site on city-owned land would be available.[83] Passage of this proposal through Council was more difficult than anticipated as old enmities were bared, and it was approved at an in-camera session in early 1983 (with, of course, councillors Eriksen and Davies present) by, it is reported, a narrow 6–5 majority. With a lease on city-owned land, and CMHC funding, the DERA executive could announce jubilantly to its membership that the fifty-six-unit DERA Co-op would be completed in 1984.[84] Symbolically it includes a six-storey mural of the history and struggles of the Downtown Eastside and the Waterfront.

The DERA Co-op powerfully extended the achievements of the past into the present, and provided precedents for the future: 'The DERA Co-op was of tremendous symbolic significance in showing what could be done with no Board, no staff, entirely self-sufficient. The City and the Feds said this is impossible that people in this district manage a $5 million budget. The Co-op is a shining example of what is possible. We just went on from there. We had a large number on the waiting list and experience that should be re-used.'[85]

The second project was equally audacious. The long recession following 1981 combined with the erosion of affordable housing had brought families to the Downtown Eastside, and the 153-unit Four Sisters Co-op was the first project planned to include families as well as seniors.[86] Once again the proposal ran into heavy criticism, from Council and some city departments, but again, thanks to the two DERA members, it was narrowly approved, was completed in 1987, and has a long waiting-list; the project has won design awards and been described as 'the model of the future.'[87] Two further renovations have been undertaken since, with joint federal-provincial funds, and by 1990 DERA was among the largest landlords in the Downtown Eastside, with 413 units in its four buildings, administration of an additional 76 units, and further plans under discussion.[88] A recent DERA thrust has been to introduce the non-profit hotel model, which has worked effectively in several U.S. cities, to Canada, through the purchase and renovation of existing hotels.[89] This initiative would introduce competition to market hotels, and also provide better management of beer parlours, a major neighbourhood problem. Reminiscent of DERA's proposal for the Stratford Hotel in 1980, the pubs could also generate subsidies and working capital for each structure. With these varied initiatives, DERA's housing portfolio amounted to some 640 units with the completion of a new subsidized rental building in 1992.

All of these achievements have been made possible by funds from various levels of the state, but the record indicates that initiatives and innovation have typically originated in the community. It was pressure from DERA that influenced by-law revisions in the 1970s and, through Alderman Rankin, DERA's Council ally, led to the formation of the Downtown Housing Implementation Committee in 1978 at the end of a concerted lobbying campaign. Initially DERA's three-point housing program of by-law enforcement, rehabilitation, and new building was resisted by Council and staff, but in the 1980s it became official policy.[90] During Mayor Harcourt's tenure (1980–6), the City acquired ten sites for non-profit housing societies, and a total of 1,244 society-operated units were built in the Downtown Eastside. A further 1,200 market units were renovated through the rent-controlled RRAP, and 1,500 others, renovated for Expo, have been returned to the local market. In 1989 revisions to the Rental Tenancy Act gave tenants' rights to Downtown Eastside residents after a fifteen-year campaign. And even the notion of using a beer parlour as a profit centre to subsidize room rentals, which 'stumped' the CMHC when suggested by DERA in 1980, became part of City–Provincial–DERA negotiations over purchase of a downtown hotel in the early 1990s. Repeatedly, if not without a struggle, the community has succeeded in impregnating the state, and has come to influence the housing agenda.

Territorial Struggles: Expo and the New Urban Reality

But this argument should not be pressed too far. Community control is contested and far from total. Indeed, by the early 1990s, there is an air of crisis as to whether the Downtown Eastside can survive the incursions of mega-projects encircling it on three sides: from the east and north the threat is the redevelopment of the waterfront by the Port of Vancouver; from the west the pressure comes from Gastown-induced gentrification and, behind it, the expansion of downtown functions, including Simon Fraser University's new downtown campus and the convention and leisure business associated with Canada Harbour Place; and to the south, on the site of the Expo lands, the beginnings of the vast Concord Pacific redevelopment project of the Hong Kong entrepreneur Li Ka-shing complete the encirclement. The capacity for displacement is substantial: 'We've got major high-rise developments coming in on three sides of us in the next few years, an invasion of well-off people, and nobody is giving a thought to the effect it will have on this neighbourhood ... Expo was bad, the worst year of my life. But this will be worse because the evictions will be more massive, and more long-term – in fact, permanent.'[91]

Expo 86, the World's Fair, marked the transition to this new urban reality, as DERA's dealings shifted from local slumlords to national and international public and private corporations. With its well-honed local knowledge, the association was not caught off guard. Indeed, when Jim

Green began as organizer in 1981, his terms of reference included, as first priority, relations with B.C. Place, the provincial Crown corporation which acquired the Expo site in 1980.[92] Equally vigilant was First United Church, which in June 1981 anticipated that hotel upgrading in the Downtown Eastside for Expo visitors would lead to evictions of 'at least 800' residents, a remarkably prescient estimate.[93] By the following January, DERA, the Carnegie Centre, and First United Church had formed a coalition, the Save the Downtown Eastside Committee, which had begun lobbying in earnest (Save the Downtown Eastside Committee 1982), and by early 1983 various departments of the city were also considering housing and other impacts, leading to a request by Mayor Harcourt to the federal government for a special disbursement of offsetting housing funds.

Meanwhile DERA had assembled its own housing strategy to divert the worst-case scenario of neighbourhood impacts. Early in 1984, DERA joined a coalition of First United Church and the Chinese Benevolent Association and approached the Expo 86 Corporation with a proposal to build 450 units of housing in converted warehouses near the Expo site, to be rented for Expo use during the fair, and then turned over to non-profit groups afterwards. This offer was declined by the corporation, which instead built delegate housing at the University of British Columbia, six miles away from the site.[94] The lobbying campaign then went into high gear with the politicians' tour of the Downtown Eastside, and DERA's eight-point proposal to secure the stability of the district in the face of mega-project threats.[95] Two of the proposals were for a rent freeze in Downtown Eastside hotels during the Expo period, and, once again, full tenancy rights for residents, thereby protecting them from summary eviction. These items were developed further and presented to the city in a report requesting that a rent freeze and no evictions during the course of the fair be incorporated in a new by-law. The mood was grim: 'What we will get from Expo are tourists, more crime, more traffic and less housing. We will not benefit from Expo one bit.'[96] The by-law was an essential base to a preventative strategy. 'A major fight coming up is for the by-law for Expo '86 – August 13, 1985. If we don't get the by-law, gloves are off for Expo ... '[97]

A similar strategy was doing the rounds of the social planning department at City Hall, and the department endorsed DERA's proposal before Council – one of many examples of a more cooperative relationship between the Association and City staff in the 1980s. The by-law's history before Council was one of prolonged frustration, in the face of tied votes, the sickness and absence, twice, of a key supporter on Council, and wranglings over legal wording. Members of Council opposed to the by-law had a long history of hostility to DERA, and charged that the Association was rumour-mongering and exaggerating Expo impacts.[98] Finally, in February 1986, with the undisputed evidence of Expo evictions now underway, Council supported DERA's reapplication for a by-law enforcing a rent and eviction freeze for established residents, and petitioned the provincial government for enabling legislation.

Not surprisingly that legislation never materialized, for both ideological and personal barriers separated DERA from the right-wing Social Credit administration. The province had been steadily drawing in its welfare net for several years, under the rubric of a restraint program, and social impacts in the Downtown Eastside were far from its list of Expo priorities. Indeed, in a radio interview, Premier Bennett declared that the exposition had achieved what the city had been unable to, to 'get rid of the slums.'[99] There were also acerbic personal relations between Cabinet members and DERA stretching back to tenants' and welfare-rights campaigns in the 1970s.[100] More recently, Jim Green had sued B.C. Place for misleading advertising in its public relations, and had been a member of a group who had occupied the premier's Vancouver office in a demonstration that was a part of the Solidarity campaign against the government's restraint program.[101] DERA's task became one of treatment rather than prevention, as it facilitated the rehousing of many evicted tenants.

Events were moving to a higher level of politicking. In Victoria, the NDP member for Vancouver Centre was removed from the Legislature for accusing the premier of lying over Expo impacts. Leaders of the main opposition parties in Ottawa visited the Downtown Eastside, and questions were raised in Parliament over the evictions. Indeed, much to the embarrassment of the provincial government, the evictions became a *cause célèbre* and were widely reported in the national and U.S. press, and even beyond.[102] The evictions themselves increased steadily, and with them exorbitant rent increases, with room charges inflating from $200–$250 a month to $45–$65 a night in some hotels. The total number of evictions is unknown, but the best estimate suggests a figure between 500 and 850 residents in the period immediately prior to the opening of the Fair.[103]

The Expo evictions represented the struggle of the previous decade writ large to protect a fragile community of the poor, the elderly, and the disabled against more powerful and destructive external forces.

DERA's local knowledge proved more reliable in the projection of impacts than the intuition of unfriendly Council members or the predictions of a wavering social planning department, and its solution of a rent and eviction freeze, juggled by Council for six months, was finally supported only when DERA's dire predictions were proven correct. But Expo also marked a transition. The escalation over the evictions brought the group added prominence, nationally and internationally, as champion of the district in numerous interviews for radio, television, and newspapers. The *Los Angeles Times, Detroit Free Press,* and other foreign newspapers, and a feature on Australian television, mindful of its own exposition in 1988 on an inner-city site in Brisbane, promoted the Association, and thus enhanced its power.

CONCLUSION: FROM CONFLICT TO CO-PRODUCTION?

As I entered DERA's office on East Hastings Street in August 1989, I was stopped by four men who were panhandling. Inside, and up the stairs of the history-shrouded building, there was discussion of a protest rally later in the week to repatriate the pocket park across the street, which has again been taken over by a sad group of mainly youthful substance abusers. Recently DERA has been campaigning across Canada for tighter controls on the possession of knives; other issues from the early years, including slum landlords and the management of beer parlours, never seem to go away. Periodic, and sometimes sensational, rediscovery of Skid Road by the media does not help to counter a selective perception that not much has changed in the Downtown Eastside, a perception which always has its takers.

But this is a misleading campaign. The hard to house, the substance abusers, the transients are no less visible for being a minority who use the neighbourhood for a night or a season before moving on. They have not been a significant base of DERA's constituency, a constituency which has included instead permanent residents – the less-visible majority for whom the district is not a short-term stop, but a home. And considering that community, an altogether different perception takes shape. The conjunction of poverty, old age, and physical or mental handicap has made residents like those of the Downtown Eastside among the least empowered in North American society. In city after city – Toronto, Montreal, Seattle, San Francisco, and many others – their neighbourhoods have been usurped by more powerful public and private interests in incremental or major redevelopment, rationalized always by the outsider's discourse of skid road. Sometimes the land-use transition has been accompanied by conflict, and occasionally, as in San Francisco's Yerba Buena project, it has been protracted.[104] What makes Vancouver's Downtown Eastside, and the groups that have championed it, so interesting and potentially informative is the degree of their success in achieving both enhancement and preservation from within.

History hangs heavily over the Downtown Eastside. It is not just the old buildings which inculcate a sense of the past. Far more powerfully, it is a place of shared sentiment and symbol, of collective memories, of Victory Square and its annual Remembrance Day parades at the cenotaph, where the sacrifices of an earlier generation are commemorated each November. But there were other collective struggles and collective sacrifices whose memories project the past into the present. Victory Square has other symbolic associations, as the site where Mayor McGeer read the Riot Act to 2,000 unemployed protesters in 1935. DERA's offices in the modest Templeton Building (1895) were used by the Relief Camp Workers' Union; from his office window Jim Green can look across the street at the Tellier Tower, formerly the Holden Building (1911), DERA's third housing project, and named after Gerry Tellier, long-time resident of the district and DERA member, and one of the four leaders of the 1935 On-to-Ottawa Trek of the Relief Camp Workers, an important episode in Canadian labour history.[105] Tellier was also one of the founders of the Canadian Seamen's Union, the Union of which Eriksen was also a member and about which Green has written a book. These intertwined biographies weave an alternative discourse, a semantic and material struggle to regain the identity of the neighbourhood, to sustain a memory and vision kept alive also by the historic mural on the DERA Co-op, by the exhibition 'East Side Story' sponsored in the mid 1970s, by a picture of the reading of the Riot Act hanging in DERA's office. In all of this the past empowers the present.

That empowerment has achieved palpable results in neighbourhood improvements, too numerous to summarize.[106] It has also led to the remarkable enfranchisement of what has been historically Vancouver's most disenfranchised district, with the election through the 1980s of two DERA leaders to City Council; a larger electorate clearly subscribes to Eriksen's view of the city as a corporation of equal shareholders where the voices of deprived neighbourhoods should be heard in their own terms. DERA's successes have been the result of a sophisticated political analysis derived from trade-union democratic socialism, energized by astute local knowledge, dogged persistence, charismatic leadership, and committed lieutenants and foot soldiers. If less than complete, its reading of the problems and opportunities of the Downtown Eastside has proven most reliable over the years, as, sooner or later, many battle-weary politicians and seasoned bureaucrats have come to recognize. DERA provides ample evidence of the capacity of a local movement to infiltrate the state, of how innovation can bubble up from below. Because such influence frequently shatters the pre-existing protocols and categories of government procedures, it is initially resisted, only later to reappear on the agenda of the state itself.

From the community perspective, this interpretation is admittedly a best-case scenario and there are plenty of examples where particular contingencies have diverted it. But this is only to reinforce the complexity of the now recursive relations between DERA and the welfare state. The Association has a history of grass-roots innovation, accomplishment, and community power which must be recognized even by those who may not always admire it. In 1985 DERA was approached by a police seniors' organization who asked for its advice in setting up an advocacy program; in 1989 staff workers assisted a tenants' group in middle-class Kerrisdale to organize to resist eviction and displacement. If it was a friendly mayor who proclaimed Downtown Eastside Day in 1983, it was members of a persistently unfriendly provincial government who identified the DERA Housing Society as 'the best in Canada' at a national housing conference five years later.[107]

DERA has itself learned and evolved over its twenty-year history. 'We left a good impression on the 15 B.C. Housing and 15 CMHC officials in attendance' notes the satisfied staff minutes, assessing DERA's presence at the housing conference. Persuasion now comes less from threatening embarrassment, and more from the power of a superior argument and reinforcing achievements. By 1991 the association's offices in the Templeton Building included a dozen rooms, with close to thirty-five staff in the office and on assignment. In Jim Green's mind, DERA has entered a new third phase, beyond the protests of the 1970s, beyond even the struggle for bricks and mortar in the first social housing projects of the early 1980s. Since Expo 86, it has become something of a gatekeeper in overseeing proposed change in the Downtown Eastside. The DERA message, broadly disseminated through the Expo evictions, continues to travel in policy and planning reviews, housing seminars, and professional meetings. Greater prominence and an established record create greater legitimacy. Joint projects have been completed with groups as diverse as the City Police, the Royal Bank, and even in the late 1980s, the housing arm of the long-hostile provincial government. From the conflict model of the 1970s, relations with the state in the late 1980s show tendencies to co-production, a model with greater opportunities to set the agenda and secure resources but also, to be sure, with greater dangers of co-optation and separation from the grass roots: 'Having been around longer, we can rely on different levels of allies now. Not just poor people. Even developers, a few anyway. I'm involved in a ton of negotiations and I have to be secretive. Not even people in the office know what's going on for 6–8 months. Otherwise, we've seen it before, a developer comes along and scoops up the site. Since Expo we've moved into, sort of a third stage of DERA. Now we're more of a partner in development. People have learned it's better to do a deal with DERA than be held up. We're becoming part of the development process.'[108] Green's statement provides a view of neocorporatism from the community perspective. DERA is now 'a partner in development,' and the price of access to the state's resources and powers is a necessary separation of leadership from the grass roots, and an agreement to play by the rules laid out by the state. Only particularly seasoned community leaders can enter this realm, simultaneously maintaining co-operative relations with the state and also credibility with the rank and file over an extended period. In our second example, the Ohalim movement in Katamon Tet, a protest organization in another multiply deprived neighbourhood has proven unable to withstand the pressures towards incorporation by the state, and with incorporation has entered a condition of political passivity.

But before leaving the Downtown Eastside, the potential cost to the state of neocorporatism should also be noted. DERA was established in 1973 from an existing, government-sponsored, self-help initiative; the same benevolent liberalism supported it through grants in its inexperienced early years. But DERA quickly developed an ideology and tactics at odds with its local sponsors, and indeed became a principal base of an oppositional socialist politics in the city. That opposition both contributed to, and benefited from, the erosion of the liberal centre party at City Hall, and the left-right polarization of civic politics. As they learned to their cost, in nurturing a political voice in the Downtown Eastside, TEAM councillors were erecting a Trojan horse at City Hall. Neocorporatism can be a two-way street, where the empowerment of the grass roots might even proceed at the cost of the local state. Neocorporatist politics in the Downtown Eastside encouraged the effective demise, not of the neighbourhood organization, but of the municipal liberal party.

7

Socializing the Grass Roots: The Ohalim Movement in Katamon Tet

On 26 June 1979, about three thousand residents of poverty neighbour-hoods gathered at Binyanei Ha'uma, a Jerusalem conference centre, to celebrate the establishment of the Ohalim (Tents) movement. A scroll styled to mimic Israel's Declaration of Independence set out the move-ment's major concerns and principles. It stated:

The basic charter of our state ... contains the following language: 'The State of Israel will labour to develop the country for the general welfare of its in-habitants, will be based on the principles of justice, freedom, and peace, in keeping with the vision of the prophets of Israel, will establish social equality ... ' You have turned your backs on the Declaration of Independence ... and instead of a democratic, egalitarian state you have divided the nation into two parts ... Therefore we, the young members of the Ohalim councils in Jerusalem's disadvantaged neighbourhoods, the second generation in the neighbourhood ghettoes, have decided to bring this situation to an end and to fight for a new society.[1]

The movement then put forward its demands for a radical revision of the system of education, official recognition of Oriental (Asian–North African) culture, as well as changes in housing policy, health, and social services.

Somewhat embarrassed by the unexpected declaration, Israel's pres-ident Yitzhak Navon, who attended the gathering as a guest of honour, refused to sign the scroll. Yet representatives of five neighbourhoods, representing Jerusalem's poverty belt, did sign it, thus symbolically ex-pressing their discontent with their country's social policy. Five months later (on 25 November), Jerusalem's traffic was brought to a standstill as hundreds of the movement's members took to the streets in protest against the government's economic policy. In a series of protests over the next two years, the Ohalim movement put its demands on the national agenda, giving rise to a new urban social force outside the institution-alized political party system.

The theoretical-empirical question that may be raised at this point is how disadvantaged social groups have been mobilized to collective action. This question has been raised by Marxists and pluralists alike, who iden-tified the missing link between structure and action, and inquired about the sociopolitical process whereby a social base is transformed into a social force (Smelser 1963; Castells 1977). Yet the answers given to the question remained quite often at the theoretical level, thus lacking em-pirical substantiation. To fill this gap, the chapter goes beyond the social conditions experienced by the neighbourhoods' residents (for a discussion of these issues, see chapters 1 and 5), and tries to decipher what Kling and Posner (1991) describe as the development of social dispositions or 'consciousness.'

At the centre of the study are, therefore, the agents of change who interpret reality and suggest new paths of action. In line with Touraine's theory of social action (1981), it is argued that social agents, in this particular case community workers, played a leading role in evoking so-cial and territorial sentiments, in developing political orientations and strategies of action, and in mobilizing the local residents for collective action. A complementary argument is that social mobilization was af-fected by the nature of the groups involved, the nature of local leadership and the prevailing authority structures, the existing informal networks, and local norms and traditions. The chapter examines these arguments through an historiographic study of the Ohalim movement from its in-ception as a community council in 1973, through its transformation into a city-wide movement in 1979, to its disbanding in 1981. In charting the movement's development, the chapter describes the changes in its social orientations: from services improvement at the neighbourhood level to a movement that seeks to pursue deeper and more general issues such as social justice, democracy, and cultural identity.

As the DERA case (chapter 6) clearly shows, such a gradual change of focus from pragmatic community issues to deeper and more general problems is not unique to Jerusalem. It may occur in other lower-class areas where liberal-radical agents of change interact with local residents, and help in drawing the links between particularistic and universal issues. But the links thus drawn, we would argue, do not necessarily lead to the adoption of a class-based perspective as some neo-Marxists would have it, nor would they lead to an alternative model of society. Rather, as this chapter shows, those liberal-radical agents of change may serve as agents of socialization, who perhaps in spite of their intended actions may help to integrate the grass roots into the existing social system. The study is based on three years of participant observation (1980–2), interviews with members, community workers, and politicians, as well as on an analysis of documents and reports produced by the parties involved.

JERUSALEM: SYMBOLS AND HARSH REALITY

Many people picture Jerusalem as a mystical entity, the world's centre, a holy city revered by Jews, Christians, and Muslims alike. Even for secular Israelis the city is laden with rich symbolic meanings: as King David's capital, the location of the Temple, the home of prophets, the remnants of past conquests. It also contains symbols associated with Israel's rebirth – the Knesset (Parliament) building; the Yad Vashem memorial to the victims of the Holocaust; the Mt Herzl cemetery, where national leaders and military heroes are buried. Yet there is another reality, one that visitors and Israelis alike tend to forget. Behind the mystical and the national symbols, and far away from the well-established neighbourhoods of Rehavia and Beit Hakerem, adjoining the pre-1967 border areas, lies another face of Jerusalem – a harsh reality built of recently constructed public-housing estates inhabited by immigrants who arrived in the 1950s and 1960s from North African and Middle Eastern countries. It is a zone populated mainly by the new working class of Sephardic origin, referred to in chapter 5. Part of the belt, stretching west to east along the city's southern rim, includes Ir Ganim, the Katamons, and southern Baka. In the northeast it includes Shumel Hanavi and the formerly Arab neighbourhood of Musrara (see figure 7.1).

Out of sight at the city's edge, the poverty belt remained unnoticed by the public and largely ignored by the country's politicians. It was, therefore, a shock to Israeli society when a group of young people from Musrara took to the streets in 1971 and, in a series of demonstrations instigated by the newly formed Israeli Black Panthers Movement (IBPM), put the issue of poverty on the public agenda (Cohen 1972; Bernstein 1972). Subsequent to the IBPM's protest, a special committee was set up to explore and make recommendations about the status of socially disadvantaged youth.

The youth of Musrara brought poverty into public awareness, and at long last the country discovered the other faces of Jerusalem and, by extension, the other faces of Israeli society. Intellectuals, students, actors,

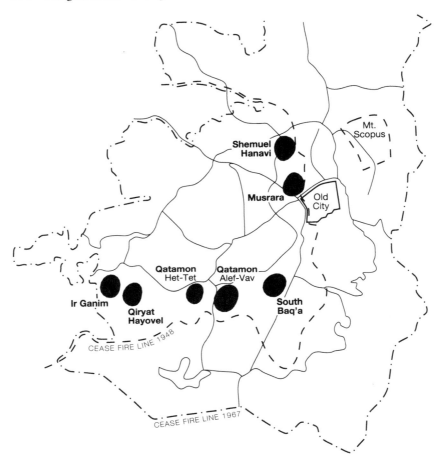

FIGURE 7.1. Jerusalem's belt of poverty. Behind the mystical and national symbols abundant in Jerusalem, and adjoining the pre-1967 borderline, there lies another face of the city – a harsh reality built of public-housing estates inhabited by lower-class immigrants who arrived in the 1950s and 1960s from North African and Middle Eastern countries.

community workers, the press, and every other kind of well-meaning agent appeared in the disadvantaged neighbourhoods, some with offers of social assistance and others probably looking for social salvation – that is, the redemption of a lost utopia buried in the ghettos.

Among the poor neighbourhoods that basked in this sudden public interest, the Katamon public-housing projects had a special position. In the mid 1960s, the entire area was considered one of the poorest in the city – 65.7 per cent of the local families were in the lowest-income group, as compared with 35.1 per cent of the population of the country as a whole (Kimchi 1970). The estate's original six sections, bureaucratically named according to the Hebrew alphabet as Katamon Alef, Katamon Bet, and so on through Katamon Vav, were laid out during the 1950s at a relatively low density. They were made up of two-storey buildings, each containing four to ten flats, ranging in size from 28 to 45 square metres. Each building had a small garden plot in front. In the 1960s the four-storey multi-family estates of Katamon Het and Tet were constructed, with the size of each flat ranging from 55 to 64 square metres. The different residential densities had an overwhelming effect on the future of the neighbourhoods. Over the years many of the residents of the low-density group of estates have been able to enlarge their apartments by expanding over the garden plots, while no such opportunity existed for the residents of the multi-storey buildings. As a result, the poverty belt experienced over the years an internal stratification manifested in relatively advantaged and less-advantaged housing estates. In 1972, for instance, the market value of flats in the multi-family units of Katamon Het and Tet was 20 per cent lower than those in Katamons Alef through Vav. Being less attractive, the multi-family estates contained a far higher level of rented apartments – 88 per cent higher than in the rest of the Katamons (Israel Central Bureau of Statistics 1972). To make matters worse, in a deliberate attempt to alleviate the housing problems of families living in overcrowded conditions, the state housing agency, Amidar, moved several hundred families to Bar Yochai Street in Katamon Tet, where relatively large flats were built in the late 1960s. In blocks 101 and 102, where the Ohalim movement had its inception, there were, in 1976, 207 families, with a thousand children. Of these, some 90 per cent were of Asian and North African origin, and 10 per cent were female single-parent families.[2] According to the local community worker, about one-third of the teenagers in the two buildings in the early 1970s had criminal records. Indeed, the entire area suffered from a high crime rate at the time – burglaries, rapes, drug trafficking, prostitution, and child abuse.[3] The employment officer reported that in 1979 about 40 per cent of the young adults, ages 18 to 26, in Katamons Het and Tet were unemployed. Indeed, many of them chose not to seek a job at all, preferring to live on social-security grants, and, for some, the underground economy.[4] This group came to form a distinct stratum of the broader Sephardic working-class group that lived in the Jerusalem poverty belt, the distinction being determined by both housing conditions and class affiliation. Residents of Katamon Het and Tet, and those on Bar Yochai Street in particular, belonged to the lower class and underclass, and formed a distinct disadvantaged housing class. As I have shown elsewhere (Hasson 1985), the Ohalim movement was largely confined to these subclasses.

THE PRE-MOVEMENT STAGE: 1972 TO OCTOBER 1973

The Ohalim movement has its roots in the early 1970s, with two groups of teenagers, most of whom lived in blocks 101 and 102 on Bar Yochai Street in Katamon Tet. The two groups supplied the movement's leadership, basic values and aspirations, and norms of behaviour, and subsequently exerted a far-reaching influence on the movement's orientations and strategies of action.

One group of fifteen- and sixteen-year-olds endorsed the central values and orientations of society at large, but felt themselves to be socially outside the mainstream. They attended school and participated in drama clubs outside the housing estate, yet felt isolated from the host society. Moshe Salach, a prominent figure in the group, who had lived for a time at a kibbutz, voiced his feelings plainly: 'There is racism at the kibbutz. At the kibbutz they treated the group I came from like unfortunates, and we didn't feel equal to the kibbutz children ... The war is between those who came from Europe and those who came from Asia and Africa, since the Orient is based on emotions and looks to the past, while the West is based on rational calculations and looks to the future.'[5]

The second group, of the same ages, utterly rejected mainstream values and orientations. Members of this group dropped out of school at an early age and some of them spent time in institutions for juvenile delinquents. In the early 1970s they were organized in a criminal gang that specialized in burglary and drug trafficking. Yamin Swissa, the gang's leader, described himself as follows:

At that time I was a leader of a criminal gang. I was a thief and terrorized the neighbourhood. The people in the gang were just like me, engaged in crime and poverty. There were 1,200 people in the two blocks where we lived. We didn't know about social services and didn't care about the law. We were marginal people who could be released and re-arrested. There was another group of Yorams

[Hebrew slang for 'cowards' or 'suckers'] who were scared of us ... they were not my friends at that time.[6]

The transformation of the two groups into the core of a social movement was a slow one. The initial catalyst is usually thought to have been the development of a community theatre in the area. In the early 1970s, several actors and directors associated with professional theatre, apparently moved by the problems of disadvantaged youth as exposed by the IBPM, went into the poor neighbourhoods and tried to establish communication with the young people. Community theatres were organized in socially distressed areas of Tel Aviv as well as in Jerusalem. Among the actors participating in this meeting of cultures was Arieh Itzhak, who in 1971 set up a community theatre in a poor section of Tel Aviv. In 1972 he arrived in Katamon Tet and, along with the mainstream-oriented group, developed a community theatre there. Itzhak did not try to eliminate the feelings of social resentment and alienation, but rather attempted to direct these emotions into symbolic-theatrical channels. As Michael Paran, the community worker in blocks 101 and 102, recalls: 'He used to talk to the guys about sex and violence. Then, suddenly, he would take off his clothes, curse, break chairs, and act like a volcano. From this extreme he would return and assume a moderate model of behaviour. The guys were stunned. I didn't understand what he was doing and felt very bad watching how he worked. But I didn't intervene because I felt that this was the only hope.'[7] One of the participants shed further light on Itzhak's strategy: 'When we rehearsed, he would suddenly change his voice and start speaking with a heavy Iraqi-Oriental accent. We were confused, because we had been taught that the Oriental accent is inappropriate and that we should speak in an Israeli accent.'[8] Only gradually has it become evident to the group's members that what he was trying to do was to restructure ethnic identity and make them proud of their Oriental heritage, to present their conditions as they really are and to communicate them to the public.

In March 1973 the group presented its first production, *Joseph Goes Down to Katamon*. The biblical Joseph's maltreatment symbolized the misfortunes of Katamon youth. As the group put it: 'Joseph went to Egypt and was saved. He then came back to Katamon to be buried with his dreams. Joseph symbolizes the unrelenting drive for social justice. He is the righteous man of Jewish tradition. And we, too, aspire to achieve justice, not charity.'[9] The play, which became a hit, presented a harsh critique of Israeli society and its disparaging attitude towards the Oriental newcomers. It also criticized the ways that the state handled disadvantaged youth. One of the scenes, for instance, illustrated police harassment, depicting the rape of one of the group's members by young adults with whom he was imprisoned. Another play, *The Dropout*, presented a self-critique of their own social behaviour. A third production, *Class Reunion*, criticized the educational system's insensitivity to Oriental values and its attempt to impose Western values and standards on Sephardic youth.

The community theatre became a form of social protest, symbolically conveying feelings of deprivation, ethnic pride, and discrimination, as well as presenting a social critique. In the course of these performances, the group came to grips with its own social history and everyday life experience, so defining its social and ethnic identity. 'I am no longer ashamed of my illiterate mother,' one of them said. 'She possesses a deep knowledge of life, making her superior to many others.'[10]

Joseph Goes Down to Katamon was well received by the public and the group was soon invited to perform on professional stages such as Jerusalem's Khan Theatre, as well as on other stages around the country. The residents of Katamon Tet did not, however, like the show. The mother whose son was raped fainted during the first performance, residents claimed that it gave the neighbourhood a bad reputation, and even Mayor Kollek was criticized by the religious parties for allowing such a presentation to be performed in public.

During the show's run, some members of the criminal gang cooperated with the mainstream-oriented group, even taking part in some of the theatre activities. 'The theatre brought me closer to the Yorams,' the gang's leader admitted.[11] The performances were followed by long discussions with the audience to further elaborate the nature of social problems faced by youth in poor areas. Some of the discussions extended over several days as members of the group were invited to continue the debate. Gradually, a group of community workers, university professors, and students gathered around the theatre group and began to explore new ways of local development. In this manner, the theatre served as a medium of communication with the public and helped evoke interest and attract forces from the outside to work in Katamon Tet. A group of overseas students living in the Freemasonry House in Katamon Tet began to explore, along with the theatre group, the deeper problems underlying its social grievances; the North American students proposed ethnic-cultural explanations, whereas the South Americans suggested political-economic ones. The students hosted members of the group in their apartments, and, when Arieh Itzhak left, one of them took over and for a while directed the theatre workshop. Ten years later, in 1981, some of the students were still involved with the movement, now helping it to establish a political party. A psychiatrist and Hebrew University professor who closely followed the theatre workshop noted that the theatre created a sense of identity and responsibility, enhanced creativity, and developed a cohesive group (Miller 1973).

'We were told many times, by different groups,' Moshe Salach conceded, 'to assume responsibility and to run the neighbourhood on our own. But we would say that it was beyond our capabilities and should be seen to by the municipality.'[12]

The change came during the Yom Kippur War, when many of the local service workers, such as teachers, youth counsellors, and community and social workers, were drafted. To prevent social chaos, members of the theatre group took upon themselves the responsibility for conducting after-school activities and served as counsellors for the young children in the two buildings. In the course of these activities, many of which were carried out in the buildings' bomb shelters, a youth council was formed. It was called Ohel Yosef (Joseph's Tent), the term 'tent' being chosen, its members would later explain, to allude to feelings of temporary residence.[13] However, a synagogue in block 101 bears the same name, which may suggest another explanation.

THE YOUTH COUNCIL OF OHEL YOSEF:
OCTOBER 1973 TO APRIL 1974

The theatre group reorganized itself as the Youth Council of Ohel Yosef and set up a variety of local services: after-school clubs, a club for eight-to thirteen-year-olds, a club for boys aged fourteen to eighteen, another for teenage girls, a women's circle, a bakery, a baby-sitting service, and, of course, a community theatre.[14] Most of these activities were planned at the grass-roots level by members of the group and by volunteers and a community worker. The municipality aided the group by covering some of the expenses and by allocating community workers to work with the council. Additional resources were mobilized in France, where Michael Paran, the community worker for the two apartment buildings, made contacts with left-wing Jewish intellectuals at the Sorbonne, and along with them established a 'Friends of' committee known as Katamon France.

Commenting on the youth council activities, Moshe Hizkyah, another community worker who cooperated with the group, said:

Ohel Yosef went far beyond the Israeli Black Panthers Movement in its con-structive activities. Unlike the Black Panthers Movement, which mainly resorted to violence and demonstrations, the members of Ohel Yosef created productive services ... They demonstrated that the neighbourhood can produce not only drug addicts and prostitutes but also some nice things ... Personally, I felt en-couraged by those young people and wholeheartedly cooperated with them and made sure that everything would be their own responsibility.[15]

With Moshe Hizkyah's assistance, the council in 1974 organized summer programs for 250 children from all over the neighbourhood, thereby obtaining some legitimacy from people outside blocks 101 and 102. 'People,' Moshe Hizkyah noted, 'started to ask "What is it?" They thought at the beginning that the Black Panthers were behind it. Eventually, they came to recognize the Ohel Yosef youth council.'[16]

Over the course of some of these activities, some members of the group were professionally trained as apprentice youth leaders; the youth council became institutionalized by registering as a non-profit organization, with a public council chaired by Alice Shalvy, a Hebrew University professor. The role of the public council, Shalvy observed, was 'to accompany the youth council and help them find the way ... At the beginning, Wasana, Salach, and others needed advice and counselling in order to shape their own thoughts and ideas and to establish connections with other social groups, and our role was to help them out. When the children grew up, we had to move out.'[17] Whether or not this statement is patronizing or a genuine pedagogical conception is hard to tell. One thing, though, seems to be quite obvious: some segments of mainstream society joined the movement at an early stage and brought their own values along. Shalvy, for instance, acted as the movement's treasurer for five years, from 1974 to 1979, and during this period continually tried to foster self-help activities in keeping with her British cultural experience.[18] As-sessing Ohel Yosef's impact, she said: 'The major contribution of the Ohel Council was to turn the boys at the margins of society into an integral part of the neighbourhood and society. Their entire self-image changed. The movement developed a neighbourhood leadership. The character of the neighbourhood changed and people for the first time felt that they were able to bring about social change.'[19] Shalvy's ob-servations on socialization and the creation of leadership have been cor-roborated by Shlomo Wasana, who served then as the council's chairman: 'We decided to open clubhouses for children; we were the counsellors, one serving as secretary and another as chairman. This helped us to form a definite identity, to define our roles and purposes ... All the young people in the neighbourhood and its adjoining groups grew up with Ohel Yosef ... Boys who were twelve when we were their counsellors today see us as their teachers. We educated them, we have influence over them.'[20]

What Wasana seems to suggest is an interesting interplay between self-help and socialization, whereby he and his friends acted as agents of socialization within the community at large. Although there is much empirical evidence, in the form of social services, to substantiate his claims, it is nevertheless true that at that time (1973–4) the juvenile gang did not yet accept the council's authority. On the contrary, members of the council were accused of selling themselves out by cooperating with the establishment's agents. Michael Paran, the local community worker, was threatened by one of the gang's members; activities initiated by the youth council were disrupted, and the gang demanded a substantial share in the summer program's profits.[21] The impact on the environment, though undeniable, was still limited in scope at that stage.

The gradual changes in the area did not escape the state's notice. Mayor Kollek supported the group, probably with the idea that he could buy some peace by giving the movement some money.[22] The deputy mayor, Yosef Gadish, who held the city council's neighbourhood portfolio, was disparaging of the group, regarding its members as part of 'the generation of the desert' – a generation like that of the children of Israel who wandered for forty years on the way from Egypt to Israel, until making way for a younger generation that would be ready to participate in Israeli life. Still, when it came to practicalities, Gadish was willing to cover some of their expenses.[23] Unlike the politicians, with their ambivalent stance, some community workers enthusiastically supported the organization on both ideological and practical grounds. Avner Amiel, head of the city's unit for social action, endorsed the local activity wholeheartedly, believing that it was the best way to promote equality and social justice. In his view, which he elaborated in much detail later on, the organization signified the beginning of a social struggle based on local issues. Hence, he saw himself as an agent of social change working to universalize local problems, thereby directing the organization's attention to deeper social issues.[24] Based on this interpretation, which uses social and territorial metaphors, Avner went on to reinforce the organization with a community worker (Moshe Hizkiyah) and saw to it that the leaders received some training.

Another community worker who was deeply involved with the Ohel Yosef Youth Council was Michael Paran (then affiliated with the department of youth advancement). Before long, Paran had become the leading force behind the youth council, gaining its members' complete confidence. Moshe Salach, then the secretary of the council, described him as follows: 'At a certain point he turned into a machine and acted like a fanatic ... We were young people, while he was married with children, and therefore it was only natural that he was far more serious than we were. Yet he adjusted himself to our pace and did a lot of things. He and Avner Amiel treated us like human beings.'[25] Shlomo Wasana, then chairman of the organization, referred to Paran as 'a person who had an internal world that helped him to reach us.'[26] Moshe Hizkiyah portrayed Paran as follows: 'He is a true believer, never willing to compromise ... as stubborn as a mule with a very solid world-view.'[27] Other residents described him as 'trustworthy' and as a person whom they 'deeply respect.'[28]

Michael Paran, at that time in his early forties, was indeed a unique personality to the young Sephardic boys of Ohel Yosef. He had been born in Poland and grew up in France, where he also studied political science and law and worked for a while as a lawyer. Affected by the rise of the Black Panthers in Musrara, he emigrated from France to Israel and asked to be employed as a community worker in socially distressed areas. Lacking professional skills, he was recruited by the youth advancement department as a special community worker to work with families in the 101 and 102 blocks in Katamon Tet. Looking back at his experience in the two blocks, he observed:

I became the main address for the residents and all I could do was just listen and get angry. I was torn apart watching each family with its problems, each child with his multiple problems. My family life became a shambles. My wife didn't see me because I would arrive late at night. I had a chequebook at that time and I used to write cheques for the boys ... They soon learned that I was with them ... In fact, I was deeply involved with the boys, the criminals, and the establishment ... I hate the establishment that sent me there, I hate the system, they should all be prosecuted because they are murderers.[29]

As Paran argued, the state had shredded the traditional social fabric of the Sephardic communities in order to control votes, undermining the supportive networks operating with the community and thus enforcing social disorganization (as we saw in chapter 5, the fostering of local bosses dependent on the state was part of this process).[30] On the basis of this specific community-oriented interpretation, Paran had been developing his counter-strategy of grass-roots mobilization. 'Criminal activity,' Paran argued, 'is essentially a protest against society. If we open the possibility of social protest, they will renounce their criminal activity. I always told them that, if you want revenge, you can be far more effective through social protest.'[31]

There is an interesting parallel between the group's theatrical performances and Paran's ideas of social protest. In both cases a medium of communication, tolerable to mainstream society, was used to define and express social grievances, thereby channelling what the theatre director and community worker saw as 'negative energies' in positive and effective directions. Contrary to Avner Amiel's philosophy of class conflict and his pursuit of social justice, Paran sought to create a territorial ideology. He described his 'philosophy' as follows: 'A poor man must stick to his environment. Here he knows every corner; here he is tension-free. This explains the attacks upon outsiders. It's nationalism ... At the first stage, you have to tell these people that all outsiders must go ... You have to take over the community centre, the clinic. Only at the second stage can you open windows ... The intention is to create an ideology of territory ... You become the neighbourhood authorities.'[32]

Moving from ideology to practice, Paran assisted the group greatly by helping to set up the organization Katamon France at the Sorbonne, by establishing contacts with the public, and by continually encouraging the group to become more active. Five years later, in 1979, he was, in a display of appreciation, elected the movement's president, and to this day is a symbol to those he nurtured in Katamon during the 1970s.[33] Not everyone, however, endorsed Paran's activity. He attracted much criticism and opposition from his fellow community and social workers. Moshe Hizkiyah, who worked in tandem with him, contended: 'To achieve his goals he would not hesitate to fake evidence, for example, by showing a schoolboy doing his homework on the toilet seat. He never fostered a positive image of the neighbourhood, never showed the positive ethnic aspects of the local heritage, like the synagogue. Indeed, he presented a distorted reality and always talked to me as if in a dream ... the martyr who carried the Katamons on his back.'[34] Instead of assuming a sober, realistic, and pragmatic approach, Hizkiyah seems to suggest, Paran indulged in unrealistic dreams. Alice Shalvy further elaborated on this, pointing out that 'Michael Paran visualized an empire of the Katamons and became too central a figure in the council.'[35] Paran's position further deteriorated as the young founders of Ohel Yosef reached the age of eighteen and, in April 1974, were called up for military service. Three adults were asked to head the Ohel Yosef council to guarantee its continuous operation, and none of them seemed to sympathize with Paran's ideology or strategy of action. The head of the council, Shimon Gotlieb, who was in his forties, severely criticized Paran:

I suggested having the youth sent to training centres outside the neighbourhood, but Michael would object, saying 'we won't get out, we are going to stay here ... ' I wanted them to participate in activities at the local Youth Centre [Beit Cagan], which was located in a respectable area of Katamon Tet, where there were good facilities, excellent youth counsellors, and mainstream social groups. But Michael objected, maintaining that 'we have to stick to the group's turf, and to work in the bomb shelters.' Then I suggested bringing in youth movement leaders to lead the youngsters, but Michael said 'we will develop our own leaders.' He thought the neighbourhood could do it on its own. I didn't agree, since in my view counselling and education should be provided by professionals coming in from the outside.[36]

In a nutshell, this dead-end discourse elucidates two entirely different strategies towards socialization: top-down socialization as represented by Gotlieb, versus bottom-up socialization as represented by Paran. The discourse also exposes the deep-seated disagreement over the nature of a distressed neighbourhood. For Gotlieb, the neighbourhood appears to be a trap: 'If the place they live in is a gutter it is our duty to help them get out.'[37] For Paran, in contrast, the neighbourhood is a source of power, since local problems can be effectively utilized to channel energies into protest activities. Finally, the discourse encapsulated two different political visions. Whereas Gotlieb conceived his role as an advocate, a mediator between mainstream society and the local community, Paran, so it appears, conceived of his role as that of a local politician trying to build grass-roots power.

It was precisely these features in Paran's conception that collided head-on with the prevailing orthodoxy in the community-work field. He was, consequently, charged by his supervisors with professional misconduct and in late 1974 Paran's supervisor and the Ohel Yosef council planned to meet to move for his dismissal. In an attempt to prevent this, Paran went to the leader of the juvenile delinquent gang, Yamin Swissa, informed him about the upcoming meeting, presented the move's possible implications for the neighbourhood were he forced to move out, and asked for his support. As Swissa reported: 'He finally realized that the real power rests with the criminals, and that they were the only force that could bring about social change. He asked for assistance in order to advance the neighbourhood's welfare, and I accepted his point.'[38] To-gether with several other members of the gang, Swissa disrupted the meeting, and new elections for the youth council were called in which Wasana was elected chairman and Swissa deputy chairman. With Wasana's resignation in early 1975, Swissa took charge (without having been for-mally elected to the office). Paran, who openly defied his supervisor, was moved to Avner Amiel's social action unit, and the two of them, along with Swissa, set the council on a new track.

FROM A TWO-BUILDING COUNCIL TO A NEIGHBOURHOOD
MOVEMENT, 1975–1976

Swissa's leadership brought with it some significant changes in the social composition, orientations, and strategies of action of the youth council. To begin with, members of the gang followed their leader, as Swissa explained: 'When the criminals saw that I had joined in, they immediately followed me, and I helped the Yorams. I saw to it that the criminals wouldn't cause disturbances.'[39] The council gained a strong leader and a committed and obedient following, as well as a preference for militant confrontation with agents of the state. In the years to come, the gang would initiate and lead most of the movement's protest activities. The gang's involvement did not imply a radical change in old patterns of behaviour. Criminal activity continued, and a few members of the gang lived at that time in both worlds. Swissa himself was imprisoned in 1980 on charges of drug possession, but he relentlessly argued that this was a frame-up by the police following a clash during one of the 1979 demonstrations.

These changes gave the movement a negative image and repelled some of the mainstream-oriented residents. The founders of the organization, for instance, scaled down their activity, and Moshe Salach stayed out of it for a long time, working as a theatre director in development towns. Swissa's leadership had, in other words, both a positive and a negative impact on the movement's development. He was born in 1955 in Israel to a Moroccan family, the oldest of eleven children. His father served for a short time in the border police and then became permanently un-employed and frequently drank. The burden of the family fell on his mother, who worked as a cleaning lady and seamstress. Since her salary was not enough to feed the family, she had to accept welfare support. Life at home was tense and violent, and the children used to unite around the mother. The family's instability massively affected the development of the children, especially of Yamin, who was an active participant in the family's life.[40]

Michael Paran described Swissa as 'a predator creature who imposed his authority on everyone. He hates the system, hence his violence and criminal activity.' Other community workers who worked with Swissa attributed his aggression to the tense social environment he suffered during childhood.[41] Yet, as both Amiel and Paran argued, the activity in the movement served as a sublimated outlet for this aggression. Indeed, both of them served as agents of change, catalysing the sublimation process. This point is directly expressed by Swissa, who concedes: 'I became attracted to Michael Paran. We have learned together what kind of services are needed, and then we learned the class issue. I then established a youth council, attended an apprentice youth leader course, and became a youth leader in the club.'[42] Social change has been augmented by the student group at the Freemasonry House in Katamon Tet who, as Swissa said, 'worked with us, instructed us, and gave the people a feeling of freedom.' It was through this group that he was exposed to the ideology of the left, and subsequently to Sheli, a small party to the left of Labour.[43]

The major task defined at this stage was to gain the confidence of the residents, thereby expanding the organization's sphere of influence over a larger area. Commenting on this, Paran said: 'I knew quite well that a revolution cannot be carried out with two buildings. Every day I told the guys that they would not get support from the outside unless they managed to expand the organization territorially. I told them that they had to represent Katamon Tet in its entirety and then the rest of the Katamons. I developed "neighbourhood nationalism" and, in the end, the message got through.'[44]

To further develop the council's authority in the area, Avner Amiel and members of Ohel Yosef asked the municipality to send in another community worker, David Meiry. In the late 1960s, David Meiry had worked with the Musrara neighbourhood gang around which the IBPM formed, and he gained a reputation there for being unconventional. Upon arriving in Katamon Tet in early 1976, he initiated a 'self-survey' as a vehicle for defining local problems and raising social consciousness. 'The goal has been,' Meiry commented, 'to educate the people and to prepare them for possible social action.'[45] The self-survey, carried out in blocks 101 and 102, was undertaken in collaboration with community workers, who interpreted its meaning and practical implications. One of the findings, for instance, was the existence of dampness-plagued flats with a relatively high proportion of children suffering rheumatic diseases.

Out of 207 families surveyed, 146 had suffered some dampness. The dilapidated housing conditions exposed by the survey led to social mobilization, both by residents and community workers. One of them published a series of protest poems describing the misfortunes of street-corner gangs and the insecurity created by housing policy, and calling for community support and social protest (Ross, n.d.).

The students in the Freemasonry House held daily meetings with residents, where they discussed socio-ideological issues. Following these activities, a large group of residents from the area, headed by the Ohel Yosef council, met with managers of the Prazot urban housing company to discuss local housing conditions. Prazot's failure to put forward practical solutions worsened the already existing local resentment. Capitalizing on those feelings, the Ohel Yosef council launched a protest, squatting in an adjacent public-housing project then under construction.

One hundred families, about four hundred people, took part in the squatting episode. It lasted for four days, from 28 April to 2 May 1976. Agents of the state played a leading role: David Meiry served as a spokesperson, Michael Paran took care of food supply, and Avner Amiel handled the communication with the media. In addition, members of the student group at the Freemasonry House, the IBPM, and the leftist Sheli Party joined in to assist the squatters. The harmonious relations among the squatters led to the establishment of a local commune called the 'Paris Commune.' On the fourth day of the protest, a contingent of policemen forcibly evicted the squatters, arresting some of them. The general feeling was one of despair, in Meiry's view: 'People felt defeated. They'd lost the battle, so they came to me and asked, "What should we do next?" It was very important to encourage them. They said, "We shall stick with you to the end, but show us what to do."'[46]

Meiry thus clearly indicated that state agents led the protest activities, thereby creating contradictory state responses. The police enforced law and order, while a counter-force of community workers agitated and organized against the state. One may argue with Saunders (1986) that those contradictory responses reflect the familiar tension between the central and local state, with the former largely concerned with wealth creation and the latter with social welfare. According to this explanation, Meiry, Paran, and Amiel were local state agents agitating against a central state housing policy. There is much empirical evidence in the preceding section to support such an interpretation. What seems peculiar to the present case is that, within the local state itself, the supervisors of the three community workers ostensibly objected to their activity. Meiry was reprimanded by his supervisors, Paran was warned not to enter Katamon Tet, and Amiel was openly criticized by the mayor. Yet none of them left Katamon Tet.

On the contrary, following the eviction of the squatters, there was a series of meetings with Knesset members and the media to put Katamon Tet's problems on the public agenda. On 3 May 1976, *Al Hamishmar*, the daily newspaper, announced: 'The squatters will continue their struggle.' The most effective coverage was given by *Ma'ariv*, the popular daily, in a series of in-depth reports published over four weeks. Its correspondent, Aharon Dolev, conveyed to the public the hardships endured by the youth of Katamon Tet. The first article, which appeared on 9 July 1976, bore the headline 'The Curse of Katamon' and the second, 'We Are Trapped.' The public was moved. The Knesset held an open discussion on the issue and set up a special committee to examine the problems. A senior member of the Likud Party, then in the opposition, visited Katamon Tet and arranged a meeting with party leader Menachem Begin. The meeting was paternalistic and ineffective: 'Begin turned to each member personally and asked "what is your problem?" and we tried to tell him that this was not a personal but a general problem that affected the entire neighbourhood.'[47] A year later, upon becoming prime minister, Begin declared that thousands of families were living in shameful housing conditions and announced the beginning of the Neighbourhood Renewal Programme. It is hard to say whether Begin's decision was influenced by the council's activity, as some of its members openly suggested, but it is evident that the Ohel Yosef council's activities put Katamon Tet's malaise on the national agenda. Ohel Yosef's leadership, though still suspect to some residents, had practically turned into a local force. For instance, families participating in the squatting arrived from different parts of Katamon Tet and though, as one of them said, 'they did not sympathize with the council's leaders, they still largely endorsed the organization's activity.'[48] Assessing the overall achievements of the Ohel Yosef council during this period, Meiry observed: 'We put the issue of poverty on the public agenda, and I think it affected Begin's decision to initiate the Neighbourhood Renewal Programme. Many young couples were provided with housing. The experience taught the residents how to present a problem, and how to cope with local issues within the existing democratic system. Residents were exposed to other social groups, to the intelligentsia, which helped heighten their self-esteem. And, finally, a local leadership had been formed.'[49] Meiry's assessment is important in that it elucidates both the instrumental and sociopersonal changes occurring in the area and the delicate interplay between material and subjective transformations. Meiry also indicated the direction of sociopersonal changes: learning how to act within the existing democratic system. Protest appears in this light as a means to a contradictory end, that is, acceptance of the basic norms and values by rejecting their practical concrete manifestations, e.g., housing conditions.

But the squatting and the political activity that followed have had some other consequences: the students in the Freemasonry House who accompanied the council through its formative stages were evacuated by the municipal housing company from their residence and dispersed all over the city (some of them left the country). Michael Paran and David Meiry were transferred to other neighbourhoods, and Avner Amiel's career, at the time very promising, was halted. Tougher measures were not imposed on them because, as the deputy mayor pointed out, 'We didn't want to turn them into martyrs.'[50] The residents were ready to confront the state at this point. An army sergeant-major who had participated in the squatting said: 'I deeply respect Michael. He left his wife and children and came over to work with us. We told him we would organize and prevent his removal, but he disagreed and said, "Let the dust settle." '[51] It appears that, where the local leaders failed, Michael Paran complemented them by being a symbol, a charismatic figure, with whom many mainstream-oriented residents could identify.

FROM NEIGHBOURHOOD ORGANIZATION TO URBAN MOVEMENT, 1977-1981

From 1977 to 1979, members of the Ohel Yosef council operated as diffusion agents, spreading the idea of local Ohel councils to other distressed neighbourhoods. Once again, Michael Paran came to play a leading role. 'Time and again,' Paran said, 'people told me that Ohel Yosef was a mere passing incident. You have, they would say, without a doubt contributed quite a lot, but in essence this was coincidental. I felt that I had to show them that an Ohel council could be established anywhere.'[52] Paran's drive for power, for leadership, is vigorously manifested in these lines. Not only poverty is at stake, but also Paran's own prestige as an organizer and, perhaps, as a leader. Transferred to the Shmuel Hanavi housing estate, he used the experience he gained in Katamon Tet to establish a second local youth council. He then approached the young leaders of the Nachlat Achim neighbourhood and suggested the establishment of a third Ohel council. As Paran put it: 'South, Katamon;

north, Shmuel Hanavi; Nachlat Achim at the centre – then to establish a federation. The struggle is to expand, from blocks 101 and 102 to the rest of the Katamons, and from there to other parts of the city.'[53]

Paran's ideology at the time had some strikingly anarchistic tones. 'Obviously,' he said, 'I read Proudhon and was influenced by him.' Members of Ohel Yosef followed in Paran's footsteps. They met with the members of the new Ohel councils, offered their assistance in setting up programs, and offered some financial help. From February 1979 onward, members of the Ohel Yosef council held weekly meetings in the Pargod Theatre in Jerusalem, during which Moshe Salach, who had returned to grassroots activity, elaborated in detail the Ohel's ideology. Young people and community workers from distressed neighbourhoods attended the meetings, and some of them started to organize Ohel councils on their own turf. Members of Ohel Yosef assisted the young councils by offering advice and guidance, and by heightening local motivation.

Each new Ohel council had to adopt the Ohel's constitution, which set out in detail the organization's objectives, strategies of action, membership conditions, and internal structure. Following the Ohel Yosef precedent, each council was expected to become the leading power in its area by initiating a variety of services: a youth club, extracurricular classes, and creative workshops, and by improving local conditions in housing, health, culture, education, and judicial affairs. To attain these goals, each council was expected to mobilize resources, purchase assets, organize seminars and conferences, and negotiate with public institutions.[54]

Throughout the intensive activity between 1977 and 1979, Yamin Swissa was out of the picture. He had resigned as Ohel Yosef chairman in late 1976, left his job at the municipality, and ultimately, as Amiel indicated, 'regressed to his previous condition.'[55] A deliberate attempt was undertaken by Avner Amiel in 1979 to draw Swissa back to grassroots activity. As Amiel said: 'At the beginning of 1979 I resumed my activity with the Ohalim movement, which now operated on a city-wide scale. In May I contacted Yamin Swissa and thereafter put much effort into drawing him back to public activity in the movement, this time as a secretary of an urban movement that included five neighbourhoods.'[56]

About the same time, Michael Paran approached the president of the World Sephardic Federation, who lives in Geneva, and gained his wholehearted support for the movement. The president supplied the movement with a luxury apartment and a secretary to facilitate its activities, and covered most of its expenses. Agents of the state thus acted as mobilizers of human and financial resources.

In June 1979, residents of the five neighbourhoods gathered at Binyanei Ha'uma, a Jerusalem conference centre, to celebrate the establishment of the Ohalim movement, officially called 'The Tent (Ohel) Neighbourhood and Community Centre.' The movement's charter explicitly stated that it 'would initiate social activities in distressed areas all over the country.'[57] In the framework of the movement, neighbourhoods exchanged information, formulated urban policy, and coordinated their activities. City-wide activities focused on such issues as lower standards of education in poor neighbourhoods, housing conditions of young couples, the rising prices of basic commodities, and the government's settlement policy in the administered territories. In addition, the Ohalim movement initiated a series of militant protest activities. In 1979, members of the movement squatted in an abandoned school building at the entrance to Jerusalem and demanded the establishment of a college for the poor neighbourhoods. In November of the same year, residents of the five neighbourhoods took to the streets to protest the government's economic policy. These confrontational activities culminated in 1980 in the protest known as Ohel Moreh. Mimicking Gush Emunim (a nationalist-orthodox movement that, in defiance of government policy, established new settlements in the administered territories, the first of them named Elon Moreh), the Ohalim movement set up, within Israel's borders, a tent settlement. Forty young couples organized by the movement squatted on an unsettled state-owned area and claimed the land for themselves. In doing so the movement sought to draw public attention to the harsh housing conditions of young couples and to criticize the massive investments in settlements in the territories. Members of the Peace Now movement and of kibbutzim, politicians, journalists, and other sympathizers came to express solidarity with the movement and to offer assistance. Given the massive public support, the police refrained from physically evicting the squatters. The ensuing negotiations involved the prime minister, the ministers of housing and defence, the deputy mayor of Jerusalem, and the president of the World Sephardic Federation. Subsequent to this protest the movement was allotted land at the edge of the city, upon which it was to establish a cooperative neighbourhood. The plan never materialized, however, possibly indicating that the movement's major aim was not material achievement but a moral-political one – putting the housing grievances of young couples on the national agenda.

There was another squatting episode in 1980, but this time the police acted resolutely and immediately evicted the squatters. Police surveillance of the neighbourhoods has been increased; Swissa was arrested on a drug charge and sent to prison. Yet the movement was not affected significantly. A former member of Swissa's gang took the lead and formed a city-wide forum of the Ohalim movement, neighbourhood committees, and local activists. The forum met every other week to discuss such city-wide issues as the closing of an institution for battered children in Baka, the municipality's plan to transform the residential area of Mekor Haim into an industrial area, and the social policy of community centres. Assessing the forum's impact on land-use change, the chairman of the Mekor Haim committee noted: 'The municipality takes into consideration the Ohalim movement's demands. When we went in to [Mayor] Teddy Kollek and asked him to prevent the proposed land use change, he didn't listen to our demand. Things have changed radically since we joined up with the Ohalim movement.'[58] In fact, the city engineer was instructed by Kollek to preserve the status quo in Mekor Haim. There was a feeling among the participants of those meetings that they constituted another city-wide organization functioning in parallel with City Hall. This point was clearly illustrated on 30 April 1981, when a hundred members of the forum occupied the Beit Hanoar Ha'ivry (the Hebrew Youth Centre) in Katamon, demanding a radical change in the élitist policy assumed by these centres.

Aside from negotiations, advocacy, lobbying, and protest, the movement founded three cooperative plants in which socially detached youth and young delinquents were employed. The movement's community theatre performed in different places all over the country. The movement has also organized a meeting between the residents of poor neighbourhoods and Israeli Arabs in order to bridge the deep rift between the two groups. In the course of these activities, Katamon Tet, the cradle of the Ohalim movement, turned into a symbol of power. Shlomo Wasana, then the director of the movement's community theatre, pointed out that 'the activity in the field turned Katamon into a centre of power.'[59] A Shmuel Hanavi activist argued that 'the Ohalim movement changed the system of power relations in the city,'[60] and pointed to the growing cooperation between the movement and the local authority acting against the central government. In a lecture before Israeli soldiers after being released from prison, Yamin Swissa contended: 'They never believed that power would come from this ghetto.'[61]

The political activity at the urban level was supplemented by programmatic activity at the neighbourhood level. The Ohel councils negotiated on local issues with the local and central state, and with the advent of the Neighbourhood Renewal Programme (NRP), comprised the steering committees that made policy at the neighbourhood level. In this manner, the movement adopted a dualistic orientation: programmatic and instrumental at the neighbourhood level, and a political-power orientation at the urban level. Accordingly, the strategies of action ranged from co-production to protest, thus simultaneously accepting and defying the system's rules.

Since it operated both within and outside the established political system, any attempt to categorize the movement would be simplistic. This complexity resulted in tension and conflict within the state as to the appropriate attitude towards the Ohalim. Elad Peled, the then newly elected deputy mayor, described the municipality's ambivalence:

Within the municipality there are two different conceptions of cooperation with neighbourhood organizations. One conception, characteristic of the parties, is that neighbourhoods should be represented and administered by the old bosses to whom you give something and get something in return. Another conception, which owes its ideology to Avner Amiel at the department of youth, leisure, and community, argues that it is far better to cooperate with the rising tide instead of pretending not to see it. The orthodox establishment accuses Amiel of agitation.[62]

Peled then distinguished between different streams within the anti-orthodox approach:

There is a certain level of consensus with Avner's approach, but there is no consensus whatsoever with Michael Paran's approach. My own conception is quite close to Amiel's ... The neighbourhoods have set themselves on the track of peaceful revolution and it is both necessary and desirable to have them express their authentic and justified protest. We should therefore cooperate with the O-halim movement and assist them as long as they follow the rules of the game. The orthodox establishment (made up of former deputy mayor Yosef Gadish and other senior officials) rejects these ideas. But Teddy Kollek supported my view. I met with their leaders, prevented the police from attacking the Ohel Moreh tent settlement, and helped them establish cooperative and working groups in the framework of the Neighbourhood Renewal Programme.[63]

As a colonel in the Israeli Army with a doctorate in education, Peled was quite sensitive to the plight of youth in distressed neighbourhoods and was consequently willing to adopt new approaches to neighbourhood management. During his short term as deputy mayor, the municipality continued to finance the movement's social services. But Peled sought to go far beyond this, to the decentralization of other services, in order to advance what he called 'universalization and democracy.' The real power, as he put it, did not lie in the 'ephemeral services' developed by the movement, but in central services given to the neighbourhoods by the welfare state, such as medical clinics (Kupat Holim), social-security grants, and employment bureaus. As long as these services remained centralized, Peled argued, decentralization and universalization were doomed to be limited in scope. Hence his demand 'to further universalize [i.e., decentralize] the provision of services through local organizations.'[64] In his view, members of the Ohalim movement have already comprehended this principle: 'They grasped the idea of power; they understood that power implies control over resources ... Their intention is to develop population dependence on the Ohel council instead of on the state. What Mapai's (Labour's) dinosaurs realized several decades ago was that they have to control the tap. Now the leader of Ohel Yosef wants to control all the taps.'[65]

Indeed, Peled intensified the contact with the movement, and behind the scenes even supported its anti-government protest activities. For example, some of the equipment for the Ohel Moreh tent settlement was supplied by the municipality itself in a well-planned move that was agreed upon in advance. Peled became popular in the neighbourhood, where he was described as 'trustworthy,' but was condemned by the old-time politicians. Eventually, he resigned his job, and in January 1982 became the chairman of the re-established public council of the Ohalim movement. Addressing the council, he said: 'My own inclination is to work with a social movement and not with a neighbourhood committee. The 1974 form of activity is inappropriate now. I don't want to deal with refuse collection and local services.'[66] Peled never specified what precisely he wanted to achieve, and much like those of other leaders, his positive vision, as opposed to his articulated critique, remained vague and unclear. This, perhaps, is one of the predicaments of such movements – a sophisticated critique of state bureaucracy and politics dwelling side by side with a deep longing for an alternative but vaguely conceived future.

The interaction with the state has not been confined to the local authority alone. The Neighbourhood Renewal Programme provided contact with the central state as well. Members of the Ohel councils became involved in local steering committees, in decision making concerning the allocation of resources, and in negotiations with national officials and politicians. As a result, there has been, much as in the DERA case (see chapter 6) a shift of emphasis from self-help services initiated from below to co-production of large-scale projects financed by massive state resources. In the course of this change, some of the movement's activists and leaders have been absorbed into the bureaucratic system, becoming state wage-earners. Criticizing this process, Shlomo Wassana observed: 'It's the establishment's bear hug ... it's pollution: controlled local initiative that prevents you from operating according to your own basic inclinations.'[67] Yamin Swissa conceded that 'the Ohel's activities were eroded by the NRP.'[68] Alice Shalvy further contended that 'the NRP destroyed the spontaneous process of self-help by co-opting local residents into large-scale physical projects.'[69]

Despite the severe critique, co-production with state agencies has increasingly become the major feature of the Ohel councils, thus enhancing institutionalization within the existing political system. The NRP has, in other words, acted as a powerful tool in pulling the Ohalim movement inward towards the existing bureaucratic centre. The institutionalization process has been furthered by the political parties. Attracted by the movement's popularity, several attempts have been made to incorporate the movement's leaders, Michael Paran and Yamin Swissa. In 1981, Swissa, supported by the Labour Party but opposed by the other Ohel councils, established the Ohalim Party. This deepened the existing dissatisfaction with Swissa's authoritarian leadership and eventually led to an internal split. Cooperation at the urban level came to a halt, embryonic Ohel councils withered away, and by September 1981, Michael Paran bluntly conceded that 'there isn't any movement any more; it has simply vanished.'[70] Commenting on the downfall of the movement, Avner Amiel said: 'Doing business with a subculture is a difficult task ... The subculture somewhat ruins things ... it is interested in immediate achievements. Their id is also a bit stronger; a party gives out money, so they go to work [for it] immediately.'[71]

In 1989, when this study was concluded, the Ohel councils in Katamon Tet and Shumel Hanavi were still functioning, although without any cooperation or exchange between them. Yamin Swissa has managed to climb up the political ladder and become a member of the Labour Party's central committee. Moshe Salah has become an orthodox Jew and turned to religious studies, Michael Paran has returned to his old profession and works as a lawyer, occasionally defending young delinquents from disadvantaged neighbourhoods. Avner Amiel has continued, as enthusiastic as ever, to establish new forums and groups, trying with them to advance the values of liberal democracy and social tolerance towards other groups, and especially towards Palestinian Arabs. Alice Shalvy has become the chairperson of Israel's feminist lobby.

Unlike its position in the early 1970s, Israeli society at the beginning of the 1990s is turning a cold shoulder to lower-class groups, and poverty is not a significant issue on the public agenda. There are several possible ways of accounting for this change. The intelligentsia, frustrated perhaps by the ongoing political support that the poor neighbourhoods give to the right-wing parties, has retreated into its books. The movement's leaders have failed to develop into major political figures and, now that the dust has settled, look like ordinary party activists. Finally, Israeli society is preoccupied with the uprising in the occupied territories and with the ongoing public debate over the future of the territories, and has relegated poverty to a lower priority.

CONCLUSION

The historical circumstances of immigrant absorption have created a specific social setting that has immensely influenced social protest. The salient features of this setting were:

a / The arrival of a mass wave of immigrants originating in pre-modern 'Oriental' societies into a relatively modern 'Western' society. The unavoidable result has been the crystalization of the newcomers (of Sephardic origin) in the lower echelons of the economic system, and hence the relatively high correlation between ethnic origin and lower economic status.
b / Massive state intervention in absorbing the newcomers and in socializing urban costs by providing housing and urban services to the newcomers.
c / The spatial concentration of this lower-class ethnic group in isolated enclaves at the city's periphery.
d / The emergence of a notable social gap between the newly arrived Sephardic residents and the old-time Ashkenazic residents.

The spatial concentration of lower-class people in isolated and dilapidated housing estates acted as a necessary trigger for social protest. But,
in and of themselves these conditions were insufficient to produce social
action. To transform an underclass living in substandard housing into
a social movement required, as Touraine's theory (1981) clearly shows,
the intervention of a human agent. Indeed, state agents (community
workers and politicians), civil society actors (volunteers, including artists,
students, and university professors), and the movement's leaders, drawing
on their rules (norms and values) and resources (knowledge, skills, networks, and available funds), played a leading role in transforming the
existing social base into a social force. Analysing the role of state agents
reveals that this group was the driving force behind the movement in
its preliminary stage. Unlike their counterparts in Ir Ganim, who failed
to acquire the confidence of the local social base (see chapter 5), those
operating in Katamon Tet established close contacts with the local residents; disseminated ethnic, territorial, and housing messages that were
easily absorbed by the local constituency; and fostered a strong
leadership.

Assisted by other social actors, the state agents worked to modify well-
entrenched interpretative schemes and to deroutinize old patterns of behaviour that sustained asymmetrical power relations. They thus signalled
the possibility of sublimating feelings of anger, revenge, and discontent
into organized social activity; clarified the opportunities embodied in
assuming local responsibility and territorial self-management; and provided a set of meanings and symbols – ethnic, class, and territorial –
with which to identify. State agents thus played an important role not
only in social mobilization, but also in the search for the movement's
meaning.

It would be a mistake, however, to attribute too much rationality (i.e.,
correspondence between means and ends) to the activity of state agents.
Although serving as the real instigators behind the movement, they operated under conditions not entirely acknowledged, and their activity
bore some unintended consequences. To begin with, the local leaders
and their associates brought into the movement old norms and patterns
of behaviour that clashed strikingly with the idea of social liberation
or class struggle as postulated by some of the state agents. Members
of the former gang, for instance, brought along old habits of social conformity, obedience, a tendency for confrontation, and authoritarian patterns of leadership. Moreover, the prevailing attitude among the leaders
and other members of the group was that their social and physical prob-

lems were rooted in ethnic discrimination. Any attempt to mould the local problems in class terms was greeted with suspicion, and only a few members adopted a class-based approach (most notably, the leaders of the movement). The attempt by some of the state agents and radical students to create a radical left-wing movement was thus diverted to a certain extent by traditional norms and values rooted in the universe of daily life experience (the life world) that permeated the movement.

The activity of the state agents was further hampered by some unintended consequences. Protest has been utilized as a means of socialization and even as a way of incorporating peripheral groups into mainstream society, and into the state apparatus. What may appear at a particular time as defiance of state authority – e.g., confrontation with state bureaucrats, politicians, laws, and norms – appears over a longer period as acceptance of the state's rules, values, and power centres. This may suggest that studies of urban social movements should stop celebrating the incidental and short-term events – e.g., specific demonstrations or squatting operations – and start tackling seriously the historical development of such movements, thus exposing the contradictory meanings of social protest.

Limited as the present case may be, it still suggests that, when viewed historically, protest has become a means to an opposite end, that is, to attaining legitimacy, co-production, and political neutralization. The state, in other words, has succeeded in expropriating even its critics, and when viewed historically, community work appears to be another form of political control. Yet it is necessary to state a reservation. We do not mean to suggest that such a process was planned or deliberated, or intended by the state. Indeed, the empirical evidence points to the contrary, that protest exposed deep conflicts between opponents and proponents of the movement within the state. It appears that the movement's supporters within the state genuinely expressed the liberal ideas prevailing among certain segments within civil society. Along with representatives of those liberal segments, including artists, students, and professors, state agents have intervened in social life and disseminated their cultural values, only to ultimately produce another mainstream-oriented movement!

PART FOUR

The Equivocal History of
Neighbourhood Participation

The rhetoric of partnership has been an abiding element in urban discourse over the past twenty-five years, referring variously to relations between central government and local government, to contacts between the local state and neighbourhood interests, and, increasingly through the 1980s, to joint projects like waterfront redevelopment linking the public and private sectors. In this book, the second of these partnerships, between City Hall and its constituent neighbourhoods, has provided a backdrop for several earlier case studies, notably in Shaughnessy, Rehavia, and Ir Ganim. In this final section we focus squarely on the decentralization of planning and other functions, from state bureaucracies to neighbourhood organizations; one of the key issues we explore is the assessment of the extent to which functional devolution (to the extent it has really occurred) has been accompanied by the devolution of power; in short, to consider the politics of partnership.

These and related issues are examined in the inner-city neighbourhoods of Kitsilano and Baka. Both districts have experienced considerable social change since the 1960s as a result of their location and amenities. Both are placed within easy reach of burgeoning downtown office employment; Kitsilano's environmental amenities of beaches and ocean and mountain views are accompanied by the residential amenity of Baka's large old houses built by a now displaced Arab middle class. These attributes have encouraged gentrification to take place in both districts, though the process remains incomplete, so that considerable social diversity has remained. Kitsilano, historically a lower-middle-class community of homeowners, became the centre of Vancouver's counterculture in the 1960s and, as has so often been the case, this group was succeeded by in-migrating middle-class professionals. In 1972 a protest group, the West Broadway Citizens' Committee (WBCC), was formed to resist this embourgeoisement, as an alliance of older homeowners and younger para-professionals and counter-culture members. They found themselves in disagreement with a long-established ratepayers' association in its twilight years. While the ratepayers were quickly outnumbered and became inconsequential, other divisions in the community emerged as WBCC stood firmly behind Alinsky-style protest. In Baka, division was built into the fabric of the neighbourhood council as the primarily Ashkenazi gentrifiers of north Baka were set in the same territory as the established and poorer Sephardic community.

In British Columbia the period from 1968 to 1975 was the high-water mark in the decentralization of public services as new governments (at all three levels) responded to the community pressures which had elected them in a participatory process that was inspired from both above and below. Kitsilano was a designated area for two federal community-enrichment initiatives, one of which, the Neighbourhood Improvement Programme, required resident participation in establishing local projects for funding; provincially, the new NDP government introduced community resources boards, in which elected local committees administered and funded a range of social services; and municipally, a reform council introduced a participatory model of neighbourhood land-use planning. These tendencies towards decentralization had begun in the United States a decade earlier and diffused widely throughout the Western world (Sharpe 1979). By the end of the decade they were taken up by conservative as well as left-liberal administrations, although often reworked for different purposes; the inner-city partnership program in Britain, for example, was quickly seen as a means of increasing the direct control of central government. In Israel, the conservative Likud Party initiated its Neighbourhood Renewal Programme around the same time, while in Jerusalem the distinctive vision of Mayor Kollek led to a top-down policy of neighbourhood self-management which began in 1980. The Jerusalem program created neighbourhood councils charged with establishing local priorities for public services; the Baka council, one of the first, was constituted in 1982.

Mayor Kollek's vision acknowledged, and to a degree, empowered local cultures in a diverse and divided city. But it also made the city more governable by showing an acceptable face to City Council. These conflicting motives mean that neighbourhood participation is placed on a precariously fine line between protest and incorporation, or, from the state's perspective, between disruption and governability. This tension has permitted varying interpretations to be made of community participation. To some it is a cynical venture of social control by the state, which permits an extension of its reach further into the realms of daily life.[1] This was the eventual conclusion also of WBCC and led to its withdrawal from the co-production activities of local area planning and neighbourhood improvement. But, in severing its ties with the state (and state funds) and reasserting itself as a protest organization, the WBCC became politically isolated and underresourced, so that, despite initial achievements, it dissolved after four years of community activism. A more nuanced view of participation sees both empowerment and co-optation as simultaneous and contradictory tendencies in the state.[2] To the extent that state funding permits group survival, it provides a form of political empowerment. To the extent that community needs are addressed by the state, however imperfectly, a measure of social and economic empowerment is attained. This latter view sees the outcomes of participation as more contingent as community organizations struggle to turn to advantage the opportunities and constraints before them.

Moreover, there are additional issues of both practical and theoretical importance which muddy the waters still further. In its reluctance to share power with neighbourhood groups, the state has legitimate questions of its own. How widespread is the grass-roots call for empowerment, and how representative are the 'professional citizens' (as a member of City Council dismissively described the WBCC)? In Kitsilano's resources board election, for example, fewer than 10 per cent of the population cast their ballot. In professional north Baka, 80 per cent of residents were aware of the neighbourhood council, but in south Baka only a quarter of residents who were surveyed knew of its existence. Nor do neighbourhood groups always escape the temptation to pursue interests that are not only self-seeking, but exclusively so. The pursuit of school curricula reform by liberal Baka gentrifiers was not shared by longer-established Sephardic residents. More generally neighbourhoods may seek power for privatistic ends; Shaughnessy's pursuit of land-use controls to exclude others is not unusual, and sullies some of the perhaps too neatly drawn political (and ethical) conclusions of the 1970s.

The use of liberal means to secure conservative ends also alerts us to the importance of longitudinal research which is not limited to the study of a particular conflict or flashpoint. While the WBCC was terminated in 1976, its leadership moved on to related initiatives in developing social housing and promoting more democratic ward politics. As we saw earlier in Strathcona, the Downtown Eastside, and Katamon

Tet, one should not overlook the incubator effect of neighbourhood organizations, educating and nurturing leaders for new projects, and in some instances, political careers. In this latter outcome, we need to acknowledge also the possibility that the lessons of the lifeworld may infiltrate the policies of the state.

8

The Limits of Neighbourhood Empowerment: Gentrification, Resistance, and Burn-out in Kitsilano

The 1967–72 struggle over first the Chinatown freeway and then urban renewal and rehabilitation in Strathcona prepared the way for a new departure in civic politics in Vancouver. As we saw in chapter 1, these events were not unique but part of a broader, if far from complete, movement towards urban reform and citizen empowerment in certain Canadian cities. Moreover, the Canadian story was repeated internationally, with the so-called neighbourhood movement in the United States, and Mayor Kollek's concept of neighbourhood self-government, which introduced to areas of Jerusalem like Baka (see chapter 9) a similar set of opportunities – and frustrations.

In Vancouver the liberal reform slogans of the Council majority in 1972 promised new departures in both policy and process. Policy would include a range of strategies of growth management during a cycle of rapid development. The maxim of the highest and best use in land development would be qualified by the plural objectives of the 'livable city.' This liberal ideology included a concern with environmental aesthetics (parks, landscaping, pollution control), social justice (notably an enlightened concern for small-scale social housing), transportation (public transit, not freeways), cultural pluralism in an increasingly cosmopolitan city, and attention to the scale of development, with medium density, and a human scale, favoured over high density construction.[1] The process of local government appeared far more open, with practical steps taken to heighten public awareness of civic issues, to disperse information, and to award citizens greater empowerment in decision-making procedures. The attitude of the dominant reform group on council towards participation had been anticipated by the apprenticeship served by a number of its leaders in Chinatown-Strathcona.[2] Like those of other Canadian cities, Vancouver's reform council introduced a form of decentralized local area, or neighbourhood, planning in the early 1970s.[3] A public decision-making process was an integral element of the reform platform: the first of eight points in the policy paper of The Electors Action Movement (TEAM) on planning and development in the 1976 civic election was 'to encourage participation in the planning process of persons and organizations,' while a later item was 'to give to the occupants of neighbourhoods as strong a voice as possible.'[4] Here, then, was a new initiative of the local state, attempting to institutionalize the community participation forced upon it by protest movements. Was this a genuine offer of an enhanced local democracy, or a veiled strategy of the state to restore governability through a still deeper involvement in everyday life?

There was no shortage of willing takers for this apparent offer of local empowerment among the city's neighbourhoods and interest groups. In the context of the 1972–4 development boom, land-use conflict spread quickly from the late 1960s origin of Chinatown-Strathcona. From the beginning of 1973 to the end of 1975 close to one hundred locational conflicts were reported in the daily press, concentrated in, but not limited to, the downtown and inner-city districts (Ley and Mercer 1980). The map of conflict was not, however, a simple replica of the pattern of land-use change. Conflict was disproportionately concentrated in the white-collar districts on the city's west side, where a vigilant and educated citizenry were active contestants of proposed development. Nowhere was this more evident than in the inner-city district of Kitsilano, where a mobilized community vigorously tested the limits of neighbourhood power.

KITSILANO: GROWTH VERSUS THE COUNTER-CULTURE

One of the first suburbs built outside the downtown peninsula, Kitsilano had always been a socially mixed, Anglo-Saxon neighbourhood. But, by the 1950s, as the district aged, the cycle of down-filtering led to a declining number of middle-class households, and a growing proportion of widows and the retired. During the 1960s, student numbers increased substantially; from 1961 to 1971 the population aged between twenty and twenty-four years more than doubled in the eastern, apartment-zoned section. By the end of the decade, Fourth Avenue had become Vancouver's principal youth thoroughfare, and during the 1970s included such counter-culture emblems as the Divine Light Mission, craft shops, the Soft Rock Cafe, and the founding office of the international environmental group, the Greenpeace Foundation. Neighbourhood school attendance plummeted by almost one-third, from a peak of 4,400 in 1959 to 3,000 in 1975. Kitsilano, the family neighbourhood, became a district of non-family households; even in the areas of single-family dwellings, families with children at home were a minority group by 1971 (Stobie 1979, 65).

But a second change was also in progress, for in more ways than one the youth culture was an avant-garde. In 1971 Kitsilano remained an area of modest incomes, with the average family income more than 10 per cent below the city mean. However broader contexts speedily transformed this status. Rapid economic growth in the metropolitan area was associated with a characteristic shift towards a post-industrial landscape and employment profile. A downtown office boom accommodated large numbers of new professional and managerial jobs in both the private and the public sector. Young high-status households were selectively drawn to neighbourhoods like Kitsilano, close to downtown, yet with high levels of environmental amenity provided by the beach, mountain, and ocean views, and with the specialty stores and restaurants of an adult-oriented lifestyle. Like many inner-city neighbourhoods throughout Canada and the Western world, in the early 1970s Kitsilano faced the rapid onset of gentrification. Since then it has been identified by both academic and literary writers as one of Canada's most distinctive neighbourhoods of young urban professionals.[5] Redevelopment rather than renovation was the normal transition process. In place of rental apartments, market condominiums became the principal expression of inner-city embourgeoisement, and Kitsilano led other districts with almost 1,500 units (on close to 50 sites) constructed in the five years to 1976. In contrast, only four new rental apartment projects were registered. In the rental market, growing demand was frustrated by declining supply as new condominiums required the demolition or conversion of existing rental units. More than 1,250 rental units disappeared in this manner between 1968 and 1976, and for much of the 1974-6 period the official vacancy rate was zero per cent.

Gentrification clearly indicated class succession in the housing market. Whereas in 1971 inner-city rents and inner-city incomes were both beneath the city mean, by the mid 1970s it was estimated that the cost of a condominium required an income of 25-50 per cent above the city mean. In the midst of a crisis of affordable rental housing, in the face of the apparent injustice of gentrification, and with evidence of manipulation of the housing market by property interests, a segment of the community resisted. With slogans of 'We aim to stay' and 'Housing for everyone not just the rich,' the West Broadway Citizens' Committee entered the fray and made redevelopment a political issue in the autumn of 1972.

Kitsilano has experienced a long history of neighbourhood associations and other supportive expressions of an institutionally complete community, including the Kitsilano Ratepayers' Association (KRA), founded in 1909.[6] Despite its longevity, the representativeness of the Association in the broader neighbourhood is a moot point. Members were disproportionately drawn from the ranks of local small-business people, a number of them with property interests. The executive typically included at least one sitting member of City Council, providing direct access to elected officials. During much of this long period the council was similarly constituted primarily of the managers of small businesses, belonging to the Non-Partisan Association (NPA) and sharing similar values with the KRA. Despite a membership peak in 1956, the seeds of the KRA's demise were then in place. In that year almost 60 per cent of the executive were widows or retired members, symptomatic of the ageing of the generation who had opened up the district.[7] With their ageing came a change of priorities. Earlier resistance to rezoning for higher densities began to give way to support and even lobbying in favour of rezoning. In retirement the family home took on a new meaning as a nest egg, which, under more intensive forms of zoning, would guarantee financial security in old age. Thus, in April 1973 the KRA presented a brief to City Council, supporting the ongoing redevelopment of the district, and specifically the high-rise zoning in northeast Kitsilano; KRA announced its opposition to any down-zoning of the area.[8] Nine months later, the rump of the KRA, reduced by that time to two principal and ageing advocates, once again spoke forcefully at a public meeting in favour of redevelopment and against down-zoning of districts zoned for high-rise apartments. From their perspective, redevelopment represented progress and was consistent with the 'upgrading' of Kitsilano the Residents' Association had been committed to for almost seventy years.[9] Three days later, before Council in the packed auditorium of Kitsilano Secondary School, the KRA spokesman presented a strong brief against down-zoning, and against 'those transients who claim to represent the community.'[10] But the 500 Kitsilano residents present were on the side of the 'transients'; they roared approval for a petition in favour of down-zoning presented by the West Broadway Citizens' Committee (WBCC) and endorsed by other speakers. Overriding KRA protest and criticism from real estate representatives, Council voted unanimously to approve residential down-zoning for Kitsilano. A redefinition of the neighbourhood had occurred, and a political succession was under way to fight for it.

The origins of the WBCC were inauspicious enough, though in the context of rapid neighbourhood change, the emergence of a protest group is scarcely surprising, particularly in an era when a dominant liberal ideology sustained the slogans of public participation and neighbourhood empowerment in decision making. In 1972, The Electors Action Movement (TEAM), a liberal reform party of young professionals and managers, founded in 1968, won control of City Hall in a landslide of popular support, sweeping aside the dynasty of the Non-Partisan Association who had exercised power since 1935 (Ley 1980). Key issues in the election campaign were greater public participation in decision making, environmental quality, and a critique of the power of the development lobby and their secretive allies at City Hall, an alliance starkly revealed in the built environment during a land boom. The provincial government was led by the New Democratic Party (NDP), who won a surprising election victory in autumn 1972, the first time that a social-democratic party had acceded to power in British Columbia. Federally, Pierre Trudeau's Liberals remained in office, and even if the initial excitement of Trudeaumania in spring 1968 was somewhat tarnished, commitments to decentralization and a more open society remained in place. At all levels of the state, then, there were well-grounded expectations for more open government and greater attention to social justice in public policy.

The broader politics of urban development was played out in sharper focus in Kitsilano where strong redevelopment pressures ran up against the generation and the values which had fed counter-cultural social movements. The event which triggered neighbourhood mobilization was a proposal in 1972 to upgrade the commercial strip of West Broadway, a typical streetcar thoroughfare of small retail stores with a local market. A development study, sponsored jointly by the City of Vancouver and local merchants, proposed 'to revitalize Broadway by creating all the amenities and some of the character of a regional shopping centre without the gigantic surrounding car park.'[11] Associated with this twenty-year strategy was a more immediate beautification plan. As part of this overall process, space for car parking would require expropriation of nearby single-family homes. The project was typical of urban planning during the NPA period. The unwritten assumption was that planning was synonymous with growth, and thus the city would encourage private-sector initiatives even to the extent of cost-sharing in meeting development expenses such as consultants' reports. This process would unfold quietly, and the public would be informed (not consulted) only when considerable momentum had been attained, even though serious impacts might well ensue; in the case of the West Broadway plan these impacts included the expropriation of owner-occupied houses for commercial expansion.

At the end of a public hearing in November 1972 five or six residents gathered in the lobby of Kitsilano Secondary School, angered at the expropriation of private housing. They were joined by Nathan Karmel, a community development organizer assigned to Kitsilano by the locally funded United Community Services. He convinced the group that joint action to resist the project was feasible. At the end of the month, forty residents met to elect an executive, identify goals, and select a name – the West Broadway Citizens' Committee. The group spent the next eight months in research and analysis, and following a number of conflict-ridden meetings with representatives of the city and the merchants, persuaded Council (now, of course, with a TEAM majority) to adopt ten guidelines for retail development on West Broadway. Meanwhile, membership, including a strong component of homeowners, had risen to seventy. At this stage a decision was reached not to become a single-issue organization, but to intervene more broadly to resist and redefine changes in the built environment. An aggressive stand was taken against high-rise redevelopment as the most massive form of neighbourhood transition. The activism of the WBCC was widely reported in the media, and in a polarizing situation of edacious private development, serious shortages of affordable housing, and active recruitment drives, membership grew rapidly, reaching a probable peak of 441 in late 1974.[12]

Who were these citizens and how representative were they of the broader community of 34,000? Critics of the WBCC (of which there were many) constantly charged that its members were counter-cultural transients, opportunistic and not representative of the neighbourhood at large; this was certainly the view of the KRA. In a celebrated outburst, a newspaper columnist accused the WBCC leadership of being political opportunists, who were taking advantage of senior citizens and their housing needs to advance their own political aspirations.[13] Later, as relations with the reform council soured, elected officials began to speak sarcastically of the 'professional citizens' in Kitsilano. Yet there is abundant evidence that the WBCC enjoyed broad grass-roots support, and that its objectives (if not always its tactics) were widely shared. At public hearings it spoke with the voice of the majority in attendance. At the planned demonstration which evoked the language of 'dirty tricks' and 'Watergate' from the conservative columnist, the WBCC had the endorsement of twenty-three community groups, including the Catholic parish priest, a pre-school, and five senior citizens' associations.[14] A reform alderman who later spoke harshly of the WBCC did not challenge its representativeness as a much smaller association in June 1973 at a community meeting to discuss Broadway commercial redevelopment. Contrasting the potential retail developer with the WBCC, he observed: 'Mr Orr is not as representative of the community as you people who live here are. His main interest is in profit and economics. Well, that has some place in our society, but that should never be the all-important consideration in planning any area of the city.'[15]

The most convincing demonstration of the alderman's assessment came a year later. The provincial NDP government decided to decentralize aspects of its social and welfare programs to elected community resources boards, which would administer them. This innovation was a further sign of the political context of the times and its commitment to community participation in both decision making and management, though the experiment was short-lived and was terminated only two years later by a newly elected conservative government in the province. None the less, the Kitsilano Resources Board election of June 1974 was an indicator of local political endorsement. Emphasizing the housing issue under the slogan 'We aim to stay' the WBCC ran a slate of twelve candidates for the fourteen-person board, including several members of its leadership. In a field of thirty-nine, all twelve were elected.[16]

Though the WBCC records are incomplete, some further analysis is possible of the 1974 membership list. Homeowners remained an important element, especially among the leadership, but tenants were numerically dominant. Partial occupational data indicated a lower-middle-class grouping of service workers, including a number of public-service employees, and representatives of the 'soft' professions and para-professions, including teachers, nurses, and artists. There was a smaller group of blue-collar workers, often established homeowners, and an admixture of students and members of the counter-culture. The association was not financially privileged, including as it did, the retired, single parents, and the underemployed. The differences in social class with the business and professional orientation of KRA membership a generation earlier is marked. In age the largest single grouping was the cohort of those aged twenty-five to thirty-five, precisely the cohort which had grown so rapidly in Kitsilano that, by 1976, it comprised 50 per cent of the population in the apartment area, 40 per cent in the conversion area, and 30 per cent in the single-family area. Although senior citizens were a minority, a number were active in the organization. Three were successful candidates on the resources-board slate, while others were visible in various actions. At one demonstration which temporarily stopped work at a condominium construction site, ten of the eighty protesters were senior citizens.[17]

The WBCC enjoyed energetic leadership which showed theoretical sophistication in interpreting urban change. The elected chair of the organization, following its augural meeting in November 1972, was Jacques Khouri, who had moved into Kitsilano in 1970 and had subsequently bought his own house. Khouri was in his mid twenties, and a graduate of the Urban Land Economics program at the University of British Columbia. At the time he was an employee of the federal government, but his political sympathies were revealed by his unsuccessful candidacy in the 1972 municipal elections for the left-wing Committee of Progressive Electors (COPE). By 1974 he described himself as a radio broadcaster, and indeed ran through several short-term jobs for the next ten years while he pursued his real vocation, the preservation and supply of affordable housing. In pursuit of community objectives Khouri was decisive, visionary, resourceful, and never intimidated; on one occasion he posed as a speculative property investor in order to purchase a site for cooperative housing. He became chair of the elected Community Resources Board in 1974 and inspired several housing action groups spun off from the WBCC.

Part of the theoretical interpretation of events in Kitsilano was provided by Nathan Karmel, community organizer for the WBCC. The same age as Khouri, Karmel had grown up in Kitsilano and spent a year at the University of British Columbia Law School before completing a Master's degree in Social Work in Montreal. Karmel was influenced by the radical community development strategy of Saul Alinsky. 'There's no point in sitting down and dealing with people on a one-to-one basis who have problems as the result of the system. It's smarter to organize people to change the system.'[18] It was Karmel who had convinced the original homeowners to organize to resist commercial redevelopment on Broadway; indeed he had posed the questions during the public hearing in

November 1972 which showed that the city was considering expropriation of houses to expedite the development.[19] A consummate professional, he led the occupation of one muddy construction site in suit and overcoat while clutching a briefcase full of press releases in anticipation of the arrival of the media. A complementary theoretical analysis was provided by Donald Gutstein, an instructor in the School of Architecture at the university. Born in 1939, Gutstein arrived in Kitsilano from Toronto in 1968 and was also one of the founding members of the association. He was a meticulous researcher of development issues and uncovered a number of examples of block-busting and other forms of manipulation of the real estate market. His book, *Vancouver Ltd.*, was a trenchant exposition of the manipulated-city thesis, positing an interlocking élite of developers and politicians who conspired in their plans for the built environment. This semi-popular volume received wide distribution across Canada and contributed towards an influential theory of élite conspiracy in the interpretation of urban development.[20]

While this triumvirate of Khouri, Karmel, and Gutstein provided both charismatic leadership and a convincing theoretical interpretation of change, they were supported by an active cast of workers. Beatrice Kellie, a nurse in her sixties and homeowner for more than ten years in Kitsilano, had been a founding member of the WBCC and was elected as the group's second chairperson. Frank Hyde, also a long-established homeowner, radicalized by the threat of expropriation of his home for the Broadway project, was a frequent spokesperson for the group. Carl Lehan, WBCC treasurer and neighbour of Bea Kellie, was a retired resident who had lived in Kitsilano for more than twenty years; the spectre of rapid development drew him to his first demonstration at age sixty-six. Susan Hoeppner, WBCC staff coordinator, was a single parent and tenant; like the other three she was elected to the resources board where she acted as liaison with a WBCC-sponsored subsidiary, Renters United for Secure Housing (RUSH). The elected leadership was accountable to its members through monthly meetings and an annual general meeting, where attendances ranged from twenty to seventy.

Ideological Orientations, Political Strategies

In true Alinsky fashion, the WBCC's central objective was community control. Its founding goals were frequently repeated in minutes and reports.[21]

1. To ensure that local area residents are consulted before any decisions on major developments in Kitsilano are made.
2. To involve residents in an ongoing program of planning for the future development of Kitsilano.
3. To organize citizens in the community to better meet their diverse needs.

The crux of this, of course, is community control.

The same message was distributed in a news release within a few weeks of the group's formation: 'Call it grass-roots planning or participatory planning or whatever you want, the main ingredient is people and the objective is controlling the growth of the city according to our needs and priorities ... If we can take an active part in planning, then we *can* control the future shape of our community.'[22]

This ideology was pursued unwaveringly through the history of the WBCC and its spin-off groups, and permits an understanding of its unwillingness to compromise its principles which, like DERA's (chapter 6), so frequently led to division and conflict both with other community groups and with different arms of the state. Gutstein (1975, 183) observed that it may be necessary to alienate middle-class sympathizers in the pursuit of direct action, such as demonstrations: 'Tough actions will eventually drive the liberals from the group.' The alternative is the 'liberalization' of the group from strong action to a more cooperative relation with the state and 'a comfortable period of decline' (ibid). This rejection of co-production with the state on any terms other than those held by the group itself does alert the community to the dangers of co-optation (Ley 1974). This was certainly the view of local area planning which led to the withdrawal of the WBCC from the Kitsilano planning process only a few months after it had begun: 'we pulled out of the group that we had helped form, to show City Council that we would not take part in a sham attempt to dupe citizens into being manipulated by civic bureaucrats.'[23] But ideological purity is a political assumption open to scrutiny, and the experience of citizens elsewhere in the city, in low-income Strathcona and high-income Shaughnessy, show the possibilities of a more flexible approach to co-production.

Alinsky-inspired theoretical analysis of neighbourhood change drew upon a wide range of strategies of resistance. Integral to these was local power emerging out of local organizations around issues of community significance. Such a project was, however, daunting in a community becoming dominated by tenants with rapid residential turnover. Apathy was seen as 'a problem of ignorance, of lack of understanding and lack of choices,'[24] and, to counteract it, the WBCC and affiliated groups engaged in a detailed program of research, communication, and education. A spate of free community newspapers, *Around Kitsilano*, *RUSH News*, and *Kitsilano Resources*, claimed to reach 10,000 residents apiece and set out the parameters of neighbourhood change, while information bulletins distributed to WBCC members filled in the details. The leadership made effective use of the media as a means of promoting awareness, including radio broadcasts by Khouri and popular articles by Gutstein: 'On March 18, we stopped construction of the Imperial Ventures high rise at 3rd and Larch – and immediately launched a dramatic case for the need to preserve our community in the eyes of hundreds of thousands of sympathizers who saw us on television that night ... Our actions brought us scores of new members.'[25]

Events were staged self-consciously for media consumption and distribution. In summer 1975 a series of press releases identifying a development 'profiteer of the month' was successfully initiated. A June report noted with satisfaction 'Extensive media coverage – Wall and Redekop "Profiteer of the month" got coverage in the Sun, Province, Western News, CBC and CTV.'[26] The coverage prompted a response by the developer, thus extending the project's publicity value. Perhaps the most audacious action was a boycott of a zoning hearing before Council, when sixty members of RUSH (WBCC) set up a picket line discouraging the public from entering the auditorium. They were invited instead to radical theatre – a mock Council meeting acted out by RUSH members in the foyer in which developers and community residents presented their opposing visions for the future of Kitsilano before rostrums identifiable as Mayor Phillips and members of council. 'Mayor Flip-Flop controlled the mock council in his usual off-handed bored manner wielding his tennis racket with impatience.'[27] Following this farce the audience was invited to an information party explaining the alternative RUSH plan for the community: a Kitsilano development permit board consisting of six elected residents and one appointed member of Council with powers to approve or disapprove demolition and development applications. Democratic local control remained the guiding principle.

Detailed research brought immediate relevance and convincing case histories of displacement to the process of community education (see figure 8.1).[28] Meticulous scrutiny of land sales and development appli-

JUST ONE PROBLEM TENANTS FACE: EVICTION

WHAT CAN I DO?

- JOIN RENTERS UNITED FOR SECURE HOUSING........ SOON!

- TALK TO OTHER TENANTS ABOUT JOINING
  A MASS TENANTS' ORGANIZATION.

- HELP TO ORGANIZE OTHER TENANTS IN
  YOUR BUILDING & NEIGHBOURHOOD
  (Our staff will help if needed)

- VOLUNTEER A FEW HOURS PER WEEK - ALL
  KINDS OF THINGS TO DO - research, telephone
  work, distribution of flyers and newsletters, organizing,
  newsletter-writing, typing, photography, etc.

- FEEL FREE TO CALL 736-2944.

- DROP-IN TO 2150 W. 4th AVENUE, VANCOUVER V6K 1N6.

- OPEN MONDAY TO FRIDAY, 1:00 - 9:00 p.m., and
  SATURDAY, 12:00 - 5:00 p.m.

INDIVIDUALLY, WE CAN'T DO IT: TOGETHER WE STAND
A GOOD CHANCE.

HELPING TENANTS TO MANAGE BETTER!

D. Donnelly photo courtesy The Province

DOROTHY SHEPHERD [senior on Mincome] her home, 14 years.
- 2476 - 2486 W. 3rd: 20 Tenants; Rents $95. - $150.
- DEMOLITION: 17 luxury, high-priced condominiums going up.
- DEVELOPER: Wall & Redekop: Profit on deal - $200,000.

IN KITSILANO MANY MORE WILL BE EVICTED

FIGURE 8.1. 'Just One Problem Tenants Face: Eviction' (Source: RUSH flier, summer 1975)

cations enabled residents to understand the broader patterns and major actors implicated in neighbourhood change (Gutstein 1975, 180). In one public-relations triumph, research revealed a scam which made front-page news in the city newspaper and attracted television coverage, where several realtors operated a network of companies in the zone of housing conversions, buying and selling property in intercompany trading at a dizzy pace, with each transaction involving remortgaging, rent increases, frequent evictions, and sales commissions.[29] In another superb example of community research, the WBCC uncovered close business relations between the president of a service organization proposing to build a subsidized senior citizens' high-rise building, and a developer who had been thwarted the previous year in an attempt to penetrate another section of Kitsilano with a high rise.[30] The research provided strong circumstantial evidence that the senior's project was to provide an innocuous precedent for further high-rise redevelopment in the district. This disclosure, plus widespread community mobilization, led to the downscaling of the building, although it had already been approved by the city and the federal agency, Canada Mortgage and Housing Corporation (CMHC).

Occasional newsletters, notifications of meetings, and some twenty numbered circulars were distributed around the community. Information circulars were not empty exercises in rhetoric but included specific details of planned developments, underlined the implication of tenant displacement, and ended with an appeal to mobilization (figure 8.1). Circulars were often headed by an attention-grabbing illustration, either a cartoon or a photograph. These illustrations were usually locally inspired, but cartoons were sometimes employed from other sources, and a powerful photograph which appeared on at least two circulars of a distraught woman who was denied entrance to her expropriated home was taken in Winnipeg.[31] The image crystallized the issues in a simpler form. The theme of destruction of a stable community and sound housing was perhaps the most constant element of discourse. The bulldozer as the symbolic agent of destruction was commonly featured in illustrations, a semantically loaded text, where systemic power, intrusion, and inhumanity were counterposed against the displacement and demoralization of a family unit.

In figure 8.2 the message is perhaps more sophisticated, attempting to problematize existing attitudes and redirect privatistic orientations towards a shared political project – a fundamental task, as we saw for the community developers of the Downtown Eastside and Katamon Tet. The edacious bulldozer is visible through an apartment window. Inside the apartment lounges a young woman, an eviction notice in her hand. 'What me worry? It can't happen to me ... anyway I can go anywhere.' The circular, distributed by Renters United for Secure Housing, is challenging the apathy which confronts any tenants' organization. 'Apathy is a historical reality,' Khouri had noted during this period, and to countervail it, the community organizer had to begin with the tenants' inherent privatism: 'it's in your own self interest to get involved, and it's fun to get involved.'[32] A threat which destabilizes a resident in her most

RENTERS UNITED for SECURE HOUSING

2150 WEST 4th AVENUE, VANCOUVER, BRITISH COLUMBIA V6K 1N6, TELEPHONE 736-2944

If you're a TENANT....WHERE WILL YOU GO WHEN YOUR EVICTION COMES ???

' what, me worry ?

it can't happen to me..
anyway..
I can go anywhere.'

GUESS AGAIN--Here are some facts:

FIGURE 8.2.   'What Me Worry?' (Source: RUSH circular, summer 1975)

intimate place (reclining in a favourite living-room chair beneath a Home
Sweet Home wall hanging) is a stimulus to dislodge the complacency
of individualism and to open one's eyes to the broader social reality un-
folding on the other side of the window. The text below the illustration
trenchantly reinforces the image, with carefully compiled statistics which
outline the trends under way; a map of the apartment district is added,
identifying the large number of sites where condominium development
had occurred or, through the issue of development permits, was
imminent.

   To encourage mobilization the potential for success had to be demonstrated, and in most fliers past victories were advertised. 'The one
way to counteract apathy is to give people hope that they will have some
effect.'[33] Public statements by the WBCC staff were an exercise in positive thinking. Block-busting, a real estate strategy to destabilize a neighbourhood and hasten land assembly, was widely exposed and became
a household word in Kitsilano. In a letter to the mayor and Council,
a senior citizen who had formerly been a homeowner and Kitsilano

resident for fifty-seven years referred critically to the destruction by developers of blocks of good housing 'some by the process of "block busting."' This letter, from a WBCC member, repeats a discourse appearing prominently in community fliers: (a) the destruction of a beautiful environment; (b) the responsibility of Council in this destruction; (c) the greater culpability of developers, concerned not with livability but with profits; (d) the transition to a high-density 'concrete jungle' comparable with the high-rise West End district (an emotive object lesson commonly drawn by the WBCC);[34] (e) the displacement of family housing; and (f) the necessity for strong intervention by the state.

Reflecting and generalizing upon the experience of the WBCC up to 1974, Donald Gutstein (1975, 179) outlined six steps in the escalating process of community organizing. First, build up membership by taking on smaller and winnable issues that are salient in everyday life. Second, spread knowledge 'about how the system works' and how to confront it successfully. Third, construct an organization that is constantly developing community leadership. Fourth, move on to more challenging problems, affecting more people, that 'strike closer to the roots of the problems.' Fifth, sustain an ongoing program of community education and awareness raising. Finally, engage in proactive initiatives, not only reactive responses, to show the possibilities of community power to accomplish community needs. This stage model was a blueprint for the life history of the WBCC and bears several implications that explain much of its activity, successes, and eventual demise.

First, there is an implication for the specification of issues. Initially the issue was local, the commercial redevelopment of a section of West Broadway, or a pedestrian crossing at a busy intersection. The ensuing decision to challenge two separate high-rise projects was undertaken not simply because of local consequences (though these were, of course, important) but because of what they represented: in one case, at Third and Balsam, tenant displacement and the injustice of class succession in a tight inner-city housing market; in the other case, at Seventh and Maple, more delicate because it was a project to build social housing for the elderly, the interpretation was woven around the inappropriateness of the site and the building design for the elderly, and the block-busting effects of constructing the first high rise in a low-rise district by a developer who had previously tried, unsuccessfully, to build market high rises in Kitsilano.

From here a further abstraction occurred: 'The issue in Kitsilano is purely and simply redevelopment.'[35] This abstraction led to a discourse at the level of 'system.' As Nathan Karmel had put it: rather than dealing always with effects on a single basis, 'it's smarter to organize people to change the system.'[36] This discourse led to the far more challenging task of changing the allocation rules controlling both private redevelopment and public decision making. Efforts to revise the zoning map were a first step in the former direction; a second was the formation of a tenants' organization, Renters United for Secure Housing (RUSH), which would form a separate and offsetting power bloc to the property industry. In relations with the state, local area planning and the community resources boards were seen as promising vehicles to enhance community discretion over decision making. Both were lobbied for by the WBCC, who then, through further mobilization, gained a dominant position on each, before rejecting both as essentially agencies of co-optation which denied the objective of community control, while distracting scarce community resources into meaningless deliberations: 'We will not allow our energy to be drained in a committee only to find its decisions are totally meaningless and its job short circuited by ambitious politicians.'[37]

The final step in Gutstein's model is a pro-active and not merely reactive posture by a community group, and as time passed the scale of the WBCC initiatives became far more ambitious. The RUSH campaign was one attempt to move onto the offensive, but equally ambitious was the endeavour of the Kitsilano Housing Society, another WBCC affiliate, to build its own affordable housing. Through preservation, renovation, and infill, the society's aims were to supply low- and moderate-income housing for displaced Kitsilano tenants, while encouraging self-help rather than government dependency.

There were two other implications to the organizational spiral the WBCC and its affiliates followed between 1972 and 1976. The first was the level of available resources as objectives became more general and more challenging. The initial project against Broadway beautification had involved a few dozen volunteers who were lent a community organizer and shared a desk at the Kitsilano Information Centre. As the program, first of resistance, and then of reconstruction, grew more ambitious, so did the resources required to sustain the effort. The successes of downzoning were won with a membership of 400–500 at its maximum. But, for tenant organization, more were required. For almost two years RUSH was an effective trouble-shooter for individual grievances in individual buildings. In the first few months some 150 tenant units were organized, rising to a maximum claimed membership of about 300. But for systemic change these numbers were insufficient. 'We need larger and larger numbers to be involved – not just a couple of hundred, but a couple of thousand ... unless we get this number we will not have enough people to countervail the powers that be.'[38] This confidence in the law of large numbers, a radical commitment to grass-roots democracy, drove the organization as a charter belief. Its first failure (though it led indirectly to down-zoning) was attributed to inadequate numbers: 'When we took on Imperial Ventures, we knew that we could beat them finally, only if we had enough people – which we didn't!'[39]

But greater numbers demanded a more thorough organizational effort than part-time volunteers could muster. It required full-time staff, an office, supplies, and equipment. Very quickly the WBCC ran into budgetary problems, and solutions were only ever short-term and below expected costs. An endless series of requests for funding fell on deaf ears. Allocations never met the budgeted need, far less the aspirations of visionaries. Against the experience of a 1973–4 income of $13,500 (and a deficit of $750), a target of $110,000 was specified for the RUSH initiative; eventually $10,000 came through from the Kitsilano Resources Board. The next year, the Kitsilano Housing Society applied to City Council for $100,000 in seed money to purchase $2 million worth of rental property; after rejection from the city, $8,000 was received from CMHC (Stobie 1979, 141). An air of financial crisis was continuous, sapping morale and dampening the early excitement of achieving attainable goals. 'Where do we go from here?' asked an information circular in the spring of 1975. 'Financially we are close to bankruptcy. We have no money for rent or staff.'[40] At the same time the stakes were becoming higher. The ascending ladder of community organization, the seeking out of more systemic targets, was stretching the group beyond its resource base. 'We are facing the future demolition of approximately 1,500 housing units in this area. Stopping this demolition is the biggest and toughest issue West Broadway has taken on so far. If we can be successful here, we will be very close to the realization of our goals – COMMUNITY CONTROL OF DEVELOPMENT. This is a crucial stage in our history, and will inevitably "make or break" us as a citizens' group. With enough support we can do it.'[41] Six months later, with twenty-three members in attendance, the WBCC held its last general meeting.[42] Energies then passed entirely to the RUSH initiative of tenant organization, but within a year these energies, too, were spent.

Tactics were a final corollary of the group's theoretical analysis and escalating objectives. During the initial phase of resisting West Broadway beautification, tactics involved by and large conventional, if firm, negotiations. But the shift to broader objectives seemed to imply more confrontational tactics. As the Broadway issue was winding down, Nathan Karmel made a presentation to a monthly meeting that, in the face of continuous political procrastination, the group 'had gone as far as we could through the negotiation process.'[43] Further forms of community organization were needed, and he offered to show a film of Alinsky-inspired community development.[44] Over the next twelve months, petitions, demonstrations, picketing, the occupation of building sites, and confrontational meetings with Council and the CMHC took place (see figure 8.3). 'We were forced to use tactics that some of the faint-hearted would disapprove of,' noted Khouri, 'but those of us who could see the need for action were not deterred, and emerged from each battle a little stronger.'[45] With RUSH came a promise of escalating confrontation: 'Because our past methods have not been tough enough to stop these more serious and challenging problems, the new organization will be organizing members whose situation is less secure and would therefore be willing to take a few more risks.'[46] Landlords and developers were shamed in the media and taken to court, and to the provincial rentalsman's office; building sites were occupied to prevent demolitions; the profiteer-of-the-month award was started as a publicity stunt. RUSH was working towards, but unable to achieve, the ultimate tenant weapon of a rent strike. Relations with Council soured further; even the provincial NDP government was criticized. The WBCC majority on the Kitsilano Resources Board split, and acrimonious accusations were hurled back and forth. The liberals had indeed withdrawn. The Kitsilano activists had isolated themselves from tactical alliances with the only groups who could supply their resource base.

Relations with the State

Initially relations with government were characterized by an atmosphere of cautious co-production. The election of a reform City Council in November 1972 seemingly ushered in a new era of citizen participation, and with a sense of expectancy, relations between the WBCC and council members were civil. The tone of early briefs and letters to Council was appreciative of the new and more open political process, even in the face of disappointments.[47] Expectations on the community side were inflated further by the promise of local area planning where participation would occur across a broad swath of issues. These promises were aired by a reform alderman who answered questions posed by WBCC members

FIGURE 8.3. WBCC demonstration, attempting to halt work at a high-rise condominium site, March 1974. Jacques Khouri, bearded and wearing a tie, appears at the centre of the action. The slogans give a clear sense of WBCC's discourse, and the photograph suggests a profile of its activists (Photograph: *Vancouver Sun*, 18 March 1974).

in a meeting prior to the start-up of local area planning. 'We're not going to make any decisions without consultation ... Whatever changes we feel are going to be desired [are those] desirable for Kitsilano and wanted by people in Kitsilano ... presumably people who live here don't want to increase density in the area: presumably you don't want arterial streets crashing through your area here: presumably you don't want to have regional shopping facilities around here which would decrease livability ... Presumably you don't want high rise buildings – you want more amenities and things like that.'[48]

This vision for the future of Kitsilano, which, the alderman confided, was that of 'a majority' of Council, seemed to emphasize preservation, the lack of massive change, and an enhancement of existing livability in consultation with citizens. It was a view closely in conformity with the preferences of the broader Kitsilano community, revealed in a survey of 150 households early the next year (Ley 1981). Overall responses showed a strong preservation and anti-development bias. The maintenance and improvement of existing homes was the top priority, followed by services to aid families, seniors, and tenants, all households under pressure from neighbourhood change. High-rise development was uniformly rejected, and interestingly there was widespread resistance against high house resale prices, which were seen as a factor destabilizing the community. This resistance was expressed in both tenant and homeowner districts; indeed, there was consistent agreement across tenure groups even for group-specific issues like home-improvement grants, rent controls, and the legalization of illegal suites.

It seemed there was ground for considerable optimism of a consensus between Council, the community, and the WBCC's development policy, and armed with its knowledge of Council's inclinations, the WBCC was able to mount a community strategy with considerable hope of success. It pressed, and received priority designation, for local area planning and down-zoning. Following the successful resolution of the beautification issue, these additional successes were a source of buoyancy for the citizens, and through carefully managed public relations contributed legitimacy and momentum to the WBCC. The gains for the community were significant, and the WBCC could take credit for pro-actively setting the agenda, even if there were already prior indication of Council's willingness to act. In a classic case of co-production, Council was a willing suitor, waiting to be asked.

Far more contentious was the WBCC's challenge to two high-rise apartment projects which had already begun to pass through the city's approval process prior to down-zoning hearings. The issues at stake seemed serious and general enough that the citizens decided to engage in more confrontational 'touch actions' (figure 8.3). Forceful delegations were sent to City Council where the WBCC could count on two or three allies from the most left-leaning of the reform group. But this bloc was repeatedly outvoted in the months that followed on the eleven-person council, and the WBCC did not engage in attempts to coax councillors to their side but, rather, engaged in shouting matches at City Hall.[49] Their approach rapidly alienated them from council members, the more so as taunts and personal insults were hurled by frustrated citizens who perceived they had the stronger case, but neither power nor the force of the law on their side. For its part Council felt it was meeting its obligations in promising down-zoning for future developments, and had no legal grounds for overturning development permits it had already issued.

During the spring and summer of 1974 opportunities for co-production were re-established with the beginning of the local area planning process and the inauguration of the WBCC-controlled Kitsilano Resources Board, a vehicle to administer neighbourhood social services. Both bore considerable initial promise, particularly when Kitsilano was designated a neighbourhood improvement area and allocated federal funds of $1.2 million. The local area planning committee, set up by the city, was invited to recommend priority areas for neighbourhood-improvement funding. In July 1974, Donald Gutstein, one of the two WBCC representatives to the Kitsilano local area planning committee, announced that the committee was making 'good progress.'[50] But the pace of discussions became disturbingly slow, while evictions and demolitions continued unabated; during 1974 demolition permits were issued for eighteen projects, or an estimated 10 per cent of redevelopable sites in the apartment zone.[51] In July the Kitsilano planning committee sent a motion to Council urging a six-month moratorium on condominium development pending completion of the local area plan. The motion was denied, and at its October monthly meeting the WBCC passed a strongly worded resolution to bring before Council, urging demolition controls unless comparable replacement housing was offered to residents within the same general area. The resolution was endorsed by the local area planning committee.[52] The WBCC's tactics sheet for its presentation at City Hall on 22 October 1974 throws an informative light upon its style of dealing with the city:

... City Council will be expecting a noisy, angry crowd tonight.
3. With your cooperation, bearing in mind our usual approach to City Council, we can throw them slightly off balance by 'coming on' differently.
4. Our approach is to be *courteous* tonight! No yelling out, no catcalls, boos or hisses. Allow our speakers to put forth our stand.
5. If there is a necessity to change this approach, you will be instructed by marshals in the crowd.

In the event a motion for a further temporary down-zoning to block condominium construction was defeated 5–3. In a polarized and alienated council, the WBCC was again unable to build upon its base of three allies. Council endorsed a weaker resolution to scrutinize each demolition permit individually, but this convinced no one.[53] One practical obstacle facing the city was uncertainty of legal authority in its charter to introduce demolition controls. As a result its capacity to check redevelopment was limited, and with no licence to levy taxes for a housing fund, its discretion was minimal. The director of planning, frequently sympathetic to the WBCC's case if not its methods, acknowledged before Council that his department did not know how the housing problem could be solved.[54] But the call for demolition controls did not go away, for it was a fundamental plank in any strategy for affordable housing. Delegations appeared repeatedly before Council in 1974, and variants of the original WBCC motion were revived by sympathetic councillors but always lost. Finally, in October 1975, following briefs from twenty-three delegations, including RUSH, a compromise resolution was passed directing the city to seek a charter amendment from the provincial legislature to empower it to withhold issuance of demolition permits on rental structures until certain conditions had been met.[55]

But, by then, the WBCC and RUSH had become strident opponents of local area planning as conducted in Kitsilano. In a press release dated 22 October 1974, the same day as the evening council meeting, the WBCC announced its withdrawal from local area planning, 'a process which neutralises and subverts true community participation.'[56] From this point on, relations with the council majority became increasingly acerbic, and included personal attacks. In December 1974, Alderman Bowers sent a letter to Khouri in reply to a hostile letter that Khouri had published in a local newspaper. Bowers enclosed his successes in Kitsilano in recent civic elections: 'I don't see how these figures indicate a protest vote of Kitsilano residents against my policies,' he concluded. 'You might bear this in mind the next time you address Council indignantly "on behalf of the residents of Kitsilano."'[57] Several months earlier he had disparagingly queried whether an official delegation of the Kitsilano planning committee, appointed by Council itself, were 'twenty kooks' or true community representatives.[58] The WBCC did nothing to temper such hostility. Each liberal on Council was singled out for criticism, and often ridicule. One published letter referred disparagingly to the mayor as 'our incumbent Bourbon' and concluded: 'I suggest we be allowed to impeach elected officials for the abuse of public office.'[59] The press campaign against Council came thick and fast: 'City hall accused of wasting $1 million,' 'Kits group raps Penta decision,' 'Confrontation tactics planned over housing.'[60] A stinging attack on Alderman Cowie for alleged conflict of interest concerning property in

Kitsilano drew response from the alderman's lawyers, demanding a retraction; none the less, RUSH pressed the case up to the B.C. Supreme Court, seeking to invalidate a new by-law benefiting the alderman.[61] Even the New Democratic Alderman Harcourt, one of the WBCC's three Council allies, came under fire.[62] And then, incredibly in the context of this media campaign, 'Kits group asks City for $100,000,' a request for a low-interest loan of $100,000 was submitted to Council by the Kitsilano Housing Society (a WBCC affiliate) for low-cost housing.[63] When the proposal came before the city's five-person Housing Committee, it foundered on a 2-2 tie vote; the critical fifth vote was held by Alderman Cowie, the very alderman RUSH was bringing to the B.C. Supreme Court two weeks later on conflict-of-interest charges! He abstained, and the motion failed to pass.[64]

If community activists held initial optimism in working with the liberal reform council, their hopes were much higher of enjoying a constructive relationship with the provincial government. The New Democratic Party had won election for the first time in British Columbia in 1972 on a platform which included strong commitments to citizen participation, redistribution, and social justice. In the Canadian constitution, the province is a much stronger arm of government than the city and, with the federal government, is responsible for social programs, including housing. Here then was the opportunity to cultivate and draw upon the services of a powerful ally. Moreover, Kitsilano was part of a constituency which had returned two high-ranking New Democrats, including Norman Levi, minister of human resources, and Rosemary Brown, a prominent activist for minority rights. The WBCC had good relations with the local NDP riding association and enjoyed endorsement for several of its actions, beginning with opposition to the proposed senior citizens' high rise at Seventh and Maple. Part of the funding for this project came from the province, and with financial and political commitment to the project also granted by the city and the CMHC, the WBCC quickly turned to the provincial government for support.

In a letter of September 1973, Rosemary Brown thanked the WBCC 'for the splendid work you are doing.'[65] The next month, and following a meeting with a WBCC delegation, Levi and Brown issued a press release endorsing the down-scaling of the Seventh and Maple high rise to three storeys, as requested by the citizens. Drawing directly upon the WBCC's argument and its discourse, they continued: 'We must view the decision of the Vancouver City Council to approve this project as what may be characterized as "block busting" ... to permit the building of a high rise in the area could well lead to applications and decisions to allow more high rise structures.'[66] Their advice was accepted by the minister of housing, and the WBCC action was successful. The association again appealed over the head of council to block the high-rise condominium at Third and Balsam, where opposition had been more confrontational, including on-site demonstrations (figure 8.3); the minister of housing wavered over an expropriation order before announcing his office would not enter the dispute.[67] The WBCC, never gracious in defeat, informed the media they were 'shocked and outraged that they were lied to so blatantly' by the minister's representative.

Mr Levi made his endorsement of the WBCC more tangible by awarding the group a one-year grant to rent a storefront and hire a part-time worker. Yet more encouraging was his introduction of the community resources boards as a decentralized agency for social-service delivery. Running on a housing platform, the WBCC swept the Kitsilano Resources Board elections. With an increasingly ambitious community program, and shut out in other funding applications, the WBCC made heavy use of the flexibility offered by its control of the board. Three of its staff were hired in various functions by the board, and the WBCC itself was awarded a grant of $10,000 and allowed to use space in the board office. As the directors of the board were WBCC members and nominees who had run on the housing issue, in essence the WBCC was given a new lease on life. Indeed, the WBCC, RUSH, the Kitsilano Resources Board, and the Kitsilano Housing Society had identical goals and, it seemed, a common leadership. Ironically the citizens were replaying the private-sector game of holding companies with interlocking directorships which they had so effectively exposed in the development industry. Indeed, charges of conflict of interest were sent to Minister Levi's office, and in early 1975 he blocked any resource-board expenditures aimed at housing issues. Representations to the housing minister were fruitless, and resident frustrations again made their way to the press. The housing minister, charged Khouri, 'has taken the same policy as the developers – tear down one house and build a more expensive one'; the Kitsilano Resources Board had been 'betrayed' by the provincial government.[68]

Events reached a climax in August 1975. Levi, as minister responsible, and Rosemary Brown met with RUSH board members in a closed meeting. The minister subsequently told reporters his office would follow up conflict-of-interest allegations. However, simultaneously, RUSH counter-attacked at a second meeting the next evening with its own agenda: that 3,000 residents would face eviction if the local area plan endorsed by Council was officially adopted.[69] While the down-zoning clause for Kitsilano was retained, no provision was made in the plan to check demolition of affordable housing and its replacement by three-storey condominiums. In its place, the resources board, RUSH, and the WBCC had a counter-proposal, a housing program emphasizing preservation, mandatory replacement units for displaced tenants, community participation, and a higher quota of social housing.

A week later, six WBCC-backed members of the Kitsilano Resources Board and board manager Nathan Karmel resigned, as Minister Levi brought down new regulations for the conduct of resources boards, including conflict-of-interest guidelines.[70] Speaking for the group, Jacques Khouri argued that they had been elected on the housing issue and had been frustrated by the provincial government in pursuit of a just housing policy.[71] At the same time he called for Levi's department to assume responsibility for housing and fund 'community housing groups like RUSH.'[72] Four more moderate members of the WBCC slate remained on the board and became a butt of criticism as RUSH challenged the board's priorities.[73] But worse was shortly to follow. In late 1975, the NDP government was defeated in a provincial election, and its right-wing successor announced the termination of the resources-board program. The entire Kitsilano Resources Board resigned in protest at the end of February 1976, noting that 'the decision was made against the people and in favour of centralized bureaucratic control and the established political forces.'[74] With the WBCC/RUSH resistant to the end, the Kitsilano Local Area Plan was also adopted by City Council.[75] It was the end of an era. In June, RUSH published its last community newspaper and closed its office, announcing that all attempts to raise funds from government had been thwarted.

In Retrospect

And yet, this was not quite the end. Like a many-headed hydra, the Kitsilano Housing Society (KHS) now took the place of the WBCC, RUSH, and the resources board. The last issue of *RUSH News* announced the stirring of this new arm of the WBCC, with Jacques Khouri as president. Half the pages of the newsheet were given over to the first KHS project, a renovation-infill structure with fifteen units, at First and Maple in the apartment district. This project was funded by a $16,500 down-payment raised from community subscriptions, lent at 8 per cent, to the Buy Back Kitsilano fund. In this manner, affordable housing would be retained and condominium redevelopment thwarted (KHS outbid a well-known condominium developer for the First and Maple site). A non-profit co-op was established with KHS, and the tenants jointly establishing a rent structure to cover costs of debt servicing, taxes, and maintenance.[76] After extensive negotiations, Canada Mortgage and Housing Corporation (CMHC) awarded a seed grant for the project, and later provided funds for the infill portion. This enabled the initial downpayment to be regained, and with close to $40,000 in the Buy Back Kitsilano fund (60 per cent of it raised by mortgaging Khouri's house), a second site was secured, aided by a low-interest second mortgage from the United Church.[77] Again funding support was provided by the CMHC, with a demonstration grant from the National Research Council for a solar-heating system. The project, completed in 1978, contained seventeen moderate-priced cooperative units, most of them built for families. This promising relationship with the CMHC did not, however, proceed far enough, for the corporation declined to establish new funds which would make start-up money available for non-profit-housing societies to engage in their own purchase and renovation program. Instead, any application would have to be referred to Vancouver's allocation of existing co-op funds.[78]

In April 1976, Khouri offered an eight-week night-school course in Kitsilano, with the title 'How to Buy Out Your Landlord and Start a Co-op.' Two years later, and building on the expertise gained from the two KHS projects, the Inner City Housing Society was founded, as a sponsor to encourage the formation of cooperatives, and give practical guidance in all aspects of getting a cooperative off the ground. Until 1984, Khouri directed Inner City Housing and successfully incorporated some 25 cooperatives with 1,200 units, principally in Kitsilano and other inner-city districts. But the co-op program had been a product of the social experimentation of the early Trudeau years, and by the 1980s both Trudeau and his idealism no longer matched the political mood of the times. Controls were tightened on the co-op program by the federal government. At the same time new responsibilities had arrived; Khouri had married and a son had been born. In 1983 he became a licensed real estate agent.

After doing co-ops for a while, I asked myself why am I doing this? Begging to governments and getting into hassles. Somewhere along the line co-ops have lost the vision.[79]

I stopped doing co-ops in 1984. Strictly private now. That's the way the world's going. That's the way co-ops are going. They've been co-opted. I realised a lot of people are only in co-ops for themselves. You develop this special information and you see some other guy, no smarter than you, making say $300,000 while you're making $30,000. You think you're pure or something, but all the time you're doing deals with these guys to get co-op jobs done, they take you out for lunch. They can't figure you out, why anyone would do anything not for profit. They don't understand it, they figure you must have an angle. Then they think you're either crooked or stupid.

And one day I figured maybe I am stupid. I'm being used by the government to keep their costs down, and every year they turn the screws further. And there's no power here with poor people and tenants to force political change. With political will anything can happen, but it doesn't happen here.

It was right at the time, I wouldn't do it now. Your motivations change. I'm not that motivated any more, unless you think you're on the side of God or something. And then, there's you know burn out, from always going against the current.[80]

Jacques Khouri still lives in Kitsilano, but other members of the original leadership have departed. Donald Gutstein led a city-wide referendum to introduce a ward system to Vancouver in 1978 which would bring stronger representation to neighbourhood interests on Council. His popular writing on urban development and community politics earned him a teaching position at Simon Fraser University, and he moved to the east side of the city. Following his resignation as manager of the Kitsilano Resources Board, Nathan Karmel took a job with the provincial government in Victoria. Other former WBCC activists remain in Kitsilano, several of them living at the cooperative at First and Maple built by the Kitsilano Housing Society. For them the WBCC slogan 'We Aim to Stay' has become a continuing reality.

Others like them still remain. In the civic elections in 1988, one section of Kitsilano included the only polling district on Vancouver's west side to endorse for mayor the left-wing COPE candidate, the party for which Khouri had run for office in 1972. But, as predicted by the WBCC, the tide of condominiums, Vancouver's manifestation of gentrification, has swept across much of the apartment district.[81] On Fourth Avenue, the Soft Rock Café and the Divine Light Mission have given way to chic, up-market stores; a Pentecostal church has been replaced by a neighbourhood pub, a union hall by a private medical building, a rock-music club by an exercise and fitness facility.

Yet it would be a mistake to see the accomplishments of the citizens in the 1972–6 period as totally ineffectual. 'Stop Kitsilano from Becoming Another West End' ran the headline of the WBCC's first information circular, drawing attention to the high-density, high-rise landscape of the West End neighbourhood facing Kitsilano across English Bay on the downtown peninsula.[82] During the 1960s, high-rise redevelopment began to diffuse into Kitsilano, and there is no doubt that, without community resistance, such buildings would have multiplied. Similar success against massive redevelopment was won on the West Broadway retail strip, again in the face of opposition from the development industry. The publicity which the WBCC gave to development issues hastened the arrival of the state, and the co-production ventures of local area planning and the resources board. By the summer of 1974, the WBCC was in a dominant position on both of those agencies. Its actions also expedited Kitsilano's designation as a recipient of federal Neighbourhood Improvement funds ($1.2 million) and as a target area for the Residential Rehabilitation Assistance Programme, another federal program offering loans and grants for home and apartment maintenance. By the end of 1979, more than 1,000 Kitsilano homeowners and landlords had applied for RRAP support; more than 2,000 units had been rehabilitated, representing an investment of over $8 million in state aid to the neighbourhood (Leithead 1980; Ley 1981).

In the two years after November 1972 much had been accomplished. The West Broadway Citizens' Committee had 400–500 members, a versatile and talented leadership, proven depth in researching issues, organizational sophistication, and important successes. If weakening in their commitment, reform impulses at the civic and national levels provided openings where new initiatives in the built environment could be (and were) supported (Ley 1980, 1987). The WBCC had blazed a trail across the night sky over the evening sessions of Council. Yet, eighteen months later, by the summer of 1976, like any short-lived meteor, it had burned out. Why was such a promising beginning in such an enabling context so quickly compromised?

The WBCC foundered on the limits of what was possible. Its resources of people and finances could not match the scope of its ambitious objectives of community control. Indeed, a critical contradiction existed between its ideology and its strategy. Its systemic analysis of community change and resistance required substantial resources, but its aggressive tactics and inability to compromise isolated it from the political alliances essential for those resources to be secured. As Jacques Khouri put it: 'The Alinsky model got results. When we talk to the NDP they always ask "Is it politically correct?" Political theories make you immobile. Alinsky is issue-oriented. More pragmatic. You don't get labelled as this party or that. You're independent. But we were outcasts. Not even members of the NDP. You have to ally yourselves with somebody to get money from them. We paid the price for our independence.'[83] Put simply, the WBCC's program required a strategy of co-production, but its strategy was that of confrontation, to drive the state rather than proceed in locked arm. But the state can be driven, in a democracy, only by the force of large numbers. The WBCC was keenly aware of this numerical logic, but the really large numbers never materialized. Moreover, confrontational tactics lost the group its legitimacy not only with the state, but also with less militant members of the community. The WBCC would answer this assessment with the claim that resorting to liberal tactics of consensus or co-production was a prescription for failure. As Jacques Khouri said: 'We're intelligent people, we can see grey, we can compromise. But grey doesn't motivate. We need black and white to get results. Stroking political egos would not have helped. The political middle would have watered us down. We had to keep it black and white.'[84]

The protracted nature of negotiations with the city had been a frustration in the initial conflict over retail redevelopment on West Broadway. These frustrations were multiplied many times over by local area planning, the process offering the clearest path to empowerment. Discussion was slow, progress partial, and on occasion City Hall's intent to set the agenda was disruptive to the point of subversion[85] The urgency of the problem, and the energy of community problem solvers, ran into the seemingly impenetrable and cumbersome machinery of bureaucracy, and a liberal council that was withdrawing from its initial position on citizen participation.[86] When, after several months' work, the Kitsilano planning committee had brought its first resolution to Council, a unanimous motion for a six-month development moratorium which was endorsed by the city planning department and the planning commission, the motion was defeated by an 8–3 margin. Gutstein, the WBCC's member on the local planning committee, drew a conclusion which would be pursued vigorously over the next two years: 'City hall isn't going to give local area committees any power ... not unless we go out and get it through strong actions with broad citizen support.'[87] A renewed phase of adversarial relations between concerned citizens and back-peddling liberals on Council was guaranteed. Like neighbourhood planning elsewhere in government, and indeed elsewhere in Canada, citizen expectations were high and invariably disappointed by the process (Anderson 1977).

The tardiness of Council represented in part the limits to which a liberal ideology could be stretched by Alinsky-style analysis, in part the limits of what the local state could accomplish. The profundity of the citizens' analysis was pushing the city into uncharted waters where its own legal powers were restricted. In a heated exchange at a council meeting, a WBCC-inspired resolution to check demolitions moved by one council member was challenged by another as breaking the law by prescribing an action beyond the city's constitutional powers.[88] 'These [development] pressures,' noted the planning department, 'are largely outside the City's Charter authority.'[89] Neither did the city have the resources to engage in affordable housing production. Its only asset was scattered land holdings which were commonly made available to co-ops at below-market rates. As a result the director of planning acknowledged that he had no solution for the housing problem.[90]

But the city did have modest resources which would have aided WBCC activities. It makes small grants to community organizations which the WBCC (unlike DERA, chapter 6) was never able to secure; it was prepared to discuss the WBCC's proposal for a low-interest loan for housing by the Kitsilano Housing Society, a proposal which failed by one vote in subcommittee. It is clear that Council was prejudiced by the WBCC's methods of embarrassment and intimidation; one of the dissenting aldermen against the KHS proposal observed that he was 'totally opposed' to any support for KHS: 'a lot of people in Kitsilano don't appreciate this organization.'[91] Council's prejudice obscured its vision, but its prejudice was inflamed by the personal attacks on councillors. Its response was commonly an *ad hominem* retaliation which overlooked the sound analysis which WBCC research had uncovered. For example, the organizational structure which the KHS assembled for its first housing project led to an estimated saving of between a third and a half over per-unit housing costs built by the state.[92] But the strength of a good argument could not compensate for the veil of hostility which isolated the WBCC from project funding.

And of course that isolation was in part self-induced. While the KHS was seeking desperately for funds to establish affordable co-op housing, the Kitsilano Planning Committee was looking for a non-profit housing society to use almost $600,000 in Neighbourhood Improvement funds to build affordable family co-ops. But the WBCC members, having pressed successfully for local area planning, for Neighbourhood Improvement designation, and for establishing housing as a funding priority, had withdrawn from Kitsilano local area planning, and secured their isolation by their trenchant criticism of the planning office, including its Neighbourhood Improvement priorities.[93] The chairman of the Kitsilano Planning Committee responded in kind: 'It is regrettable that this community organization refuses to participate in planning for Kitsilano ... There is the waste. Instead of raising public awareness they merely raise hell.'[94]

The ultimate failure of the West Broadway Citizens' Committee contrasts sharply with the successes and longevity of DERA. Both were established under the sponsorship of municipal social workers in the climate of benevolent liberalism in 1972–3. Both assumed the mantle of protest organizations, struggling to displace traditional and conservative neighbourhood associations, and providing candidates for the left-wing COPE party in municipal elections. Both quickly became the dominant, though not the undisputed, neighbourhood voice. Both experienced predictably turbulent relations with the state, including the withdrawal of financial support. The local cultures from which their leaders were drawn provided, however, a major line of demarcation. The influential leaders of West Broadway were young professionals, recent university graduates with a middle-class education but not yet a middle-class income. In adopting the Alinsky blueprint of community development, they selected a model that was itself achievement-oriented, aiming to build success upon success and ambition upon ambition in an upward spiral which would expand over ever-broader domains. The model mimicked, even as it resisted, a mainstream model, the inflating ambitions of the successful entrepreneur. West Broadway was a group in a hurry, a group that was driven. Its firm adherence to a theoretical model, foreclosing options for compromise, also reveals its middle-class, indeed intellectual, presuppositions. Its principles overrode any prospect of pragmatic negotiation. Astutely it diagnosed the neocorporatism within the state's strategy of local area planning as 'a sham attempt to dupe citizens into being manipulated by civic bureaucrats.' And yet social control was not the whole story. The local state was offering not only negotiations, but also limited funds and services. In withdrawing from co-production ventures, rejecting negotiation in favour of 'direct action', West Broadway was selecting a protest route that it had neither the funds nor the personnel to pursue. Its single-mindedness alienated politicians, and even Kitsilano residents.

In treading the path of theoretical purity it achieved political oblivion, while leaving traces enough on the Kitsilano landscape of what might have been. In contrast to the summary dismissal of neocorporatism in Kitsilano, we turn now to a more patient exploration of its possibilities by the neighbourhood council of Baka.

9

An Uneasy Partnership: The Case of Baka Neighbourhood Government

The idea of neighbourhood government arose against a background of political and social conceptions which emerged in Jerusalem in the late 1960s and early 1970s. In 1968, in an attempt to devise a political solution to the problem of Jerusalem, Meron Benvenisti, then serving as the municipal official responsible for East Jerusalem, wrote a memorandum detailing a program for binational but unimunicipal administration of the city. The main points of his program were the expansion of Jerusalem's municipal boundaries by incorporating nearby villages and towns, dividing the city into five submunicipalities or cantons (Jewish Jerusalem, Arab Jerusalem, villages, Bethlehem, and Beit Jalla) and creating an umbrella council for them under the auspices of Israel and Jordan. Local government was thus conceived within the framework of a metropolitan authority governed symmetrically by Israel and Jordan (Benvenisti 1988).

In retrospect, the only practical effect the report had was to draw attention to the possibility of a decentralized municipal administration operating within the framework of a metropolitan government. However, the operational definition of 'decentralization' and its translation into organizational terms did not suit the report's spirit. The decentralization considered today is not geopolitical, as Benvenisti sought, but rather concerns administration of local services and expression of the cultural values developed by social-welfare professionals and students who, in the spirit of the 1960s, warned against the weaknesses of welfare policies.

The new neighbourhoods established after the 1967 war to reinforce Jerusalem constituted a fertile field for protest. In late 1973, a team from the School of Social Work at the Hebrew University of Jerusalem, involved in field-work in one of these neighbourhoods, was shocked to discover the utter neglect in neighbourhood services: some services were lacking and others were duplicated; senior officials were apathetic and hardly accessible, and did not coordinate with one another. In reaction to the problems discovered, it was suggested that the mayor establish a local project for service and community development. This project, which commenced in the new neighbourhood of East Talpiot in 1974, involved a wide range of social and community activity and included formulation of key ideas for neighbourhood self-management (Salzberger 1988). A parallel experiment was undertaken in the old neighbourhood of Baka in 1975–82, attempting to combine social planning and physical renewal. On the basis of accumulated experience in East Talpiot and Baka and the problems revealed in the provision of welfare services in other neighbourhoods, the Social Workers' Association in Jerusalem drew up a proposal for reorganizing neighbourhood community-service systems.[1] This proposal primarily called for establishment of a neighbourhood umbrella organization to coordinate and integrate services on the local level, thereby improving them and rendering them more efficient.

The program's formulators advanced a bold vision: comprehensive administration and coordination of services through a leading neighbourhood organization, which integrates and operates the entire system and as such (even though not stated explicitly) transcends the various organizational affinities, power interests, and professional conceptions. Accordingly, the neighbourhood council was charged with 'overall responsibility for planning and supervising all services in each of the neighbourhoods included in the project ... Training employees of all neighbourhoods in comprehensive perception of residents' needs ... Comprehensive planning through the coordinated combined activity of service representatives and residents.'[2] The goal of self-managed administration and policy making was supplemented by several additional objectives, such as community and leadership development and intensifying residents' participation in local affairs.

The overall guidelines of Meron Benvenisti's program and the idea of neighbourhood self-management as propounded by the social reformers were adopted following substantial modifications to fit Mayor Teddy Kollek's conception of Jerusalem as a 'cultural mosaic.' During the late 1970s, the mayor derived some ideas from the two (political and social) proposals and wove them into his basic world-view. This outlook, expressed on various occasions, declares that Jerusalem is a pluralistic city with a delicate and fragile ecological and social texture. 'Most of the [city's] population, Jewish and Arab alike,' as Kollek writes, 'lacks democratic traditions. Jews from Muslim countries, from Afghanistan to Morocco, from Eastern Europe and Latin America, have always distrusted the state apparatus; they survived by creating self-contained communities whose leaders represented them to the outside world and the state' (1988, 163).

To maintain the integrity of this urban system, one should display, as Kollek suggests, sensitivity and open-mindedness towards local cultures. According to this conception, neighbourhood government (in Hebrew *Minhalot*) can encourage values of self-expression and local management and thereby fulfil an educational and moderating role. The cultural-mosaic conception thus has two faces. Its more overt aspect emphasizes a humanistic, broad-horizon approach, which recognizes cultural variety and allows each environment to conduct its local life according to its own values and aspirations. This is the social-humanistic side of the mayor's conception. The other side of the coin is both pragmatic and political, developing and responding to values of consumption (residents' involvement in provision of services), thus ensuring acceptance (legitimization) of the local government. From the geopolitical point of view, this approach guarantees continued Israeli control of all parts of Jerusalem and preserves the integrity of the municipal system. In the mayor's words: 'An expanded system of Minhalot could eventually play a role in a permanent arrangement by becoming the framework for self-administration by the different autonomous communities within one municipality.' Autonomy in provision of services, which Kollek calls 'functional authority,' is supposed to ensure both the social and the geopolitical integrity of Jerusalem. 'There can be no geographic division of sovereignty,' Kollek declares. 'I believe that further sharing of functional authority and greater decentralization within Jerusalem is possible and very desirable ... Israeli sovereignty need not interfere with the Arab community's institutions and economic, cultural and even political life' (1988, 163). This is the essence of the geopolitical principle underlying the conception of neighbourhood government.

The local-government conception was apparently conceived against the background of several other forces liable to divide the city: social movements in distressed neighbourhoods like Katamon Tet (chapter 7) which challenged the status quo, large neighbourhoods in the outer envelope of Jerusalem whose residents complained about the poor level of public services, and Project Renewal activists associated with central-government authorities, who to a certain extent side-stepped the local authorities. In these processes, there were some threats to the city's integrity and to the local political leadership. The neighbourhood government program, created from the top, allowed City Hall to regain control. It created a convenient platform for dialogue with part of the Arab population, moderated pressure by residents of new neighbourhoods, and enabled the mayor to establish direct contact with neighbourhoods, while bypassing the cumbersome bureaucratic apparatus. It is doubtful, though, whether these ideologies could have been realized had Jerusalem's politics remained overshadowed by central-government policy. Indeed, one essential ingredient in advancing the neighbourhood-government idea was the rise of a strong municipality which managed to assume control over local affairs (see chapter 1).

In 1980, the Jerusalem municipality, financially supported by the Jewish Development Committee (JDC – an international philanthropic Jewish organization), embarked upon the Jerusalem Project of Neighbourhood Self-Management (JPNSM). The project's general goals were to foster self-administration and citizen participation, to improve local services, and to promote coordination among local agencies engaged in human services.[3] To attain these goals, the municipality established an independent association, the Jerusalem Association for Neighbourhood Self-Management (JANSM), whose responsibilities are to formulate a general policy for the JPNSM, to establish new neighbourhood councils, the *Minhalot* (singular *Minhelet*), to provide the necessary guidance and training to professional staff and community leaders, to resolve conflicts, to act as liaison between neighbourhood councils and municipal departments, to examine budgetary plans made by neighbourhood councils, and finally to allocate resources to the councils (Kerem 1987). The deputy mayor, Yosef Gadish, was appointed as the JANSM's chairman and acted as a liaison between the municipality and the neighbourhood councils (NCs).

At present there are thirteen neighbourhoods affiliated with the JPNSM: three Arab neighbourhoods, one Jewish Orthodox neighbourhood, five new Jewish neighbourhoods built at the outskirts of the city, and four older Jewish neighbourhoods located in inner-city areas. Each neighbourhood council consists of two components: a professional staff, whole salaries are paid by the municipality, and a residents' council, initially appointed and later elected, whose members serve on a voluntary basis. The professional staff includes a manager, an architect, a community worker, and a secretary. The residents' council makes policy, while the professional staff is responsible for implementation and for handling routine affairs. In addition, there are several committees charged with specific issues such as environmental quality, the elderly, education, and social welfare (Hasson 1989). Apart from paying the staff's salaries, the municipality allocates on a matching basis some resources, known as seed money, for the development of new neighbourhood projects. From the inception of the JPNSM in 1980 up to 1988, the NCs have managed to mobilize $1.5 million (U.S.) for the development of such projects, while the total expenditure of the municipality and the JDC amounted to $3 million.[4] The NCs are not statutory organizations, and therefore are not recognized by the law, as official municipal agencies. Nevertheless, they have been officially mandated by City Hall as authorized and legitimate representatives of their neighbourhood.[5]

Obviously, a wide array of questions concerning the activity and meaning of such an institutionalized form of neighbourhood government may be raised at this point. For the purposes of this chapter, however, these questions will be reduced to three major ones: performance, citizen participation, and relations with the state. We focus on these issues because arguments concerning top-down initiatives, undertaken by local authorities, revolve around the effectiveness of such formalized councils and around their ability to enhance citizen participation and to become politically significant in the urban arena (Hallman 1974; Rich 1988). I will elaborate on each of these specific issues, through a detailed case-study carried out in Baka, one of the first neighbourhoods included in the Jerusalem Project of Neighbourhood Self-Management.

A NEIGHBOURHOOD OF TWO COMMUNITIES

First, there is the name – El-Baka'a – which means in Arabic, a plain, and beyond the name there is a specific history of a well-to-do Muslim community that lived in the area until the outbreak of the 1948 war. In the late nineteenth century, groups of Muslim Arabs, much like their Christian and Jewish counterparts, started to build new neighbourhoods outside the Old City walls. Rich Muslim families, who took part in the process, chose to build their houses at the flat area of El-Baka'a because of its nearness to the train station and its location on the roads leading to Bethlehem and Hebron.[6] At the northern part of the neighbourhood some luxurious family houses were constructed and landscaped in a typical local style: one- or two-storey buildings faced with massive local stone, a large staircase leading to a colonnaded veranda which lies at the front entrance to the house, bougainvillaea shrubs climbing the outer walls, and carefully maintained Mediterranean gardens and orchards surrounding the house. During the 1948 war most of the Arab population evacuated the area, and Jewish refugees from the Old City as well as new immigrants from North African and Middle Eastern countries occupied the houses that had been left behind. Many of the luxurious houses have subsequently become subdivided into small apartment units: new partitions were hastily raised, corridors were blocked, and kitchens and bathrooms were added to accommodate the lower-class newcomers. When the existing Arab housing stock had been exhausted, large and low-quality housing estates were built, mainly at the southern end of the Baka (as it is now pronounced in Hebrew), to absorb the ongoing waves of migration. For the next thirty years the Baka neighbourhood consisted mainly of North African and Middle Eastern immigrants, and has been considered one of the lower-class areas of the city.

A 1975 survey showed that 67 per cent of the neighbourhood's 8,000 residents were of Asian-African origin, 22 per cent of European-American descent, and 11 per cent Israeli-born. Only 13 per cent of the local families had a car, and 60 per cent of the families were tenants.[7] It was only in the late 1970s that the immense residential potential of this inner-city area became apparent to Israeli and North American middle-class families. Within the last decade many old Arab houses have been purchased and renovated, and the whole area witnessed a remarkable social upgrading. Private nursery schools were created, new school curricula were designed, and higher-status cafés and restaurants were opened to furnish the new local needs. Capitalizing on the gentrification wave, private developers went on to purchase undeveloped lots and to build new cottages to feed the rapidly growing demand for housing in Baka. As a result, Baka has become socially divided into two distinct communities (almost equal in size – each including about 4,000 residents), locally referred to as 'northern' and 'southern' Baka. Northern Baka, which has witnessed gentrification, possesses the quality of a country village within the city. Southern Baka, in contrast, is by and large an area of large, low-income housing estates (see figure 9.1). Some of the social features of the two communities are outlined in table 9.1.

The notable distinction between the two communities is revealed at the level of schooling, as north Baka has twice as many residents who went through higher (college or university) education. A minor distinction is discerned in length of residence, where northern Baka has a relatively higher proportion of newcomers. The fact that the newcomers who have a higher education level live in respectable housing whereas the old-timers with a lower education level live on housing estates has

FIGURE 9.1.   Gentrified Arab Housing, northern Baka. A typical Arab villa in Baka, 1930s. The spacious and vernacular architecture of these buildings has made the neighbourhood attractive for middle-class families (Source: David Kroyanker).

TABLE 9.1.   Social Characteristics of the Northern and Southern Communities in Baka, 1988 (percentages)

	North Baka	South Baka
Length of residence		
less than two years	27.8	8.8
2–9	27.8	38.3
10–19	8.3	38.2
20+	36.1	14.7
Owner occupiers	72.2	73.5
Years of schooling		
0–8	5.6	11.8
9–11	5.6	17.6
12	36.1	44.1
13+	52.8	26.5

Source: Residents' Survey, 1988

served to intensify feelings of deprivation and social resentment. In 1981, Fanny Ruash, a local activist, along with several local youngsters joined the Ohalim grass-roots movement (see chapter 7), and in 1983, she went on to accuse the neighbourhood council of neglecting the problems of the young people in Baka.[8] Eventually, the NC itself absorbed and reflected some of these tensions.

All but one of the five northern representatives in the years 1985-7 were newcomers of Ashkenazic (European or North American) descent who had a university or college degree. In sharp contrast, all but one of the five southern representatives were old-timers, some of them raised in Baka since childhood, of Sephardic (Middle Eastern or North African) origin and had completed high school or gone on to teachers' college. As the NC manager noted, the social differences have produced a deep-seated tension among local representatives, which sometimes showed itself in such ethnic expressions as 'northern-Ashkanazic' and 'southern-Sephardic.'[9] In the 1985 elections slogans like 'We will show the Northerners who we are' were quite prevalent, while after the 1987 elections the chairman of the education committee defined the main problem of the NC as an ethnic one.[10]

The evolution of a formal neighbourhood organization in Baka began with the Committee to Improve the Environment of Baka, headed by Sara Kaminker, then a planner in the city planning department. Kaminker contends that, at that time, a growing social and physical gap emerged between the newly formed neighbourhoods (built in East Jerusalem after the 1967 war) and older neighbourhoods like Baka, which for a long time remained physically neglected. Confronting this situation, the then deputy mayor and Kaminker decided to initiate a showcase project of urban revitalization in one of the older neighbourhoods, in order to contain the emerging pattern of sociophysical inequality. The neighbourhood of Baka, at that time largely settled by socially disadvantaged groups, was targeted for this process. A planning proposal, put forward by Kaminker, recommended the demolition of several dilapidated houses and the renovation of some others, the development of green areas in different sections of the neighbourhood, the strengthening of local social services, and the improvement of local roads.

To secure the residents' involvement in these proposed changes, Kaminker created a small committee made up mainly of gentrifiers, who had at that time discovered and penetrated the neighbourhood. This committee served as the base on which the formal neighbourhood council was developed.[11]

Although the revitalization project was primarily attuned to the needs of the older, disadvantaged group, the major impetus for resident involvement in local affairs came from the newly arrived group and was oriented towards middle-class needs and aspirations. Since their arrival in the late 1970s, the gentrifiers, many of them young couples in their mid-thirties, sought to reshape the environment according to their values and aspirations. One of the main targets for their local activity was the local educational system, which failed to match their needs and values. Parents of both secular and religious orientation organized as early as 1980 into lobbying groups that criticized the prevailing curriculum in the secular and religious schools, challenged the professional capacity of the principals, and sought to introduce a new curriculum and staff that would better match their orientation. Their proposals for change, as revealed in their leaflets, disclose typical middle-class values: tolerance, openness, democracy, mutual help, and education in accordance with the values of the Zionist labour parties (in the case of the secular group) and the values of Jewish tradition (in the case of the religious groups).

The early 1980s thus saw the rise of a formal organization, geared towards the needs of the less-advantaged group located mainly in southern Baka, and informal organization created from below that sought to advance the interests of the newly arrived middle-class residents. In 1982, Sara Kaminker, the general director of the JANSM, and Yosef Gadish, the then deputy mayor and chairperson of the JANSM, declared the foundation of the Baka neighbourhood council (NC). Avi Armony, a lawyer and gentrifier, was appointed as the NC's chairperson, and served in this office until the first elections, in 1985. (In 1986, upon Gadish's death and Kaminker's resignation, Armony took over Kaminker's position and, four months later, in 1987, was appointed by Mayor Teddy Kollek as chairperson of JANSM and special aide for neighbourhood affairs.)

Aware of the unequal balance of power within the community, members of the NC sought to secure proportional representation of the different social groups and interests in the area. This was done through neighbourhood elections based on regional representation. The neighbourhood was divided into ten regions, each electing three representatives to sit in the thirty-member general assembly. The ten nominees, who received the largest number of votes in their region, served on the council committee, which is the policy-making body. During the 1987 elections, forty candidates ran for the ten seats of the council committee and for the thirty seats of the general assembly. In most regions, four to five candidates competed. Out of roughly 5,000 eligible residents, 1,002 (20 per cent) voted. In this manner formal representation of northern and southern Baka was secured.

But formal representation is not necessarily coterminous with an equal say and equal benefit, nor does it imply fully fledged support and co-operation on the part of the state. Three questions still require an answer. First, how responsive and effective has the NC been while dealing with the preferences of its two communities? Second, to what extent was it able to enhance citizen participation and to attain legitimation? Finally, to what extent was the state, through its different levels and organs, ready to give neighbourhood democracy a fair chance, that is, to make neighbourhood government practically, as opposed to ideologically, possible? The following sections take each of these questions in turn, and through a detailed case-study, based on a residents' survey (seventy household representatives), an analysis of services, and interviews with politicians and senior officials, as well as with staff and representatives of the neighbourhood council, seek to highlight the nature of Baka neighbourhood government.

PERFORMANCE

Underlying the development of a formal neighbourhood council (NC) in Baka was a municipal decision to initiate on its own an urban revitalization process in the area. Such an operation stood in sharp contrast to other urban-renewal projects sponsored by the Israeli government and the Jewish Agency in six of Jerusalem's neighbourhoods, and perhaps was designed to show the central government that what the municipality can do on its own may be even much better (see chapter 1). To this end, funds were obtained from the Buxenbaum family, and municipal resources were made available.

The major idea was to improve the physical infrastructure (road, sewage, and lighting systems), to enlarge small apartments in the immigrant housing estates, to improve housing maintenance and gardening, and to control the pace of construction in the area.[12] Although some of these activities have a neighbourhood-wide implication, special attention was given to the needs of less-advantaged social groups located in southern Baka. Social assistance to this group was particularly felt in the sphere of housing and education, where a special fund was formed to help disadvantaged students. As noted before, all these activities preceded the establishment of the residents' neighbourhood council and were carried out by the Committee to Improve the Environment of Baka, headed by municipal administrators.

Handing over authority to the residents' neighbourhood council in 1982 brought about some marked changes in social orientation. Active middle-class residents in the northern section of Baka started to reshape the neighbourhood council agenda. Consequently, the northern Baka interest groups, formed around educational issues, applied to the NC and asked for its organizational and political support in establishing two parent-run nursery schools after North American models, and to help in changing the curriculum of one of the local schools so that it would adopt a Labour Party ideology.[13] By extending its help to these interest groups, the NC has gradually shifted its activities towards social needs advanced by well-to-do residents in the northern section.

A North American–style parents' nursery school, which involves a certain tuition fee, is beyond the economic capacity of less-advantaged social groups located in southern Baka, and a Labour-oriented curriculum is not highly favoured by a Middle Eastern poor community, which traditionally has tended to vote for the right-win Likud party. True, the state, through the ministry of education, stipulated the opening of Baka parents' nursery schools on the condition that they would serve the two communities in line with the principle of educational integration. Reality, however, proved to be quite different. The two nursery schools, whose creation was supported by the NC, soon became highly segregated, serving mainly children of well-to-do families coming either from northern Baka or from adjacent neighbourhoods. Small wonder then that social tension has been steadily increasing within the neighbourhood council. Reacting to the proposed change in the school curriculum, the head of the Parent-Teacher Association (PTA), a resident of southern Baka and one of the area representatives in the NC, said: 'I am the head of the PTA and I will not let this change happen in our school. I am going to teach you [the northern residents] a lesson you will never forget.'[14] The conflict between the two groups culminated in the NC's decision in 1985 to close down the local youth centre, which served the southern Baka youth, and to concentrate all cultural and informal educational activities in a modern community centre. Objecting to this decision, residents of southern Baka pointed to the important services administered by the youth centre to socially detached youth.[15] But in spite of their objections, which were supported by Mayor Kollek, the youth centre was shut down.

These short illustrations vividly indicate the social transformation

TABLE 9.2.   Types of Projects and Their Areal Distribution

Neighbourhood-wide projects	Area-specific projects
Project 'Safe Neighbourhood'	Walkway/South Baka
Land-use plan	Expanding housing/South Baka
Walkway	Physical improvements/South Baka
Curriculum enrichment programs	Yehuda Street/South Baka
Extracurricular programs	Mekor Chaim/West Baka
Upgrading of schoolyards	
Heating supplies for the elderly	
Newspaper	

Source: Projects Survey, 1988

which occurred in the NC's orientation, and point to the deep rift that separates the two communities of Baka. However, despite their apparent polarity, delegates of the two groups managed to develop some basic points in common: first, that the southern section would have a priority in physical development, and second, that there is a need for several projects that would serve the neighbourhood as a whole. Table 9.2 highlights these two points by presenting neighbourhood-wide and area-specific projects.

The area-specific projects undertaken reveal a clear preference for problems and target groups located in the southern end of Baka. The projects, a large number of which were initiated by the NC, addressed some of the more pressing problems in the area. For example, the renovation of some of the entrances to the immigrant housing blocks improved the quality of life for many southern Baka residents. The role of the NC in attaining these outcomes was quite crucial insofar as it organized the residents, launched the renovation plans, and handled the project through lengthy bureaucratic procedures. In the case of the Mekor Chaim area, located at the outskirts of Baka, the NC acting as a lobby group was able to bring pressure on City Hall to prevent the further encroachment of industrial uses into the neighbourhood. In Yehuda Street, the NC negotiated a reduction in the widening of the road that otherwise would have entailed the demolition of some homes and yards.

Apart from the southern Baka targeted projects, representatives of the two communities have collaborated to produce certain neighbourhood-wide plans and services to the benefit of different social groups. One of the most significant outcomes of this cooperation has been the development of a statutory land-use plan, which articulated a vision for the neighbourhood as a whole. The plan, which was drawn up between 1982 and 1987 by both residents and the NC's professional staff, was described by the manager of the NC as 'providing a basis for the prevention of decisions that might threaten or entail a negative impact on the neighbourhood.'[16] However, beyond this reactive conception, the plan signifies the return of the public to political life. This has been the first time since the demise of pre-state neighbourhood organizations that a statutory city plan was created from below with the full endorsement and support of the state apparatus, i.e., the Jerusalem municipality and the Israeli Land Administration.

Another neighbourhood-wide project wherein the two groups have invested a considerable amount of energy is a 900-metre pedestrian walkway planned to traverse the neighbourhood from north to south. At the root of the plan are two social goals; first, to foster a sense of neighbourhood unity by physically integrating north and south Baka, and, second, to provide southern Baka with a social centre to be used for meetings, play, and recreation. The first section of the project, planned and partially funded by the NC, was recently completed. With a one-block area in southern Baka now closed to traffic, a landscaped plaza was laid to serve the surrounding densely populated housing estates.

There is nothing in these illustrations to suggest that Baka is another manifestation of Moynihan's (1969) well-known dictum of 'maximum feasible misunderstanding.' This is by no means a situation where an active minority utilizes the NC to pursue its own narrow interests at the expense of a weaker group. The case examined here is much more complex insofar as the NC both reflects and distorts neighbourhood-wide polarities, and serves as a locus of conflict as well as a centre for cooperation. This duality stems from the NC's unconscious adoption of three different social orientations, which correspond to three distinct rungs in Maslow's (1970) hierarchy of needs. At the very lowest level, the NC developed a kind of urban-renewal policy attuned to the basic security and physical needs of less-advantaged residents in southern Baka, indicated by the importance attached to the upgrading of housing blocks and to the creation of playgrounds and public open space. At the intermediate level, the NC catered to the needs for community and belonging of the middle-class residents, located at the northern end, by creating new educational and cultural institutions and by modifying the school curriculum. Finally, at the upper level, the NC offered the neighbourhood an opportunity to shape its own destiny by becoming involved in the formulation of a local master plan and by producing several

TABLE 9.3.   Indicators of Citizen Participation in Northern and Southern Baka, 1988

	Northern Baka	Southern Baka
	(percentages)	
Knew of the existence of the NC in the neighbourhood*	80.6	26.5
Had knowledge of the NC activities**	82.8	22.2
Participated in NC activity**	10.3	0.0

*Percentage of total interviewees
**Percentage of those who knew of the existence of the NC
Source: Residents' Survey, 1988

neighbourhood-wide projects. Carried out simultaneously, these orientations ensure some tangible benefits for each social group and for the neighbourhood public as a whole. This may account for the tendency observed in the course of this research to play down social conflicts, to relegate them to the background and to focus on pragmatic action. Representatives from both northern and southern Baka think that the NC has been quite effective in handling local needs and give it a score of 5 on a 7-point scale where 7 indicates high evaluation.[17]

CITIZEN PARTICIPATION AND SOCIAL LEGITIMATION

One of the major goals at the root of the JPNSM has been to advance citizen participation through local organizations which manage to attain neighbourhood-wide legitimation. Were these goals achieved in Baka? A residents' poll of 70 residents, which included 36 residents in northern Baka and 34 residents in southern Baka, addresses some aspects of this question (table 9.3). There are striking differences between the two communities in terms of social awareness and active participation in the NC's activities. Southern Baka presents the lowest rate of citizen awareness of the NC's existence, whereas northern Baka displays the highest in Jerusalem (26.5 per cent and 80.6 per cent, respectively). Moreover, of those aware of the existence of the NC, only 22.2 per cent in southern Baka had knowledge of the NC's activities as compared with 82.8 per cent in northern Baka, and 56.7 per cent in the JPNSM councils as a whole. Actual participation in the southern Baka area among those who knew of the NC's existence was the lowest in the city, while the respective figure for northern Baka equaled the Jerusalem Project's average.

TABLE 9.4.   Degree of Legitimation Accorded to the NC by Northern and Southern Baka Residents, 1988

	Northern Baka	Southern Baka
	% of interviewees in agreement	
Do you support the idea of neighbourhood self-management through neighbourhood councils?	94.4	52.9
The public can express its needs better to the municipality through the NC.	66.7	38.2
The NC makes for more effective control of the neighbourhood by City Hall.	30.6	50.0
The NC is not in touch with the public.	16.7	55.9
The neighbourhood would not be harmed if no NC exists.	16.7	61.8

Source: Residents' Survey, 1988

Given the significant differences in terms of social awareness and participation, it is of interest to examine the degree of legitimation accorded to the NC by members of the two communities (table 9.4).

The findings in table 9.4 should be interpreted cautiously. Given that only 26.5 per cent of the respondents in southern Baka knew that the council existed, it seems that their answers to the questions in table 9.4 reflect general attitudes towards the concept of neighbourhood self-administration rather than an attitude based upon knowledge and experience. Bearing this warning in mind, there still seems to be a consistent gap between the two communities in terms of the legitimation accorded to the council. Although both groups recognize the positive aspects associated with existence of the NC, they are nevertheless markedly divided over the council's legitimacy. Whereas the majority of northern Baka residents support the idea of self-management and think that the NC is well attuned to public needs and that it generally represents local interests before the city government, residents of southern Baka express ambivalent and even opposite views. In particular, there is a significant disagreement as to whether the NC is sensitive enough to public needs. Indeed, the survey of residents exposes two different sets of local values, one which enthusiastically endorses the institution and another which is reserved or even quite critical of it. Given the dichotomy, it is not surprising to find that the majority of southern Baka residents (61.8 per cent) think the neighbourhood would not be harmed if the NC were to close down.

THE CONTRADICTION BETWEEN PERFORMANCE AND LEGITIMATION

The overall impression conveyed by the findings on performance and citizen participation is somewhat disturbing. On the one hand, the NC appears quite effective in addressing critical needs in southern Baka (housing, open space, and educational needs); on the other, it failed to achieve legitimation, and most of its activities passed unnoticed. A similar feeling of uneasiness has been expressed in a letter sent to the JANSM by the chairman of Baka's NC, wherein he challenged the findings which show that residents of southern Baka are unaware of the NC's activities in their areas.[18] He himself, as he noted in an interview, had helped these residents in improving their surroundings.[19]

This contradiction between effectiveness and legitimation, which has been also discerned by Rich's (1986) study in U.S. cities, seems to be rooted in a deeper tension between the much-exalted goal of participatory democracy and the reality of representative democracy prevailing in Baka. In other words, the failure to attain legitimation and to evoke large-scale citizen participation is an outcome of the representative democratic model adopted. Judged by the interests pursued and by their sociodemographic characteristics, Baka's elected delegates appear to be genuine representatives of their communities. Much like the residents of the communities from which they come, the elected representatives indicated that problems of planning and infrastructure should be accorded top priority on the NC's agenda.[20] As far as their sociodemographic characteristics are concerned, the local delegates are drawn from the rank and file of the local communities. Northern Baka council members (in the 1985–7 period) indicate a large proportion of intellectuals of North American or Israeli descent, among them the head of the social science department in the ministry of science and a designer, both of whom arrived from the United States, and a television reporter, an artist, and a teacher, all of whom were born in Israel and arrived in Baka recently as gentrifiers. Among those representing the southern Baka area, one could find a maintenance person born in Iran, an elementary-school teacher born in Yemen, a senior activist of Sephardic origin born in Jerusalem, and a senior official in the ministry of education who belongs to the Greek community of Baka.[21] The chairman at present is a southern Baka resident of Sephardic origin who possesses a long record of public activity.

All these delegates, as they themselves indicated, are quite familiar with neighbourhood problems and values, and perhaps think they are in a position to express community opinions even without consulting and involving the residents. Meetings with the regional constituency are rare and were held mainly before elections, a point quite openly admitted by local representatives. Indeed, all of them evaluated their interaction with the community as average or mediocre (4.1 and 4.2, respectively, on a 7-point scale). Moreover, all the residents interviewed in southern Baka and 79.3 per cent of those interviewed in northern Baka indicated that they had not received information on the NC's activity (Hasson and Altman 1989). The walkway project, specifically designated to provide for southern Baka's open space needs, highlights the problems associated with a lack of accountability. Unaware of the project's purpose, residents of adjacent housing estates signed a petition to halt construction. It was only in response to the petition that a meeting was held between the NC's representatives and the residents, and the goals of the project were clarified. Once informed, the residents endorsed the project, with some minor revisions, but also found it necessary to express dissatisfaction with the way they had been treated by the NC. One of the residents commented: 'No one knew about it [i.e., the walkway]; we were angry and thought about tearing it down ... We did not know about the project until we saw it ... We raised a petition and went to the meeting at the Community Centre where we asked, "What is going on here?"' In response to this charge, the manager of the NC said: 'A petition was brought forward charging that the walkway would disturb the neighbourhood. They were upset, claiming that the NC never informed them about the project. I have to admit that we made a mistake in not informing the residents until the last minute' (Hasson and Altman 1989, 125).

In a nutshell, this incident elucidates a basic weakness of the NC, that is, its tendency to become bureaucratized and inward-looking. A similar tendency has been noted by Cooper in his Los Angeles study, where he observed that 'even when agencies approach the community with the best intentions, they are still the carriers of the modern bureaucratic, legal and technical mentality' (1980, 439). This technical mentality has been checked in northern Baka, where a plethora of interest groups has sprung up outside the NC's confines. Residents of this section, traditionally less dependent on the council, have organized themselves spontaneously and used the NC as a vehicle to promote their particular interests. In southern Baka, however, where such a spontaneous initiative seems to be missing, bureaucratization and lack of communication tend to impair the council's visibility and to undermine its legitimacy. The new manager summarizes the existing state of affairs as follows: 'When

I entered this position, I found that the organs of communication between the NC and the community were non-existent.'[22]

In summary, the formal structure of participation has not stimulated large-scale resident involvement in the NC's activities. The residents' role has been generally conceived to be quite passive, limited to the reception of benefits. Such a top-down process, felt particularly by less-advantaged groups in southern Baka, transformed the NC to a semi-bureaucratic body which plans projects *for*, as opposed to *with*, the residents. From a theoretical point of view, several features in the model closely resemble Dahl's (1961) pluralist-élitist theory of city politics. First, there is a small leading minority which has been elected to office through a democratic procedure. Second, this élite has proved to be responsible and sensitive to local needs. Finally, the pluralist-élitist model has shown to be quite effective in delivering the necessary services. However, from a normative point of view, this form of local democracy failed to evoke legitimation on the part of less-advantaged groups located in southern Baka, and indeed the major complaint raised by residents of this section against the NC focused on social detachment from the community. The pluralist-élitist model, of which Baka is a fine example, stands in sharp contrast to the participatory model of local democracy that sees residents as partners in the assessment of community needs and in the creation of projects (Hain 1980; Ventriss and Pecorella 1984). Consequently, despite its tangible products, the NC appears to residents of southern Baka as another 'iron oligarchy' aloft and detached from community needs.

RELATIONS WITH THE LOCAL STATE

Beyond the sphere of horizontal democracy, which concerns the relationships between the NC and local residents, lies the sphere of vertical democracy, which concerns the relationships between the state and NCs. Several questions may be raised at this point. First, to what extent is Baka NC recognized by politicians and senior officials as a legitimate representative of neighbourhood concerns? Second, to what extent has the NC become a genuine partner in co-production of services? Finally, has the NC been politically institutionalized by becoming involved in urban decisions concerning neighbourhood development? These questions represent three distinct dimensions of state-neighbourhood relationships: a normative dimension of legitimation, an administrative dimension of service delivery, and a political dimension of power sharing. We will take each of these dimensions separately and examine the specific strategies and interactions pertaining to it. Since some of these strategies and interactions are general in scope, the discussion will broaden at certain points to encompass the general urban policy towards neighbourhood government.

The Normative Dimension

Teddy Kollek, the major political supporter of the neighbourhood self-management idea, wrote in 1978 of 'a future structure for Jerusalem, in which the city will be run through a system of sub-municipalities in each quarter, with autonomy in the management of municipal services and way of life' (Benvenisti 1988, 124). This position fits in with the mayor's urban mosaic view, according to which co-existence in the city can be made possible by displaying tolerance and giving each group the possibility of local cultural expression. Moreover, involvement in the management of services will encourage, the mayor believes, local responsibility and will contribute to increasing democratization not only in the city, but in Israeli society as a whole.[23] In 1981 the principles of self-management were included in the platform of the mayor's One Jerusalem party, and in 1986 the city directorate and city council announced their support of the neighbourhood councils and their recognition of them as the only bodies authorized to represent the residents of the neighbourhoods. Within the establishment there are, however, elements that oppose the neighbourhood councils. The representatives of the right-wing Likud party believe that the term 'autonomy' in the management of services may be broadened to include political matters, and sometimes see the neighbourhood councils as the harbingers of a repartition of Jerusalem.

Important as it is, City Hall's announcement of 1986 – which may be interpreted as symbolic legitimacy – is not sufficient to ensure smooth operation of the NCs. To realize the democratic principle of neighbourhood self-management, there is a vital need to attain legitimacy and co-operation from the municipal departments as well. Without such cooperation, as Ronen, formerly adviser to the mayor, remarked, 'it is not possible to advance the project.' Given the mayor's position, one might expect that recognition of, and support for, the NCs from the department heads should immediately follow. Things are not, however, so simple, as Ronen says:

You can't advance a subject in the municipality today because it is run like private estates, and they [the department heads] will not give up any power ... There are department heads who are afraid of Teddy. He has the power to make them feel threatened, but he does not, in fact, take advantage of his authority. Teddy does not go back to ask whether things have been done, and the department heads know this. As a result, inconvenient decisions, from the department heads' point of view, will not be accepted.[24]

Time and again it has been shown that heads of departments are anxious to retain their power positions and strongly opposed any political attempt to advance political devolution of power. Interviews held with three department heads, who possess close ties with the NCs, reveal that, although all of them support cooperation, they nevertheless insist on maintaining authority and final decision in their hands. 'I'm a partner' claims the head of the youth, sport and community department. 'We need to establish mini-municipalities' says the head of the city improvement department. 'Education services are not sensitive enough' says the head of the education department. In reality, however, continuing central control is sought while allowing the NCs some degree of freedom in areas designated in advance. As the head of the youth, sport and community department bluntly puts it: 'I am the professional element in the city ... I can't allow any neighbourhood body to make decisions instead of me.' In a similar vein, the head of the education department says, 'there is no room in an urban system with a complex fabric to disperse authority.' And, finally, the head of the city improvement department concedes: 'There will always be a need for a central body to take care of upkeep, landscaping and the development of large parks. The neighbourhood councils can take care of smaller things, and then I'll need fewer workers.'[25] These statements clearly define the normative context for co-production as set by senior administrators: retention of authority, that is, policy making, in the hands of the departments and relegating the NCs to information gathering, non-committed consultation and operation in areas formerly designated by the departments.

The Administrative Dimension

Despite their declarations, department heads were ready to cooperate closely with the NCs in the daily provision of services. The improvement department asked for NIS 300,000 (U.S. $150,000) to be designated for neighbourhood council landscaping projects. The head of the sanitation department asked for the equivalent of the salaries of twenty workers to assist the councils in upkeep and cleaning. The education depart-

TABLE 9.5. The Range of Projects Undertaken by the NC in 1988*

	Municipal	Local	Independent
Physical improvement	3		1
Land use	3		
Educational/social		4	3

*'Municipal' refers to projects undertaken in cooperation with municipal departments. 'Local' refers to projects undertaken in cooperation with institutions such as schools that are located within the neighbourhood. 'Independent' refers to projects that the NC produced on its own.
Source: Projects Survey, 1989

ment head asked for funds for three education coordinators in the neighbourhood councils. A closer look at the range of activities and initiatives undertaken by the Baka NC reveals how limited the normative dimension may be, and consequently how risky it would be to rely solely on what people say and ignore what they actually do. During the fiscal year 1988, the Baka NC was involved, as shown in table 9.5, in fourteen projects, six of which were carried out in cooperation with municipal departments. In carrying out these projects, the NC assumed a wide variety of strategies, ranging from initiation through planning to implementation.

Table 9.5 and the strategies of action assumed by the NC clearly demonstrate that the NC domain is much larger than the level that the heads of departments would like to see. To begin with, the NC has been able to go beyond the municipal sphere of influence by developing services either independently or in cooperation with neighbourhood-based agencies, such as neighbourhood schools, the local community centre, or the Centre for the Elderly. The pedestrian walkway, for instance, has been initiated and planned by the NC, and partnership was established with the city improvement department, but only at a later stage, in order to finance and implement the construction. Along with the Centre for the Elderly, to cite another example, the NC distributed heating supplies. It appears that even when cooperating with municipal departments, the NC refused to accept the minor, passive roles assigned for it by senior officials, and proved to be very active in initiating, organizing, and planning local projects. This tendency culminated in drawing up the neighbourhood land-use plan. Such an undertaking signifies a pragmatic legitimation attained by the NC, which stands in sharp contrast to the disparaging views conveyed by senior officials at the normative level.

From a pragmatic point of view, then, the Baka NC has not been just an organizational framework for gathering information and exchanging ideas with city departments, but has also demonstrated creativity and activism in shaping the nature of its local environment. The administrative level, in sharp contrast to its belittling normative view, has been willing to cooperate on higher participation rungs, and to tolerate the NC's involvement in certain spheres of policy making, i.e., in shaping certain aspects of social life. Such a co-production tendency stems from a mutual interest, shared by both sides, in improving local services. Yet co-production should not be viewed as the end of a conflict over power alluded to at the normative level. Beyond the common interest in service improvement lies the political sphere which separates the neighbourhood from the city.

The Political Dimension

Co-production, we will argue, stops short of genuine power sharing and a policy-making partnership. Both the former and present managers of Baka NC argued that the organization has not yet been recognized as a legitimate partner to policy makers. As an example, they both cited the neighbourhood budget for the 1988 fiscal year prepared by the NC upon municipal request. For the neighbourhood representatives, budget planning has become associated with policy making in so far as it envisaged a set of goals, priorities, and plans made up by an elected local body. The psychological effect of budget making on the participants was to generate rising expectations. These expectations, the NC managers stated, have soon turned into disappointment as the NC has not received any commitment for funding from city departments. Instead, heads of departments made it clear that they would consider this policy as a mere recommendation that might not be realized. The result has been sharp criticism from neighbourhood representatives.[26] Reacting to a similar experience, Rimon Lavie, one of the elected representatives of Rehavia-Nahlat-Ahim NC, wrote:

I thought naively that when we received representative legitimacy we would be able to take part in discussion about clarifying municipal policy in areas that we would identify as important to the neighbourhood residents ... I was disappointed to discover that, as far as I know, we have not yet succeeded in any given case in achieving a real participation of this type, and of course I cannot point to any case in which we succeeded in changing the city's policy on planning, development of services, legislation, enforcement and upkeep ... The municipal departments utterly reject any attempt we made to challenge, or even question [a] position or plans that have already been decided, or to be formal and legitimate partners in the process of planning and formulation of programmes that will be carried out later by them. There was even one official who reacted to our demands by saying that these were not the kind of neighbourhood councils he had hoped for. (1988, 3)

Beyond co-production in service provision lies the power-field of agenda setting and neighbourhood policy making, and it is precisely over the entrance into this field that the struggle is currently launched. It is true, no doubt, that in this struggle department heads seek to retain power and tend to be suspicious of any neighbourhood's infiltration into what they regard as their own political domain. Reality, however, seems to be more complex than what they or their critics in the neighbourhood say. The steadily growing functions undertaken by the NCs and their increasing ability to initiate local projects have led to an informal devolution of authority to the neighbourhoods. As indicated above, Baka council, as well as other NCs, have been quite often involved in policy making and have managed to shape the landscape, the educational programs, and the land-use patterns of their neighbourhood. The Baka land-use plan has been officially endorsed recently and has become a statutory document, while programs for the spatial deployment of public institutions (such as synagogues or kindergartens), envisaged by other NCs, have been approved by the political system. True, this is not a formal legitimation for power sharing, but it still attests to a deep change in city politics. In an informal way, that is, without any formal change in the existing law, there occurred a significant normative change in the conduct of service provision, whereby neighbourhood councils have gradually become partners in shaping local life.

Rabbi Nissim Zeev, a member of the city council, has been quite sensitive to this gradual transformation. In an address to the city council in December 1987, he challenged 'the legality of neighbourhood councils, their limitations and power,' and said:

I want to know whether the authority of the neighbourhood councils is legal ... The question is what legal authority the neighbourhood council has, what law provides that it can make decisions. Is there not here a direct circumvention of the authority of the municipal council ... So we, actually, indirectly, won't need a mayor, perhaps, and perhaps not even a city council. The elections will be direct in the existing neighbourhood councils.[27]

What started out as an experiment in administrative decentralization guided formally from the top has apparently been transformed, as Rabbi Nissim Zeev seems to suggest, into a reality of informal political decentralization advanced from the bottom.

CONCLUSION

Neighbourhood organizations are quite often portrayed as monolithic entities whose members tend to work cooperatively in order to promote shared community interests (see chapter 1). The Baka case casts some doubts on this somewhat mystified conception. Living together in the same neighbourhood does not necessarily breed a sense of community among local residents, and different social groups may pursue different projects, depending on their needs, norms, and values. This point was strikingly illustrated in Baka, which during the last decade experienced a significant social change as a result of massive gentrification. As a result, the neighbourhood witnessed the rise of an internal sociospatial division between recently arrived middle-class members, located mainly in northern Baka, and old-time less-advantaged groups, mainly in southern Baka. The decision to integrate the two communities into one neighbourhood council reflects (a) a political decision imposed from the outside, and (b) a recognition that both groups share the same urban infrastructure (roads, community centre, kindergartens, and schools). The integration thus produced within the confines of a neighbourhood organization had its risks and merits. For one thing, it intensified and brought into the open internal conflicts within the neighbourhood with regard to the NC's orientations. The gentrifiers were mainly interested in sociocultural change, whereas the old-timers were largely concerned with physical upgrading of their turf and showed less, if any, interest in sociocultural innovation. This conflict broke out on certain occasions in tense confrontation between the two groups at council meetings. Another facet of this conflict is manifested in the remarkable differences existing between the two communities in terms of citizen participation and legitimation accorded to the NC. While the northern, well-to-do residents seem to be quite aware of the NC and endorse its pattern of activities, the southern, less-advantaged residents tend to remain somewhat reserved, and even alienated.

Yet it would be an oversimplification to interpret these findings as an indication of a minority northern rule over the neighbourhood. A closer examination of the NC's performance reveals that, over time, representatives of the two communities managed to transcend parochial interests and developed a broader conception of what the neighbourhood should look like in both physical and social terms. In other words, they managed to serve the interests of both groups and to overcome, though not without a struggle, their specific interests. In the last instance, a decision imposed from the outside, which charted the nature of the organization and its geographic boundaries, brought about a certain level of intraneighbourhood cooperation between the two communities.

What are the implications of this finding? First, contrary to other neighbourhood organizations discussed in this book, organizations which developed within the confines of well-defined communities, the Baka NC is a territorial organization shared by at least two different social groups. Therefore, in order to sustain itself over time, it had to develop a broader, neighbourhood-wide vision that transcended any particularistic, community-based interest. Geographic boundaries imposed from the outside may thus, in the long run, create some mutual interests. Second, unlike other organizations spontaneously created from below, the Baka NC owes its existence to a deliberate governmental attempt to improve the handling of urban affairs through closer cooperation with urban neighbourhoods. As such, the Baka council, like several other officially created neighbourhood councils, represents the emergence onto the urban stage of a new generation of mainstream and managerial rather than charismatic and protest-oriented neighbourhood organizations. Unlike their predecessors (the neighbourhood boss and the urban social movement – see chapters 5 and 7), these councils steer a middle course between city-wide requirements and neighbourhood demands. For politicians and senior officials, they ensure avoidance of strategic conflict, mobilization of support, and governability. For local residents, they work to improve the quality of life by making service delivery more effective and sensitive to human needs.

Yet, as is quite often the case, a middle course is fraught with sociopolitical tensions. By referring to tensions we do not intend to repeat the 'who governs the neighbourhood' debate, nor seek to discuss whether neighbourhood government is democratic in orientation or prone to manipulation.[28] At the heart of the self-management experience, exposed here through the Baka case, there seems to lie a deeper contrast between neighbourhood government as it exists and neighbourhood government as it is represented. At the intraneighbourhood level, the rift appears as one between performance and visibility, or between effectiveness and legitimation. Relying solely on what residents of southern Baka say, the NC appears to be disconnected from community needs and therefore negligible in community eyes. In reality, however, southern Baka's interests are well served by an elected group which both materially and sociodemographically represents its constituency. A similar tension between what people say and what has actually been performed re-emerges at the urban level. Senior officials, while expressing disparaging views towards neighbourhood councils at the symbolic level, tend to work closely with them when moving to the pragmatic level. As a result, there has developed during the 1980s far-reaching cooperation between municipal departments and neighbourhood councils, and the latter have slowly and informally penetrated the area of policy making.

The apparent contrast between action and representation raises several practical and theoretical questions. There is no doubt that the current debate over neighbourhood government tends to ignore the two different discourses, pragmatic and symbolic, in which the experiment is deeply imbued. The result has been contradictory descriptions, which bypass the complexity and ambiguity surrounding the experiment. In a rather preliminary manner, it may be suggested that, beyond the façade of symbolic expressions and political declarations, there seems to exist a pragmatic exchange between neighbourhoods and government in the course of which new patterns of service provision and informal rules of cooperation and power sharing are gradually produced. Through this delicate and somewhat hidden pragmatic process, co-production forms are filled with urban political content. Theorists, too, might probably recognize the change at the end of the day.

PART FIVE

Conclusion

10

Local Democracy: A Cross-Cultural Perspective

In recent years, the achievements, failures, and yet-to-be realized possibilities of democratic states have been reconsidered in the light of new political and theoretical developments. The astonishing success of the democracy movement in Eastern Europe and the former Soviet Union, unimaginable five years ago, and the lethargy of socialist parties in electoral politics in advanced industrial societies, have reopened with some urgency the issue of radical democratic politics.[1] Closely related has been the intense intellectual debate around modernity and the enlightenment project, a debate with profound implications not only for epistemology and aesthetics, but also for politics. As has been the case with so much social theory of the past twenty years, Jürgen Habermas has been a central figure in these exchanges. The English translation of his 1962 monograph, *The Structural Transformation of the Public Sphere*, has provided a focus for concentrated assessment of the democratic character of the public sphere enunciated through the enlightenment in Western societies (Habermas 1989). In a meticulous examination, Nancy Fraser (1991) has shown that the bourgeois public sphere manifests only a partial political rationality in ways which go beyond Habermas's own critique. Exclusions from the public sphere occurred not only on the basis of explicit social categories such as gender, but also in more covert forms. The public sphere as a speech community offered minimal access to groups unable to engage its specialized linguistic culture, or indeed to share the sensibility, manners, and mannerisms of male, middle-class debating societies. Indeed, Fraser suggests these exclusions were not innocent, but deliberate, a vehicle of class privilege. The public sphere, then, came to define 'the new, hegemonic mode of domination.' From this perspective Fraser concludes that the predilection of Habermas for a reformulated and unitary public sphere to replace the cacophony of voices of a fragmented public of interest groups may not be desirable after all. A single public sphere may surreptitiously, but decisively, pass into the control of a dominant group, despite protestations to the contrary.

Now this abstract discussion provides an illuminating perspective upon relations between neighbourhood organizations and the modern state. In North America the rationalization of the local state dates from the period of so-called Progressive reform between 1880 and 1930. Among the multifaceted objectives of reform was the elimination of special interests, a euphemism for ward politicians (Hays 1964). The corruption of the ward system has been amply documented, but what perhaps has been concealed is the local accountability of ward politicians to local publics. The reformers, whom Hays identifies as middle-class professional and business men, sought to replace these multiple publics with a single public interest, an interest rationally conceived and executed by a professional civil service. Despite a formal democracy with electoral politics, power inevitably gravitated to a male power élite. To some extent this transmission of power was anticipated, indeed intended. Reviewing the Chicago of the 1920s, the sociologist Harvey Zorbaugh (1929), having documented to his satisfaction the collapse of *Gemeinschaft* local community in the industrial city, looked for a new principle of social order at an enlarged and unified scale, the scale of the entire city. But who could forge such a unifying public vision above the flotsam and jetsam of a myriad of local interests? Only those, reflected Zorbaugh, who dreamed dreams for the city as a whole, the public-spirited élite of the high-status Gold Coast district.

The posture of disinterested servants of the people was advertised by business élites. In Vancouver, as we have seen, the businessmen's party named itself the Non-Partisan Association and exercised single-party rule, and a single public interest, for thirty years. More broadly, as has been noted for the whole of western Canada, 'the reform model of urban government was anti-democratic in the extreme' (Anderson 1979). Nancy Fraser's cautions about the desirability of a singular public sphere seem apposite indeed. The business lobby and its neighbourhood counterpart, the ratepayers' association, became a dominant hegemony. Power emanated from, and sustained, a political culture whose configuration was defined by middle-class, property-owning Anglo-Canadian men. Interests that were peripheral to this hegemony were politically marginalized: the interests of lower-income groups, tenants, visible minorities, and, in a more complex manner, the interests of women. The growth of a municipal civil service, a professional bureaucracy, enhanced this marginalization by promoting a superior public interest in a discourse of instrumental rationality incomprehensible to a disqualified public. And so the residents of the Downtown Eastside might uneasily anticipate the consequences of designation as a 'tax sink' by the city's director of planning in the 1960s, just as an earlier city document had disparagingly noted that 'the Chinese quarter to the east of Main Street is at present of significance only to the people who live there.' A greater public good, conceived in splendid isolation from an inclusive public sphere, could disqualify such local public interests. The attainment of a formal democracy through electoral politics could not conceal forms of practical disenfranchisement. On occasion even elected officials were captive to the inaccessible logic of professional discourse – disclosed most powerfully when the protests of Chinatown residents against a freeway network that would dismember their district revealed that city councillors themselves did not understand the technical reasoning of consultants and their own officials which justified the entire proposal.

At the same time it would be naïve to conceive of the modernization of the local state in entirely critical terms. The counterpoint is provided in Jerusalem during the British mandate. The modernization of a traditional administration was shaped not only through the implementation of master plans and the design of garden suburbs like Rehavia, but also by the provision of public services, including modern health care which eradicated endemic malaria in the city in little more than a decade. The distinction to be drawn of course is between those functions of the state, such as health care, where a unitary public interest is more easily (but not unproblematically) definable, and those functions where there are competing interests and where existing biases in the state serve persistently, and even structurally, to disqualify some publics but not others.

The rise of protest movements in the 1960s, and the attempt by the state variously to institutionalize and to socialize those movements in the co-production events of the 1970s and 1980s, highlighted such structural inequalities in the public sphere. Protests were directed not merely at the outcome, the product, of state policy, but also at political process, the model of cloistered decision making dominated by instrumental rationality. In challenging the decision-making process, protest movements sought to redefine the boundary between civil society and the state, urging new forms of political accountability, including various degrees of neighbourhood self-management.[2] As a result, urban political life has been reshaped in some important, if partial, ways in the past thirty years and the changing urban landscape points to these attempts to redefine the traditional public sphere by voices from the margins.

To account for these attempts at transformation and their impact on society and place, we embarked upon a comparative historical study of neighbourhood organizations in Canada and Israel. Both nations, as mentioned in the Introduction, are welfare states based upon mass democracy, a market economy, and a pluralist society. With their mixed economic systems, the governments of Canada and Israel are beset by basic tensions and double codes as they seek simultaneously to advance wealth creation and wealth redistribution, while confirming their own political legitimacy in an often volatile environment. Other tensions are associated with the fact that both countries are young nations still engaged in a process of nation building in societies which are highly plural, both culturally and socially. If both the Arab question and the diversity of immigrant groups challenge Israel's identity and national integrity, in Canada the massive proximity of the United States (accentuated by the 1989 free-trade agreement) and fissiparous regionalism continue to make the national project a precarious one. In the preceding chapters we presented eight case-studies, four from Vancouver and four from Jerusalem, through which we explored the structural conditions under which neighbourhood organizations develop, the sociohistorical process whereby they have been constructed by purposeful human agents, their meanings, and the interrelations between organizations and the state. In this concluding chapter, these findings are placed in a broader theoretical discussion, and new possibilities for democratizing social life are briefly explored.

THE RISE OF NEIGHBOURHOOD ORGANIZATIONS

The Structural Contexts

In this study, we have surveyed local organizations of varying groups in differing locations, active for periods ranging from a few years to more than five decades. Obviously, the macrosocietal conditions under which the organizations arose have markedly changed over space and time (see table 10.1). In both Canada and Israel, the first forms of neighbourhood organizations, which developed in the late nineteenth and early twentieth centuries, were the products of the colonization of territories hitherto settled by traditional societies, the advent of a capitalist system, the beginning of urbanization, and the emergence of a bourgeois group in search of a distinctive place. The neighbourhood organization of Rehavia was thus supported by the Zionist Organization precisely because it was considered to be a means of furthering the policy of colonization. In Vancouver, the founders of Shaughnessy Heights were senior officials of the Canadian Pacific Railway (CPR), a company that was both a symbolic and actual representative of the concerted economic and political colonization of Canada.

No doubt Vancouver possessed at this stage a much stronger link to the European capitalist core, whereas events in Jerusalem took place in the framework of a transition from a traditional (Ottoman) to a modern society. However, the British mandate and the arrival of European Jews brought in their wake strong European influence, among other things notable in modern administrative, planning, and architectural styles. Those colonial landscapes were carved out as aristocratic and spatially isolated enclaves settled by cohesive and well-organized communities. Uncertainties of land development and the absence of public services made necessary a high degree of autonomy in the management of everyday life. This is, in fact, the typical situation of frontier communities, where cultural life (values and norms), provision of services, and negotiation with external forces are handled by the community. Small wonder, then, that this reality was described sixty years later as a *Gemeinschaft*-type community (Katan and Cnaan 1986). Historians and social scientists, on occasion isolating the communal organizations from their specific context, have turned them into the forerunners of local democracies (Turner 1962 [1894]). This kind of nostalgia still sometimes nourishes a feeling that a lost utopia of neighbourhood life waits, perhaps, to be redeemed in the future.

But this is, of course, a myopic observation. At the time when Rehavia and Shaughnessy Heights flourished, other communities witnessed the dismaying conditions associated with the rise of competitive capitalism and urbanization. A case in point is the Chinese community in Vancouver, present there before the last spike of the transcontinental railway was driven into the ground. Serving as a cheap labour force in constructing the Canadian Pacific Railway, they arrived in Vancouver as a unique social stratum, socially and spatially segregated from the rest of society and denied basic social and political rights. Their spatial segregation was living evidence on the fate of state-sanctioned exclusion confronting ethnic groups in capitalist societies in which the principles of universal political and welfare rights had not yet struck root (Anderson 1991; Lai 1988). The later arrival of Oriental (Middle Eastern and North

TABLE 10.1.   Macrosocietal Features, the Role of the State, and Types of
Neighbourhood Organizations: A Historical Model

Macrosocietal features underlying neighbourhood organization	Welfare mode	Type of neighbourhood organization, leadership, and period	Organization's main concern
Organization, colonization, and the development of a capitalist system	Pre-welfare state: charity, philanthropic, sectoral, territorial welfare organizations	Ratepayers' associations, traditional leadership, late 19th and early 20th century	Basic services (streets utilities, etc.), leading to physical and social development, beautification, defending place and community
Immigration of marginalized ethno-class groups – cultural/political hegemony of Western groups – alienation and motivation crisis, among the 'underclass'	Vancouver: pre-welfare state to socialized mode of welfare	Vancouver: traditional organizations in Chinatown and Downtown Eastside	a) Basic needs b) individual *ad hoc* problems
	Jerusalem: socialized mode of welfare	Jerusalem: local boss operating along traditional lines 1950s and 1960s	a) securing the community its basic needs b) enlisting voters for the party
Politicization of space, political inflexibility of local state, socio-economic mobility, and rise of expectations – legitimation crisis	Socialized mode of welfare with greater emphasis on universalism	Protest evolving later to co-production. Late 1960s to early 1980s	Amelioration of housing and ecological conditions; participation in decision making, maintaining ethnic and local identity
Mainstream and political critique of the bureaucratic state – rationality crisis; economic restraint and privatization	Corporate decentralized mode of welfare	Decentralized forms of neighbourhood management. Vancouver: neighbourhood area planning. Jerusalem: neighbourhood government	Physical and social development.

TABLE 10.1. *continued*

Relationship with the state	Social actors (leadership)	State agents	State theory
Very diffuse and informal	Middle and upper class	Power-élite Vancouver: representatives of the private sector; Jerusalem: dignitaries	Elites and the minimal state
Paternalism, clientelism and domination of local interests	Vancouver: exclusion; Jerusalem: inclusion	Traditional ethno-class leadership; In Vancouver, Chinatown benevolent societies and Downtown Eastside religious groups; In Jerusalem, neighbourhood bosses	Power-élite; Vancouver: Economic and social élite; Jerusalem: delegates of the parties of the central and local state	Power-élite and instrumentalism, corporatism
Conflict to co-production		Marginalized ethno-class young-charismatic leadership; middle-class social animators	Plural groups: politicians and bureaucrats at different levels of the state	Pluralism and managerialism
Co-production to liberal corporatism		Different social classes; more mainstream oriented	Vancouver: government bureaucrats at various levels of the state; Jerusalem: bureaucrats of the local authority	Neocorporatism and managerialism

African) immigrants in Jerusalem after 1948 took place under entirely different conditions: a centralist and welfare-oriented government that had vowed to absorb and integrate the newcomers (see chapter 1). It provided housing and social services, and the immigrants were also formally entitled to every political right. While the Chinese community had to compete for a place within the framework of a capitalist and somewhat racist system, the Oriental Jews, although relegated to housing projects constructed by the state, were formally seen as an integral part of the nation.

These differences, important as they may be, mask certain interesting parallels between the two groups (table 10.1). In everyday, practical life, members of the two communities encountered a dominant European culture (Anglophile in Vancouver, Eastern European in Jerusalem), a culture that held a disparaging view of the Orientals' cultural orientations. Members of the two communities formed the lowest social stratum in the urban economy. Although their spatial location was shaped under different structural conditions (a market mechanism in Vancouver, state intervention in Jerusalem), both communities found themselves socially segregated, occupying the miserable sections of the cities (neglected inner-city areas in the Chinese case and the underserviced urban periphery in the Jewish Oriental case). Under these economic, cultural, and physical conditions, a traditional leadership developed (benevolent societies and the local boss) to serve community needs. In Jerusalem, the rise of such a leadership was further augmented by the political drive of the leading (state) party to strengthen its grip on the newcomers' votes. The local boss thus played a double role, simultaneously serving both the party and the community. Unlike the ratepayers' organizations of Shaughnessy and Rehavia, which possessed high levels of local autonomy and self-management, those of the ethnic/lower-class groups were highly controlled and dominated from the top, featured conservative patterns of activity, and operated within traditional communities largely alienated from mainstream society.

The crisis of motivation, as postulated by Habermas (1982), is associated with cultural alienation, the absence of a sense of social solidarity, and some pathologies at the personal level. It would seem that such a crisis characterized certain segments of the Oriental community in Israel, notably among the members of the underclass that later formed the core of the Ohalim movement. In Chinatown, poverty and the overwhelming male majority (legislated by immigration laws) defined a favourable context for opium-smoking, drunkenness, and prostitution, although the clients and coordinators of the 'ills of Chinatown' represented a much broader racial cross-section. The same motivation crisis was equally evident in the Downtown Eastside, where, prior to DERA's appearance, the subculture of tavern life dulled the political sense of a large number of residents.

Alienation and the crisis of motivation were, however, only two components in a much broader set of societal conditions. Over the years, the young generation of Chinese and Oriental groups acquired education and skills and experienced upward social mobility. The Chinese were enfranchised in 1947 (municipally in 1949), and the emergence of a welfare state brought social and economic benefits in its wake. It was the younger and often more educated generation in Vancouver and Jerusalem that challenged traditional leadership and confronted the state.

The protest of the younger generation arising in areas settled by ethnic/lower-class groups should not be viewed, however, in isolation from general changes that occurred about the same time (late 1960s and early 1970s) in society as a whole (table 10.1). These years were marked by growing discontent, even in mainstream, upper-class groups. State decisions on the deployment of social facilities, high-density development, urban renewal, and the construction of freeways were challenged by single issue–oriented groups that sought to defend their territory. Within this milieu, the protest of ethnic and lower-class groups has a special position precisely because it exposed the state to the sharpest critique – a critique that challenged not only the performance of the welfare state, but also its goals and principles in damaging already vulnerable communities. These organizations attracted public attention to the inflexibility and rigidity of the state, its inadequate response to local needs, its contempt for local values and ethnic heritage. The main conflict was not with capitalists, but with the state, and the protest groups managed to rouse public support primarily from among liberal and left-wing professionals. It is hard to tell whether this was a large-scale legitimation crisis, but there can be no doubt that legitimation wore thin among a large segment of the public; this was often expressed by militant activities in Jerusalem and abrupt political shifts in election returns for local and more senior levels of government in Vancouver. It is not surprising, then, to discover a dramatic change in state response to local organizations, manifested in the adoption of an open style and co-productive patterns. Indeed, in all the cases examined, most of the protest and defensive groups entered swiftly into co-productive relations with the state. In subsequent years, the state tightened its contacts with the organizations, provided them with economic resources (grants), professional guidance, and in certain cases with political support. Community life has thus been penetrated by the state, a process that culminated with the advent of decentralized forms of neighbourhood management (local area planning and neighbourhood government) created by the local state.

Decentralized forms of neighbourhood management developed under the circumstances of a growing critique among liberal and social-democratic professionals in civil society, and within the state itself, of bureaucratic rigidity, lack of responsiveness, insensitivity to human needs, and lack of efficiency. In essence, this critique, especially when originating within the state, points to a rationality crisis, that is, growing impatience with the administration's inability to deal responsively and efficiently with local needs (table 10.1). Another source for the political change has to do with the fiscal crisis confronting the welfare state. The increasing gap between rising expectations and stable and even declining welfare expenditures leads to a further legitimacy problem at the local level. Hence the continuous attempt to grapple with these problems by ongoing modifications in the operation of the state at the neighbourhood level, and by constant change in the nature of these organizations.

The initial results were to open up the local state by ensuring that different forms of decentralization took place, representing a deliberate attempt to democratize social life by establishing representative neighbourhood committees. This form of populist politics, sometimes expressed in such slogans as community participation, empowerment, pluralism, and social justice, also enabled the incorporation of diverse cultures into mainstream culture. The state played a leading role in these processes, and one could argue that this is a phase at which local initiatives are directed and even manipulated from the top.[3] The situation is one of decentralization (primarily administrative in nature), democratization, and strong state intervention. Much like the trade unions, the neighbourhood organizations appear in this light as partners and are allowed a certain range of discretion as long as they operate within the agreed political framework. This pattern of local activism may be termed neocorporatism, which differs from pluralism in that local power is not diffused and the local state is accorded a greater steering capacity in urban affairs. Political integration of interest groups is attempted through representation and the cooperative interaction of leadership, together with the mobilization and social control of the rank and file.[4]

The neocorporatist phase was later marked by a state tendency to privatize the supply of social services. Decentralization and privatization signify new modes in the development of the welfare state and the neighbourhood organization (Laws 1988; Wolch 1990). They imply a retreat from socialized welfare, simultaneously advancing greater communalism, while operating services in accordance with market principles. In the long run, however, privatism and communalism may collide, thereby leading to a new mode of protest.

From a historical point of view, there appears to be a gradual change in the nature of the neighbourhood organizations and the mode of the welfare state. We do not, however, postulate this as a general evolutionary model of paternalism, protest, and co-production, nor should table 10.1 be taken too literally. For one thing, protest has not disappeared from the urban scene; it could erupt again if privatization continues unchecked.[5] Indeed, the revival of community politics and anti-growth coalitions in Canadian cities like Toronto and Montreal in the late 1980s and the renewed protest of homeless young couples in Israel warn us of the pitfalls of any linear evolutionary model. Neither has bossism entirely disappeared, and one may still find it when delving deeply into the nature of protest or co-production organizations. Michels's iron law of oligarchy (1962) seems to hold true with regard to contemporary, supposedly progressive organizations.

What seems to be more interesting from a historical-cultural perspective is that characteristics of the life-world (the taken-for-granted values and norms and routinized patterns of behaviour) may militate against linear progress towards decentralization and the development of neocorporatist organs at the neighbourhood level. Thus there was remarkably little popular support for the community resources boards which decentralized some social services to neighbourhood committees in Vancouver in the early 1970s. Or, again, despite the large-scale penetration of offices into Rehavia and the municipal attempt to encourage local government in the area, a substantial part of the population remained apathetic and inactive. The failure to mobilize in Rehavia had to do with feelings of helplessness, disbelief in the ability to reverse the trend, and routinized patterns of inaction which characterized the elderly population of Rehavia. What appears to be a gradual evolution towards neocorporatist, co-productive forms of neighbourhood government may thus be hampered by well-entrenched values and norms.

Over the course of the changes in the form of neighbourhood organization, group objectives seemed to move from the material to the postmaterial sphere.[6] The ratepayers' associations focused on housing, planning, and physical infrastructure. The traditional associations and the local boss sought to provide their constituency with basic needs, primarily in the spheres of housing and employment. The protest and co-production organizations added to basic needs new values and demands associated with political participation, communal responsibility, and democratization. The decentralized forms of neighbourhood organization focus on self-management in cooperation with the state, embracing a broader spectrum of local life: policy making, provision of services, and conflict management.

To sum up, the changes in the forms of neighbourhood organizations were associated with the operation of several structural forces within society (table 10.1):

a / the shift from competitive capitalism and pre-welfare modes of state operation to a mixed economy where the state plays an important role in socializing urban costs, and finally to a gradual withdrawal of the welfare state;

b / the social mobility of lower-class groups and the growing concern of the middle-class public with land-use and environmental issues in an era of urban growth;

c / the opening up of the dominant culture, allowing the incorporation of popular cultures associated with ethnic minorities and lower-class groups;

d / legitimation, rationality, and fiscal crises that led to the adoption of new forms of urban management by the state.

The disparate conditions under which neighbourhood organizations arose resulted in a growing diversification of local activism in terms of the groups involved, their orientations, strategies of action, and relations with the state – a diversity that has survived to the present. This is, perhaps, one of the salient features of our times, on occasion vaguely referred to as 'new times' and designated by a range of transition theories (e.g., post-industrialism, post-modernism, post-Fordism). If there is any common thread running through all these propositions, it would seem to include rebellion against any dominant system and the recognition of the diversity of cultures and their role in shaping urban life.

The Role of Human Agency

Important as they may be, structural conditions do not necessary breed social action. This is a simple truism that could have been left unsaid were it not so frequently forgotten by structuralists and functionalists alike, when they try to account for social mobilization. It was as if the essential first part of Marx's aphorism 'Men make history, but not in circumstances of their own choosing' had been overshadowed by the second part, even in the case of those professing allegiance to human agency. Although aware (often, brilliantly so) of the role of the human agent in his empirical chapters, Castells, for example, chose in his theoretical discussion to expand on the structural forces underlying urban social movements. He thus fails to theorize the complex process whereby structural or macrosocietal features are read, deconstructed, and reconstructed by active human beings. As a result, the reader is finally left with but a vague notion as to the process whereby a meaningful purposive action is produced. It is interesting to note that, despite their theoretical disagreement, both Castells (1983) and Pickvance (1985) shared at base a common epistemological orientation, that is, a search for the proper structural forces shaping social organization. Though acknowledgement is made to human agents, they remain enigmatic and obscure in both schemes.

In contrast, our starting-point is the simple proposition that people may react to structural forces, changes, and even crises in varied ways, by opting for exit, resistance, or adaptation, or by retreating into apathy. The discussion will highlight how the complex processes associated with organization differ markedly along social-class lines (table 10.2). Quite often, as seen in the pre-organizational state, people tended to follow the routine patterns they had become accustomed to over time. This phenomenon was particularly notable among ethnic and lower-class groups (in Chinatown until the late 1960s and in the Downtown Eastside, Ir Ganim, and Katamon Tet until the 1970s), and found expression in ideological utterances such as the ones made by two leaders of the Ohalim movement:

We were told many times ... to assume responsibility and to run the neighbourhood on our own. But we would say that it was beyond our capabilities and should be seen to by the municipality ...

The people in the gang were just like me, engaged in crime and poverty. We didn't know about social services and didn't care about the law. We were marginal people who could be arrested and re-arrested.[7]

Similar voices could be heard among economically and racially marginal groups in Vancouver. Prior to his recruitment to the People's Aide program in 1972, Bruce Eriksen's world in the Downtown Eastside was one that fell outside the bounds of political participation: 'Before that time when I went past City Hall I thought it was some high class place that I couldn't even go into. I don't think I even voted up to that time.'[8]

These utterances are of crucial importance in that they indicate routine

TABLE 10.2.   Differences in the Construction of Neighbourhood Organizations among Social Classes

Parameters	Lower class	Upper class
Life-world: cultural sphere	Deconstruction through reinterpretation of preinterpreted sets of beliefs, thus deroutinizing well-established norms and patterns of behaviour	Reconstruction of local myths, values, and norms, thus modifying old patterns of behaviour
Role of organizers and leaders	Crucial – tend to be charismatic. Important role of professionals in community development and of the media	Minor – utilization of existing social network. Normally, limited use of the media
Life-world: Internal relations	Enhancing solidarity among members of the community in order to exert greater political pressure on the system	Social solidarity is less essential, and political influence may be attained through personal networks
Life-world: external relations	From system challenge to system integration	Segments of the system are part of local life-world.

patterns of action guided by deeply entrenched beliefs, norms, and values, which help to sustain asymmetrical power relations. Members of the groups, through day-to-day life experiences, unintentionally reproduced the existing set of values, and hence the prevailing political relations. This is precisely the recursive nature of structure which, so Giddens (1984) argues, both enables and constrains. The constraining element, however, the tenacious conservatism of the taken-for-granted life-world, is apparently far more evident, demonstrated, through the medium of language, in the seeming absence of any counter-beliefs in the group's capacity to deroutinize already existing patterns of social action.

These expressions are ideological in the sense that they express an internalization of existing power relations. Put another way, social marginality and compliance with existing relations had become part of a set of values, norms, and behaviours that were taken for granted (that is, part of the life-world). Obviously, such utterances could not be found among members of the middle- and upper-class organizations, because their links to the economic and political system, and their universe of daily life experiences, were entirely different. Evidently, the asymmetrical power relations and the extent to which they were internalized in the life-world vary significantly among the social classes (table 10.2). As one moves from lower to higher classes, the asymmetry in power relations diminishes significantly and is almost reversed in the case of the upper- or upper-middle classes of Shaughnessy and Rehavia, where strong political agents acted as advocates of the neighbourhood interest. Social-class position is not, however, the only factor that accounts for ideological internalization or unequal social relations. The language of the elderly middle-class residents of Rehavia, much like those of lower-class people in Katamon Tet, discloses a loss of faith in their capacity to control local life and their reluctant acquiescence in the commercialism of their neighbourhood.

It is apparent, then, that ideological and symbolic configurations implicated in routine activity are recursively reproduced, and that they are geographically variable, reflecting the social make-up (for instance, class structure and age distribution) of the actors involved. The crucial question that ties together pre-mobilization and social action is whether these routinized social behaviours can be modified in a way that breaks with deeply entrenched daily life conventions and with old patterns of interaction with the political-economic system. This question is particularly important in the case of ethnic and lower-class groups where, as we have shown, pre-interpreted schemes tend to sustain traditional and conservative patterns of political behaviour (table 10.2). It is precisely at this point that an understanding of the deconstruction of old ideological notions and the process of identity transformation is most needed. This critical role of enabling ideologies in the mobilization process has recently been emphasized (Lowe 1986). So too has the stultifying effect of their absence. Why has a broad coalition not formed to resist the costs of economic restructuring in U.S. cities? A major reason is that within the United States 'no tendency exists to put the situation of poor New Yorkers within a context of meaningful action' (Fainstein and Fainstein 1985; Cox 1988).

Casting new light on old conventions and social practices was aided by the use of myths, ironies, and jokes. Moroccan tradition, occasionally looked down upon by mainstream Israeli culture, was elevated and self-consciously mythified to become associated with the virtues of modesty, voluntarism, and brotherly relations between Jews and Arabs. Ironies were skilfully utilized to identify adversaries and reorient social action. Similarly, in the Downtown Eastside, working-class humour and irony were able to problematize the taken-for-granted life-world and thus bare its political edge (figure 6.2). Consider, for example, DERA's Crummy Cockroach Haven Contest, a playful competition inviting residents to nominate the 'three sleaziest dives' in the district. The subversive face of this contest was revealed when widespread publicity obliged the city to prosecute the 'winner' of the competition and other premises, and soon after to set up an interdepartmental team to establish a downtown housing strategy. The interrogation of everyday life was also accomplished by cartoons (e.g., figure 8.2) and radical theatre. The West Broadway Citizens' Committee engaged in such 'pranks' as holding a mock council meeting, a farce acted out by members in the foyer of a school hall, to divert residents entering the building from a public hearing before Council under way in the main hall. A more sustained strategy was the use of community theatre by professional actors and directors in Katamon Tet as the catalyst of a social movement among underclass youth. The semantically loaded theatre productions (with such titles as *Joseph Goes Down to Katamon*, *The Dropout*, and *Class Reunion*) projected everyday life into an entirely new symbolic and political realm.

Through these acts, new images and symbols that convey a sense of power and challenge were created among the marginalized groups. As the leader of the Ohalim movement said, 'They never believed that a power would emerge from the ghetto.' An ICL pamphlet called on the residents to topple the 'party pimps from the immigrant transit camps era and to act so as to make possible greater public involvement in neighbourhood affairs, in order to allow for the demonstration of our life.' In a similar, if less polemical, vein, one of the leaders of SPOTA claimed: 'My husband said ... the Chinese have to show that they're capable of winning the fight with City Hall, and we mustn't look down on ourselves as a people – we can do it.'

Sometimes, particularly in lower-class and ethnic communities, the deconstruction and politicization of everyday life were accomplished by a particularly charismatic figure (table 10.2). The Downtown Eastside's need for a 'big man' was met by the radicalizing of Bruce Eriksen. A neighbourhood resident imbued by the apolitical norms of everyday life, Eriksen underwent a political awakening that began with conversations with community workers placed in the district by the state, but in its radicalism quickly exceeded their reformist strategies. As we move to upper-class organizations like those of Rehavia and Shaughnessy, power resides more with the office than the personality. The group rather than the leader speaks with authority.

We should not assume, however, that the power of personality is limited to the grass roots. Charismatic figures in government, such as Mayor Kollek in Jerusalem during the 1980s and Prime Minister Trudeau, particularly in the innovative 1969–72 period, similarly have the capacity to reshape the enabling environment of community organizations. We noted earlier the unusually direct and enabling links between Trudeau's cabinet minister and SPOTA, and Kollek's personal initiative was similarly a factor in the process of neighbourhood self-management in Rehavia. Teddy Kollek, as he himself concedes, sought to deroutinize old patterns of social behaviour by initiating self-management patterns at the neighbourhood level. 'Most of the [city's] population, Jewish and Arab alike,' he wrote, 'lacks democratic tradition' (1988, 158). Hence, Kollek conceived of his role as educational, one of fostering such values as participation, tolerance, and self-administration. Not only did Kollek criticize the sphere of life-world; he also went on to challenge the political bureaucratic system, which in his view failed to respond sensitively to citizens' needs. He has defended the interests of the Arab population in Jerusalem, criticized the encroachment of Jewish settlers into Arab areas, and lent political and economic support to neighbourhood organs of self-government throughout the city. In the Rehavia case, he openly sided with the local residents in the struggle to halt the penetration of offices into their territory, even though this meant clashing with business interests. Both his initiative on behalf of Rehavia and his status as a neighbourhood resident underscore the interlocking character of élite neighbourhoods and the welfare state. Similarly, the cordial relations between Shaughnessy property owners, planners, and members of council in establishing the Shaughnessy Plan were undoubtedly aided by the office of Mayor Volrich, leader of an earlier anti-development action by Shaughnessy residents. In both instances the boundaries of system and life-world are blurred; personal networks become significant political resources.

Nor, despite the above examples, should we ignore the gender composition of neighbourhood leaders and facilitators. A frequently critical literature has explored the relations between women and the welfare state.[9] Community is a key concept in the discourse of the welfare state, and it is invariably presented in gendered terms, contrasting the private and domestic realm of women with the public and economic realm of men (Walker 1990). The term has also been employed ideologically, most recently in state privatization schemes which speak of 'restoring' responsibility to 'the community,' in effect to a frequently unpaid and overextended constituency of women. Certainly the politics of consumption of neighbourhood groups is a politics to which women have made powerful contributions (Fincher and McQuillen 1989). In our own studies, women played an important role in leadership in three of the four Vancouver neighbourhoods, including the Downtown Eastside with its predominantly male population; only in upper-class Shaughnessy did more traditional gender roles prevail, with men dominating the organization's leadership, while women acted as its 'foot soldiers.' They were equally prominent as community workers and other professional facilitators to the neighbourhood organizations in both cities. The role of professional women in Jerusalem is particularly noteworthy, for women were much less visible in positions of grass-roots leadership. These professional women were all of Ashkenazi origin, but even in affluent Ashkenazi neighbourhoods, organizations have male leadership; all the principal leaders of Rehavia since its beginnings in 1922 have been men. In the Sephardic immigrant communities, a traditional patriarchy has continued to prevail, and this status did not change, nor indeed was it seriously challenged, in the protest movements. The constitution of the Ohalim movement did call for a woman to be appointed as deputy chairperson, but such a post was never filled.

The empirical evidence from Chinatown, the Downtown Eastside, Kitsilano, Ir Ganim, and Katamon Tet points to the significant role played by outside professionals working in conjunction with a newly formed local leadership. These agents, occasionally assisted by the media, developed new sets of images and symbols that challenged old conventions and reoriented ideological configurations and social action. Sometimes, their role was a simple as to pinpoint the existence of an alternative. 'Margaret Mitchell' (a community worker in Chinatown), noted Bessie Lee, later a leader of SPOTA, 'happened to be sitting near me and she said, "Look, if you really want to find out more and do something about this, give your name to the girl over there."' Nathan Karmel, a community development organizer assigned to Kitsilano by the City of Vancouver, convinced local residents to form an organization to resist the city as it sought to make space for automobile parking by expropriation of nearby single-family homes. Influenced by the radical community-development strategy of Saul Alinsky, Karmel asserted: 'There's no point in sitting down and dealing with people on a one-to-one basis who have problems as a result of the system. It's smarter to organize people to change the system.' Michael Paran, a community worker in Katamon Tet, saw criminal activity as a protest against society. Therefore, he said, 'I always told them that, if you want revenge, you can be far more effective through social protest.'

Alongside their role in deconstructing pre-interpreted schemes, community organizers, local leaders, and certain politicians were deeply engaged in reconstruction and institution building (table 10.2). Particularly for poorer or more radical groups, strength lies in large numbers, and efforts at institution building were tireless, most self-consciously in the West Broadway group with its close adherence to the Alinsky model of community mobilization. Institution building involved internal and external sets of activities. The internal set extended over four spheres of activity.

The ideological sphere: Activity involved the constant reshaping of local values, norms, and patterns of behaviour, thus reinterpreting local schemes, providing alternative readings, demystifying old notions, and developing a vision that informed the orientation and strategies of action of the organization. Sometimes there were several groups engaged in this process, offering competing readings and visions. In the case of the Ohalim movement, for instance, the South American students offered political-economic interpretations, the North American students offered ethnic and cultural interpretations, one community worker developed a somewhat exclusionary territorial vision, and another strove to develop cognitive-moral links with the left. In Kitsilano, too, there were competing liberal and radical ideologies of community resistance, eventually resolved in favour of the Alinsky model. In an élite neighbourhood like Shaughnessy, the task in contrast was to promote continuity rather than change, to reassert traditional patrician values, using the landscape myth of the English country estate as an ideological rallying point.

The social sphere: Activity at this level involved organization of local residents around tangible problems and symbolic configurations. This was done through face-to-face encounters, the distribution of leaflets, the dissemination of information through social networks, regular community meetings, and the utilizing of notable local figures. The YFN leadership, for instance, effectively used the rabbis and synagogue networks to mobilize the local population. These activities were partly didactic. This was the explicit purpose of the West Broadway group in the showing of Alinsky films, and in a more veiled manner, one aim of Shaughnessy owners in commissioning a consultant to prepare a land-use and landscape plan for the district, around which a neighbourhood consensus might be consolidated.

The organizational sphere: Actions included the development of norms, strategies, an internal division of labour, and authority and leadership styles. This process involved varying degrees of formalization, ranging from very amorphous structures and behaviour in the case of the single-issue organizations, to very formal structures in the case of local area planning and neighbourhood government. The development over time in this sphere appears to be hyperbolic. The ratepayers' association and the current decentralized forms of local planning and administration possess a highly formal structure frequently specified in a constitution or terms of reference, and a well-defined division of labour. In contrast, the protest organizations seem to be less structured, being quite often organized around a charismatic figure. But even in this type of organization there has been a tendency to develop more formal structures. The survival of the organization thus involved degrees of bureaucratization that at a certain level contradicted original anticipations, and subsequently led to internal conflicts.

The economic sphere: The mobilization of resources in order to sustain the organization's existence was the first preoccupation. This process lies at the interface between internal and external activity, because it involves engaging both internal and external social environments. The organizations that developed in the pre-welfare period drew most of their resources from the internal environment, whereas the decentralized forms of organizations rely heavily on state resources. Within the protest and defensive organizations, resources were mobilized from both the internal and external environments. Protest organizations isolated from state funding are extremely vulnerable, as was evident from the experience of DERA and the West Broadway group.

The *external set* of relations implied a link, whether confrontational or cooperative, with different levels of government (table 10.2). Demands, norms, mutual legitimation or delegitimation, personnel, professional knowledge, and economic resources were exchanged through this link. Frequently, the skills and networks of community workers facilitated the connection between the organization and external agencies (recall the role of Darlene Marzari and Margaret Mitchell in Chinatown-Strathcona, and the role of Yair Fidel and Avner Amiel in Ir Ganim). The role of radical community workers appears paradoxical in this light.

On the one hand, they invoke social critique and help to produce a counter-ideology. On the other hand, they perhaps unintentionally bring about greater integration into the system and enhance conformist action. More rational integration of the life-world and system appears in this light as a dialectical process in which integration complements confrontation. For élite groups, of course, a high level of existing integration usually precludes the necessity for confrontation.

Throughout this process of institution building, the media played an important role in publicizing local demands, and sometimes even mystifying them. Recall Jim Green's reference to a strategic use of the media by DERA or the West Broadway group's 'developer of the month' award, directed as a tactic to gain media attention. On another occasion, a group of five people lacking a support base (ICL) was presented by the Jerusalem media as the resurgence of the Black Panthers and as a challenge to the right-wing Likud party's dominance in poor neighbourhoods. Publicity, whether accurate or not, operated as an empowering resource in raising local issues on the agenda and in exerting social pressures on government. The media acted, in other words, as another power centre, partly informing and partly manipulating public opinion.

The Diversity of Organizational Culture

Institution building was performed under conditions of which the organizers and leaders were not entirely conscious, and produced some unintended consequences. At times the organization's structure and behaviour were shaped by latent orientations rooted deeply in the life-world permeating the process of institution building. For example, the Ohalim movement crystallized around two social groupings, one mainstream-oriented (in the sense of accepting the centre's authority and the values it represented), while the other, made up of gang members, was oriented towards marginalized groups. The values of each cluster, formed through specific experiences, affected the movement in remarkably different ways. The mainstream-oriented group sought to counter socio-economic deprivation through cooperation with the state in developing local services, while its rival confronted the state, and so put the issue of poverty and housing on the public agenda. The groups' differences were also revealed in patterns of leadership. Whereas the mainstream members were inclined towards non-hierarchical and anti-authoritarian organization, the other group, bringing in traditions and norms nurtured in the gang, reversed the trend. The result has been internal tension within the organization that led to the exclusion of the mainstream group and, later, to the collapse of the organization.

The penetration of the life-world into the organization caused some frustration among social organizers, one of whom contended: 'The subculture somewhat ruins things ... A party gives out money, so they go to work [for it]immediately.' Thus old values (Giddens's rules) acquired through specific personal and collective trajectories, continued to be implicated in human activity. Another example of the effect of life-world on the organization is drawn from the Ir Ganim case. Trying to transform conventions in Ir Ganim by drawing a cognitive link between local housing problems and massive governmental expenditures in the West Bank, ICL and its supporters on the left encountered hostile reaction from local rabbis. So, too, both DERA and SPOTA not infrequently found themselves in opposition with traditional and more conservative groups (the religious missions and benevolent associations) in their analysis of local problems and prescriptions of appropriate actions.

There are rare cases, where only one set of values rooted in the life-world permeated the organization. Failing to notice the exceptionality of this situation is one of the major weaknesses of the existing literature on neighbourhood organizations (and, by extension, on urban social movements), precisely because the researchers of supposed 'liberation' movements seem to ignore or unintentionally obliterate all competing and opposing sets of values. We have already encountered the dual cultures within the Ohalim movement. Baka neighbourhood government provides another example, as the values of older residents sharply collided with those of recently arrived gentrifiers; in Kitsilano the distinction was between liberal reformers and Alinsky-style activists. In Ir Ganim, the modification of the chairperson's values and his retreat into a local boss style of leadership were confronted by members of the organization. The selling of apartments by the elderly to business people was justified by the chairperson of the Rehavia neighbourhood council, although it was opposed by the rest of the council. Even in Shaughnessy, with its carefully cultivated political connections, the appearance of a minority splinter group at the eleventh hour created an unexpected air of uncertainty at a public hearing to approve the recommendations of the Shaughnessy Plan. These contradictory sets of values are closely associated with the social make-up of the discrete groups involved in the organization. In defending the right of local residents in Rehavia to sell their apartments to businesses, the chairperson represented the interests of the elderly group in the area, for whom housing sales had become the major means of funding health and social expenditures. In contrast, the struggle to keep Rehavia residential and to prevent the establishment of more offices represented the interests of groups that wished to continue to live there. The study of conflicting values within the neighbourhood militates against the one-dimensional, quasi-average view imposed quite often by researchers. Some of the most interesting debates, as these cases show, take place within or between local organizations.[10]

Such heterogeneity informs not only the organization's vision but also its strategy of interaction with local residents, and with the political-administrative system. Values may be modified to a lesser or greater degree so that a new organization is conceived in the womb of an existing one. A striking example is the Ohalim movement. Starting as a reform organization, mainly engaged in the provision of services, it was exposed to socialist ideas when joined by the gang and radical intellectuals, including community workers, students, and university teachers, an encounter which radicalized its orientation. Finally, through constant exchange with politicians and bureaucrats, piecemeal procedures were adopted, culminating in co-production with the state. Indeed, it is interesting to note the swiftness with which even the most radical groups modify their original values and assume co-productive patterns of activity. One may observe the same transition in DERA's twenty-year history; its strong conflict voice of the 1970s evolved into a dominantly co-productive mode in the 1980s. In Jim Green's view, the organization's strategy is flexible; it is simply a pragmatic question of what works: 'There's less necessity for picketing and rallies now. We can often accomplish with a telephone call what took a picket line in the 1970s. But when we need to, we will do it. I'm involved in a lot of negotiations, meetings with government, and so on. I expect to get what I ask for. I tell them I'd rather not embarrass them with 500 pickets and the media.'

It appears that linkages created between the organizations and the political-administrative system led unintentionally not only to greater dependence on the state and its redistributive power, but also to a modification of original norms, an enhancement of socialization in terms of the centre, and a change of personal orientations. At the same time, as Green's statement indicates, the gain for the organization is access to material resources such as the close to 650 social housing units built, under construction or managed by DERA in 1991, or the funding provided by the state for SPOTA's renovation program. Organizations (like West Broadway) that decline the co-productive option are ignored by the state, unless they attract very large numbers. More often than not, bereft of resources, they wither away.[11]

The longitudinal approach adopted in this book contributes to more than the sense of organizational evolution. Any assessment of the effectiveness and impact of local action also requires the long view. The restricted time horizon of locational conflict studies, for example, excludes all but short-term consequences. Longer-term impacts may well be more subtle and also more decisive. The neighbourhood zoning victories of the WBCC and SPOTA in the early 1970s created an enhanced sense of place which arguably encouraged middle-class reinvestment and displacement of former residents. But in both neighbourhoods the radicalization of key individuals also introduced countervailing tendencies. Jacques Khouri in Kitsilano and Michael Harcourt in Strathcona consolidated careers that would later bring neighbourhood benefits, from Khouri as a co-operative housing specialist, and from Harcourt as a social-democratic politician who would a decade later become mayor of Vancouver, and twenty years later attain the office of premier of British Columbia. Both careers must be seen as outcomes of an earlier apprenticeship in neighbourhood organization.

THE NEXUS OF PLACE

Despite their numerous sociocultural differences, all of the organizations we have studied are concerned to secure the preservation and enhancement of a local community in a specific territory: to stop the construction of a freeway and the demolition of a neighbourhood (Chinatown), to halt office penetration (Rehavia) or the infiltration of undesired *nouveaux riches* (Shaughnessy Heights), to secure better housing and social services (Ir Ganim and Katamon Tet), to provide affordable rental accommodation (Downtown Eastside and Kitsilano), and to upgrade the physical infrastructure and the school system (Baka).

Such goals, through place-oriented action, are loaded with material, ideological, and political content. In the material sphere, they entail such activity as land-use regulation, developing a pedestrian walkway, enlarging an apartment, or stopping a freeway. In the ideological sphere, a message is directed both inwards and outwards. Traditional leadership, instructed from powerful central agencies, conveyed a message of a place that was dominated and controlled by outsiders. However, protest organizations conveyed a symbolic-political message of a territorial challenge in which place has been turned into a centre of power. For the residents of Rehavia and Shaughnessy Heights, the message delivered is one which asserts the unique aristocratic nature of their neighbourhood, a place which should therefore remain intact. For the residents of the Downtown Eastside, a major symbolic struggle has been waged over the meaning of their territory; against the mainstream rhetoric of skid row is pitted the voice of the marginal other, asserting the presence of community. This symbolic struggle is critical, for the dominant interpretation will shape the dominant material reality.

In the political sphere, all eight organizations delivered a message of struggle and negotiation over the human capacity to shape and act upon their environment. With the exception of the traditional organizations in ethnic/lower-class areas, all the others sought to assert a certain level of local autonomy. In certain cases, this has been performed by trying to halt or rectify processes associated with market mechanisms or state decisions. These processes, as demonstrated in Kitsilano, Chinatown, Rehavia, or Shaughnessy, threatened old environments through rezoning, urban renewal, encroachment of business into residential areas, and penetration of mass culture into old 'high culture' areas. Confronting these processes, neighbourhood organizations seem to post a barrier by seeking to 'freeze' time and defend place. Obviously, they follow different strategies, whether opposing state decisions, struggling against the business sector, or manipulating public opinion and the state by emphasizing the aestheticization of local life. The political message in all these cases was particularistic in orientation – that is, largely confined to the territory in which the organizations operated. In a few cases, however, such as DERA, the Ohalim, and the ICL, local autonomy has been asserted in a much more radical form. Members of the movements managed to transcend local boundaries and develop universalistic messages that relate to broader groups within society. In Jerusalem, they took up the housing problems of young couples and the government settlement policy in the occupied territories, and criticized state performance in the welfare sphere. For the duration of their activity, these organizations resorted to mass demonstrations, collaboration with the political left – Peace Now in Israel, a range of causes including the Solidarity Coalition in Vancouver – and cognitively tied local conditions with broader political-economic processes.

Despite the marked differences between the particularistic and more universalistic organizations, they have all basically been involved in a struggle to extend citizenship rights. The development of neighbourhood organization over time evinces, in our view, the gradual, though not unproblematic, extension of civil, political, and social rights. The civil right of equal legal status (secured not only by law but also by actual practice), and the political right of participation in urban life, which has long (from the 1920s to the 1950s) been confined to a privileged few, were extended – albeit haltingly and incompletely – over the 1960s and 1970s to lower-class and minority groups. Moreover, the ascendency of active groups in disadvantaged and minority areas marks a deliberate attempt to secure social rights. Politically speaking, then, the historical changes discerned in the nature of neighbourhood organizations attest to the gradual progress of democratic reform in the countries studied here. Moreover, in so doing, local groups plainly asserted what Foucault (1983) would call the right to be different, resisting market and state pressures in asserting, admittedly often through parochial discourse, local identity, communal heritage, and historical values.

Alongside the political discourse over the extension of citizenship rights, neighbourhood organizations had to struggle with no less conspicuous impediments rooted in the life-world. As shown above, they had to grapple with old traditions that fostered conformity to system values, with routinized patterns of behaviour responsible for inaction, with individualism, apathy, and the absence of motivation. In the course of these struggles, some fundamental changes have occurred in the cultural and social spheres of daily life. In the cultural sphere, groups that previously felt alienated and who suffered loss of meaning – for instance, groups in the Downtown Eastside and Katamon Tet – developed meaningful interpretative schemes as to the nature of society and their role in it. The leaders have undergone a process of relearning, adopted new orientations towards society, and acquired new behavioural patterns. In the social sphere, members of successful groups have proceeded to develop new obligations, to establish new social contacts, to assume greater responsibility, and to transcend the original issue that triggered social mobilization.

With few exceptions, these cultural and social changes were associated with socialization and political integration. Contacts and negotiation with the political-bureaucratic system increased the motivation for conformist actions, accelerated the incorporation of local cultures into mainstream culture, and increased the capability for exchange with individuals and groups belonging to other sectors of society. It follows, then, that the changes in the system and the life-world are interwoven. The development of new interpretative schemes, the redefinition of orientations, the processes of relearning and self-formation, the broadening of social contacts, and the adoption of new obligations have closely affected political action. We therefore conclude, from the broader national perspective, that these processes have contributed in the last instance to nation building. Peripheral groups have been incorporated through local activism into the centre, partly modified the dominant values, and partly changed their own original values, orientations, and goals.

All these changes were produced in conjunction with the construction of places. This implies that, through the construction of place (via neighbourhood activism), human beings seek to satisfy material needs and fulfil political and cultural desires. Social action has thus turned place into a major subject through which it reveals itself. Place, in other words, is not just a passive element to be socially constructed, but also an active element, since through the realization of its potentialities (material, political, and ideological), human beings assert themselves. If several decades of neighbourhood organization tell us anything, it is less the vague promise of an alternative society than the constant struggle of past and present generations to assert themselves as human beings, in part through the dialectical processes of self- and collective realization by shaping and reshaping their places. That this meaning is quite often passed over by actors and researchers alike has to do with the swiftness with which these realizations seep into the complex matrix of the life-world. For instance, in Vancouver, the fact that Mayor Harcourt's office found it necessary in the 1980s routinely to consult the Shaughnessy property owners or DERA on issues and decisions concerning their territories has become part of the taken-for-granted matrix.

RELATIONS WITH THE STATE

The role of the local state, as noted in table 10.1, has undergone some fundamental changes over time. The earlier apparatus headed by the local power élite (economic boosters in Vancouver and dignitaries in Jerusalem) was steadily replaced by a welfare state headed by a paternalistic and rigid bureaucracy. Confronted with social protest and public criticism, the political-administrative apparatus opened up during the late 1960s and 1970s and assumed a more pluralistic approach. This process became quite evident in the case of ethnic and lower-class groups supported by community and social workers employed by the state. The opening up of the local state was augmented by changes that occurred at the upper echelons of government – the rise of the Trudeau Liberals and the British Columbia NDP to power at the federal and provincial levels, respectively, and the decline of central state power in Israel. During the 1970s and 1980s, the state, and particularly the local governments, adopted co-productive patterns while working with neighbourhood organizations, and encouraged administrative decentralization. In Vancouver, this initiative peaked in the mid-1970s with the decentralized efforts of local area planning at the municipal scale, the community resources boards that represented a devolution of provincial social services, and the community-level funding and priority setting enabled by the federal programs of neighbourhood improvement and, in a funding sense at least, of residential renovation. In Jerusalem, administrative decentralization increased throughout the 1980s as a result of the central government's project of neighbourhood renewal and the deliberate municipal attempt to further democratization and local responsibility through the Jerusalem Project for Neighbourhood Self-Management.

Kitsilano's local area planning, the experience of the Downtown Eastside Residents' Association (DERA), and the neighbourhood government of Baka are three notable examples of this process. The three organizations also illustrate some of the initial tensions involved in neocorporatism. Who runs the neighbourhood, the civic bureaucracy or the local residents? Which policy guides the organization, the policy shaped at the neighbourhood level or the one developed by City Hall? Could the organization rely on public resources, especially when confronting the state? Could a corporate form of neighbourhood organization accommodate conflict with local government, or is it bound to break up when conflict occurs? The ways in which the organizations in Kitsilano, the Downtown Eastside, and Baka grappled with these issues are illustrative of the impediments and opportunities inherent in the new institutional arrangements. Faced with the arduous task of negotiation with government officials, members of the more radical, Alinsky-style West Broadway Citizens' Committee lost their faith in the co-productive pattern, and accused the local area planning process of being manipulated by civic politicians. Erosion of the initial ideals of local area planning has also been identified in a number of Canadian cities (Anderson 1977).

Perhaps the most convincing counter-example has been DERA's success in electing its leaders to the city council, thereby forcing a redefinition of the state's agenda and decisions. Its disciplined trades-union model of organization also permitted a process of co-production without co-optation to take place through the 1980s. The Baka group developed a different strategy of action. It embarked on a long-range and comprehensive process of negotiation with the local and central state, fostered friendly relations with politicians and bureaucrats, and penetrated local government, notably when one of its members was named to a senior civic position. In the course of this process, the group managed to launch a new master plan for the area, to upgrade the neighbourhood, and to transform the school curriculum in the area. The answers to the questions we have posed depend, so it seems, on the basic orientations of the group involved (confrontation, participation, or negotiation), their former experiences (Alinsky-type activism, trade unionism, or local advocacy), and their world-view (social change from below, reform from within, or middle-of-the-road positions). Apparently, neocorporatism may take varying forms, depending on the specific sociocultural context in which it is experienced. In Kitsilano it appeared, at least in the eyes of the radical activists, as a conservative form which stifled the grass roots. In the Downtown Eastside it revealed itself as a liberal enterprise through which trades-union traditions could infiltrate the state. Finally, in Baka, it emerged as a synthesis between pluralism and corporatism, where interest groups (struggling over school curricula), neighbourhood government, community groups (of the northern and southern communities), bureaucrats, and politicians were loosely connected to the organization's activity. The general and somewhat abstract reference to neocorporatism should therefore be replaced, so we suggest, by a more refined definition that carefully distinguishes between the conservative, liberal, and pluralist forms it takes (cf. Savitch 1988).

The changes in the relationships between neighbourhood organizations and the state suggest the utility of employing different theories of the state that range from power-élite theories, prevailing in the pre-welfare mode; through a tendency to pluralism, characterizing state response to protest; and finally to neocorporatism, prevailing at the present (table 10.1). The transition from a closed-rigid system to a pluralist, and even to a corporatist, one entails growing state intervention in social life. Basically, the state in its latest phase penetrated local organizations in numerous ways, thereby assuming a significant role in the moral-political, social, cultural, economic, and environmental-aesthetic spheres. This engagement is frequently recursive: in the process of structuring, the state may itself be structured.

The *moral-political sphere* implies the regulation, if not creation of local organizations – for example, the Baka neighbourhood government and the renewed SPOTA and Kitsilano organizations (re-created through local area planning in 1989) – according the organizations legitimacy and sometimes even a monopoly, in practical terms, over activity in a given territory.

The *cultural sphere* implies the incorporation of popular and grass-roots cultures into mainstream culture, such as the incorporation of the underclass culture through protest theatre and grass-roots services, or the incorporation of Chinese culture into the mainstream through the notion of multiculturalism. This process is carried out by politicians, at various levels of government, and by social and community workers at the local level. Such incorporation may, however, redefine mainstream norms. Multiculturalism, for example, has progressed from a harmless celebration of ethnic food and festivals to increasingly successful challenges to the cultural hegemony of Anglo- and Franco-Canadians (Kobayashi 1993).

The *social sphere* implies the socialization and integration of local leadership into the dominant sociopolitical ideology and into the institutional (that is, the bureaucratic and political) system. This process expresses itself in political or bureaucratic careers pursued by many of the leaders involved. It is not surprising, therefore, to find from our case-studies neighbourhood leaders serving as city councillors, senior officials, special aides to the prime minister, members of the central committees of national parties, and members of parliament. The crucial question arising at this point is whether the entry of neighbourhood leaders into the system has also entailed changes in the state's agenda and style of action with regard to the neighbourhoods. The answer is by no means uniform. The leaders of DERA and of the Baka neighbourhood government, who penetrated the local authority, remained faithful to their original visions, continued to serve their local constituency in the spirit of the organization from which they came, managed to shape governmental decisions, and obtained large resources for their constituents. The leaders of YFN and ICL in Ir Ganim seem to have been entirely co-opted and to have severed their ties with the local community. The leader of the Ohalim movement is in an ambivalent position, being partly co-opted and partly independent. While maintaining such a double position, he has succeeded in increasing the allocation of resources to Katamon Tet, but became an ephemeral figure at both the neighbourhood and the state levels. The leader of the West Broadway group, frustrated, gave up his later position in providing social housing and moved into the private sector. Dismayed at the evolution of the co-operative housing program in Canada during the 1980s, he said: 'After doing co-ops for a while, I asked myself, why am I doing this? Begging to governments and getting into hassles. Somewhere along the line co-ops have lost the vision ... I'm being used by the government to keep their costs down, and every year they turn the screws further.'

In sum, in their newly elevated position *vis-à-vis* the state, some local leaders have managed to keep their original vision, increased their neighbourhood resource base, and had some effect on city-wide decision making. Others have turned their neighbourhood positions into a springboard for the development of their own political careers. Still another group has been burned out and has moved, frustrated, into alternative occupations.

The *economic sphere* implies a redistribution of resources, subsidizing local activities, and strengthening the provision of public services. These gains may be substantial. By 1991, DERA had become the largest landlord in the Downtown Eastside and, with thirty-five staff in advocacy, research, and housing management, was a not insignificant local employer (Gerecke 1991); in Kitsilano the lobbying of the WBCC brought close to $10 million in federal home-renovation and neighbourhood-improvement funds into the district in the 1970s. The level of improvement of public services is an important entry in the balance sheet evaluating participation, providing a measure of the organization's effectiveness and the state's good faith.

Finally, *environmental-aesthetic development* implies co-production in environmental schemes, protecting heritage, and in defending the neighbourhood from unwanted redevelopment, as shown in the cases of Shaughnessy Heights, Rehavia, and Chinatown-Strathcona.

The massive intervention of government in these different spheres of social life, through cooperation with neighbourhood organizations, seems to defy any simplistic categorization of the present role of the state. On the one hand, the state appears as centralist and even manipulative, and, on the other, as open to new experiments of decentralization and democratization. This is perhaps one of the salient features of neocorporatism, where citizens' groups are allowed a high level of political discretion as long as they follow the prevailing rules of the game. But the situation is much more complex. Within this vague line of demarcation between civil society and the state, there seems to develop an interesting struggle between two contradictory projects: effective state control through administrative decentralization, and decentralization initiated from below. Organizations like DERA, the West Broadway group, and Rehavia neighbourhood government, though partly aided and financed by the state, waged a fierce struggle against the state's programs (Hasson

1989; Wolch 1990). On certain occasions, as in the Rehavia case, these struggles permeated the state itself and caused an internal split within it. These developments militate against any swift generalization that depicts the state as overly centralist and impermeable. Although the state's officials may approve advancing recentralization and effective control, they may end up, as the Baka case shows, negotiating more pragmatically other terms of reference. Indeed, in an open-ended partnership, neocorporatism may bring risks to the state as well as to the neighbourhood organization. The two rounds of local area planning in Kitsilano in 1974 and 1989 raised expectations and provided a focus for the mobilization of protest groups. The state was even less able to contain its coproduction venture in the Downtown Eastside, where an initiative by a liberal council was decisively outflanked by the political subject it created, the Downtown Eastside Residents' Association.

Neither does government intervention seem to corroborate Saunders's (1986) hypothesis concerning a clear division of labour between different tiers of the state. Both in Canada and in Israel, the upper levels of the state (or at least certain segments of it) have been deeply involved with neighbourhood organizations and provided them with grants and professional support. For instance, when the Vancouver City Council turned against SPOTA in an attempt to advance urban renewal and to build the freeway and, later, the firehall, the federal and provincial governments sided with the organization and helped resolve the impasse created by the municipality. Another example is how the leaders of the right-wing national Likud party helped put the grievances of the Ohalim movement on the public agenda. Moreover, in both countries the larger financial grants to neighbourhoods and their organizations were provided by the upper levels of the state (in itself testimony to the fragile financial position of local authorities in both countries).

This is not to question the validity of the dual function of the state – wealth creation and wealth redistribution, economic growth, and political legitimation. What we find unsatisfactory, at least in Canada and Israel, is an ideal type formulation that relates this division, perhaps too unproblematically, to state levels. Our findings suggest a more complex pattern of relations that cuts across the politicians, departments, and bureaucrats at various levels of government. Whether different segments of the state support or confront popular demands appears to depend to a large extent on the political-economic interests and ideology of the different officials, internal conflicts within the state, the social connections between politicians and local constituencies, and economic constraints.

Put in another way, the duality of politics seems to characterize each level of the state, the local state being no exception. Many issues raised by the local organizations brought about internal debates within the local state itself and led to deep conflicts among competing actors and factions. For instance, the mayor of Jerusalem and the head of the planning department, who supported the demands of Rehavia's residents to halt the penetration of offices into the area, had to struggle and finally compromise with other politicians who supported business interests. The struggle over the civic grant to DERA produced significant rifts in City Council during the 1970s. The social workers who assisted the Ohalim movement and the West Broadway Citizens' Committee collided at the local level with politicians and bureaucrats who opposed them. Throughout the conflict, the Ohalim were supported by the deputy mayor and opposition national parties from the right and left, but criticized by the mayor, the West Broadway group were supported in a number of actions by the provincial NDP government, the city planning department, and an opposition minority on Council, but opposed by a back-treading liberal majority on Council. To reduce the duality of politics to a local/central division appears in this light to be an oversimplification that ignores the wide range of possibilities open to organizations in building coalitions with different agents at different state levels.

What are the ramifications of growing state intervention in neighbourhood life? The answer seems to be somewhat complex, disclosing different and even contradictory tendencies. One tendency to be observed has to do with the shift in the state's attitudes towards the city. In the past, the state socialized the costs of urban life by building schools, health clinics, community centres, roads, etc., whereas neighbourhood organizations played a minor role in decision making. At present, though, it seems that the state has moved in an opposite direction by privatizing some of the costs of urban life while socializing neighbourhood activity. Local consultation is sustained, but public services are reduced. In this way, the state is apparently seeking to resolve both economic and legitimation crises, that is, to reduce its social expenditures and at the same time to foster political loyalty through collaboration with informal and formal organizations. With such a neocorporatist structure neighbourhood organizations cooperate with the state in regulating the reproduction aspects of daily life. Developed unchecked, this process may result in co-optation, bureaucratization, organizational closure, and professional leadership. A second tendency is that the state is losing its ability to govern. The enormous growth of the state, and its penetration into every sphere of daily life, create problems of coordination and steering capacity. What seems, then, at the surface to be benevolent patronage may appear, upon closer examination, as a loss of governability (Offe 1984, ch. 2).

TOWARDS A NEW POLITY

Neither of these tendencies is likely to contribute to advancing citizenship rights.[12] With the first tendency, a new form of state domination through organizations initiated, financed, and controlled from the top would impinge on human rights. On the other hand, the second tendency, the loss of governability and the weakening of liberal welfare policy, would put social rights at risk. What seems to be needed, then, is a transformation within both civil society and the state, and the restructuring of relationships between the two sides. Within this framework, state intervention is viewed as a major device in securing civil rights, the redistribution of resources, the regulation of conflicts, cultural incorporation, socialization, and environmental management. The other side of our argument is that neighbourhood and community organizations should be strengthened as well in order to advance citizenship rights in areas that are often overlooked by the state (including the parties) and other groups in civil society. The new social movements have undoubtedly put some critical issues on the public agenda in recent years, including gender relations, environmental protection, and racial and ethnic rights, and have thus contributed to the multiplicity of power centres and allowed for greater representation of hitherto marginalized social groups. Yet many other areas raised by neighbourhood organizations, such as services for the elderly, development of child care and playgrounds, housing issues, sensitive urban development, local or historical heritage, and a range of social and cultural services at the local level remained almost untouched by the new social movements. The strengthening of neighbourhood organizations may contribute, therefore, to the diversification of power centres and, along with the new social movements, may advance the principles of participatory democracy and social welfare.

It is apposite to ask in conclusion to what extent neighbourhood organizations *have* created a more democratic public sphere, a task for which Fraser's four criticisms of the public sphere in 'actual existing democracies' provide a ready frame of reference.[13] First, neighbourhood organizations are consistent with her endorsement of a multiple, not unitary, public interest. Protest organizations have exploded the ideological view of the 'non-partisan' reformers of the Progressive era that there is only a single public interest, attainable through the privileged insights of a professional bureaucracy. Second, the traditional distinction between private and public interests has been fundamentally challenged. The modernization of civic administration in the period from 1880 to 1930 counterposed unfavourably the 'special' (i.e., private) interests of the ward against the preferred at-large (i.e., public) interests of the city. But, as urban historians have convincingly shown, the public ends of the reformers were in reality in close harmony with the private interests of property-owning élites. The neighbourhood movement has legitimized the reinstatement of the private interest of the neighbourhood in urban politics. Third, neighbourhood organizations have challenged the sharp distinction between civil society and the state, which Fraser identifies as a questionable character of current democracies – a distinction captured perfectly in its ideological form by the proposal of a Vancouver councillor to halve the civic grant to DERA's organizer because he spent half his time at work in the Downtown Eastside and half of it politicking at City Hall. It is precisely such a colonization of the corridors of power that protest and neocorporatist associations in the city have insisted upon. Fourth, Fraser requires that multiple publics be allowed political access substantively, and not only formally. Institutional arrangements must not impede entry to the public sphere. The demotion of technical rationality as a monopoly discourse, and the enhanced role of local committees and public hearings which meet in neighbourhood settings go some distance towards attaining this goal.

Of course, this theoretical endorsement of neighbourhood associations may or may not be confirmed in practice. Co-production ventures may be entered into in bad faith by the state; neighbourhood organizations may exhibit not only parochialism, but also an exclusionary privatism; and a range of other contingencies may deflect the democratic promise of local action. None the less, we agree with Held, who maintains that 'the central issue today is not the old alternative between liberalism and Marxism, reformism or revolution to abolish the state. Rather, it is the question of how to enact the "double sided" process of creative reform protected by state action and innovation from below through radical social initiatives' (1989, 168).

It is within such a framework of a 'double sided' reform that the concepts and practice of co-production and liberal corporatism from below merit further elaboration. Liberal corporatism has, no doubt, its merits and pitfalls. It may curtail, in the short run, residents' capability to set the local agenda by themselves, lengthen discussions, and slow down progress. At the discursive level, it may appear too vague a notion to stimulate and attract a large number of supporters. Alinsky's rhetoric would probably do this much more successfully. As one of Alinsky's followers in Kitsilano argues: 'We need black and white to get results ... The political middle would have watered us down.' Not only residents are suspicious of co-production; so are politicians and bureaucrats. In Jerusalem, members of the city council and department heads reacted with suspicion and criticism to the municipal project of neighbourhood government. At the symbolic level, heads of departments interpreted the experiment as nothing more than bureaucratic decentralization within their own jurisdiction. At the political level, politicians and bureaucrats fought against losing a part of their power. As one politician put it: 'We, actually, indirectly, won't need a mayor, perhaps, and perhaps not even a city council. The elections will be direct in the existing neighbourhood councils.'

The suspicions arising within civil society and the state towards liberal corporatism are not without a sound base, yet there remains the potential of expanding participatory democracy while strengthening the steering capacity of the local state. Liberal corporatism, guided by the principles of a welfare democracy, decentralization, and the democratization of local life, may signal a new way of expanding human rights. This may involve entrusting the neighbourhood organization with greater responsibility for producing services (as, for example, with DERA's housing society), for decision making concerning local affairs (for instance, Baka's self-initiated master plan), for coordination of services at the local level, for competition with the private sector in running local institutions if and when privatized, for opposition to state decisions seen as threatening, and for conflict management at the local level. At the same time, city-wide decisions, universal aspects of welfare, and the authority to intervene in order to secure the rights of minorities will be carried out by the state. Such a scenario is, of course, rife with conflicts, and requires a rational procedure for dispute and arbitration among the parties involved. It is a scenario that might, however, address the disturbing rebuke that 'urban government has never performed the democratic functions traditionally attributed to it' (Magnusson 1981, 61).

Notes

1 Evers and Rodrigues 1978; Castells 1983. In the United States, community associations grew in numbers from fewer than 10,000 in the late 1960s to 130,000 in 1989. Even allowing for the permissive definition which includes condominium organizations, the scale and steady growth of associations remains impressive (Davies and Herbert 1993, 186).

2 For the United States, see Banfield and Wilson 1967; for Canada, see chapter 4; for Israel, see Hasson 1987.

3 Many of the observations in this paragraph are consistent with the arguments in Offe 1984, especially ch. 7.

4 See the essays in Lustiger-Thaler 1992 for the philosophical and practical currency of local politics in Canada. For a Montreal-based discussion, see Hamel 1991.

5 For a detailed summary of these studies, see Lowe 1986, 64–6; see also Warren 1978.

6 Rex's position is revised and extended by Davis (1991).

7 This distinction underlies, for example, the debate between Harris (1987) and Caulfield (1988) over political reform movements in Canadian cities. While Harris identifies systemic forces, Caulfield argues for the place of local coalitions and contingencies in urban reform.

8 Goldrick 1978, or the treatment of social movements in Harvey 1989.

9 For leaders and professionals, see Alinsky 1971, Friedmann and Goetz 1981, Davis 1991; for the media, see Lipsky 1972; for communities, see Oberschall 1973.

10 For example, the divergent effects of variable housing tenure are discussed by Heskin (1991); the significance of tenure in mobilization is also emphasized by Davis (1991).

11 See also Evers and Rodrigues 1978, 176, and Offe 1984, ch. 7.

12 Keller 1968; Pateman 1970; Rowland 1973; Eyles 1981; McCarthy 1981

13 Moderate tasks: Hunter and Suttles 1972, 44; Warren and Warren 1977, 33; Perlman 1979. Piecemeal revolution: Gottschalk 1975. Radical challenge to the status quo: Dunleavy 1981, 161; Castells 1983

14 Castells 1983, 331. Magnusson and Walker (1988) similarly see the progressive potential of social movements that begin as locality-based, then make global connections but also avoid capture by the state, a point that we shall see has some relevance for co-production strategies of the state in relations with urban protest movements. For other generally optimistic views of the progressive political impacts of social movements, see Touraine 1981 and Offe 1984, and the more recent writing on post-modern politics: Laclau and Mouffe 1985 and Ross 1988. In a recent article Boggs (1991) welcomes the rise of new social movements in the urban domain, interpreting them as signs of mature and stable representation of local democracy, community, and culture renewal that grew out of 1960s radicalism.

15 Cox 1976, 182; Saunders 1979, 111, and 1981, 275–6; Kirk 1980, 172–4

16 A variant of neo-élitism has been particularly influential in examining development and resistance in Canadian cities. Among others, see Lorimer 1972, Gutstein 1975, and Aubin 1977.

17 O'Connor 1973; Offe 1984. For a spirited account in the Canadian context, see Ng, Walker, and Muller 1990.

18 See, however, Lowe 1986, ch. 3, which moves beyond such a dualistic model of the state and local organizations.

19 See also Savitch 1988; Savitch makes extensive use of a corporatist model to discuss politics and planning in New York, Paris, and London. Despite Panitch's (1979) eloquent plea, it no longer seems justifiable to limit the neo-corporatist model to the tripartism of the state, capital, and labour.

20 For various views on the Canadian welfare state, see Banting 1982; Moscovitch and Albert 1987; Myles 1988; Ng, Walker, and Muller 1990; and Lemon 1993.

21 Provincial social-service staff tripled between 1966 and 1978, together with the growth of metropolitan social planning councils. See Lemon 1993. For the role of the New Left in urban politics in this period, see Harris 1988.

22 See, for example, Lemon 1974 for Toronto, Gutstein 1975 for Vancouver, and Léonard and Léveillée 1986 for Montreal. More generally, see Higgins 1977 and Magnusson and Sancton 1983.

23 Riches 1987. The social geography of Canadian cities is reviewed in Bourne and Ley 1993.

24 For the history of development in Vancouver, see Hardwick 1974 and Roy

1980. For a history of Vancouver municipal politics, see Tennant 1980 and Gutstein 1983.

25 For the new middle class and the rise of TEAM, see Ley 1980.

26 Both Vancouver mayors during the 1980s – Michael Harcourt (1980-6) and Gordon Campbell (1986-93) – were former TEAM members. In 1991 Harcourt was elected premier of an NDP provincial government. One of his cabinet ministers is Darlene Marzari, a fellow TEAM councillor in the 1970s. Campbell became provincial leader of the Liberals, the official opposition, in 1993.

27 Kollek was eventually defeated in the November 1993 election, as this book was going to press.

PART ONE

1 The classic case of Boston's Beacon Hill is discussed in Firey 1945. In the Canadian context, see Ley 1993.

CHAPTER 2

1 Other studies of élite neighbourhood groups include Duncan 1986 and Firey 1945. See Ley 1993 for a study of élite districts in Canada.

2 For further discussion, see Hardwick 1974; Holdsworth 1981; Roy 1980.

3 This area is now known as First or Old Shaughnessy, since the CPR subsequently extended its development south to Thirty-Third Avenue in the 1930s (Second Shaughnessy) and further south to Forty-First Avenue in the 1940s (Third Shaughnessy). These latter developments, although considered part of greater Shaughnessy, have never had the size nor the social *cachet* that First Shaughnessy has. The rezoning and design guidelines that I discuss in the latter part of this chapter pertain only to First Shaughnessy.

4 French and Vaughan 1971. This information is drawn from an interview conducted in 1971 by P. French and M. Vaughan with D.P. Shepherd, the land administrator for the CPR and a company employee for forty years.

5 For a discussion of the movement of élite residents from the fashionable West End to the new development in Shaughnessy, see Robertson 1977.

6 City of Vancouver Archives, Shaughnessy File, Document no. 1; also Province of British Columbia 1914.

7 City of Vancouver Planning Department 1979, 2. Background material on Shaughnessy during the early years is to be found in City of Vancouver Archives, Shaughnessy File. See also Roy 1980 and Robertson 1977.

8 The smaller lots which were laid out in the original CPR development were

one-fifth of an acre in size. The early development of Shaughnessy focused upon the larger lots of up to one and a half acres. It is interesting that the CPR, no doubt with an eye to increasing its profit, should have designed into the original layout of Shaughnessy a place for middle-class housing.

9 There are no exact figures on membership at this time. A long-time member of the association estimated that there were between 300 and 400 members in the mid 1950s.

10 Personal communication from a member of the board of the SHPOA. Although a new president is elected every year, a core of activists has remained on the board for the past decade. New members are brought on the board if they are particularly interested in the neighbourhood, and of course share the common point of view. The all-important position of secretary has been occupied by the same person since the late 1960s. Virtually all of the day-to-day business of the SHPOA is funnelled through her, and she along with several others are the most active members of the Association.

11 'Societies Act,' Shaughnessy Heights Property Owners' Association, 1939, By-law number 40

12 *Vancouver Sun*, 24 January 1959, 8

13 For the anglophilia of North American élites, see Duncan and Duncan 1984 and Ley 1993.

14 Author of the letter was Mrs Helen Boyce, Chair of the Membership Committee of the Botanical Gardens Association. Mrs Boyce has for long been a Shaughnessy resident, and was an alderwoman during the 1970s.

15 Shaughnessy Heights Property Owners' Association *vs* Grosek and City of Vancouver 1980; Grosek *vs* City of Vancouver and Ray Spaxman 1980. SHPOA File

16 City of Vancouver Department of Permits and Licenses, letter to SHPOA, 20 January 1972

17 Jack Volrich, who served as mayor from 1976 to 1980, was a former leader of the fight by Shaughnessy residents against the Arbutus Village shopping centre in the late 1960s.

18 SHPOA's membership rose from 496 in 1968 to 600 in 1978. By 1982 it was over 700.

19 For a discussion of the social geography of Shaughnessy in the late 1970s and of the active role of women in neighbourhood activities, see Cooper 1971 and Pratt 1981.

20 See Ley (1980, 1987) for the ideology of the livable city and the impact of TEAM on the fabric of the city.

21 Interview with member of the First Shaughnessy Study Planning Committee. From 1979 until its termination in early 1981, I was a participant observer at committee meetings.

22 City of Vancouver Planning Department, 1982a, 36. This rating system was designed by Bruno Freschi Architects, who were hired by the planning department to prepare design guidelines for Shaughnessy. The properties (both house and grounds) were assigned a rating based upon their approximation to the English-country-house ideal.

23 Field notes, First Shaughnessy Study Planning Committee, 2 April 1980

24 Ibid, 14 May 1980

25 Ibid, 27 February 1980

26 Ibid, 31 July 1980

27 Ibid

28 Ibid, 12 March 1980

29 Ibid, 21 August 1980

30 Ibid, 6 August 1980

31 Ibid, 12 March 1980

32 Poverty is a relative term. When SHPOA people refer to 'poor people' in Shaughnessy they usually mean widows on fixed pensions who can not afford the upkeep on their million-dollar-plus houses. These people are often seen as tragic and heroic figures who demonstrate great love of the area by not selling out.

33 Field notes, First Shaughnessy Study Planning Committee, 19 March 1980

34 See Kalman and Roaf 1974, Duncan and Duncan 1984, and Ley 1993 for a broader discussion of landscape taste in traditional élite districts.

35 Field notes, First Shaughnessy Study Planning Committee, 5 March 1980

36 Ibid, 10 December 1980

37 Ibid, 19 November 1980

38 Ibid, 10 December 1980

39 City of Vancouver Council Meeting, 31 December 1981

CHAPTER 3

1 'The Statute of the Mutual Aid Association of Rehavia Ltd.,' 1925, The Jerusalem Municipal Archive

2 Ibid

3 Letter of the Mutual Association of Rehavia Ltd. to Sha'arei Hessed and Nahlat Ahim, 1942, The Jerusalem Municipal Archive (henceforth JMA)

4 Planning and Building Law, 1965, and the town plan, 1936

5 Letter of Mr Valero, 22 July 1942, and letter of Professor Zundak, 24 March 1946, JMA

6 Council letter addressed to the residents, 1943, JMA

7 Council letter to the residents, 1944, JMA

8 Council letter on the allocation of policemen, and a letter to the residents

concerning tax payments to support the police force, 9 August 1936, JMA

9 Interview on 2 February 1988 with E. Eliashar, a member of the neighbour-hood council from 1929 to 1949

10 Ibid

11 B. Kochba, 'Any Remaining Apartment Is Turned into an Office,' *Kol Yeru-shalaim*, 2 August 1983

12 Central Bureau of Statistics, Population and Housing Census for 1961 and 1982, Hamadpis Hamemshalti, Jerusalem

13 The first communication distributed by the neighbourhood council to the residents of Nahlat Ahim and Rehavia, March 1983 (Yedion No. 1)

14 Jerusalem Master Plan, No. 62, part of item 6, 1965

15 Survey carried out by the neighbourhood council in 1982 and 1986

16 Data provided by the neighbourhood council for 1986. Source: The Jerusa-lem Municipality, Department of System Analysis. Data from the 1983 cen-sus show a slightly lower figure of 25.3 per cent.

17 Data provided by the neighbourhood council on the number of students at the local school, October 1987

18 Kochba, 'Any Remaining Apartment ... '

19 An interview on 28 February 1988 with Mr Shalgy, head of the neighbour-hood council during the years 1969–81

20 This section relies on the documentation reports produced by the Jerusalem Association for Neighbourhood Self-Management (JANSM). The activities of each neighbourhood council were documented and publications appeared regularly every three months. For Nahlat Ahim–Rehavia, we relied on docu-mentation reports 1–12.

21 For another study on a local organization in an affluent area, see Burton and Morley 1979.

22 Yedion (a municipal report), No. 1, March 1983, p. 11

23 Information sheet on new plans, Jerusalem City Information Department, 13 March 1983

24 N. Banai, 'The Self-Management Project in Nahlat Ahim–Rehavia' (He-brew), Documentation Report No. 10, May/August 1985

25 N. Banai, 'The Self-Management Project in Nahlat Ahim–Rehavia' (He-brew), Documentation Report No. 11, September/November 1985, p. 13

26 I. Cherniavsky and A. Edgar, Private Offices in Jerusalem, City Planning Department, 1976; I. Cherniavsky, 'The Spatial Distribution of Private Offi-ces in Jerusalem,' City Planning Department, 1981

27 Interview on 18 October 1987 with Irit Cherniavsky, head of the city's plan-ning department

28 Plan No. 3327, Amendment to the Jerusalem Master Plan No. 14/83, 1983

29 Letter sent by the Institute of Architects and Town Planners in Israel to its members, 6 November 1985

30 N. Banai, Documentation Report No. 11, p. 13; letter sent by D. Vind (head of the BSC) to E. Zissman (chairman of the Yerushalaim Ahat faction), 7 July 1985

31 Letter sent by D. Vind to the BSC's members regarding plan 3327, 14 July 1985

32 Letter sent by D. Vind to E. Zissman, 7 July 1985

33 Letter sent by D. Vind to E. Amir, 10 November 1985

34 Quoted by S. Fiermont, 'Plan No. 3327,' M.A. seminar, the Institute of Urban and Regional Studies, The Hebrew University, from minutes of the town planning subcommittee, 31 August 1988

35 Memorandum of city manager, 15 April 1983

36 Letter sent by Y.S. Ziv, municipal legal counsel, to the Rehavia neighbour-hood council, 27 November 1986

37 I. Schachar, 'The Plan Was Adjusted to the Lawyers,' *Kol Ha'ir*, 1 July 1987

38 N. Banai, Documentation Report No. 11, 1985, p. 13

39 Minutes of the town planning subcommittee, 29 June 1987

40 Schachar, 'The Plan Was Adjusted to the Lawyers'

41 Letter sent by Mayor Teddy Kollek to the head of the town planning sub-committee, 6 July 1987

42 Minutes of the town planning subcommittee, 13 July 1987

43 Interview with the head of the town planning subcommittee, conducted by S. Fiermont, 1983

44 Interview with the secretary of the district planning commission, 28 October 1988

45 Interview conducted by S. Fiermont, 1989

46 Cox 1976, Yates 1977, Lineberry and Sharkansky 1971

47 'The Offices Problem in the Neighbourhood – A New Phase,' editorial, Nahlat Ahim-Rehavia newspaper, Summer 1989

PART TWO

1 See, for example, Smith and Thrift 1990 and Kobayashi 1993.

CHAPTER 4

1 For Chinatown and the Chinese, see Anderson 1986, 1987, 1988, 1991; Lai 1988; Wickberg et al. 1982; and Yee 1988. The classic statement on 'Orien-talism' remains Said 1978.

2 Willmott 1964, 1970. Wickberg (1980) records that 'disunity and factionalism' characterized social relations within Chinatown during the first half of this century.

3 For a recent review, see Smith and Moore 1993.

4 Nann 1970. Richard Nann's doctorate in social work examined the social costs of displacement. Nann was also one of the consultants to SPOTA (and one of the five professionals listed in note 14, below).

5 This account is taken from one of the participants, a university professor of planning: Pendakur 1972. He was an elected TEAM alderman from 1972 to 1974.

6 Pendakur 1972, 61, citing a newspaper account: 'Council Reneged on Promise - Chinese Seethe over Freeway,' *Vancouver Sun*, 18 October 1967

7 *Vancouver Province*, 2 December 1967

8 A participant's view is expressed in Hardwick and Hardwick 1974. Hardwick, a university geographer, was a prominent opponent of the freeway, and was elected TEAM alderman, serving from 1968 to 1974.

9 G. Peloquin, 'Freeway Meet Called by Council,' *Vancouver Sun*, 1 November 1967. Cited in Pendakur 1972, 65

10 Also K. Alsop, 'The Eloquent Battler,' *Vancouver Province*, 6 January 1972

11 Interview with Shirley Chan, 23 November 1989. For a similar transition in leadership in New York's Chinatown, see Wong 1977.

12 City of Vancouver Archives (CVA), ADD Mss 734, Vol. 1, File 6

13 Minutes of SPOTA general meeting, 17 April 1969 (CVA 734/6/6)

14 *SPOTA Journal*, pp. 66-9 (CVA 734/31/5). The group also included three architects and Dick Nann (see note 4 above).

15 *SPOTA Journal*, 4 (CVA 734/31/5)

16 Brief to Vancouver City Council from Strathcona Property Owners' and Tenants' Association, 27 January 1969 (CVA 734/6/3)

17 Minutes of the City of Vancouver Town Planning Commission, 20 December 1968 (CVA 734/6/2)

18 *SPOTA Journal*, 28 (CVA 734/31/5)

19 Brief to Vancouver City Council from Strathcona Property Owners' and Tenants' Association, 16 May 1969 (CVA 734/6/6)

20 Letter to Harry Con from Hon. Robert Andras, 14 July 1969 (CVA 734/6/7). In light of Shirley Chan's designation of Mr Con's 'good Liberal connections' it is interesting to note his centrality in correspondence with Ottawa.

21 Bell 1975, 16; 'A Brief History of Strathcona Site C and D (Old Fire Hall Site), CVA 734/19/5; Yee 1983

22 See, for example, H. Leiren, 'Council Airs New Firehalls,' *Vancouver Sun*, 8 November 1972; S. Kass, 'Chinatown Lights Match under Election,'

Vancouver Province, 11 December 1972. It was discovered that the developer had not submitted, as required, details of his firm's experience and financial status. In addition he was an employee of the city's engineering department: Yee 1983.

23 S. Fralic, 'Hopeful Housing,' *Vancouver Sun*, 1 April 1982

24 'Strathcona Renewal Launched by Basford,' *Vancouver Sun*, 8 October 1971; Bell 1975; Ptarmigan 1977

25 Interview with Nora Curry of SPOTA, 23 June 1983

26 Minutes of SPOTA general meeting, 11 April 1976 (CVA 734/1/7)

27 The developer was Jacques Khouri, leader of the West Broadway Citizens' Committee in the 1970s (chapter 8)! 'Synagogue Reconstruction Wins Heritage Award,' *Westender*, 11 February 1988. If Khouri was a pioneer, other upgrading activity has begun to follow his lead in strata titling remaining heritage buildings: Fitzgerald 1990.

28 Among recent work, see Jackson 1987, Smith 1989, and Anderson 1991.

29 Government of Canada, *Debates of the House of Commons*, 12 November 1963, 4647

30 Ibid, 8 October 1971, 8545

31 City of Vancouver Social Planning Department, File 17, Director's report, 12 June 1970

32 *Chinatown News*, Vol. 20, No. 6, 18 November 1972

33 Ibid

34 *Chinatown News*, Vol. 20, No. 9, 18 January 1973

35 City of Vancouver Planning Department, Chinatown Beautification file, Pickstone to Egan, 27 March 1973

36 Ibid, memorandum from Kemble, 20 June 1973

37 City of Vancouver Planning Department, historic area zoning schedules, F, appendix B, July 1974

38 City of Vancouver Planning Department, Chinatown Beautification file, minutes of special public meeting of Council, 9 July 1974. David Ley was a member of CHAPC in 1983–4.

39 Ibid, Goldberg to Planning Department, 25 September 1974

40 *Chinatown News*, Vol. 21, No. 21, 18 July 1974

41 *Chinatown News*, Vol. 24, No. 9, 18 January 1977

42 Government of Canada 1978, p. 14

43 *Chinatown News*, Vol. 20, No. 3, 3 October 1972

44 *Chinatown News*, Vol. 20, No. 12, 3 March 1973

45 City of Vancouver Planning Department, Chinese Cultural Centre file, Mah to Mayor and Council, 22 July 1976. The site of the Cultural Centre and Garden were of considerable symbolic significance in an assertion of Chinese

turf, located on land that would have been alienated for the Chinatown Freeway, and at the original focus of Chinese settlement in Vancouver, a site where revolutionary leader Sun Yat-sen resided during a visit to Canada.

46 *Chinatown News*, Vol. 24, No. 3, 3 November 1976
47 City of Vancouver Planning Department, Chinese Cultural Centre file, agreement of 12 September 1978
48 Ibid, Kemble to Chee, 27 June 1978. As in the SPOTA struggles, external allies were of key importance. CHAPC member, Marwyn Samuels, a university geography professor and China specialist, was a major source of inspiration and fund-raising activity.
49 Rule 1981; City of Vancouver Planning Department, Chinese Cultural Centre file, Volrich to Yi Zhu, 6 May 1980
50 City of Vancouver Planning Department, Chinese Cultural Centre file, Kemble to Chee, 17 April 1979
51 Mike Kemble, personal communication
52 *Chinatown News*, Vol. 26, No. 17, 18 May 1979
53 *Chinatown News*, Vol. 28, No. 2, 18 September 1980
54 A Chinatown property owner, and CHAPC member. Field notes (David Ley), meeting of the Chinatown Historic Area Planning Committee, 21 November 1984
55 A Chinatown architect, and CHAPC member, speaking at the same meeting. By the early 1990s the arrival of new Chinatown entrepreneurs from Hong Kong and Taiwan had hardened this scepticism towards an imagined cultural past. They requested relaxation of the historical designation of Chinatown, and its ethnic signature, as too confining for current business needs and as too antiquated as a representation of a vibrant commercial culture. Their resistance raises once more the question that has run through this chapter: who does multiculturalism serve?

CHAPTER 5

1 Interview with David Ohayon, 19 February 1985
2 Ibid
3 Ibid
4 Ibid
5 Ibid
6 Ibid
7 Interview with Benjamin Hayman, director of the NRP, 18 September 1981
8 Meeting between the director of the NRP and the 81 Planning Team (Field notes, Shlomo Hasson).

9 *Ganim*, Ir Ganim newspaper, September 1982, 3

10 *Ganim*, November 1981, 6

11 Meeting between the local planning team and members of the NRP's steering committee, 21 October 1981

12 Interview with David Ohayon, 19 February 1985

13 Interview with Benjamin Hayman, 18 September 1981

14 Meeting with the local community workers, 21 September 1981

15 A detailed description of the 77 circle activities in the Bucharim neighbourhood was made by the local community worker Chaym Zemach. His file is in the possession of the author.

16 There were several meetings in which municipal support was ensured. The last one took place in October 1981. Detailed minutes of the meeting are in the possession of the author.

17 A leaflet handed out by the ICL movement in 1981 (n.d.)

18 Interview with Chaim Amar, 26 June 1985

19 Ibid

20 Chaim Amar documented carefully the activities of the movement in a file titled 'The Chairman's Records.' This section relies partly on these reports.

21 Leaflet No. 2 distributed to the public in 1981 (n.d.)

22 Minute from the YFN meeting on 3 April 1982

23 Letter of the chairman of the YFN to the city mayor, March 1984

24 The registration form of the YFN as a non-profit organization

25 The development of the ICL movement was documented by a community worker employed as a research assistant by the author. These documents, filed under 'Reports of a Community Worker, 1981–1983,' are held by the author.

26 Meeting with Ir Ganim's community workers, 21 September 1981

27 Ibid

28 Meeting with Ir Ganim's community workers, 24 September 1981

29 In private communications Amiel described community worker B as a reactionary.

30 Reports of a Community Worker, 1981–1983.

31 Ibid

32 Leaflet calling for residents to attend an ICL demonstration, 1982 (no exact date)

33 Letter of Chaim Amar to Mayor Teddy Kollek, March 1984

34 Letter of a resident to Chaim Amar, 12 December 1984

35 Speech of Dede Ben-Shitrit at the Peace Now demonstration in Efrat, 15 January 1983. The speech was later typed and distributed to the public by the ICL.

36 Interview with Dede Ben-Shitrit in the *Kol Hayir* weekly newspaper, 4 February 1983
37 D. Meiry, 'Pantherim Now,' *Ma'ariv* (a daily newspaper), 7 March 1983
38 Articles and reports portraying such an image were quite abundant in 1983; see, for example, *Ha'aretz* (a daily newspaper), 24 June 1983; *Kol Hayir* (a weekly newspaper), 21 June 1983; *Ma'ariv* (a daily newspaper), 7 March 1983.
39 Reports of a Community Worker, 1981–1983
40 Interview with Chaim Amar, 26 June 1985
41 Ibid
42 Letter of the deputy chairman of the YFN to the movement's secretary, 19 July 1984

CHAPTER 6

1 The title of an unpublished social history of the Downtown Eastside by DERA (Priest, Harris, and Wong 1983); it is also the name of a large mural at the DERA Co-op.
2 Covering letter by W.E. Graham, in City of Vancouver Planning Department 1965, 4
3 For early history, see Matthews 1932; Roy 1980; Working Lives Collective 1985.
4 See the oral history of Willis Sharpala, one of the occupiers of the Carnegie Building in Canning-Dew 1987, 60–71.
5 See the oral history of John Turvey, youth social worker, in Canning-Dew 1987, 150–8.
6 See the oral history of Frank White, 'Hauling around Town,' in Knight 1980, 97–109.
7 City of Vancouver 1965. The terms 'skid row' and 'skid road' are used interchangeably here, as they are in the Downtown Eastside.
8 City of Vancouver Planning Department 1965; see also B. Power, 'A Night at The Travellers Makes a Night to Remember,' *Vancouver Sun*, 16 April 1983.
9 See the oral history of Archie Miaishita, in Canning-Dew 1987, 92–102.
10 'Negligent Politicians Cause Early Deaths,' *Downtown East* 55, February 1979
11 DERA 1988, 16; J. Armstrong, 'Inside the Downtown East Side,' *Vancouver Sun*, 12 August 1989
12 Interview with Bruce Eriksen, 19 August 1989

13 Ibid; also S. Persky, 'The Alderman from Skid Road,' *Today Magazine* (*Vancouver Sun*), 30 May 1981, 12, 14

14 Interview with Bruce Eriksen, 19 August 1989

15 'Peoples Aid,' *Downtown East* 1/1, May 1973. The newspaper published eleven issues in 1973. At the beginning of 1974 it was taken over by DERA and restarted its numbering sequence with issue 1 in January 1974. Its final issue was November 1980, the month in which Eriksen was elected to Council.

16 *Downtown Community Resources Board* 2, June 1975

17 Interview with Jim Green, 22 August 1989; S. Rossiter, 'DERA Ten Years On and Establishment-Prone,' *Vancouver*, June 1983, 20–1; M. Hume, 'The Notoriety Helps DERA,' *Vancouver Sun*, 23 April 1986

18 Hume, 'The Notoriety Helps DERA'

19 'Peoples Aid,' *Downtown East* 1/1, May 1973

20 Various DERA sources, 1973–89

21 For a detailed discussion of the neighbourhood planning process in the Downtown Eastside, see Huzel 1982.

22 P. McMartin, 'Protecting Turf on the Eastside,' *Vancouver Sun*, 23 March 1987

23 Martin (1987) offers a sympathetic assessment of the roles and objectives of the missions in the Downtown Eastside.

24 'A Brief History,' *Downtown East* 4, August 1974

25 J. Swanson, 'Hunger, Handouts and Humiliation,' *Downtown East* 47, June 1978; also D. Salter, 'Harbour Light Mission,' *Downtown East* 1/5, 15–30 August 1973

26 'DERA Disruptive, Inefficient, Misdirected Says Cox–Davies Replies: DERA Disrupted Cox Not Community,' *Downtown East* 45, April 1978

27 J. Todd, 'Council Rejects DERA Grant,' *West Ender*, 17 March 1983

28 McMartin, 'Protecting Turf on the Eastside'; T. Tevlin, 'Cost Share Job Program for Eastside,' *Vancouver Courier*, 24 January 1988. Its politically inspired opposition to DEEDS has provided one of the very few occasions when the media have been critical of DERA and its advocates.

29 'A Brief History,' *Downtown East* 4, August 1974

30 'One Down Many to Go,' *Downtown East* 3, July 1974

31 L. Davies, 'More Hired Hands,' *Downtown East* 1/5, 15–31 August 1973

32 *Downtown East* 1/3, 1–15 July 1973

33 Interview with Jim Green, 22 August 1989

34 Minutes of DERA Annual General Meeting, 30 October 1983

35 Interview with Jim Green, 22 August 1989
36 L. Davies, 'DERA Won't Quit,' *Downtown Eastside* 20, March 1976
37 Interview with Bruce Eriksen, 19 August 1989
38 Jim Green, cited in Hume, 'The Notoriety Helps DERA'
39 M. Goodhand, 'Like a Trip Down Memory Lane,' *East Ender*, 26 July 1984; 'Politicians See Expo Impacts' and 'Programme Urged to Save Neighbourhood,' *Downtown News*, August 1984
40 Glenn Bullard to Margaret Mitchell, MP, and Pat Carney, MP, 8 July 1983
41 M. Mitchell, 'D.E.R.A.,' *Downtown East* 9, April 1975
42 Interview with Bruce Eriksen, 18 August 1989
43 Persky, 'The Alderman from Skid Road'
44 'Pickets Shut Down Granville Mall Work,' *Vancouver Province*, 19 June 1974
45 See various articles in the *Vancouver Province*, 19–26 June 1974, and a satirical editorial, 'The Peoples Mall,' on 28 June. There are also several features in *Downtown East* 3, July 1974, including 'Granville for Oppenheimer' where the political bargaining is explicit.
46 See features in *Downtown East* 43 and 44, February and March 1978
47 'Hotel Fire Deaths: Who Cares?' *Downtown East* 17, December 1975
48 Interview with Jim Green, 22 August 1989
49 Cited in Hume, 'The Notoriety Helps DERA'
50 CRAB (Create a Real Available Beach), a group largely energized by DERA, attempted, eventually with success, to turn waterfront industrial land owned by the Port of Vancouver into a neighbourhood park (see also figure 6.3); D. Konrad, 'Overpasse Impasse: The Making and Taking of CRAB Park,' paper presented to the Western Division, Canadian Association of Geographers, Vancouver, March 1990
51 Glenn Bullard to Margaret Mitchell, MP, and Pat Carney, MP, 8 July 1983
52 'The Mall, the Police, and Traffic,' *Downtown East* 5, September 1974
53 For example, M. Armstrong, 'Inside the Downtown Eastside,' *Vancouver Sun*, 11 August (Part One) and 12 August (Part Two) 1989
54 Glenn Bullard to Max Beck, 3 January 1984
55 'Head Planner Rejects Institutional Use in Area,' *Downtown East* 55, February 1979
56 City of Vancouver, Office of the Mayor, 'Proclamation: Downtown Eastside Day,' August 1983
57 The organizers were Eriksen and Larry Bantleman, the latter returning to DERA a decade later, after a spell with First United Church.
58 'Council Scorns City-Wide Opinion,' *Downtown East* 21, April 1976. For a detailed account of the 1977 request and appeal, see Persky 1980, 123–8.
59 'DERA Grant Slashed,' *Downtown East* 45, April 1978

60 'Brown Supports DERA Appeal,' *West Ender*, 9 June 1983

61 'DERA to Fight On without City Grant,' *Vancouver Province*, 17 March 1983

62 'Skid Road Fires – 1973,' *Downtown East* 3, July 1974. See also several accounts in *Downtown East* 1/10, 1–14 November 1973.

63 '20 Deaths Too Many – 150 People Demonstrate,' *Downtown East* 7, November 1974

64 B. Power, 'Ailing Landmark in Peril,' *Vancouver Sun*, 19 July 1982

65 For example, the following stories in *Downtown East* during 1978; 'Committee Goes Easy on Slum Housing,' 44, March; 'Council Stalls on Slum Clean-Up,' 45, April; 'Wanted: Fewer Excuses, More Enforcement,' 48, July. See also notes 67 and 68, below.

66 'Wanted … '

67 'Proving the Obvious: What the Survey Shows,' *Downtown East* 50, September 1978

68 'Court Lets Lawbreaker Off Hook Cheaply,' *Downtown East* 47, June 1978; 'Smiling Slumlord Drives Off in Cadillac,' *Downtown East* 49, August 1978. See also DERA 1979, 32.

69 'East Hotel Eviction,' *Downtown East* 2, June 1974; J. Swanson, 'Former East Hotel Tenants Get Nominal Damages,' *Downtown East* 14, September 1975; also DERA 1979, 41

70 'Fighting Closure,' *Downtown East* 6, October 1974; B. Eriksen and L. Davies, 'Millions Worth of Housing Lies Vacant,' *Downtown East* 28, November 1976

71 M. Moya, '30 Tenants of Rundown Rooming House Suddenly Thrust Out with Little Warning,' *Vancouver Sun*, 5 June 1985; D. Bramham, 'Hotel Residents Evicted,' *Vancouver Sun*, 21 October 1989

72 J. Swanson, 'Victoria House Tenants Win Fight Against 118% Rent Hike,' *Downtown East* 12, July 1975

73 'Borgstad Decision to Be Appealed,' *Downtown East* 40, November 1977

74 K. Bolan, 'Laws to Aid Hotel Tenants Praised,' *Vancouver Sun*, 2 August 1989. It should be added, however, that protective clauses for all tenants in the act had been eroded by 1989.

75 'Danson Waffles on Slum Upgrading,' *Downtown East* 24, July 1976; 'Oullet Says Hotels to Get Renovation $,' *Downtown East* 32, March 1977. With bureaucratic delays (including the disbanding of the federal ministry of urban affairs), RRAP did not become available until 1979.

76 D. Purdy, 'New Affordable Housing for Low-Income Inner City Residents: Transforming Skid Road in Vancouver, B.C.,' paper presented to the Mak-

ing Cities Livable Conference, Charleston, South Carolina, March 1988 (Purdy was deputy director of Vancouver's social planning department at the time). See also Howard 1984.

77 L. Davies, 'Housing Foundation Becomes New Landlord,' *Downtown East* 1/4, August 1973

78 'Fighting Closure,' *Downtown East* 6, October 1974

79 'What DERA Wants: How We Can Eliminate Slum Housing in Three Easy Steps,' *Downtown East* 50, September 1978; also J. Swanson, 'Bureaucrats Reverse Stand on Housing,' *Downtown East* 51, October 1978

80 'Costly 42 Page Report Skips Housing Facts,' *Downtown East* 57, April 1979

81 'CMHC Stumped by Beer Parlour Bid,' *Vancouver Sun*, 2 May 1980; 'DERA Seeking Federal Help to Take Over Downtown Hotel,' *Vancouver Sun*, 30 July 1980

82 Interview with Jim Green, 22 August 1989

83 Minutes of DERA Executive Meeting, 5 January 1983

84 Minutes of DERA Membership Meeting, 25 March 1983; for a more detailed statement on aspects of DERA's housing program, see McLean 1988.

85 Interview with Jim Green, 22 August 1989. Green elaborated on the symbolic significance of the DERA Co-op on a separate occasion: 'The resident control model can lead to the creation of new people ... a new type of human being, who have pride in themselves, know they can change things.' The remaking of identity was thus a project at the level of the individual, as well as at the level of the neighbourhood. Address to the Conference on Affordable Housing in B.C., November 1985

86 R. Sarti, 'Families Returning to Skid Road,' *Vancouver Sun*, 13 February 1986, and 'Kids Are Odd Men Out in This Area,' *Vancouver Sun*, 9 September 1987

87 J. Callwood, 'Four Sisters Project a Haven of Sanity and Repose,' *Globe and Mail*, 17 November 1987; also Purdy, 'New Affordable Housing ... '

88 'Housing Project Changes Hands for a Dollar,' *Vancouver Sun*, 17 December 1988

89 DERA 1988. A first step was to take over the management, though not the ownership, of the 72-room Rainbow Hotel: R. Sarti, 'DERA to Take Over Management of Hotel,' *Vancouver Sun*, 13 February 1991

90 Purdy, 'New Affordable Housing ... '; Howard 1984; Aird 1982

91 Jim Green, cited in R. Sarti, 'Residents' Organizer Fears New Evictions,' *Vancouver Sun*, 27 October 1988

92 Minutes of DERA Executive Meeting, 8 July 1981; for the motivation and development of Expo 86, see Ley 1987, and Ley and Olds 1988

93 Olds 1988, 'Appendix II. A Chronology of Events: The Expo 86 Eviction Crisis'; this chronology also appears in DERA 1987.

94 Minutes of DERA Membership Meetings, March, April, and June 1984; see also 'Social Housing Plans Proceed,' *Downtown News*, July 1984.

95 'Programme Urged to Save Neighbourhood,' *Downtown News*, August 1984

96 Minutes of DERA Membership Meeting, 26 April 1985

97 Minutes of DERA Planning Meeting, 3 July 1985

98 DERA 1987, Chapter III, 'The Evictions,' 2–3; Minutes of DERA Staff Meeting, 25 November 1985

99 The claim was made in a CBC radio interview, 11 April 1986: see Olds 1988, 'Appendix II.'

100 See, for example, the acrimonious tone of an exchange of letters in 1979 between Bruce Eriksen and William Vander Zalm, then minister of human resources, later elected premier of British Columbia in 1986: *Downtown East* 56, March 1979. For further incidents between DERA and Vander Zalm, see 'DERA Plans Protest at Vander Zalm's Home,' *Vancouver Sun*, 25 April 1977; 'Minister Drops Protesters into Job,' *Vancouver Province*, 10 March 1978.

101 Predictably the occupation did not pass unnoticed by DERA's opponents on Council. In an explanatory letter to the director of social planning, DERA's president observed that Green's actions had been those of a private citizen, as he had requested and received a one-day leave of absence from his duties as DERA organizer, a legal nicety which critics found less than convincing. Bullard to Beck, 7 October 1983. For the premier's personal commitment to Expo 86, see Ley 1987.

102 See, for example, the lengthy article in the *Toronto Star* (10 March 1986) by Rosemary Eng: 'Expo Greed Blamed as Transients Lose Homes.' The death of Olaf Solheim, aged 88 years, two weeks after his eviction from the Patricia Hotel, his home for 62 years, was reported on the front page of dailies in his native Norway: see DERA 1987. True to its practice of using historical memory to promote present solidarity, DERA's current housing project (1992) is named after him.

103 Olds 1988, 'Appendix II'

104 Hartman 1974; Hartman and Kessler 1978. On the contraction of American skid rows in the 1960s and 1970s, see Bahr 1967, and on Seattle, Miller 1982. The rise of homelessness in the 1980s has produced a new reality on skid row; in the Canadian context, see Dear and Wolch 1993, and note 86, above.

105 DERA, n.d. [1989?]; Priest, Harris, and Wong 1983; Sharpala oral history

in Canning-Dew, 1987. According to some accounts the idea of the Trek was put forward by Stan Lowe, a long-time DERA member.

106 See DERA 1979 and 1985 for a selection of programs and projects.

107 Minutes of DERA Staff Meeting, 31 May 1988, in reference to the annual conference of the Canadian Association of Housing and Renewal Officers, held in Vancouver a week earlier.

108 Interview with Jim Green, 22 August 1989. By 1992 Green's identification of a third stage in DERA's history had been amply confirmed. The high-water mark of the November 1990 civic election for DERA supporters was followed in 1992 by labour strife among staff and the departure of Green into a provincially funded position to establish a community-based bank in the Downtown Eastside. In his first visible challenge in this position, Green was unable to assemble the financing to purchase the site of the Woodward's department store for community ends in the heart of the Downtown East-side. The stakes have been raised in the balance between co-optation and infiltration of the state. DERA's new organizer, Barb Daniel, faced a di-vided and demoralized association, though one much stronger than Green had encountered in 1980: M. Usinger, 'DERA's Green Turns Banker,' *Vancouver Courier*, 1 November 1992; E. Aird, 'Green Up Against Wall over Future of Old Woodward's Store,' *Vancouver Sun*, 11 February 1993; M. Parry, 'DERA AGM Could Test Mettle of New Organizer,' *Vancouver Sun*, 28 January 1993.

CHAPTER 7

1 The Declaration of Independence of the Ohalim Movement, 26 June 1979
2 The data are based on a survey carried out by the local residents in 1976
3 Interview with Michael Paran, 30 October 1980
4 Report of the Employment Officer, 1981
5 Interview with Moshe Salach, 19 October 1980
6 Interview with Yamin Swissa, 10 May 1981
7 Interview with Michael Paran, 30 October 1980
8 Interview with Mosh Salach, 19 October 1980
9 Journal of the Ohalim Movement, special edition, March 1980
10 Interview with Moshe Salach, 19 October 1980
11 Interview with Yamin Swissa, 10 May 1981
12 Interview with Mosh Salach, 19 October 1980
13 Interview with Shlomo Wasana, 26 February 1981

14 Budget proposals for Ohel Yosef in various years
15 Interview with Moshe Hizkyah, 27 January 1981
16 Ibid
17 Interview with Alice Shalvy, 12 February 1981
18 Ibid
19 Ibid
20 Interview with Shlomo Wasana, 26 February 1981
21 Interview with Michael Paran, 30 October 1980
22 Ibid
23 Private communication with Yosef Gadish
24 Interview with Avner Amiel, 24 October 1980
25 Interview with Moshe Salach, 19 October 1980
26 Interview with Shlomo Wasana, 26 February 1981
27 Interview with Moshe Salach, 19 October 1980
28 Interview with Daniel Avichzer, a participant in the protest squat of 1976 at the Pat housing estate, 23 February 1981
29 Interview with Michael Paran, 7 November 1980
30 Interview with Michael Paran, 30 October 1980
31 Interview with Michael Paran, 7 November 1980
32 Ibid
33 Interviews with participants in the protest squat of 1976 at the Pat housing estate, 23 February 1981
34 Interview with Moshe Hizkyah, 27 January 1981
35 Interview with Alice Shalvy, 12 February 1981
36 Interview with Shlomo Gotlieb, 10 March 1981
37 Ibid
38 Interview with Yamin Swissa, 10 May 1981
39 Ibid
40 Ibid
41 Interview with Michael Paran, 7 November 1980
42 Interview with Yamin Swissa, 10 May 1981
43 Ibid
44 Interview with Michael Paran, 7 November 1980
45 Interview with David Meiry, 15 January 1981
46 Ibid
47 Ibid
48 Interviews with participants in the protest squat of 1976 at the Pat housing estate, 23 February 1981
49 Interview with David Meiry, 15 January 1981

50 Interview with Deputy Mayor Elad Peled, 12 February 1981
51 Interviews with participants in the protest squat of 1976 at the Pat housing estate, 23 February 1981
52 Interview with Michael Paran, 7 November 1980
53 Interview with Michael Paran, 14 November 1980
54 Constitution of 'The Tent (Ha-Ohel) Neighbourhood and Community Center,' 1981
55 Letter from Avner Amiel to the District Court, 26 September 1980
56 Ibid
57 Constitution of 'The Tent (Ha-Ohel) Neighbourhood and Community Center,' 1981
58 Minutes of the forum of the Ohalim Movement, neighbourhood committees, and local activists, 1 March 1981
59 Interview with Shlomo Wasana, 26 February 1981
60 Interview with Ester Dover (a Shmuel Hanavi activist), 22 February 1981
61 Yamin Swissa's lecture to Israeli soldiers, 6 June 1981
62 Interview with Elad Peled, 12 February 1981
63 Ibid
64 Ibid
65 Ibid
66 Address of Elad Peled to the public council of Ohel Yosef, 3 January 1982
67 Interview with Shlomo Wasana, 26 February 1981
68 Minutes of the meeting of the public council of Ohel Yosef, 3 January 1982
69 Interview with Alice Shalvy, 12 February 1981
70 Minutes from Ohel Yosef meeting, 27 September 1981
71 Interview with Avner Amiel, 17 October 1980

PART FOUR

1 Loney (1977) inclines towards this view as do several contributors in Ng, Walker, and Muller 1990.
2 See Gough 1979 and, for a Canadian example, Christiansen-Ruffman 1990.

CHAPTER 8

1 Ley 1980, and compare, for Toronto, Lemon 1974.
2 Aldermen Hardwick, Harcourt, and Pendakur, and Alderwoman Marzari, or half the TEAM councillors in 1972, had been prominent in the Chinatown-Strathcona struggles, prior to their election.
3 For a national review of neighbourhood planning, see Anderson 1977.

4 The Electors Action Movement, 'Policy on Planning and Development,' 1976

5 Carr 1980; Gutstein 1975; Ley 1981, 1988; Mercer and Phillips 1981; Stobie 1979; also Snukal's play *Talking Dirty* (1982) and John Gray's novel *Dazzled*(1984). David Ley was a resident of Kitsilano in 1972-4, and a participant observer during that period of the West Broadway Citizens' Committee.

6 For a detailed study of the Kitsilano Ratepayers' Association and the social geography of Kitsilano to the 1960s, see Carr 1980.

7 Ibid

8 Kitsilano Area Resources Association, 'Apartment Zoning,' *Newsletter*, May 1973

9 Speech by George Moul, president, Kitsilano Ratepayers' Association at Kitsilano United Church, 18 January 1974

10 Brief presented to Council by George Moul, Kitsilano Secondary School, 21 January 1974. Compare note 75, below.

11 P. Wilson, 'A Beautiful Broadway to Be,' *Vancouver Sun*, 3 November 1972

12 These trends were compiled from a variety of unpublished documents of the West Broadway Citizens' Committee.

13 J. Wasserman, 'Blueprint for a Screw-up,' *Vancouver Sun*, 21 November 1973. See also the reply by Harry Rankin, West Broadway's most dependable ally on council: H. Rankin, 'Wasserman's Dirty Tricks Attacks on West Broadway Citizens,' *Georgia Straight*, 6 December 1973

14 A. Smith, 'High Rise Protests: Dirty Tricks in Kitsilano?' *Western Voice*, 4-17 December 1973

15 Alderman Jack Volrich to West Broadway Citizens' Committee. Transcript of the meeting of 11 June 1973

16 S. Persky and L. Beckmann, 'Housing Activists Sweep 12 of 14 Seats in Kits Resource Board Contest,' *Western Voice*, 26 June-9 July 1974; see also West Broadway Citizens' Committee, Information Circular No. 10, 5 July 1974.

17 'Tempers Flare at Protest at Kitsilano High Rise Site,' *Vancouver Sun*, 18 March 1974; see also 'Elderly Storm CMHC in Protest,' *Vancouver Sun*, 23 October 1973.

18 C. Gordon, 'Profile on the Kits Area Manager,' *Kitsilano Resources* 1, August 1975. For a discussion of the WBCC's use of Alinsky-style organizing, see Muller 1985. A broader discussion of Alinsky's legacy appears in Reitzes and Reitzes 1987.

19 West Broadway Citizens' Committee, Information Circular No. 6, April 1974 (draft)

20 See, for example, Lorimer 1970, 1972; Caulfield 1974; Aubin 1977.

21 See S. Hoeppner, 'West Broadway Citizens' Committee Progress Report to the Kitsilano Community Resources Board for the Months of April and May,' Mimeo, 1975. Compare DERA's similar objectives, enunciated during the same period (pp. 183–4).

22 Khouri, Jacques, and West Broadway Citizens' Committee, 'News Release,' January 1973

23 Jacques Khouri, 'Chairman's Report to West Broadway Citizens' Committee AGM,' 13 November 1974

24 Jacques Khouri interview in C. Gordon, 'The Issue in Kitsilano Is Redevelopment,' *Kitsilano Resources* 1, August 1975

25 Khouri, 'Chairman's Report ... '

26 S. Hoeppner, 'West Broadway Citizens' Committee Progress Report to the Kitsilano Community Resources Board for the Month of June,' Mimeo 1975

27 'Rush Boycotts Meeting,' *RUSH News* 1, (December 1975); 'Kitsilano Rezoning Wins Qualified Approval,' *West Side Courier*, 10 December 1975

28 A number of incidents involved the eviction of seniors, especially widows: for example, 'Home, Happiness Destroyed,' *Vancouver Province*, 14 June 1975; 'Tenant in Kitsilano for 14 Years Sees Home Wrecked for Condominium,' *Western News*, 19 June 1975.

29 Gutstein 1975, 107–10. The story was broken on the front page of the *Vancouver Sun*, 14 February 1974.

30 West Broadway Citizens' Committee, 'Press Release,' 30 October 1973; also the 7th and Maple file in the WBCC archive.

31 The photograph, by *Winnipeg Tribune* photographer Frank Chalmers, appears on the back cover and p. 205 of Lorimer 1972.

32 Khouri interview in Gordon, 'The Issue in Kitsilano ... '

33 Ibid

34 W.A. Weaver, letter to Council, 6 May 1975; West Broadway Citizens' Committee, Information Circular No. 1, April 1973, 'Stop Kitsilano from Becoming Another West End'

35 Khouri interview in Gordon, 'The Issue in Kitsilano ... '

36 C. Gordon, 'Profile on the Kits Area Manager,' *Kitsilano Resources* 1, August 1975

37 West Broadway Citizens' Committee, 'Press Release,'' 22 October 1974

38 Khouri interview in Gordon, 'The Issue in Kitsilano ... '

39 West Broadway Citizens' Committee, staff memo, 16 April 1974

40 West Broadway Citizens' Committee, Information Circular No. 18, April 1975. Finances were saved on this occasion by a $10,000 grant from the (WBCC-controlled) Kitsilano Resources Board.

41 West Broadway Citizens' Committee, Information Circular No. 17, January 1975

42 Minutes of the monthly membership meeting, West Broadway Citizens' Committee, 11 June 1975

43 Minutes of the monthly membership meeting, West Broadway Citizens' Committee, 25 June 1973

44 Later, as plans for tenant organization were discussed at a strategy meeting, the minutes end with the statement: 'Sometime in the near future we will have a marathon showing of the Alinsky films.' Minutes of a strategy meeting, West Broadway Citizens' Committee, 17 February 1975. See also Muller 1985 (and note 18, above).

45 Khouri, 'Chairman's Report ... '

46 West Broadway Citizens' Committee, Information Circular No. 19, June 1975

47 For example, as expressed in a letter from Jacques Khouri to Council, 1 March 1973

48 Alderman Jack Volrich to West Broadway Citizens' Committee, Transcript of the meeting of 11 June 1973

49 'City Won't Block Kits Condominiums,' *Vancouver Province*, 5 December 1973

50 West Broadway Citizens' Committee, Information Circular No. 10, 5 July 1974

51 H. Botham, 'New Blood for Resource Board Due,' *West Side Courier*, 28 August 1975

52 West Broadway Citizens' Committee, Information Circular No. 14, 9 October 1974; 'Kitsilano Planners Urge Replacement of Housing,' *Vancouver Sun*, 3 October 1974

53 'West Broadway Citizens' Committee Quit Kitsilano Area Planning Team,' *Western News*, 24 October 1974

54 Ibid

55 'City Council Votes to Seek Controls Over Demolition,' *Vancouver Sun*, 29 October 1975

56 West Broadway Citizens' Committee, 'Press Release,' 22 October 1974; D. Gutstein, 'An Open Letter of Resignation to the Kitsilano Citizens' Planning Committee,' 22 October 1974

57 Alderman Bowers to J. Khouri, 5 December 1974

58 *Vancouver Province*, 2 August 1974

59 L. Bantleman, 'Out of the Ordinary,' Letter to the Editor, *Vancouver Sun*, 6 October 1975

60 *Vancouver Sun*, 26 June 1975; *Western News*, 3 July 1975; *Vancouver Sun*, 6 June 1975

61 The issue prompted a spate of newspaper stories between February and April 1976, including: 'Come Clean Cowie,' *RUSH News*, 1 (February 1976); 'Renters' Group Asks City Alderman to Resign,' *Vancouver Sun*, 17 February 1976; '[Mayor] Phillips Supports Cowie Against "Conflict" Charge,' *West Side Courier*, 19 February 1976; 'Court Hearing Set March 30 to Consider RUSH Bid on Bylaw,' *West Side Courier*, 4 March 1976.

62 J. Khouri, 'Enough to Make a Crocodile Weep,' Letter to the Editor, *Vancouver Sun*, 9 September 1975

63 *Western News*, 9 October 1975; also 'Kits Housing Information Asked,' *West Side Courier*, 13 November 1975

64 'United Church Aids Kits Housing Group,' *Western News*, 18 March 1976

65 Rosemary Brown, MLA, to Susan Hoeppner and Peter Beaudin (WBCC coordinators), 25 September 1974

66 N. Levi and R. Brown, MLAs for Vancouver-Burrard, 'Press Release,' 24 October 1974; 'MLAs Accuse Vancouver of "Block Busting,"' *Vancouver Sun*, 25 October 1974

67 'Adviser to Seek Scaled-Down Projects,' *Vancouver Sun*, 8 March 1974; 'High Rise Opponents Rap Nicholson,' *Vancouver Sun*, 14 March 1974

68 'Housing Minister Censured,' *Vancouver Sun*, 4 July 1975; 'Kits Board "Betrayed" by Government,' *Vancouver Sun*, 6 July 1975.

69 'Levi Plans Kits Talks: "Conflict of Interests" Reports Under Study'; also 'MLAs at "Private" Meeting,' both in *West Side Courier*, 14 August 1975

70 'In Kits "We're a Community Again,"' *West Side Courier*, 28 July 1975

71 'Chairman, Three Others Resign from Kits Board,' *Vancouver Province*, 22 August 1975. (Two others resigned shortly after.)

72 'In Kits "We're a Community ... "'

73 'Expediency Wins Again: $253,784 for Band-Aid Programs in Kitsilano,' *RUSH News* 1, (February 1976)

74 'Open Letter from Kitsilano Community Resources Board,' *Around Kitsilano* 2 (March 1976).

75 The apartment area plan was approved by Council in December 1975. While RUSH opposed the plan with its mock court to protest the need for further down-zoning to prevent the demolition of affordable housing, George Moul, president of the Kitsilano Ratepayers' Association, criticized the plan as too restrictive of potential development. 'Apartment Zone Okayed,' *Vancouver Province*, 5 December 1975

76 Kitsilano Housing Society, 'Buy Back Kitsilano: Invest $500 to $1000 at 8% in your Community through the Kitsilano Housing Society,' Mimeo, n.d.;

'Resident Group Launches "Buy Back Kitsilano Fund,"' *Western News*, 2 October 1975; see also features in *RUSH News* 1 (December 1975), 1 (June 1976). Stobie 1979, 139-43

77 'United Church Aids Kits Housing Group,' *Western News*, 18 March 1976. In addition to Khouri, charter investors in BBK included Gutstein and Karmel; among the seven-person board of KHS were the familiar names of Khouri, Gutstein, Karmel, Susan Hoeppner, and Frank Hyde.

78 'Ottawa Aids Kits Housing,' *West Side Courier*, 12 February 1976

79 Interview with Jacques Khouri, 27 November 1985

80 Interview with Jacques Khouri, 15 November 1988. See also chapter 4, note 27.

81 Ley 1981. In 1989 a development boom and a renewed round of local area planning led to the formation of the Kitsilano Residents' Association, with Mel Lehan, son of the WBCC treasurer, among its leaders. There is considerable continuity with WBCC objectives, though today Kitsilano is a more divided community. M. Lehan, 'Kits Residents Alarmed by Development,' Letter to the Editor, *Vancouver Sun*, 16 February 1990; also P. McMartin, 'Blockbusters,' *Vancouver Sun*, 3 February 1990; J. Lee, 'Refusal to Stop Demolitions Riles Kits Residents,' *Vancouver Sun*, 27 June 1990

82 West Broadway Citizens' Committee, Information Circular No. 1, April 1973

83 Interview with Jacques Khouri, 2 February 1989. For a review of criticisms of the Alinsky model, see Castells 1983.

84 Interview with Jacques Khouri, 2 February 1989

85 At a public hearing in the apartment district, to the astonishment of residents who had gathered to discuss housing, pride of place on the agenda was given over by the city to discussion of the Burrard-Arbutus Connector, a major new roadway through the district. While this topic had not surfaced in community discussion (indeed, it was fiercely resisted and eventually dropped by the city), the Connector had been on the shelf of the city engineer's office for over forty years. In a spirited example of setting the agenda, WBCC members in the audience insisted that housing displace the Connector as the main agenda item. 'Kits Homes Issue Stirs Some Opposition,' *Vancouver Sun*, 30 May 1975

86 For an interpretation from one of the aldermen, see Hardwick and Hardwick 1974; also Stobie 1979, 144-8.

87 'Council Says "No" to Kits Downzoning,' *Western Voice*, 26 July 1974

88 'City Won't Block Kits Condominiums,' *Vancouver Province*, 5 December 1973

89 Vancouver City Planning Department, 1979, Section III b, p. 28

90 'West Broadway Citizens Quit Kitsilano Planning Team,' *Western News*, 24 October 1974
91 'City Fails to Act on KHS Housing – Again,' *RUSH News* 1 (June 1976)
92 These estimates were made by KHS members in *RUSH News* 1 (June 1976); also Stobie 1979, 141.
93 'City Hall Accused of Wasting $1 million,' *Vancouver Sun*, 26 June 1975
94 T. Hinkle, 'Distorted Picture Given on Use of NIP Funds,' Letter to the Editor, *Vancouver Province*, 17 July 1975

CHAPTER 9

1 The Social Workers Association in Jerusalem, *A Proposal for a Comprehensive Reorganization of Local Welfare Services*, 1977
2 Jerusalem Neighbourhood Advancement and Self-Management Programme, *A Plan for the Development of Neighbourhood Self Management*, 1979, 2–3
3 The Jerusalem Association for Neighbourhood Self-Management, Work Programme for the 1988 fiscal year
4 Data provided by the accountant of the JANSM
5 City Hall decision of 30 March 1986
6 The Jerusalem Municipality, City Planning Department, 1975
7 Ibid, 8
8 A letter sent to Yosef Gadis, deputy mayor, by Fanny Ruash, 1983
9 Private interview held with Yeffet Uzeri, the 1985–7 manager, on 20 July 1986
10 Reports based on evaluation research carried out in the period 1986–8. The reports were based on participant observation carried throughout the NC's meetings.
11 The Jerusalem Association for Neighbourhood Self-Management and the Baka Neighbourhood Council, 1985, 6–5; interview with Sara Kaminker
12 Dotten, Documentation Report No. 3, February–July 1983
13 Minutes from the meeting of the JANSM, 17 October 1983
14 Katz-Shiban, Documentation Report No. 8, September–November 1984
15 Minutes from the meeting of the Baka Neighbourhood Council, 24 June 1985
16 An interview with the NC's manager, 4 December 1988
17 Representatives' survey, 1988, carried out by the author
18 A letter from Aharon Cohen, NC's chairman, to Shalom Amoyal, director of the JANSM, 16 May 1989
19 Interview with Aharon Cohen, NC's chairman, 22 June 1989
20 Residents' and representatives' surveys, 1988, carried out by the author

21 Based upon personal profiles of the candidates who ran in the 1985 elections

22 Interview held with the manager of Baka NC, 20 February 1989

23 Interview held with Teddy Kollek, 20 July 1988

24 Interview held with David Ronen, formerly adviser to the mayor, on 8 December 1986

25 Interviews held with heads of the departments of education; youth, sport and community; and city improvement in 1987

26 Interview held with the present and former manager of Baka NC by Altman, 1989

27 Minute No. 64 from the meeting of the ninth City Council, 27 December 1987

28 Some aspects of this debate are presented by Hallman 1974 and Rich 1988.

CHAPTER 10

1 A catalyst in this reassessment was Laclau and Mouffe 1985. Among many subsequent explorations see Ross 1988, Smith 1989, and *New Formations* 1991.

2 A failure to redefine this boundary is one of Fraser's four criticisms of the public sphere as enunciated by Habermas.

3 The more recent history of the Inner City Partnerships in Britain seems to be characterized by such manipulation: see Byrne 1986; further evidence from the United States and West Germany is provided by Clarke and Meyer 1986.

4 This definition is provided by Panitch (1979). His concern, however, that if extended beyond the narrow tripartism of labour, capital, and the state, the term degenerates into an amorphous pluralism seems unwarranted. Savitch (1988) clarifies the distinctions in his study of urban planning and politics.

5 This suggestion has been made in the context of homelessness by Dear and Wolch 1993.

6 A point also noted by Offe (1984) in his discussion of social movements.

7 Interviews with Mosh Salach and Yamin Swissa: see chapter 7, notes 12, 6.

8 Interview with Bruce Eriksen: see chapter 6, note 12.

9 For example, Dale and Foster 1986; Baldock and Cass 1988; Fraser 1989, chs. 7 and 8; and, for Canada, Ng, Walker and Muller 1990.

10 Inter- or intra-organizational differences provide a major theme in Davis 1991.

11 The rapid growth and collapse of the Riverdale Community Association in Toronto, also an Alinsky-style group, provides an instructive comparison: Keating 1975, 1978. For the shift from conflict to co-production with state funding, and eventual co-optation, see Freeman 1977.

12 For recent discussions, see Smith 1989, and Smith and Thrift 1990.
13 For present purposes we are reordering the sequence of the four criticisms of Habermas's public sphere in Fraser 1991.

References

Agnew, J., J. Mercer, and D. Sopher, eds. 1984. *The City in Cultural Context.* Boston: Allen and Unwin

Aird, E. 1982. Gimme Shelter. *Urban Reader* 10/3-4, 14-18

Alinsky, S.C. 1971. *Rules for Radicals.* New York: Vintage Books

Ames, H. 1972 [1897]. *The City Below the Hill.* Toronto: University of Toronto Press

Amiran, D. 1973. The development of Jerusalem. In *Urban Geography of Jerusalem*, eds. D. Amiran, A. Shachar, and I. Kimhi. Berlin and New York: Walter de Gruyter

Anderson, G. 1977. Local area planning: The dream and the reality. *City Magazine* 2/7, 35-43

Anderson, J. 1979. The municipal government reform movement in Western Canada, 1880-1920. In *The Usable Urban Past*, eds. A. Artibise and G. Stelter, pp. 73-111. Toronto: Macmillan

Anderson, K. 1986. 'East' and 'West': Place, state and the institutionalisation of myth in Vancouver's Chinatown, 1880-1980. PhD thesis, University of British Columbia

- 1987. Chinatown as an idea: The power of place and institutional practice in the making of a racial category. *Annals, Association of American Geographers* 77, 580-98

- 1988. Cultural hegemony and the race-definition process in Chinatown, Vancouver: 1880-1980. *Society and Space* 6, 127-49

- 1991. *Vancouver's Chinatown: Racial Discourse in Canada, 1875-1980.* Montreal and Kingston: McGill-Queen's University Press

Astles, A. 1972. The role of historical and architectural preservation in the Vancouver townscape. In *Peoples of the Living Land*, ed. J. Minghi, pp. 145-62. Vancouver: Tantalus

Aubin, H. 1977. *City for Sale*. Toronto: James Lorimer

Bachi, R. 1977. *The Population of Israel*. Jerusalem: The Hebrew University of Jerusalem

Bachrach, P., and M.S. Baratz, 1963. Decisions and nondecisions: An analytical framework. *American Political Science Review* 57, 632–42

Bahr, H. 1967. The gradual disappearance of skid row. *Social Problems* 15, 41–5

Baldcock, C., and B. Cass, eds., 1988. *Women, Social Welfare and the State in Australia*. Sydney: Allen and Unwin

Banfield, E., and J.A. Wilson 1967. *City Politics*. Cambridge, MA: Harvard University Press

Banting, K. 1982. *The Welfare State and Canadian Federalism*. Montreal and Kingston: McGill-Queen's University Press

Bar Yosef, R. 1985. Welfare and integration in Israel. In *The Welfare State and Its Aftermath*, eds. S.N. Eisenstadt and A. Ahimeir, pp. 247–61. London: Croom Helm, in association with the Jerusalem Institute for Israel Studies

Bell, L. 1975. *The Strathcona Rehabilitation Project: Documentation and Analysis*. Vancouver: The United Way

Benvenisti, M. 1988. *The Sling and the Club*. Jerusalem: Keter

Bernstein, D. 1972. The Israeli Black Panthers: From a street corner society to social movement. PhD thesis, The Hebrew University of Jerusalem

Bernstein, R.J. 1989. Social theory as critique. In *Social Theory of Modern Societies: Anthony Giddens and His Critics*, eds. D. Held and J.B. Thompson, pp. 19–33. Cambridge: Cambridge University Press

Bigger, G. 1977. Garden suburbs in Jerusalem –planning and development under early British rule 1917–1929. *Cathedra* 6, 108–32

– 1981. *Urban Planning and Enforcement of Building Codes*. Jerusalem: Jerusalem Institute for Israel Studies

Boggs, C. 1991. Rethinking the sixties legacy: From new left to new social movements. In *Breaking Chains: Social Movements and Collective Action*, ed. M.P. Smith, pp. 50–68. New Brunswick, NJ: Transaction Publishers

Bourne, L., and D. Ley, eds. 1993. *The Changing Social Geography of Canadian Cities*. Montreal and Kingston: McGill-Queen's University Press

Boyte, H. 1980. *The Backyard Revolution*. Philadelphia: Temple University Press

Burton, L., and D. Morley. 1979. Neighbourhood survival in Toronto. *Landscape* 23, 33–40

Byrne, D. 1986. State-sponsored control: Managers, poverty professionals and the inner-city working class. In *Politics, Geography and Social Stratification*, eds. K. Hoggart and E. Kofman, pp. 144–67. London: Croom Helm

Canada, Government of. 1978. *Multiculturalism Update*. Ottawa: Department of the Secretary of State

Canning-Dew, J., ed. 1987. *Hastings and Main: Stories from an Inner City Neigh-bourhood.* Vancouver: New Star Books

Carmon, N. 1988. Deliberate social change: Evaluation of Israel's project re-newal. *Megamot* 31, 299–321

Carr, A. 1980. The development of neighbourhood in Kitsilano: Ideas, actors and the landscape. MA thesis, University of British Columbia

Castells, M. 1976. Theoretical propositions for an experimental study of urban social movements. In *Urban Sociology: Critical Essays*, ed. C.G. Pickvance, pp. 147–73. London: Tavistock

- 1977. *The Urban Question.* New York: Edward Arnold and MIT Press

- 1983. *The City and the Grassroots.* London: Edward Arnold

Caulfield, J. 1974. *The Tiny Perfect Mayor.* Toronto: James Lorimer

- 1988. Canadian urban 'reform' and local conditions. *International Journal of Urban and Regional Research* 12, 477–84

Christiansen-Ruffman, C. 1990. On the contradictions of state-sponsored partic-ipation. In *Community Organization and the Canadian State*, eds. R. Ng, G. Walker, and J. Muller, pp. 85–107. Toronto: Garamond

Clarke, S., and M. Meyer 1986. Responding to grassroots discontent: Germany and the U.S. *International Journal of Urban and Regional Research* 10, 401–17

Cnaan, R. 1989. Horizontal and vertical democracy in neighbourhood organiza-tions. Paper prepared for presentation at the International Conference on Vo-luntarism, Non-Governmental Voluntary Organizations and Public Policy. Jerusalem, Israel

Cohen, E. 1972. The Black Panthers in Israeli society. *Jewish Journal of Sociology* 14, 93–109

Cooper, M. 1971. Residential segregation of elite groups in Vancouver, B.C. M.A. thesis, University of British Columbia

Cooper, T.L. 1980. Bureaucracy and community organization: The metamor-phosis of a relationship. *Administration and Society* 11, 411–44

Cox, K. 1973. *Conflict, Power and Politics in the City.* New York: McGraw-Hill

- 1988. Urban social movements and neighbourhood conflicts: Mobilization and structuration. *Urban Geography* 8, 416–28

Cox, W.H. 1976. *Cities: The Public Dimension.* Harmondsworth: Penguin Books

Cybriwsky, R.A. 1978. Social aspects of neighbourhood change. *Annals, Associ-ation of American Geographers* 68, 17–33

Dabrowski, I., A. Haynor, and R. Cuervo. 1986. An exchange approach to com-munity politics. In *The Egalitarian City*, ed. J.K. Boles, pp. 110–28. New York: Praeger

Dahl, R.A. 1961. *Who Governs? Democracy and Power in an American City.* New Haven, CT: Yale University Press

– 1971. *Polyarchy: Participation and Opposition*. New Haven, CT: Yale University Press

Dale, J., and P. Foster, 1986. *Feminists and State Welfare*. London: Routledge and Kegan Paul

Davies, W., and D. Herbert, 1993. *Communities within Cities: An Urban Social Geography*. London: Belhaven Press

Davis, J.E. 1991. *Contested Ground: Collective Action and the Urban Neighbourhood*. Ithaca, NY: Cornell University Press

Davis, M. 1972. Shaughnessy. Unpublished paper, School of Architecture, University of British Columbia

Dear, M.J., and J. Long. 1978. Community strategies in locational conflict. In *Urbanization and Conflict in Market Societies*, ed. K.R. Cox, pp. 113–27. Chicago: Maaroufa

Dear, M.J., and J. Wolch. 1987. *Landscapes of Despair: From Deinstitutionalization to Homelessness*. Princeton, NJ: Princeton University Press

– 1993. Homelessness in Canada. In *The Changing Social Geography of Canadian Cities*, eds. L. Bourne and D. Ley, pp. 298–308. Montreal and Kingston: McGill-Queen's University Press

DERA (Downtown Eastside Residents Association). 1979. *DERA Guide: Rights and Services for Downtown Eastside Residents*. Vancouver

– 1985. Downtown Eastside Residents' Association. Mimeo

– 1987. *Expo '86: Its Legacy to Vancouver's Downtown Eastside*. Vancouver

– n.d. [1989?]. DERA's Downtown Eastside Walking Tour. Brochure

Draper, J.A. ed., 1971. *Citizen Participation: Canada*. Toronto: New Press

Dreyfus, H.L., and P. Rabinow. 1983. *Michel Foucault: Beyond Structuralism and Hermeneutics*, 2d ed. Chicago: The University of Chicago Press

Duncan, J. 1992. Elite landscapes as cultural (re)productions: The case of Shaughnessy Heights. In *Inventing Places: Studies in Cultural Geography*, eds. K. Anderson and F. Gale, pp. 37–51. Melbourne: Longman Cheshire

Duncan, J., and N. Duncan. 1984. A cultural analysis of urban residential landscapes in North America: The case of the anglophile elite. In *The City in Cultural Context*, eds. J. Agnew, J. Mercer, and D. Sopher, pp. 255–76. Boston: Allen and Unwin

Duncan, N. 1986. Suburban Landscapes and Suburbanites. PhD thesis, Syracuse University

Dunleavy, P. 1981. *Urban Political Analysis: The Politics of Collective Consumption*. London: Macmillan

Easton, R., and P. Tennant. 1969. Vancouver civic party leadership: Backgrounds, attitudes and non-civic party affiliations. *B.C. Studies* 2, 19–29

Eaton, D. 1974. The vernacular architecture of Shaughnessy. Unpublished paper, School of Architecture, University of British Columbia

Elazar, D.J. 1980. The local dimension of government and politics in Israel. In *Local Government in Israel*, eds. D.J. Elazar and C. Kalchaim, pp. 3–26. Jerusalem: Jerusalem Center for Public Affairs

Eshbal, A. 1954. *Palestine Land Development Company: Enterprises in Israeli Cities.* Jerusalem: Palestine Land Development Company

Evans, D. 1984. Demystifying suburban landscapes. *Geography and the Urban Environment* 6, 321–48

– 1988. Social interaction and conflict over residential growth. In *Qualitative Methods in Human Geography*, eds. J. Eyles and D.M. Smith, pp. 118–35. Cambridge, Polity Press

Evers, A., and J. Rodrigues. 1978. Participation and local politics in Marxist theory and practice. In *Comparative Public Policy*, ed. C.R. Foster, pp. 162–70. Elmsford, NY: Pergamon Press

Eyles, J. 1981. Why geography cannot be Marxist: Towards an understanding of lived experience. *Environment and Planning A* 13, 1371–88

Ezrahi, Y. 1968. *City of Stone and Sky.* Tel Aviv: Ma'arachot

Fainstein, S., and N. Fainstein. 1985. Economic restructuring and the rise of urban social movements. *Urban Affairs Quarterly* 21, 187–206

– 1991. The effectiveness of community politics: New York City. In *Breaking Chains: Social Movements and Collective Action*, ed. M.P. Smith, pp. 108–32. New Brunswick, NJ: Transaction Publishers

Fincher, R., and J. McQuillen. 1989. Women in urban social movements. *Urban Geography* 10, 604–13

Firey, W. 1945. Sentiment and symbolism as ecological variables. *American Sociological Review* 10, 140–8

First Shaughnessy Rate Payers' Association. 1967. Submission of the First Shaughnessy Rate Payers' Association re Bill to extend the Shaughnessy Heights Building Restriction Act for another twenty-five years. Submitted to the Private Bill Committee, British Columbia Legislature, 3 February

Fischer, C.S. 1984. *The Urban Experience.* New York: Harcourt Brace Jovanovich

Fitzgerald, D. 1990. Architect heritage heroine. *Western Living*, January, 11

Foucault, M. 1983. Afterword: The subject and power. In *Beyond Structuralism and Hermeneutics*, eds. H.L. Dreyfus and P. Rabinow, pp. 208–28. Chicago: University of Chicago Press

Fraser, N. 1989. *Unruly Practices.* Minneapolis: University of Minnesota Press

– 1991. Rethinking the public sphere: A contribution to the critique of actually existing democracy. In *Habermas and the Public Sphere*, ed. C. Calhoun. Cambridge, MA: MIT Press

Freeman, B. 1977. The decline and fall of a community organization. *City Magazine* 2/7, 18–27

French, P., and M. Vaughan. 1971. The development of Shaughnessy Heights. Unpublished manuscript, City of Vancouver Archives, Shaughnessy File

Friedland, R. 1982. *Power and Crisis in the City: Corporations, Unions and Urban Policy*. London: Macmillan

Friedmann, J., and W. Goetz. 1981. *Notes on the Future of the World City*. Los Angeles: School of Architecture and Urban Planning. University of California

Frumkin, G. 1954. *A Way of Judge in Jerusalem*. Tel Aviv: Dvir

Gerecke, K. 1991. Success in revitalizing the inner city – the story of DERA. *City Magazine* 12/4, 11–19

Giddens, A. 1977. *Studies in Social and Political Theory*. London: Hutchinson

– 1984. *The Constitution of Societies*. Cambridge: Polity Press

Gittle, M. 1980. *Limits to Citizen Participation: The Decline of Community Organizations*. Beverly Hills: Sage

Goldrick, M. 1978. The anatomy of urban reform in Toronto. *City Magazine* 3/4–5, 29–39

Goldsmith, M. 1980. *Politics, Planning and the City*. London: Hutchinson

Gonen, A. 1982. The geography of the electoral competition between Labor Alignment and the Likud in Jewish cities of Israel, 1963–81. *State, Government and International Relations* 19–20, 63–87

Gonen, A., and S. Hasson. 1983. Housing as a spatio-political measure in urban areas: The Israeli case. *Geoforum* 14, 103–9

Gottschalk, S.S. 1975. *Communities and Alternatives – An Exploration of the Limits of Planning*. New York: John Wiley

Gough, I. 1979. *The Political Economy of the Welfare State*. London: Macmillan

Gramsci, A. 1971. *Selections from the Prison Notebooks of Antonio Gramsci*, eds. D. Hoare and G. Novell-Smith. New York: International Publishers

Gray, J. 1984. *Dazzled*. Toronto: Irwin

Green, J. 1983. Introduction. In One hundred years of struggle: A historical look at the Downtown Eastside, A. Priest, S. Harris, V. Wong, ed. C. Itter. Unpublished manuscript, Downtown Eastside Residents Association

– 1986. *Against the Tide: The Story of the Canadian Seaman's Union*. Toronto: Progress Books

Gurr, T.R. 1970. *Why Men Rebel*. Princeton, NJ: Princeton University Press

Gutstein, D. 1975. *Vancouver Ltd*. Toronto: James Lorimer

– 1983. Vancouver. In *City Politics in Canada*, eds. W. Magnusson and A. Sancton, pp. 189–221. Toronto: University of Toronto Press

Habermas, J. 1975. *Legitimation Crisis*. Boston: Beacon Press
- 1982. A reply to my critics. In *Habermas: Critical Debates*, eds. J.B. Thompson and D. Held, pp. 219–83. Cambridge, MA: MIT Press
- 1983. Neo-conservative culture criticism in the United States and West Germany. *Telos* 56, 75–89
- 1989. *The Structural Transformation of the Public Sphere*. Cambridge, MA: MIT Press
Hain, P. 1980. *Neighbourhood Participation*. London: Temple Smith
Hall, W. 1974. Spatial behaviour in Victory Square. M.A. thesis, University of British Columbia
Hallman, W.H. 1974. *Neighborhood Government in a Metropolitan Setting*. Beverly Hills: Sage
Hamel, P. 1991. *Action Collective et Démocratie Locale : Les Mouvements Urbains Montréalais*, Montréal: Les Presses de l'Universite de Montréal
Hardwick, W. 1974. *Vancouver*. Toronto: Collier-Macmillan
Hardwick, W., and D. Hardwick. 1974. Civic government: Corporate, consultative or participatory? In *Community Participation and the Spatial Order of the City*, ed. D. Ley, pp. 89–95. Vancouver: Tantalus
Harris, R. 1987. A social movement in urban politics: A reinterpretation of urban reform in Canada. *International Journal of Urban and Regional Research* 11, 363–81
- 1988. *Democracy in Kingston: A Social Movement in Urban Politics, 1965–1970*. Montreal and Kingston: McGill-Queen's University Press
Hartman, C. 1974. *Yerba Buena: Land Grab and Community Resistance in San Francisco*. San Francisco: Glide
Hartman, C., and R. Kessler. 1978. The illusion and reality of urban renewal: San Francisco's Yerba Buena center. In *Marxism and the Metropolis*, eds. W. Tabb and L. Sawers, pp. 153–78. New York: Oxford University Press
Harvey D. 1989. *The Condition of Postmodernity*. Oxford: Basil Blackwell
Hasson, S. 1984. *Locational Conflict and Community Action: The Impact of Vancouver's ALRT System*. Occasional Papers 25, The Centre for Human Settlements, University of British Columbia
- 1985. The neighbourhood organization as a pedagogic project. *Environment and Planning D: Society and Space* 3, 337–55
- 1987. *The Protest of the Second Generation: Urban Social Movements in Jerusalem*. Jerusalem: The Jerusalem Institute for Israel Studies
- 1989. *Neighbourhood Self-Government: A New Experiment in Jerusalem Politics*. Jerusalem: The Jerusalem Institute for Israel Studies
Hasson, S., and A. Altman. 1989. Impact assessment of neighbourhood government. Unpublished Report. Jerusalem: The Jerusalem Institute for Israel Studies

Hays, S. 1964. The politics of reform in municipal government in the Progressive era. *Pacific Northwest Quarterly* 55, 157–69

Held, D. 1989. *Political Theory and the Modern State: Essays on State, Power and Democracy.* Cambridge and Oxford: Polity Press, in association with Basil Blackwell

Henig, J.R. 1982. *Neighborhood Mobilization.* New Brunswick, NJ: Rutgers University Press

Heskin, A. 1991. *The Struggle for Community.* Boulder, CO: Westview Press

Higgins, D.J.H. 1977. *Urban Canada.* Toronto: Macmillan

– 1981. Progressive city politics and the citizen movement. In *After the Developers*, eds. J. Lorimer and C. MacGregor, pp. 84–95. Toronto: James Lorimer

Holdsworth, D. 1981. House and home in Vancouver: The emergence of a West Coast urban landscape. PhD thesis, University of British Columbia

Horowitz, D., and M. Lissak. 1972. *The Origins of the Israeli Polity.* Tel Aviv: Am Oved

Howard, R. 1984. Downtown-Eastside: Rehabilitation planning. *Quarterly Review* 11/1, 3–4

Hunter, A.J., and G.D. Suttles. 1972. The expanded community of limited liability. In *The Social Construction of Communities*, ed. G.D. Suttles, pp. 44–81. Chicago: University of Chicago Press

Huzel, S. 1982. Conflict and compromise: A case study of the decision-making process in the Downtown Eastside. Master's thesis, University of neighbourhood

Ishai, Y. 1982. Israel's right-wing Jewish proletariat. *The Jewish Journal of Sociology* 24, 87–98

Israel Central Bureau of Statistics. 1972. *Housing and Population Census 1972.* Jerusalem: Government Printing Office

Jackson, P., ed. 1987. *Race and Racism.* London: Allen and Unwin

Jerusalem Institute for Israel Studies and the Municipality of Jerusalem. 1991. *Statistical Yearbook of Jerusalem, No. 8.* Jerusalem

Kallen, E. 1983. The semantics of multiculturalism. In *Consciousness and Inquiry: Ethnology and Canadian Realities*, ed. F. Manning, pp. 22–46. Ottawa: National Museum of Man

Kalman, H., and J. Roaf. 1974. *Exploring Vancouver.* Vancouver: University of British Columbia Press

Kark, R. 1978. *Neighborhoods in Jerusalem.* Jerusalem: Yad Itzchak Ben Zvi

Katan, J., and R. Cnaan. 1986. Neighborhood committees in Israel and their local and external orientations. *Community Development Journal* 21, 23–32

Katznelson, I. 1981. *City Trenches: Urban Politics and the Patterning of Class in the United States.* Chicago: University of Chicago Press

Keating, D. 1975. *The Power to Make It Happen.* Toronto: Green Tree Press

- 1978. Looking back at community organizing. *City Magazine* 3/6, 36–43
Keller, S. 1968. *The Urban Neighborhood: A Sociological Perspective.* New York: Random House
Kerem, R. 1987. *General Information on the Jerusalem Association for Neighborhood Self-Management.* Jerusalem
Kim, H.C., and N. Lai. 1982. Chinese community resistance to urban renewal: The case of Strathcona in Vancouver, Canada. *Journal of Ethnic Studies* 10, 67–81
Kimchi, I. 1970. Renewal areas in Jerusalem: The example of Gonen neighborhood. PhD thesis, The Hebrew University of Jerusalem
Kirk, G. 1980. *Urban Planning in a Capitalist Society.* London: Croom Helm
Kling, J., and P. Posner. 1991. Class and community: Theories of activism in an era of urban transformation. In *Breaking Chains: Social Movements and Collective Action*, ed. M.P. Smith, pp. 26–49. New Brunswick, NJ: Transaction Publishers
Knight, R., ed. 1980. *Along the No. 20 Line: Reminiscences of the Vancouver Waterfront.* Vancouver: New Star Books
Kobayashi, A., ed. 1988. Focus: Asian migration to Canada. *Canadian Geographer* 32, 351–62
- 1993. Multiculturalism: A Canadian Institution? In *Place/Culture/Representation*, eds. J. Duncan and D. Ley, pp. 205–31. London: Routledge
Kollek, T. 1988. Sharing united Jerusalem. *Foreign Affairs* 67, 156–68
Kotler, M. 1969. *Neighborhood Government.* New York: Bobbs-Merrill
Kroyanker, D. 1989. *Jerusalem Architecture –Periods and Styles: European-Christian Buildings Outside the Old City Walls.* Jerusalem: Keter Publishing House
Laclau, E., and C. Mouffe. 1985. *Hegemony and Socialist Strategy: Towards a Radical Democratic Politics.* London: Verso
Lai, C.-Y. 1988. *Chinatowns: Towns Within Cities in Canada.* Vancouver: University of British Columbia Press
Lautens, T. 1970. Crepe suzette and cockroaches. *U.B.C. Alumni Chronicle*, Autumn, 18–22
Lavie, R. 1988. Self management or local bureaucracy. *Nachlaot-Rechavia* (neighbourhood newspaper), p. 3
Laws, G. 1988. Privatisation and the local welfare state: The case of Toronto's social services. *Transactions, Institute of British Geographers* 13, 433–48
Leithead, J. 1980. Residential Rehabilitation Assistance Program. *Quarterly Review* 7/1, 16–17
Lemon, J. 1974. Toronto: Is it a model of urban life and citizen participation? In *Community Participation and the Spatial Order of the City*, ed. D. Ley, pp. 41–58. Vancouver: Tantalus
- 1993. Social planning and the Canadian city. In *The Changing Social Geography*

of Canadian Cities, eds. L. Bourne and D. Ley, pp. 267–80. Montreal and Kingston: McGill-Queen's University Press

Léonard, J.-F., and J. Léveillée. 1986. *Montreal after Drapeau*. Montreal: Black
Rose Books

Ley, D. 1974a. *The Black Inner City as Frontier Outpost: Images and Behavior of a
Philadelphia Neighborhood*. Washington, DC: Association of American Geographers Monograph Series No. 7

– 1974b. Problems of co-optation and idolatry in the community group. In
Community Participation and the Spatial Order of the City, ed. D. Ley, pp. 75–88.
Vancouver: Tantalus

– 1980. Liberal ideology and the post-industrial city. *Annals, Association of
American Geographers* 70, 238–58

– 1981. Inner city revitalization in Canada: A Vancouver case study. *Canadian
Geographer* 25, 124–48

– 1987. Styles of the times: Liberal and neoconservative landscapes in Vancouver, 1968–1986. *Journal of Historical Geography* 14, 40–56

– 1988. Social upgrading in six Canadian inner cities. *Canadian Geographer* 31,
31–45

– 1993. Past elites and present gentry: Neighbourhoods of privilege in Canadian
inner cities. In *The Changing Social Geography of Canadian Cities*, eds. L. Bourne
and D. Ley, pp. 214–33. Montreal and Kingston: McGill-Queen's University
Press

– 1994. Gentrification and the politics of the new middle class. *Society and Space*
12

Ley, D., and J. Mercer. 1980. Locational conflict and the politics of consumption. *Economic Geography* 56, 89–109

Ley, D., and C. Mills. 1986. Gentrification and reform politics in Montreal,
1982. *Cahiers de Géographie du Québec* 30, 419–27

Ley, D., and K. Olds. 1988. Landscape as spectacle: World's fairs and the culture
of heroic consumption. *Society and Space* 6, 191–212

Lineberry, R.L., and I. Sharkansky. 1971. *Urban Politics and Public Policy*. New
York: Harper and Row

Lipsky, M. 1970. *Protest in City Politics*. Chicago: Rand McNally

– 1972. Protest as a political resource. In *Group Politics – A New Emphasis*, eds.
E.S. Malecki and H.R. Mahood, pp. 158–81. New York: Charles Scribner's
Sons

Lojkine, J. 1976. Contribution to a Marxist theory of capitalist urbanization. In
Urban Sociology: Critical Essays, ed. C.G. Pickvance, pp. 119–46. London:
Tavistock

Loney, M. 1977. A political economy of citizen participation. In *The Canadian*

State: Political Economy and Political Power, ed. L. Panitch, pp. 446–72. Toronto: University of Toronto Press

Lorimer, J. 1970. *The Real World of City Politics*. Toronto: James Lewis and Samuel

– 1972. *A Citizen's Guide to City Politics*. Toronto: James Lewis and Samuel

– 1978. *The Developers*. Toronto: James Lorimer

Lowe, S. 1986. *Urban Social Movements: The City After Castells*. London: Macmillan

Lukes, S. 1974. *Power: A Radical View*. London: Macmillan

Lustiger-Thaler, H., ed. 1992. *Political Arrangements: Power and the City*. Montreal: Black Rose Books

McCarthy, J.D., and N.N. Zald. 1977. Resource mobilization and social movements: A partial theory. *American Journal of Sociology* 86, 1212–41

McCarthy, J.J. 1981. Research on neighborhood activism: Review critique and alternatives. *South African Geographical Journal* 63, 107–31

McLean, J. 1988. Social housing consumers taking control: A community development process in the urban core. Master's thesis, University of British Columbia

Magnusson, W. 1981. Community organization and local self-government. In *Politics and Government in Urban Canada*, ed. L. Feldman, pp. 61–86. Toronto: Methuen

Magnusson, W., and A. Sancton, eds. 1983. *City Politics in Canada*. Toronto: University of Toronto Press

Magnusson, W., and R. Walker. 1988. De-centring the state: Political theory and Canadian political economy. *Studies in Political Economy* 26, 37–71

Marlatt, D., and C. Itter, eds. 1979. *Opening Doors: Vancouver's East End*. Victoria, BC: Sound Heritage, VIII (1–2)

Marsh, L. 1950. *Rebuilding A Neighbourhood*. Research Publications No. 1, Department of Sociology and Social Work, University of British Columbia

Martin, B. 1987. Skid row missions: Roles, relationships, and ideologies. Unpublished paper, Department of Geography, University of British Columbia

Maslow, A.H. 1970. *Motivation and Personality*. New York: Harper and Row

Matthews, J. 1932. *Early Vancouver*, Vol. 1. Vancouver

– n.d. Shaughnessy Dockets No. 1 and No. 2. Vancouver, City of Vancouver Archives

Mercer, J., and D. Phillips. 1981. Attitudes of homeowners and the decision to rehabilitate property. *Urban Geography* 2, 216–36

Michels, R. 1962. *Political Parties*. New York: The Free Press

Miliband, R. 1969. *The State in Capitalist Society*. London: Weidenfeld and Nicolson

Miller, F. 1975. Vancouver civic political parties: Developing a model of party-system change and stabilization. *B.C. Studies* 25, 3–31

Miller, L. 1973. Theatre and community. *Bama* 56, 82–8

Miller, R. 1982. *The Demolition of Skid Row.* Lexington, MA: D.C. Heath

Morlan, R.L. 1982. Sub-municipal governance in practice: The Rotterdam experience. *Western Political Quarterly* 35, 425–41

Moscovitch, A. and J. Albert, eds. 1987. *The 'Benevolent' State: The Growth of Welfare in Canada.* Toronto: Garamond Press

Moynihan, D.P. 1969. *Maximum Feasible Misunderstanding: Community Action in the War on Poverty.* New York: The Free Press

Muller, J. 1985. Management of urban neighbourhoods through Alinsky-style organizing: An illustration from Vancouver, Canada. *Community Development Journal* 20/2, 106–13

Myles, J. 1988. Decline or impasse? The current state of the welfare state. *Studies in Political Economy* 26, 73–107

Nanetti, R.Y. 1985. Neighborhood institutions and policy outputs: The Italian case. *International Journal of Urban and Regional Research* 9, 113–35

Nann, R. 1970. *Urban Renewal and Relocation of Chinese Community Families.* Ottawa: Department of the Secretary of State

New Formations. 1991. On democracy. 14: whole issue

Ng, R., G. Walker, and J. Muller, eds. 1990. *Community Organization and the Canadian State.* Toronto: Garamond

NRP (Neighborhood Renewal Programme). 1982. *Redevelopment Plans for Ir-Ganim.* Jerusalem

Oberschall, A. 1973. *Social Conflict and Social Movements.* Englewood Cliffs, NJ: Prentice-Hall

O'Connor, J. 1973. *The Fiscal Crisis of the State.* New York: St Martin's Press

Offe, C. 1984. *Contradictions of the Welfare State.* London: Hutchinson

Olds, K. 1988. Planning for the housing impacts of a hallmark event: A case study of Expo 86. Master's thesis, University of British Columbia

Olson, M. 1965. *The Logic of Collective Action.* Cambridge, MA: Harvard University Press

Pahl, R.E. 1975. *Whose City?* 2d ed. Harmondsworth: Penguin Books

Panitch, L. 1979. Corporatism in Canada. *Studies in Political Economy* 1/1, 43–92

Park, R., E. Burgess, and R. McKenzie. 1925. *The City.* Chicago: University of Chicago Press

Pateman, C. 1970. *Participation and Democratic Theory.* Cambridge: Cambridge University Press

Pendakur, S. 1972. *Cities, Citizens and Freeways.* Vancouver: S. Pendakur

Perlman, J. 1979. Neighborhood research: A proposed methodology. *South Atlantic Urban Studies* 4, 43-63
- 1982. Seven voices from one organization: What does it mean? Unpublished paper. Department of City and Regional Planning, University of California, Berkeley
Persky, S. 1980. *The House that Jack Built*. Vancouver: New Star Books
Pickvance, C.G. 1976. On the study of urban social movements. In *Urban Sociology: Critical Essays*, ed. C.G. Pickvance, pp. 198-218. London: Tavistock
- 1978. From 'social base' to 'social force': Some analytical issues in the study of urban protest. In *Captive Cities*, ed. M. Harloe, pp. 179-86. Chichester: John Wiley
- 1985. The rise and fall of urban movements and the role of comparative analysis. *Environment and Planning D: Society and Space* 3, 31-54
Plotkin, S. 1991. Community and alienation: Enclave consciousness and urban movements. In *Breaking Chains: Social Movements and Collective Action*, ed. M.P. Smith, pp. 5-25. New Brunswick, NJ: Transaction Publishers
Point Grey, Corporation of. 1922. *Town Planning Bylaw No. 44*. Point Grey, B.C.
Pratt, G. 1981. The house as an expression of social worlds. In *Housing and Identity*, ed. J. Duncan, pp. 135-80. London: Croom Helm
Priest, A., S. Harris, and V. Wong. 1983. One hundred years of struggle: A historical look at the Downtown Eastside. Ed. C. Itter. Unpublished manuscript, Downtown Eastside Residents' Association
Province of British Columbia. 1914. *Statutes of British Columbia*, Chapter 96, pp. 839-41. Victoria, BC: The King's Printer
- 1922. *Statutes of British Columbia*, Chapter 87, pp. 609-11. Victoria, BC: The King's Printer
Ptarmigan Planning Associates. 1976. Strathcona rehabilitation project: Evaluation stage II. Preliminary draft. Vancouver
- 1977. *Strathcona Rehabilitation Project: Stage II Evaluation*. Vancouver
Reitzes, D., and D. Reitzes. 1987. *The Alinsky Legacy: Alive and Kicking*. Greenwich, CT: JAI Press
Resnick, P. 1977. Social democracy in power: The case of British Columbia. *B.C. Studies* 34, 3-20
Rex, J.A. 1968. The sociology of a zone in transition. In *Readings in Urban Sociology*, ed. R.E. Pahl, pp. 211-31. New York: Pergamon Press
Rich, R.C. 1980. A political-economic approach to the study of neighbourhood organizations. *American Journal of Political Science* 24, 559-92
- 1986. Neighborhood-based participation in the planning process: Promise and

reality: In *Urban Neighborhoods: Research and Policy*, ed. R.B. Taylor, pp. 41–73. New York: Praeger

Riches, G. 1987. Feeding Canada's poor: The rise of the food banks and the collapse of the public safety net. In *The Canadian Welfare State*, ed. J. Ismael, pp. 126–48. Edmonton: University of Alberta Press

Robertson, A. 1977. The pursuit of power, profit and privacy: A study of Vancouver's West End elite, 1886–1914. Master's thesis, University of British Columbia

Roddan, A. 1932. *Canada's Untouchables: The Story of the Man Without a Home*. Vancouver: First United Church

Romann, M. 1973. The economic development of Jerusalem in recent times. In *Urban Geography of Jerusalem*, eds. D. Amiran, A. Schachar, and I. Kimhi. Berlin and New York: Walter de Gruyter

Romann, M., and A. Weingrod. 1991. *Living Together Separately: Arabs and Jews in Contemporary Jerusalem*. Princeton, NJ: Princeton University Press

Ross, A., ed. 1988. *Universal Abandon? The Politics of Postmodernism*. Minneapolis: University of Minnesota Press

Ross, D. n.d. *Contacts*. Jerusalem: Private Publication

Rossiter, S. 1983. Exodus reversed. *Equinox* 2/8, 48–63

Rowland, J. 1973. *Community Decay*. Harmondsworth: Penguin Books

Roy, P. 1980. *Vancouver: An Illustrated History*. Toronto: James Lorimer

Rule, C. 1981. A classical Chinese garden. *Western Living*, September, 36–40

Ruppin, A. 1936. *Three Decades of Palestine*. Jerusalem: Schocken

Said, E. 1978. *Orientalism*. New York: Random House

Sait, E.M. 1963. Machines, political. *Encyclopedia of the Social Sciences*, Vol. 9, pp. 657–61. New York: Macmillan

Salzberger, L. 1988. Social Services. In *Twenty Years in Jerusalem 1967–1987*, eds. J. Prawer and O. Ahimeir, pp. 121–61. Jerusalem: Ministry of Defence and the Jerusalem Institute for Israel Studies

Saunders, P. 1979. *Urban Politics*. London: Hutchinson

– 1986. *Social Theory and the Urban Question*, 2d ed. London: Unwin Hyman

Save the Downtown Eastside Committee. 1982. *The Downtown Eastside: A Neighbourhood Worth Saving*. Vancouver

Savitch, H.V. 1988. *Post-Industrial Cities: Politics and Planning in New York, Paris and London*. Princeton, NJ: Princeton University Press

Schmitter, P.C. 1974. Still the century of corporatism? *Review of Politics* 36/1, 85–131

Shabbetai, Z. 1986. *Rehavia: History, Founders and Challenges*. Jerusalem

Shapiro, S. 1973. Planning Jerusalem: The first generation 1917–1968. In *Urban Geography of Jerusalem*, eds. D. Amiran, A. Schachar, and I. Kimhi, 140–59. Berlin and New York: Walter de Gruyter

Sharpe, L.J., ed. 1979. *Decentralist Trends in Western Democracies.* London: Sage

Shaughnessy Heights Property Owners' Association. 1966. Why Shaughnessy Heights Building Restriction Act is good for Vancouver and British Columbia and should be extended for a further period of twenty-five years. Submitted to the Private Bill Committee, British Columbia Legislature, 1 December

- 1967. Memorandum regarding application for extension of Shaughnessy Heights Building Restriction Act. Submitted to the Private Bill Committee, British Columbia Legislature, 1 February

- 1968. Memorandum regarding application for extension of Shaughnessy Heights Building Restriction Act. Submitted to the Private Bill Committee, British Columbia Legislature, 1 February

- 1977. *Shaughnessy Planning Study.* Vancouver

Skocpol, T. 1984. Emerging agendas and recurrent strategies in historical sociology. In *Vision and Method in Historical Sociology,* ed. T. Skocpol, pp. 356-91. Cambridge: Cambridge University Press

Smelser, N. 1963. *The Theory of Collective Behavior.* New York: Free Press

Smith, P., and P. Moore. 1993. Cities as a social responsibility: Planning and its impact on urban form. In *The Changing Social Geography of Canadian Cities,* eds. L. Bourne and D. Ley, pp. 343-66. Montreal and Kingston: McGill-Queen's University Press

Smith, S. 1988. Political interpretations of 'racial segregation' in Britain. *Society and Space* 6, 423-44

- 1989. Society, space and citizenship. *Transactions, Institute of British Geographers* NS14, 144-56

Smith, S., and N. Thrift, eds. 1990. Oppressions and entitlements. *Society and Space* 8, 375-483

Snukal, S. 1982. *Talking Dirty.* Toronto: Playwrights Canada

Stobie, P. 1979. Private inner city redevelopment in Vancouver: A case study of Kitsilano. Master's thesis, University of British Columbia

Susskind, L., and M. Elliot. 1984. Paternalism, conflict and co-production: Learning from citizen action and citizen participation in Western Europe. In *Cities, Communities and Planning in the 1980s,* eds. D. Soen, F.A. Lazin, and Y. Neumann, pp. 155-201. Aldershot: Gower

Suttles, G.D. 1972. *The Social Construction of Communities.* Chicago: University of Chicago Press

Tennant, P. 1980. Vancouver civic politics, 1929-1980. *B.C. Studies* 46, 3-27

Tonnies, F. 1963. *Community and Society.* New York: Harper and Row

Touraine, A. 1981. *The Voice and the Eye: An Analysis of Social Movements.* Cambridge: Cambridge University Press

Turner, F.J. 1962. *The Frontier in American History.* New York: Holt, Rinehart and Winston

Vancouver, City of. 1966. *Skid Road: The Chronic Drunkenness Offender*. Vancouver: Subcommittee of the Special Joint Committee on Skid Road
- Planning Commission. 1980. *Goals for Vancouver*. Vancouver
- Planning Department. 1965. *Downtown-Eastside: A Preliminary Study*. Vancouver
- 1969. *Restoration Report: A Case for Renewed Life in the Old City*. Vancouver
- 1979. *First Shaughnessy Planning Study: Discussion Paper*. Vancouver
- 1982a. *The First Shaughnessy Design Guidelines*. Vancouver
- 1982b. *The First Shaughnessy Plan Background Report*. Vancouver
- Social Planning Department. 1971. *Downtown Eastside*. Vancouver
- Technical Planning Board. 1956. *Downtown Vancouver, 1955-76*. Vancouver
- 1957. *Vancouver Redevelopment Study*. Vancouver
Ventriss, C., and R. Pecorella. 1984. Community participation and modernization: A reexamination of political choices. *Public Administration Review* 44, 224-31
Walker, G. 1990. Reproducing community. In *Community Organization and the Canadian State*, eds. R. Ng, G. Walker, and J. Muller, pp. 31-46. Toronto: Garamond
Warren, R.B., and D.I. Warren. 1977. *The Neighborhood Organizer's Handbook*. Notre Dame: University of Notre Dame Press
Warren, R.L. 1978. *The Community in America*. Boston: Houghton Mifflin
Wickberg, E. 1980. Chinese and Canadian influences on Chinese politics in Vancouver, 1900-1947. *B.C. Studies* 45, 37-55
Wickberg, E., H. Con, G. Johnson, and W. Wilmott. 1982. *From China to Canada: A History of the Chinese Communities in Canada*. Toronto: McClelland and Stewart
Wiener, M. 1981. *English Culture and the Decline of the Industrial Spirit*. Cambridge: Cambridge University Press
Willmott, W. 1964. Chinese clan associations in Vancouver. *Man* 49, 33-7
- 1970. Approaches to the study of the Chinese in British Columbia. *B.C. Studies* 4, 38-52
Wolch, J. 1989. The shadow state: Transformations in the voluntary sector. In *The Power of Geography: How Territory Shapes Social Life*, eds. J. Wolch and M. Dear, pp. 197-221. Boston: Unwin Hyman
- 1990. *The Shadow State: Government and Voluntary Sector in Transition*. New York: The Foundation Center
Wong, B. 1977. Elites and ethnic boundary maintenance: A study of the role of elites in Chinatown, New York City. *Urban Anthropology* 6, 1-22
Wong, S. 1978. Urban redevelopment and rehabilitation in the Strathcona area. In *Vancouver: Western Metropolis*, ed. L. Evenden, pp. 255-69. Victoria, BC: Western Geographical Series

Woodsworth, J. 1972 [1911]. *My Neighbour*. Toronto: University of Toronto Press

Yates, D. 1973. *Neighbourhood Democracy: The Politics and Impacts of Decentralization*. Lexington, MA: D.C. Heath

– 1977. *The Ungovernable City: The Politics of Urban Problems and Policy Making*. Cambridge, MA: MIT Press

Yee, F. 1983. The social and political transformations of the Chinese community in the late 1960s to early 1970s: A case study of the firehall issue. Unpublished paper, Department of Geography, University of British Columbia

Yee, P. 1988. *Saltwater City: An Illustrated History of the Chinese in Vancouver*. Vancouver. Douglas and McIntyre

Zorbaugh, H. 1929. *The Gold Coast and the Slum*. Chicago: University of Chicago Press

Index